Tales from the Teamhouse

~True Special Forces Stories~

**Stories compiled and edited by
Jim Kelley and Bill Coombs**

**Special consideration to Bob Jack, former
Special Forces operative and Special Forces
Teamhouse (list) owner**

**Cover design by
Robert Smith**

*with special appreciation to
Ben Roberts and Charlene Iniguez*

Copyright © 2004
Ben Roberts for the Special Forces Teamhouse

All rights reserved. No part of this book may be reproduced in any form, except for the inclusion of brief quotations in a review, without permission in writing from the author, editor, or publisher. The names, characters, and, or places in this book may have been changed to protect the innocent or guilty.

Library of Congress Card Number: 2004092356

ISBN 0-9749700-0-X

First printing   April 2004

The profits from this book are intended for Save the Montagnard People (STMP). Additional copies are available by mail order. Send ten US dollars ($10.00) (plus $3.00 postage and handling) to:
Tales from the Teamhouse
c/o Ben Roberts
5671 Cielo Ave.
Goleta, CA 93117
(805) 683-4909

Printed in the U.S.A. by
Morris Publishing
3212 East Highway 30
Kearney, NE 68847
1-800-650-7888

Table of Contents

How it was……………………………1

Bar Stories……………………….193

Creature Tales…………………..217

Humor……………………………...243

Jump Stories……………………....285

Maggie……………………………...323

Oops…………………………………..331

Poetry………………………………355

Various………………………………362

You ain't gonna believe………..488

A special thank you to all the Special Forces members for contributing their stories, and for generously donating the proceeds from this book to Save the Montagnard People (STMP).

Short Stories or Remembrances
By William Foxworth

1963, Camp Poli Krong, due west of Kontum on the Dak Bla River:

We ran an operation to the South and West of the camp, but did not run into any bad guys or yards. We saw plenty of tiger pugmarks, and returned to camp three days later without any contact. About a half hour to an hour after returning to camp, about 15-20 Yards, one old man and the rest women and children had followed us back to camp.

Our senior medic, James T., and one other American took another patrol out to the same are, came to an old village site and killed a couple of water buffalo. A couple of days later, they came thru the site again and saw a tiger eating one of the dead buffalo. According to James, the whole point squad of Yards and the two Americans opened fire on the Tiger. The tiger jumped up and ran into some tall grass. They closed in on the area the tiger had jumped into, James got up on one of the old pilings for a Yard house so he could see over the high grass. He spotted the tiger lying down in the grass and shot it in the head with his M2 Carbine. Then they skinned the tiger, rolled the skin up and put it in a waterproof bag.

The tiger had been hit by one bullet in the shoulder other than the one in the head. When they arrived back at camp a couple of days later that skin was really ripe. The team sergeant threw the bag and skin in the river.

Team Intel Sgt ran an operation and we crossed a tributary chat fed into the Dak Bla River below Poli Krong. This tributary was a bout 20 feet across but very swift running in the rainy season. We strung a one-rope bridge across the stream and tied most of the CIDG onto the rope so they would not be swept away. I went to the West side to get them off the rope and put them out on a perimeter. We had about 15 of them across and out on perimeter when we started receiving fire from up the hill.

Some of the CIDG returned fire, and like a fool, I came out of the tree line at the stream to see what was going on. (Well, there were no bullets kicking up dust around me, sooo I figgered I wasn't being shot at.) One of the CIDG came down the hill with his weapon on his shoulder asking for Bacsi.

I checked him out. He had a crease across the top of one arm and had a round in his leg with no exit wound. W got him back across the stream. By this time our Intel. Sgt. had gotten across the stream and led an assault up the hill. The few VC that had been there had departed. We found blood on the trail, followed it but then lost it. Afterwards, we captured two magazines for a Chenault BAR.

Our wounded man was med-evac'd to the Pleiku CIDG hospital. At that time we were using HT-1 Radios that weren't worth two cents. Black square walkie-talkie types that took 6 or 8 "D" type batteries. W called for the MEDEVAC and they wanted to know if the WIA was an American or Indig. I told the ass hole it didn't make any difference. We had a WIA, and needed him to be evacued. That was when someone at higher rank had the decision that if it was indig, the RVN would do the evac. I do not know how long that policy was continued. At the time the Huey's were just starting to become operational. The Army H-21 and the Marine Corps H-34 were the primary means of transportation.

CB Stat Team: We had a CB Team come to Poli Krong to assist in the construction of an airstrip. The CB Team Arrived with a big 5Ton truck with trailer, a jeep, a small bulldozer, and a sheeps foot roller.

Do not remember how many men were on the team, but they had an older chief and a young Lt. (Army Capt. equivalent) who wanted his men to call him captain. Never happened.

Any who, when they arrived with their equipment, the first thing they did was try to send the 5Ton truck and trailer across the river, still loaded with all their other equipment. Promptly sunk the ferry. First major job was to re-float the ferry.

This was an old French trail ferry that consisted of two barges with a deck built on them. In the event some may not know what a Trail Ferry is or how it works, it is attached to a set of pulleys/rollers mounted on an overhead cable is anchored on each side of the river. Another cable or line is attached to rollers and then attached to the ferry. Depending on which direction you wanted to go, you would have to move the cable/line from one end of the ferry to the other end. The current of the river is what powered the ferry. In the dry season, when the river was low, it could take 10 to 15 minutes to go from one side to the other. On the other hand, it would take only about 2 minutes to swing across the river.

Afterwards, the CB's had completed the airstrip. The Det Cdr asked them to clear the mine field on the south side of the camp and the airstrip. This mine field consisted of only M-14 Toe Popper's, and was put in by the Team that we had relieved. Do not remember what group they were from.

The field was probably 30-40 feet wide by the length of one side of the camp. There was no minefield plan made that I know of. It appeared there was no standard pattern, and the mines were put in the ground as single, and double and triple stacked. We did not know this at the time when the CB's started to clear the field. They decided that they would use the little D-4 bulldozer and the sheeps foot roller to run over the mines and detonate them. The driver of the dozer made a couple of passes and had to stop to refuel. While refueling he noticed that a few pads of the track were missing; that was when we determined the mines had been stacked. Needless to say, that stopped the mine clearing. I suggested to the Detachment Commander that we should use the dozer to push them into the river or make a big pile of dirt in one place, put wire around the hill and mark it mined. That didn't happen either.

Who ever picked that site for an "A" Camp should have been court-martialed. It was on the west side of the river, on the river and no way to cross except by ferry; in addition, there were a couple of small hills that were higher than the camp on the north side. Subsequently the camp was overrun in 1964. The VC set up mortars on the west end of the airstrip and attacked from the west. The came had just received a new batch of CIDG from some place. One-half were reported to be VC after the camp was overrun.

Chinese Quartermaster Division
by Jim Laritz

The first Spring Offensive started on 22 April. I didn't get there until 14 May, one of 204 replacements. It was the battle of the Imjim River from 16-18 May '51, which was part of the Second Spring Offensive. I checked further and thought I was on the Imjim River, but the list below shows our position as the Sontang River. You see how much a 16 year old grunt knows about what is going on.

Since the Second was considered the weakest Division owing to casualties suffered in the previous 90 days, it was the Chinese intent to overrun us and drive thru to the Kansas Line. Never knew there were so many bad guys trying to hurt us. Give them credit for succeeding, but at a terrible cost. It is estimated they lost over 100K just against us, but were finally beaten when they expended the last of their energy against the third ID and the 187th. The 187th 100 mile march in 72 is an epic feat. They got there tired and exhausted but ready to fight when the Chinese hit them. Note the casualty figures below. I don't know where they got their figures, but I thought my company had that many KIA alone. I know 1st Ranger was hit really hard, and we had a lot of captured. I was aware after the war that many that I thought were KIA were released from the POW camps. It took the 2nd ID a long time to live down the reputation as being the Chinese Quartermaster Division.

The enemy rested that day, then launched a second offensive on the night of 15 May, pushing back the UN right, striking on 17 May on the UN left. Putting out thousands of tons of artillery ammunition in what came to be called "the Van Fleet load," EUSAK stabilized the front. By 19 May the enemy was at a standstill, and it was the UN's turn to take up the offensive.

Apr 22-29 CCF First Spring Offensive. Largest single battle of the Korean War. CCF launch their Spring Offensive with 250,000 men in 27 divisions. Five U.S. Army divisions (2nd, 3rd, 7th, 24th, 24th) and 1st Marine Division participate. U.S.: 314 KIA; 1,600 WIA.
May 9 U.S. Far East Air Force (FEAF) launches a 300-

plane strike on Sinuiju on the Yalu River. The largest raid of the war to date.

May 16-21 Battle of the Sontang River. "May massacre" along No Name Line. 2nd ID stems the enemy tide, inflicting severe casualties on the Chinese. 23rd Inf. Regt.— 72 KIA; 158 WIA; 190 MIA.

May 17-22 CCF Second Spring Offensive. 4 U.S. divisions (1st Marine, 2nd, 3rd and 25th) participate: 333 KIA; 888 WIA

A Good Day's Work and Other Tales of Korea by CSM William Edge

KOREA, September 12, 1950: Outside Weagwan is a small city in South Korea, which there forever, and had a stone wall completely around the city. It was built to keep out the barbarians. That did not work, as the barbarians from the North had overrun and captured the city in July. Either the people had gone over to the enemy to do the labor, had fled in panic, or held/made to work on fortifying the city for the North's Army forces. In front of the city was Hill314, measured in yards above sea level meant it was about 914 feet high and heavily fortified by the North Koreans. Now it was standing between my unit and where the Generals said we were to go. Easy to say, hard to do. The mission was given to the 7th Cavalry Regiment, part of the 1st Cavalry Division.

The Division had been stationed in Japan since 1945 as part of the Occupation forces and had grown soft and ill trained, along with the other four Infantry Divisions. When the Korean War broke out on June 25, 1950, the entire US Army was caught short. President Truman took action at once to defend the South Korean Government against the

Soviet backed North. The first unit sent to Korea from Japan was the 'Task Force Smitif', a rag tag battalion made up mostly from the 21st and 19th Infantry Battalions III. Unprepared to fight and badly trained, they were easy prey for the North Koreans. Upon encounter, the enemy forces decimated and forced them to withdraw, leaving their dead in shallow graves, marked only by map coordinates. Still their sacrifice provided little time for other units to make the move to the Korea and take their place in the lines. As each Division was stripped to fill out another, the First Cavalry went then the 25th Division, and the 24th Division.

They kept the Seventh for an amphibious landing at Inchon, along with the First Marine Division. The ground forces were pushed back into what was known as the Pusan Perimeter, a large area on the Naktong River and containing the second largest city in Korea, Pusan. Fortunately Pusan was the Major port city in Korea which allowed the troop and supply buildups to take place in relative peace because the North was very reluctant to risk its small air force that far south.

After the massive buildup, several reconstituted South Korean units were moving steadily north and cutting up the North's forces. My unit, the 7th Cav regiment, pulled up in front of Weagwan and prepped for an assault on the city. However, we were told that Hill314 came first, and 3rd Battalion was to take it.

By now we were loaded for bear, having added 3rd Battalion to augment the two battalions that had been assigned when the Division was stationed in Japan as part of the occupation forces. Tank Battalions, Engineer, Artillery and support units were up to strength and fresh from the states. All of these units had been reduced to half strength while on occupation duty in Japan. When the "Pusan

Perimetee' broke out, the U S Korea, which started the Division, lost two thirds of its NCOs to fill out the 24th Division, the first American unit to go to Korea. After all, why pay soldiers when there is no war? Who needs them? Kipling was right, "tis Tommy this and Tommy that, chuck 'em out, the brute, but its all hail Mr. Atkins when the guns begin to shoot!"

Well, that policy had given the North enough motive and Soviet equipment to invade the South, and now we were back in a fall scale shooting war - only five years after the allies had TOTALLY eliminated the bad guys of the world. Of course, the United States, in a frenzy to disband the Armed forces, was nowhere near ready to enter combat anywhere, much less Korea with its tough terrain and extreme weather conditions.

Our short sighted government policy led directly to the staggering losses suffered by the weak, ill-trained U.S. Forces in the first three months of the war. After WWII, the citizens of the United States had decreed that all the military forces were to be disbanded or at least reduced greatly in size now that PEACE was at hand; after all, why pay for an Armed force when everyone knew the wars were over for all time. The Army being the largest force paid the greatest price. Units were deactivated willy-nilly. The few units kept active were absolutely gutted in order to "save money and placate the public". The units, then in the Far East, Japan and Okinawa, were all reduced by a factor of 33%. Each regiment was short one Battalion; each Battalion was short by a Company. There was no input of new gear nor did they maintain was any ammunition load.

Therefore, when Korea erupted on an unprepared South Korea and America, we were woefully short handed and totally untrained for war. In order to fill up each Division ordered to Korea, other units were stripped. Postal clerks, cooks, administrative men, service club personnel, public affairs, and musicians were all suddenly transferred as riflemen and mortar men. These men died in appalling numbers, often giving way to blind panic, fleeing the field, and abandoning weapons while doing so. Many men tried to surrender, only to be shot down as the North Korean forces had neither food nor time to handle them.

Any how, we were set to jump off with an infantry attack at something like 0400 hours which is before God gets up. The artillery was working pretty well and the tanks were helping out from dug-in hull-down positions. They were limited from really entering the town proper, by the steep hilly terrain and wet paddies outside the city. That meant the big push was to be Infantry alone, which was to be the case most of the time in Korea. Tanks could not often leave the few passable roads, nor climb the many hills; they were heavily mined, which gave the engineers plenty to do, as well as the medics. We would be aided by the 5th RCT, part of the 24th Division. The 5th was to attack Waegwan from one side while we went in on the opposite. The largest obstacle to our attack was the hill mass named Hill314. It was loaded with North Korean troops overlooking the Village. Here is where the worst of the fighting took place, at times going actual hand to hand, bayonets, pistols, firing MI s from the hip point blank in the face of the stubborn enemy. In the fight for Hill314, my Company was reduced to less than 50% effectiveness.

It was to be two Battalions abreast with a third in reserve, 1st Batt, my original assignment; as new replacement troops arrived, a new 3rd Batt was formed. The 1st with some 60 days in country was declared an old hand and transferred to form the new third, as the officer put it, "to provide some experience and set the example for the new untested troops." What a joke. I had no idea where I was at any time, nor did I ever see the BIG picture. It was one day after another, busy just trying to merely stay alive.

First we had to clear out all the dug in positions on the low ridge lines that lay before the hill, and then take on the Hill itself. This is where most of the heavy fighting took place. Once these positions were eventually destroyed, most of the enemy force inside the city promptly pulled up stakes and moved out smartly to the North.

Good plan except the weather was clear and the US Air Force got in some good licks as they departed. Close air support by PSIs carrying Napalm and 8 -50 cal machine guns can ruin your whole day. Moreover, they did! That's where I first saw what Napalm can do when dumped on troops. T'aint pretty, but sure as hell is effective. It meant that we would have fewer enemies to kill, or less of them to kill us.

The two line battalions formed up with the 3rd on the right. We had to advance over rice paddy and terraced terrain for several hundred yards, all of it steeply upwards, before we hit the first dug in resistance. The enemy had used the two months since the capture of the city to dig in several lines of bunkers and trenches, all tied in with barbed wire as if expecting to have to fight to hold on to the new territory. From my view point they had done a good job of it. This was, as we were told later Hill314, the key to Waegwan. However, they locked the door tight.

The reason they transferred me and many others was to add some combat experienced NCOs to the new 3rd Battalion which was inexperienced. They were made up of new people right out of basic training and transfers from service units in the States. Some had only been in the Army for two months! We found bunkers everywhere, each with two or more machine guns. In addition, the big Korean and Russian mortars were there in plenty. We would learn later that the guns were Russian Detreyoff drum-fed 7.62 mm, with a high rate of fire. The bunkers were constructed of log and earth, and could and did take a lot of pounding. They also issued the new 3.5inch rocket weapon or "Bazooka" as it was called. This was a huge improvement over the older 2.36 inch bazooka we were familiar with from training.

My company was on the left side of the battalion line-up, and on our left was a company from the 1st battalion. The enemy also had some artillery of its own, plus a dozen or so T-34 Russian battle tanks in the city. They dug in behind the hill mass; so it was pretty much of a fair fight, except the North Koreans had no air power that far south. Our side had some B-26 median bombers that made low level attacks on the city itself. I don't know how many enemy they killed, but they made a hell of a mess in the city, knocking down brick and wood buildings all over. Many fires were started in the old wood and thatched roofs. I discovered later why that was important when we transitioned to "combat in cities", something they had not trained us for. It was strictly "OJT" or on the job training, i.e. learn-as-you-go, if you lasted long enough to really learn anything. 90% of the units had no combat experience longer than 30 days or so. I was an "old hand" with some 60 days on line.

An infantry assault is really very simple in concept. Your unit advances on the enemy until you can go no further, then you take cover and radio for support in the form of directed artillery fire or air support on the site that is holding you up. If the site is knocked out, you continue to advance. If the site is NOT knocked out, you have two options, you can keep up the support effort until the stubborn site is finally overcome or you can then attempt to bypass it and clean it up later, if there is a later. After taking three or four trench lines we were suddenly face to face with a series of well dug in bunkers connected by a lateral trench.

One of these bunkers was directly in front of my squad and therefore my responsibility. The platoon leader came crawling up and asked if I thought my squad of now eight out of ten men, who started with me at 0400 hours, could handle it, being young and dumb (I was nineteen at the time). I answered in the affirmative if I could have a bazooka team. He agreed and sent a runner for a team. While we waited, I checked each man for ammo, first aid packets, and water on hand. I had learned that one tended to drink a lot of water when scared and under fire, and we were both. Drinking the local water was a certain trip to sick bay with galloping dysentery, and right now, Bubba!

When the two-man bazooka team arrived it was without the Lieutenant. He had business elsewhere I suppose. I pointed out the nearest bunker which was firing steadily at us and told the gunner to knock it out. He crawled up to a better position and took aim at the bunker aperture. He hit the bunker but not the aperture where the gun was. The bunker just soaked up the blast with no apparent ill effects. He put three rounds on the bunker and only raised a lot of dust and dirt. I decided then that we had better get moving on it ourselves. I told the squad what I wanted, and we began moving up to better positions, one man moving while the others covered him by aiming at the barrel of the machine gun, hoping to get some shots inside the bunker. That short trip would cost the lives of two more of my men.

As I crawled to within ten yards of the bunker I saw a crater in front of it. The crater was from a near miss by our Air force, and could not have been better for our purpose. Well, it could have been some better if it had hit the bunker. I told

the now six-man squad to stay down and keep up the fire on the aperture while my assistant squad leader and I, Jimmy Mullaney, from Baltimore,
Maryland would try and get in grenade range. I collected a dozen grenades from the others and we started to crawl toward the bunker. I didn't think they could see us because of the crater and mounds of dirt churned up by the bombs and artillery. However, I had forgotten that the next bunker in line could see us. I remembered that when we came under fire and Mullaney took a round in his right leg. When we got to within six feet of the bunker, I told Jimmy to stay in the crater and wait for a medic.

Leaving my M1 in the hole, I took half of a dozen grenades, jumped up and ran to the bunker. I got there without getting hit, stood right next to the aperture, kicked the gun barrel to one side and stuffed a grenade in the open slot. Before that one went off I had stuffed five more inside. (Too many John Wayne movies as a kid in high school.) The grenades exploded with a roar, clouds of dust blew out, and the fire from inside stopped. I yelled for the squad to advance and open up on bunker number two. Then I ran back to get my rifle and found Mullaney gone. Thinking he had gone looking for a medic, I turned and went back to the smoking bunker.

I jumped down into the trench and found myself behind the bunker with a clear path to the rear of the second bunker. I sent the squad down the trench in both directions; two men and I went to the rear of the bunker, still working back. There was a wood door in the back wall of the bunker. One man jerked the door open, another blasted his rifle inside, and I tossed in my last six grenades. My squad closed the door as the grenades exploded and all was quiet. Suddenly I realized that most of the firing had stopped. I could see Americans in all of the trenches.

As I turned around to go back toward the other bunker, a Korean soldier jumped out, aimed his gun at me and missed; I fired back and also missed. As the clip ejected from the now empty chamber, the Korean came around a corner in the trench, just in time to get a bayonet slammed in his throat, by Jimmy Mullaney! He was standing there with a bandage on his leg and jerking on his rifle to free the bayonet. I had no idea where he came from, but I was very glad he was there.

It was not yet eight o'clock and it seemed like two weeks had passed since we started this morning's stroll. Join the Army and see the world! Well, I was getting a real close look at Korea.

Now the platoon leader was back. He said we had the trench line and were to move on up to the city wall itself, enter the city and clear it of all enemy; but first he wanted to check the now silent bunkers. In the first one we found thirty-one dead Koreans, dead from six grenades. In bunker number two we found ten dead and three wounded, all wearing GI uniforms! We made them prisoners and marched off to the rear. If they made it to the rear I would have been very surprised as we had seen what the Koreans did to our guys.

We continued on and I asked Mullaney how his leg was. He said it hurt like hell, but he could walk and came on with us. When we reached the wall we found that King Company was already there and mopping up. We were assigned two different streets to clear.

Civilians were already starting to come out of the wrecked houses, each showing some sort of white cloth. Some were shot anyhow as their sudden appearance from a blasted building or a hole in the ground caused a nervousness to shoot first and check it out later. Besides no one knew who was who anyhow. It was well known by now that the NKPA wore both civilian clothing and American fatigue uniforms. We were not stopping to verify who was who!

We continued the advance and met less and less enemy resistance as we got further and further north. About a week later we were pulled out of line, refitted with needed equipment, and given three days to rest up and clean up before we moved on.

We got the word that there would be a regimental review and we were really mad about having to stand a review for some damn general. It turned out that the General was our Division Commander, and he and a bunch of staff and photographers were there to decorate some of the troops. My Battalion sent fifteen men up to get awards; Mullaney and I were two of them. I got a Bronze Star with a V device and Jimmy got a Purple Heart. WE were HEROS!!! HOT DOG!!! Of course when the General pinned the medal on me and all the pictures were taken, he moved on to the other men. A Major came along, took it back and wrote down my name, rank, service number and unit and said I would get another one later. These were only for the ceremony.

Later we would realize that we were not heroes, just dumb grunts. Still later the Battalion would be awarded two Presidential Distinguished Unit citations. However, there weren't many left alive to wear them. But, for a time I was convinced that I was a real hero, "Look out Audie Murphy! Here I come." Well, I would get two purple Hearts and some I-been-there medals. That was it for my year in Korea. I was out of the Hero business.

They shifted me over to heavy weapons and took over a machine gun section as well as four 105mm recoilless rifles mounted on jeeps. That was a lot better because I got to ride, not march. As time passed and combat became the norm, I was actually getting used to it. We were cold, wet, tired, filthy, ragged, hungry, and rattled by the constant artillery and mortar fire from the Chinese. It became a routine, and all of us were just waiting for our number to come up and get hit bad enough to be sent to Japan or be stuffed in a mattress cover. There were no plastic body bags in Korea; that would come later. Ain't progress grand?

I was to find out later via news clippings from my Mom, two guys on my high school football team and who were real close buddies had been killed in Korea. Another one was to become a POW for three years, and another guy on the same team who played left guard while I was the right guard would lose a leg on the second jump the 187 made. They were Marvin Bowers, Harnpton Tanner, Dwight Hewitt and Jack Sealy, all from the same High School in Jacksonville, Florida. I also found out after the war about my neighbor, little Jo Jo Davis, who was a skinny meek kid who flew over a hundred bombing missions as a gunner on B-29s.
Another was Gene Sleap, a year ahead of me, survived the frozen chosin' with the
U.S.Marines. I thought that a pretty stiff price to pay for a "Police Action", and I came home with scars from a bullet hole in the ribs and several pieces of a Chinese mortar shell in my young hide. I was then all of 20 years old. In addition, my Grandmother died while I was in Korea, so I never got to see her again.

Once at a place named Chin-nam-po, where we had retreated to after the Chinese Army came across the Yalu in November, over on the west coast of Korea, not far from P'yongyang, the capitol of the North, I was out on a night patrol when we were challenged in English and I heard the bolt go forward on a machine gun. Someone challenged me in a southern drawl, so I answered back that I was on patrol and who the hell were you? He told me to come forward to be recognized and discovered that the guy behind the machine gun was Homer Blackman, also from the same high school. Here we were half way around the world from home and met at a roadblock set up by the 187th Airborne.

I had no idea the 187th was in the same area as the Cav, but they had jumped north of the capitol of the North while we blasted in from the south. The 187th made two combat drops and fought the rest of the war as ground infantry. Homer said he ought to have shot me for cutting his hair off in the school initiation ritual we went through as freshmen at Andrew Jackson High. He was a year behind me in school and had quit to join the Army. All ended well and we talk about it every time we meet.

Four days later we were told we were on a peninsula, cut off by the Chinese Army and were to be evacuated by sea in LSTs that were on the way to pick us up. My unit had been retreating steadily from a high point some 40 miles south of the Yalu River that separated North Korea from China. It was a long, long walk south with several stop and block actions that always cost us more men killed, wounded and missing.

We were less than half strength when we reached the port; and were under fire as we boarded the LSTs in the river. If the Chinese had had artillery with them, we would not have made it. As it was, the ships took a lot of hits from small arms and recoilless rifles and suffered some damage. We had people wounded even as we went back down the river.

We were some 25 miles up river from the Yellow Sea and under some fire until reaching the ocean. If the Chinese had then intervened with an air force, we would have been in deep kirnchi for certain. I was firing my 105RRs and 30 caL machine guns from the deck house at targets along the river bank as was every one else. After what seemed a very long time we were clear and out to sea. I found out much later that the 187th had gone back to an airfield at P'yongyang two days earlier and had gotten out by air.

We took hot showers on the LSTs. They were the first we had for the first time in months, real meals, and tables and benches, just like the real world that had seemed so far away only a week before. They were real slow ships but we were in no big hurry to get anywhere. After a week of very rough water, we hit the tail end of a Typhoon.

We landed back in Pusan and started back up to the front, this time in trucks. By now General Ridgeway had replaced the dead Walton Walker, who was killed in a jeep accident. There were plans to counter attack north, or so went the rumor.

Many men came and went during my time in Korea. I have difficulty remembering the names of many, but I won't forget Jimmy Mullaney, though I have not seen or heard about him since 1954 when we were at Bragg. He elected to get out while I stayed in. After all, I had found a home. Three hots and a cot. That was the life.

I do remember we had a Company Commander who carried a big Colt 1917 Army .45 revolver in a Korean made shoulder holster. One day, as he was showing the Colonel around and riding in the rear seat of a jeep, he bent over to get out. The pistol slipped out of the holster, hit the hammer on the frozen ground, fired and killed him dead on the spot. I can't recall his name, but then he was not around very long.

I also remember a guy from Kentucky, a coal miner who joined the Army to get out of the mines in Hazard County. His last name was Jones and every one called him "Casey". He made it through his year and went home. I never heard of him again. I remember him because the main character in "From Here To Eternity" was from Hazard County, Kentucky, Robert E. Lee Prewitt. I recall that name but I can no longer remember real people. Old age has taken its toll. One little known fact is that there are still some 8000 men missing from that nasty little three year police action. That's four times as many as in Vietnam. Still no one cares.

Another fact is that 58,000 Americans died in Korea in THREE years of fighting. In Vietnam 58,000 also died, but that war took over ten years to run its course. Still no one cares. The Vietnam memorial took 17 years to build; the Korean Memorial took over 40 years. Still no one cares. No one remembers. Now some forty-seven years later and even after Panama, Grenada, Somalia, our very short sighted government, led by a despicable President, is doing it all over again. Will we as a people EVER learn that there are evil forces in the world who do not think like we do?

Tet
by CSM William Edge

In most of Asia the people celebrate the lunar New Year much as we Americans celebrate New Year's. Whereas our New Year comes on December 31st, the Lunar one comes in February by our calendar. In 1968, the TET in Vietnam was the time of an wholesale attack on American and South Vietnamese forces country wide, with the North Vietnamese force suffering a tremendous loss of life.

But, to the News media and TV folks covering the war it was made to took like a victory for the North. The fact was the North LOST more than 15,000 soldiers killed or wounded, while US losses were in the 1500 range, including wounded.

The big news according to Walter Cronkite was the US Embassy had been attacked and invaded; true enough, BUT he failed to mention that the enemy NEVER got inside the building and every member (twenty-two) of the attacking team was killed versus the loss of three US MPs killed.

TETI 1969
Or Lets Celebrate

However, the mere fact that the North had been able to mount such attacks at all was of great concern to all US Forces. Once again there had been plenty of warning signs but as usual the all mighty-all knowing Saigon Generals ignored them.

So, when TET of 1969 rolled around every one was a bit nervous, wondering if the North would try again. Nevertheless, to put every one at ease, the three powers involved, The American State Dept and Hanoi as well as the government of the South all agreed on a three day truce. This was so that all the Vietnamese people could enjoy their traditional holiday in peace. Some of us lowly field soldiers, far from the air conditioned, carpeted work spaces in Saigon, had our doubts, since we had been down this road before with bad results.

At the time, I was working in the coastal city of NHA TRANG, where the Headquarters of the US Army Special Forces was located. My job was relatively a peaceful one, operations Sergeant in the Plans and Operations section. However, a side job was to take a crew of myself, six radio operators and one officer to the headquarters of the Vietnamese Special Forces to act as a coordinating unit between the two commands in the event that Nha Trang was attacked.

The fly in this ointment was the fact that the Vietnamese Headquarters was located some six miles away from ours, and was in the middle of Nha Trang city. That in turn meant we had to get there by passing through the city while the fighting was going on. Maybe we would get lucky; or maybe not. Time would tell.

Well, on the night of TET (yep, you guessed it) the North broke the truce again and attacked the major cities again, but in much less strength than they had used the prior year. Still it requires only one well placed bullet to kill you. These were not the storied "Viet Cong" the press has made so much of, but were in fact hard core regular troops from North Vietnam, hardened by their long trip down from the North. They were well equipped with small arms, rocket launchers, mortars and rockets. True, they had little or no artillery, no air support at all and no Navy. Just think what they could have done if they had all the weapons our side had. Scary.

When I received the word to go, I collected my troops and we set off in an Army three-quarter truck. All of our radios were already in position at the LLDB (Vietnamese Headquarters). We almost made it with out trouble, being fired on only once during the trip and no one was hurt. We did, however, have a few bullet holes in the truck body as a reminder. When we arrived, there was no sign of trouble at that location. We went to our positions and set up the radios and got on the air, waiting for instructions.

We could monitor all the other radios and we knew that a big fight was going on all around us. Still, there was no fighting at our place. The building we were working at was a three story stone mansion built by the French when they were in control of the country. An eight foot high stone and concrete wall all around it protected it. Inside the wall there was a platform for guards to walk around on so they could see the outside. When we arrived, a number of Vietnamese guards manned it.

At about midnight, I went outside to smoke a cigarette with one of my Sergeants, John Sutter. As I lit up he said to me, "Hey Bill, where are all the fucking guards?" Hell I didn't know. There were none visible on the walls at all. However, we soon found out. Not putting a fine a point on it, they had bugged out, scooted, and departed the scene, GONE.

While standing there wondering what was going on there was a very big explosion and a whole section of the wall disappeared, leaving a gaping hole, open to the outside. That was good! We saw people running toward the hole, and they did not look any too friendly either. They had guns and everything, and looked upset about something.

Not knowing what else to do, I jumped in the truck and drove it into the hole in the wall, almost plugging it up. That was good except for one small thing. I was now on the wrong side of the wall. Well, Setter was banging away with his M16 from the wall, and I started a mad scramble to climb upon the truck and get back inside.

The bad guys were shooting the truck all to pieces. It was a total loss, and when things quieted down we had no way to get back to our base. We had to explain that to the Motor officer, who was mighty upset that his motor pool was now short one truck.

By now, all the men from any team were on the way and blazing away at the Sappers, trying to destroy the wall and get inside. Let me explain just what a Sapper is, or was. These were North Vietnamese soldiers who had a very large-bag full of explosives STRAPPED to their backs with wire. They would run across the street, lean on the wail, pull the igniter and blow themselves and the wall into the next world. Now that requires some dedication, far more than I possess.

Duty calls, but not that loudly for me. I don't know what went wrong with their timing but they had given' us just enough time to mount the wall and defend it.

Fortunately, we were able to hold them off by ourselves while some of the Vietnamese soldiers returned to the wall to lend a hand. It was a hard night, and it went on for several hours. All the outgoing fire started in the multitude of shops across the street, and burned down with a considerable portion of the center city.

I personally killed no less than ten brave soldiers that night. Our troops killed eighteen all told. For my work that night I was recommended for a Distinguished Service Cross. I ended up with a second Silver Star and the Vietnamese Cross of Gallantry with Gold Star. I was never told anything other than the board had downgraded the award to a Silver Star. Oh well, at least I was alive and wonder of wonders unwounded. I was happy to settle for that.

We held on until dawn when we saw a company of South Korean troops coming down the street in battle formation; and those boys were taking no prisoners. They were in an ugly mood, having been in the thick of fighting all night. They machine gunned every thing and any thing that was in sight. As they approached, they would toss grenades into the burning buildings, making certain that there would be few if any enemy left behind.

As they passed their office, I looked up and they said in perfect English, "You can stop now. We will take care of the problem." Moreover, take care of it they did. Whenever a house or a shop was suspected of hiding an NVA soldier, they destroyed it with no questions asked. The Korean troops caused as much if not more damage -than the NVA did to downtown Nha Trang. The South Vietnamese troops were as terrified of the Koreans as they were of the NVA. No one dared complain.

So ended the Tet holiday of 1969. After all the fighting there was not a lot left to celebrate. The NVA had, among other things, destroyed a restaurant that was full of, people celebrating in hopes that the truce was for real. Most of them were civilians. The NVA also shot up the local hospital. There they killed all those who could escape, which was the majority. In addition, several nurses were killed alongside the wounded soldiers. Those boys play rough and for keeps. Maybe that accounts for why there were so few prisoners taken by our side. Just a thought. Still, all the US media was loudly proclaiming that the VC had scored another victory, The US should pull out; it was an immoral war, etc, and so on. Sorta makes one wonder why we fight so hard to preserve Freedom of the Press. Ours is not to reason why, ours is but to fight and die, or so the poem goes.

Bee Sting
by Bryan Furman

I remember being stung by a VC bee. In a few paces I knew I was in trouble with dizziness while walking, and not carrying any epinephrine. My airway was swelling and I couldn't breath. I quickly passed out and woke up in the 9th Hospital. At the time, an LLDB who was out with me called to camp to report my condition. The camp called a medivac that first picked up a team member and flew to haul me out. The SF team mate SFC Harry H. stayed with the CIDG. I was unconscious most of the time, and had to find out what happened when I got back to camp the same day. I was reported dead by someone, and supply had distributed my stuff and trashed my kit. I was back in camp before dusk the same day.

I was known as the guy medivacked for a bee sting. (No purple heart).

Web Gear
by John Cleckner

Our Team at Dong Tre had the very early version of the M-16 and all of our strikers had M-1 and M-2 carbines. It never occurred to me that if I went out I would have a different type of weapon from my Strikers and that would be "Bad"...

Intelligence told us that there was a lot of movement about 10 kilometers north of our Camp so we planned a short 3 day operation to see if we could find anyone moving around.

This was a day light "start" operation, which was very rare. By early afternoon we found some movement after entering a Village about 10 klicks north of us. We also found massive defensive positions. As we moved through the village, it was evident we were in a VC/NVA area. I had never seen bunkers and trenches dug around a village like this one. It was deserted, and had no fires burning or any other signs of life.

All of a sudden all hell broke loose. As we cleared the northern part of the village we had a hundred or so guys in black PJs in front of us (caught in the open). I called "District HQ" to see if they had RF-PF out on any kind of operation. The reply was "NO". These were definitely Bad Guys.

I deployed our "Stickers" along the top of the bunker complex and on my signal I told everyone to "Fire for Effect". I was firing like a wild man with no discipline and of course on full automatic. Within minutes I had NO AMMO left. The other American was also out of ammo. I cannot tell you how bad the feeling was in the pit of my stomach.

By the way, the little people were not about to give us their guns, and their ammo did not fit our weapons obviously. It

was one helluva lesson, and what made it worse was in those days resupply was almost out of the question.
I prayed the VC would not turn and attack. They didn't and the battlefield was strewn with bodies. Then I got another lessen. The LLDB said "We go" and they left the area without a BDA. I was a new 2d Lt. and didn't have the counterpart relationship routine down yet. They would not listen to a thing I had to say in this regard.
When I returned to the Camp I told my weapons man the story and asked for his advice. My thought was to design web gear to hold an incredible about of ammo and still be comfortable enough to wear in the jungle and be able to move and shot.
I built the web gear he recommended I used it to give me the maximum amount of firepower I needed. The basic web gear of the day was used in conjunction with a WWII BAR Belt. I used banana clips taped in twos and put them into the BAR pouches standing up side by side. The final product weighed about 65 pounds with two, two-quart canteens of Water. (Bullets and Water that's all I needed) I also carried an Indig Ruck with an Indig hammock and Indig poncho and some string. It didn't weight anything.

Just like the Big Guys or Smoke 'Em If Ya Got 'Em
by Charlie Broz

I was a young E-5 in CCC Recon Co., and had just been named the 1-0 of one of the Recon Teams. My best buddy was also a young E-5 1-0. Another factor that bound us together was the fact that we were 23 or 24-year old college dropouts, flunkouts, and/or kick-outs who wanted a taste of excitement, action, or whatever; hence, we ended up in SOG Recon. Perhaps stunning eloquent testimony at higher education and book learnin' sure as hell don't make you smarter.

I need to emphasize that we took our jobs as 1-0's very seriously indeed. But as young E-5 troopers, probably since time immemorial, we also had a sardonic and irreverent streak in us with which we viewed our seniors, the Army, and indeed the entire SE Asia war. In no way did the above imply a lack of respect, but when I think back, it was probably a defense mechanism that allowed us to deal with the real deal.

After missions, Sgt. Fury and I would joke around and say we were getting the 50-mission crush in our hats JUST LIKE THE BIG GUYS. Indeed anything that any RT did out in the weeds was something the BIG GUYS would do. And of course we wanted to be JUST LIKE THE BIG GUYS.

I drew a warning order for an area recon and was told that I would have a strap-hanger, an O-3 who ran on another RT. I knew that this guy was going along to check out my shit. Hey, no big deal, says I. 'Cuz if learned one thing over there, running recon, it was that I could never learn enough about running recon.

The AO turned out to be one big dry hole. Sure as hell didn't disappoint me, even one teeny bit. At the end of our 5th or 6th day, my request for exfil was granted. Now we were in some heavy jungle. Really couldn't find a good LZ. Ah no problem, says I, because I'm going to be like one of the BIG GUYS and blow an LZ. Hey, no shit! It sounded like a great idea. My 1-2 was a demo guy, and he said no sweat; he could blow a hole in the jungle to a get a slick into. And I'll be damned if I wanted to ride the ropes all the way back to Dak To (we were over the fence). He rigged a couple of claymores to do the deed. I set security, and we hunkered down to wait for extract.

I had marked my position to Covey with a shiny and told him my intent. Got word that the slicks were inbound and 05 mikes out. I was running an 8 man RT, and this was to be a triple-header extract. So we needed two slicks in. Time to blow the LZ, just like the BIG GUYS would do. Ok, CA-RUMP we denote the claymores. Beautiful, just as planned a one-ship LZ appears in the jungle. But the area is kinda dry, like really kinda dry. And a small fire starts licking at the vegetation near us...all the fucking vegetation.

The first slick gets in and four RT members get on and lift out, no problem. This leaves four of us on the ground, my 0-1, another Yard, the 0-3, me. Now we got a slight problem. The down draft from the first slick and that of the second slick flaring in have fanned the flames of the small fire. It's now a big fire, a REALLY BIG FOOKING fire. I'm talking towering inferno, the bowels of Hell. I mean the National Forest Service would need a full mobilization to put this mother out. Really big trees are on fire. The whole goddamn jungle is on fire. The four of us are nearly on fire. Oops, think I fucked up. For the first time on the whole mission, I see a look of something like panic on this O-3's face. And he says to me words to effect that we can't make it out.

And I says back to him, "Bullshit! We're getting out of here, just watch us."

Well, I'm in touch with Covey, who I knew real well and he's laughing his ass off. I see the pilots in that second slick through the plexi-glass, who brought that bird into my maelstrom, laughing like hell and they're all telling me to get my ass on that bird. Anyway, we got through the flames and into the slick and those fantastic pilots got us out of my fook-up. Looking back as we clattered and whopped back to Dak To, I knew I really did set that damn jungle on fire.

Another buddy of mine was the 1-0 in an adjacent A-O and he told me later he damned near wore out a CAC pad trying to find out what all the smoke was that blew into his target area. At any rate that was the last time I ever tried that damn stunt and I ran a bunch more missions as a 1-0. Figured I best leave blowing an LZ to the BIG GUYS. But what the hell…smoke 'em if ya got 'em.

Laos
by Darrell Hoefling

On the way across the border into Laos I would sing the "This ole man, he played one..." song over and over.

I was 19, and gripped my car-15 like the old friend it had become. I looked down into the green and remembered when it was my favorite color. Soon we crossed over the red of Khe Sahn and then over the mountains on the border where there was often AA. We slipped past that and went on to our primary landing zone. The lead chopper veered off suddenly and we were on to the secondary. The first chopper dropped in with the 1-0; and half the team, me, and the others in the second for a total of eight men: three Americans. This time, we had a new guy along. They were now below us, and we could see tracers coming up at them. I saw the door gunner open up on the landing zone and the tree line.

The helicopter hovered a few feet above the ground and the team was out of the huey, running and shooting, "Our turn is next." I stopped singing.

As we came in, we started taking fire. There was so much adrenalin pumping, I wasn't aware how scared I actually was. The helicopter blades started to whistle from bullet holes, and we jumped out. I hit the ground hard, glanced to my left and saw a bloody body. It was an NVA DZ watcher, part of the anti-recon team trained to keep us out. I sprinted low toward the rest of the team. The hueys lifted and were gone. We were in Laos, and on the run.

Adventures in Germany
by Bill Coombs

My favorite memory of Detachment: A Berlin Brigade

Two of us (sorry I can't recall who was with me) drove two of our brand new Volkswagen busses down to Bad Toelz. We loaded them up with Communist bloc nation weapons. The backs of both vehicles were filled up to the window level and we covered up the weapons with Army blankets. Then we headed back to Berlin.

At Check Point Alpha in Helmstedt, one of the MP's asked if I would be willing to take a hitchhiker back to Berlin. As long as he had his flag orders and the MP's OK'd it, it was all right with me. Turns out he was a Military Intelligence Captain who had been on TDY to West Germany.

We were about an hour into East Germany when the Captain stretched and hit his hand on something under a blanket. He asked what I had back there and I told him that they were communist weapons that we were bringing to Berlin for training.

He almost shit! There we were, in Communist East Germany with a load of commie weapons. He asked me what I would do if the VOPOs or the Russians inspected what we had back there. I told him not to worry as that very rarely happened.
Then I had an evil thought, and reminded him that he was the ranking man.

The Captain never said another word until we were safely through Checkpoint Bravo in Berlin. A couple of days later, Major Shachnow told me he had met the Captain who said that he would never accept another ride with anyone from Detachment A.

Memories. Just another day in the life of an SF Supply Sergeant.

Chaplain's Assistant
by Bill Coombs

I was the Sergeant of the Guard in Bad Toelz one evening. A Captain who was a Team Leader from Lenggries was Officer of the Day. He was a sharp guy. We had sentries from both Toelz and Lenggries. As the OD was questioning a sentry, he asked him what his job was, and asked questions based on his MOS. He asked what seemed to me to be very difficult questions: What shape is a shape charge? How many ohms in an amp? What is the rifling like in a Monrovian machine gun?
One of the guys worked at Personnel, and he asked him a question about the officer's records. He stood in front of a SP4 from HHC. The conversation went like this:

OD: "What is your job?"
Sentry: "Chaplain's Assistant, Sir."

The Captain looked at me and then back to the sentry.

OD: "What does a Chaplain's Assistant do in Special Forces?"
Sentry: "Assists the Chaplain, Sir."

The Captain must have been a heathen because he had no more questions and the Chaplain's Assistant was selected as the supernumerary (The Man).

Before Father Murphy was assigned to the 10th Group, we had no Catholic chaplain. The leg sub-post Chaplain was filling in. Chaplains, even if they are single, get quarters in the housing area. One time, the SP4, who made the man at the guard mount, was house sitting for the chaplain.

The Chaplain returned from vacation a day early and found the Chaplain's assistant having his way with one of the Bad Toelz lovelies in the Chaplain's bed. We all assist in our own way, I guess.

A- 502 Stories
by Bill Coombs

I have an A-502 story with a logistical twist. I don't recall why but they needed a stove/range for their kitchen. All I had in stock was a large stove of the type used at the Consolidated Mess. As they needed one immediately, I issued them the large one on a temporary basis until a smaller one came in. That seemed to make them happy.
A while later, in December, one of their guys comes into my office at the LSC and puts down two large paper bags filled with bottles of booze. After we finished up our business, he started to leave and I reminded him not to forget his bags. He really had forgotten about them.

He then said, "Sergeant Coombs, this is a gift to you for your support of A-502."
I asked him to stop the bullshit, and told him he was giving me that booze, not for what I had done in the past, but what they thought I would do for them in the future. I told him to take his booze with him.

Just as he was leaving, CW2 Pappy Shoe, the Property Accountable Officer, walked in and the Sergeant offered the booze to him. Mr. Shoe, being more diplomatic than me, accepted it only on the condition, that it was a contribution to the Christmas party for the "entire LSC staff" to which A-502 was invited. Ah, memories.

LTC Riggs
by Bill Coombs

I was in Co A, of the 7th in early 1961, and was with a small group when LTC Riggs approached us. I saw him coming and told an NCO. He called ATTENTION. Riggs jumped in my shit because I did not call ATTENTION.

He said, "You saw me first, Coombs, and YOU should have called ATTENTION." I was just an SP4; all I could say was something like, "Er, humma, humma."

Riggs said, "Either shape up or ship out." I got my courage up and told him I was shipping out the next week for Bad Toelz. Then he got very friendly, and he and the others spent about a half an hour telling me good things about Toelz.

Each morning, we had the Reveille Formation at O dark thirty. The only ones who had to attend were the guys living in the barracks. In Company A, that accounted for about ten of us. One morning, it was so dark; we could not see who it was taking the report. We soon found out who it was when the reports were rendered. The Captain who reported for our company said, "COMPANY A, ALL

PRESENT" rather than "ALL PRESENT AND ACCOUNTED FOR."

As the Company B report was started, Colonel Riggs interrupted and said, 'If Company A is ALL PRESENT, I will kiss your ass in the middle of the parade field." The poor Captain had to report to him after Reveille. I don't know what happened to him.

Ah, memories.

ED (Exempt from Duty)
by Bill Coombs

Like others on the list, Childress was my First Sergeant in Toelz when I was a SP4/SGT. I watched him and learned a lot about how to handle troops. He did something on duty rosters that was illegal but appreciated by most of the troops. He made sure that no married guy whose family was with him had duty on Christmas and no unmarried guy had duty on New Year's Eve regardless of where they stood on the duty roster.

I think the thing that stuck with me most during my Army career was his position on Exempt from Duty (ED). He believed that everyone in the company (with very few exceptions) would pull duty. Guys who had duties similar to the duty roster jobs (Night Dispatcher at the Motor Pool for example) did not pull CQ.

I did not witness the following, but heard it from a friend. SGM P. wanted the Colonel's driver to be ED. 1SG Childress did not agree, and told the Sergeant Major that on the days that the driver was on duty, he would provide a replacement for him. That satisfied SGM P.

In my later years, I was known for being very anti-ED. Learned it from SGM Childress.

He had his own vernacular and you had to learn it to understand him. A good example was in formation one day. He made the announcement that all 'flap dicks' had to be in the theater at a certain time and that 'hard dicks' would go to their duty stations. A new guy asked me what he meant by that. "Flap dicks' were the married guys who got plenty of pussy, and "hard dicks" were the guys who lived in the barracks.

He would brief all of the new guys in the company and he used improper grammar when he would point to his First Sergeant stripes and say, "In this company, Diamonds is trumps."

When Childress was 1SG of HHC, 10th SFG, Major Berkeley S. was one of the commanders. S. told us he reserved his punishment for serious offenses he felt junior leaders could not resolve.

He said, and I paraphrase, "If you have done something your Section Leader, Platoon Sergeant, or the First Sergeant feel they cannot mete out proper punishment for, and you get in front of my desk, you will get the max."

Remember that a field grade could really put the damn on you. Much more than a Captain. Restriction for a couple of months, retention of pay, two grade reduction, etc.

So, when one of the boys had screwed up, 1SG Childress would ask, "Would you like to go before Major S., or do you want me to handle it?"

Most of them picked the 1SG's Article 15, and he worked their asses off for many nights. We had the cleanest halls and latrines in Bavaria, but at least, the punishment did not appear on their records.

Sergeant Major Childress was a good guy.

The Infamous Battle at the SFOB
by Bill Coombs

Those folks who visited the Special Forces Operational Base in Nha Trang, Vietnam knew it was a relatively safe place to be stationed. The SFOB was located between some mountains and the US Air Force Base. On occasion, the Viet Cong would fire mortar rounds at the air base and for whatever reason, some of the rounds could not reach that distance, and the short rounds would fall on the SFOB.

As I recall during the almost four years I was at Nha Trang, there was only one attack that was definitely aimed at us. They hit our ammo dump and did a fair amount of damage. One of the results of that attack was all of the glass was blown out of the 5th SFG commander's sedan. Two things remain in my memory from that attack.

We had a very special supply system whereby we could get material quickly and could go out of regular military channels due to our funding sources. About a week after the attack, I went on leave to Waltham, MA and carried in my hot little hands, a purchase request for all of the glass for the old man's sedan. I took the request to a Chevrolet dealer in Waltham and left it with the Parts Manager. The purchase request called for air delivery. When I got back to Nha Trang about three weeks later, the CO's car looked spiffy with all brand new glass.

A few days after the attack, guys started receiving clippings from home that were printed in the *Fayetteville Observer* reported on the attack on the 5th SFG HQ. The reports had us fighting in the trenches. There was no personal contact with the Viet Cong. They popped a few mortar rounds and left. As I recall, there were a couple of guys who received minor wounds and that was the extent of it.

The reports were really blown out of proportion and I have no idea who wrote them. I think they were meant to shock the families back in the Fort Bragg area and that was a shame. Very poor reporting.

Troops Going Berserk
by Bill Coombs

When I was serving my hardship tour in Hawaii, some of my troops worked at the mortuary. I would drop in from time to time to visit them. One day, they were preparing a young sailor for burial. A Honolulu policeman came into see the body.

It seems that this 5' 10" 160 pounder was loaded up with LSD and had the strength of five or six 200 pounders. He got drunk at a club near Pearl Harbor, and did something that caused the police department to be called.

They tried to calm him down, and when they attempted to cuff him, he started tossing three or four cops around like they were stuffed animals. He did a job on a couple of them. Finally, one of them got behind him and put his billy club across his throat. The cop's feet were off of the ground the way this kid was tossing him around. Well, finally the blood must have been cut off to his brain and he dropped down dead.

I looked at the kid's body and could not believe what they were telling me. The Honolulu policeman explained they ran into this all of the time with folks who take drugs and then mix it with booze. He said some of the women in this condition are tougher than men.

The sailor's family filed a lawsuit against the Honolulu Police Department but it was dismissed. I never asked the policeman who came to the mortuary if he was the one who finally brought the sailor down.

Who Didn't Get Promoted to Sergeant Major by Bill Coombs

I will never forget the day that Childress made Sergeant Major. Dave C. was the S-4 NCO in Pleiku. He deserved the promotion and as we knew it was going to go to a Supply Sergeant, I knew he had it made. I was visiting Pleiku that day and decided to stay over because Dave was going to buy me a drink. He felt that he would not make it. We went down the list of
Master Sergeant Supply types in the 5th SFG and he had time in grade on all of them.

Later on that afternoon, Dave came over to me with a long face and said they just got the results of the board at Nha Trang. I thought he was kidding me with the long face and would say, "Surprise, Surprise." What he did say was a surprise but not a happy one for Dave. They changed Childress' MOS to 76Z and gave him the promotion.

Thinking of Dave C. after all of this time gave me a thought. In SF, for the most part, you kept running into the same guys. In Bad Toelz, I was an E-4/E-5 working at the Group S-4 and Dave was the S-4 of one of the C Teams in Lenggries. I never screwed over anyone. When he came to S-4, I took care of him.

A couple of years later, I am the Company Supply Sergeant of Co E (Signal) in Panama and who would you guess is the S-4 Sergeant? Go to the head of the class; MSG Dave C. If I had been less than professional with him in Bad Toelz, he could have made things difficult for me in Panama.

Fast speed ahead a couple of years. Dave is in Pleiku and Coombs controls the issue of supplies down in Nha Trang. Of course, I did not use it on Dave but what if I was an asshole and thought that Dave had screwed with me in Panama?

Bragging a bit, I had pretty good relations with most of the guys in Group. But we all know of the rivalries that traveled from Group to Group.

Gooey Grains
by David Stafford

A man with the balls to cast his faith and body into a pod of meat-eating Orcas states:
"...stand up and in true SF fashion, do something even if it is wrong."

I had three guys with tender knees, one with bad back troubles, and two more complaining of recently re-injured ankles. Individual vulnerability coupled with the wintry weather had provided two additional mucus-filled chests to our merry band.
Sixty-six percent of ODA-084 was fucked up...

"Dave," one of the biggest said. "This f--ken' superstar needs his shit straightened out. Do something!"

Boozers, rogues, parents, and geniuses filled our team. I had never felt more safe or comfortable in all my life. My job was to secure their best interests and make sure the world didn't kick them too hard in the ass.
"How's the knee?" I asked.

"Fuck my knee," he growled. "You need to reach inside that candy cabinet of yours and put and end to this shit...now!"

We had recently received a new team sergeant. He had a history of being a wonderful typist, of having a little man syndrome, and of acquiring a newly developed personal penchant for running.

For four straight weeks my people had bested the hilliest inclines of Fort Devens as all other members of B Company, Third Battalion broke from formation to swim in a pool's heated water, lift weights, or shoot hoops. The weather and the whining were particularly bad on this day.

"What do you want me to do?" I asked moving my eyes from him to another teammate massaging his Ace-bandaged knee.

My shoulders were grabbed hard. I read the intense eyes. "We don't give a f--k what you do. Poison the prick."

"I can't do that."

"Sure you can," my other Ace-bandaged colleague muttered. "That dickhead is using us to shine. F--kin' boot licker. He's been here a month and he just called me by your name."

I read the intensity of another pair of worried eyes. "Let me think on it," I said.

"Think fast!" four miserable guys barked in harmony.

I had observed the progression. I had marked a significant pattern. Immediately after the formation, Top Peebles would bolt into the team room, gulp two, heaping cups of java, and travel over across to the B team to smooch the CO's ass. This guy clearly needed to stand out for some reason. While shivering in a snowy formation, an idea struck.

"So you want this guy slowed down huh?" I whispered to my desperate, limping shoulder-grabber.

"Slowed down? No! I want the fucker doubled over!" he growled.

"Okay," I said. "After formation you and the others

keep him out here with some questions. I'll need a minute."

"You'll have time," he said. "We'll tackle that brown-nosing, self-serving piece of shit if we have to." Many heads nodded in agreement alongside him.

My people went swimming with the other teams that morning, lobar pneumonia was subsequently treated, and my gimps had two normal patterned weeks to deal with their swelling.

I ended up needing resupply for a missing half bottle of Ipecac syrup.

We got our old team daddy back when the superstar typist turned his ankle on the Co's steps shortly thereafter.

This non-fiction is dedicated to the nurturing spirit of Mr. Ben Roberts, Special Forces Medic, SS recipient, forearm burning taunter of Orcas.

Captain Lukow's Inventory
by Don "Val" Valentine

It was Ban Houie Sai, Laos in May and the temperature was over a hundred ten degrees twenty four hours a day every day. We were on the air strip on the banks of the Mekong River in Northern Laos. The only shade was a piece of tin on four bamboo poles which LTC Kaplan had claimed for his CP.

The Pathet Lao had overrun Nam Tha, a mountain outpost in the NNW part of Laos and was marching towards Ban Houie Sai. The Royal Lao Army had fled to Thailand. Only the USSF team and interpreters remained in Northern Laos, until LTC Kaplan, a Maggot, (nickname for a member of a Military Advisory Group) came to provide us with his superior experience, wisdom and leadership.

Captain Lukow, one of our B Team staff officers, sent a message to Captain Hank (Henry Ellison) and requested a detailed inventory of our "training aids." Captain Hank ignored it. We kept a couple of guys with our only jeep on guard on the Nam Tha Road just outside town for early warning. A couple of days later, Captain Lukow repeated his request. Captain Hank ignored it again

Then I received another brilliant order from General Tucker, "No U.S. personnel will cross into Thailand again. Regardless of what happens, you (all 21 of us) will defend the Ban Houie Sai airfield." Since we already had information that we were facing approximately 5,000 enemies, that news did not make our day.

Somebody decided that we should relocate again the next day and we kept one FTT on the airfield with their backs against the riverbank. The other guys were to stay on an island that was in the middle of the river out of range of small arms fire. Captain Hank assumed that the island was not in Thailand; at least it was not "across" the river. They had decided to play roulette again.

We soon ran out of food, and I only had four shotgun shells, six rounds for my .357 revolver, and two hand grenades. No more ammo was to be had for my rather unconventional weapons. Choosing those romantic weapons had proven to be a serious fuck up on my part. This was when I discovered that I should have chosen one of the M-1 Garands; we had plenty of ammo for them. Yes sir, I was wishing that I had a nice Garand Rifle and an army-issue forty-five automatic pistol with plenty of ammo for both. Oh well, that's how rookies learn, assuming they survive the experience of course.

No field rations were available and we were not supplied any kind of food through military channels. We were the only humans around so there were no stores or farmers from which to buy food. We definitely had a problem. Captain Hank requested food and we waited.

Captain Johnson's FTT was the first to pull duty on the airfield. Colonel Kaplan stayed with me and my trusty 109 radio set. Kaplan still loved to have me encrypt and transmit those damn novels that he called messages. The first thing that we did was dig some holes in an "L" shaped mound of dirt that was near the riverbank. That was the area where the airport people had stored gasoline drums.

Securing the left flank was my responsibility; it was level and open for about fifty yards, except for some thick tall grass. The other guys covered the airfield area with their rifles and carbines, and I think O'Rourke covered the thick underbrush along the river on the right flank with his Thompson Sub-machinegun. No one watched our rear; we were backed up against the river. The riverbank there was very steep and about 15-25 feet above the river.

Tex set about making some improvised grapeshot charges to string out in front of us. In flew a light airplane and out jumped the civilian pilot, an American, and three reporters, also Americans, from the English paper in Bangkok. Those reporters nosed around and asked us all a bunch of questions, but we weren't interested in giving them any information. Mostly we referred them to the officers. One stopped and asked Tex, "Whatcha making buddy?" Tex smiled and replied, "Mud pies!" Tex strung his blasting line, but just connected blasting caps. He wanted to test the circuit without charges to make sure that it would handle that many blasting caps. Then Tex set off the caps.

A detonated blasting cap sounds like a .22 caliber pistol muzzle blast, and this was several caps all at once. Those reporters scrambled for their plane. They grabbed their pilot, who was laughing so hard he could hardly walk much less run, and drug him to the plane and off they went. The next day that same pilot returned without any passengers to pay for the flight. He just wanted to bring us a copy of that day's paper fresh off the press. That was about a six hundred mile trip from Bangkok. I do not recall which page it was on, but there it was, a small article about the "terrible mortar barrage" that we had suffered while they were there. It was worth another laugh.

In the meantime, we had been searching by chopper all day every day for Murphy and Loobey. We took turns going with the choppers. On the third day after we had lost them, we found them. They were hungry, but otherwise okay. They had a villager's abandoned pet dog with them. The dog had taken up with them; and they didn't mind because he was potential food, and they didn't even have to carry it. They had decided to eat him that night, if they weren't picked up. That was one lucky dog.

When the enemy started to flank them, Murphy and Loobey field-stripped their A-6 machine gun, threw the parts into the brush and then tried to evade the enemy.
All of their troops had already bugged out. They mostly hid. When they decided to move again, Murphy crept through some underbrush and came face-to-face with an enemy soldier. Murphy and the Pathet Lao soldier were muzzle-to-muzzle. It was a no win situation. Without saying a word both men backed off until they were out of sight of each other: then they both fled.

We sure were glad to see Murphy and Loobey, especially the guys on their team. In flew the choppers with several cases of C-Rations that had been found someplace in southern Laos. It had been three days since we had eaten. We issued the rations and I opened mine. The rations were dated 1952. In my can of crackers there was only dust and dead moths. I have no idea how those moths got into a sealed can. The C-Rations were inedible so we were still hungry.

We also had no fresh drinking water. The temperature was over one hundred degrees Fahrenheit day and night. There was no well or spring anywhere near the airfield, and the village was too far away because now we had no idea where the commie horde was located. A water party could be cut off and never get back to us. So we filled five gallon cans from that muddy river - boy, was it muddy. We spiked it with enough water purification pills to kill a horse and then let it set for a couple of days, hoping that the mud would settle to the bottom. It didn't and it tasted like shit and I tried not to think of what I had seen in that damn river just a few days ago.

Captain Lukow repeated his request again. By now Captain Hank was hot, hungry, tired, thirsty and pissed-off. This time Captain Hank wrote a message for me to send to Captain Lukow. It read something like this, "To Luke the Gook! Our training aids consist of the following: One battalion of Royal Laotian Soldiers who just finished practicing their river crossing techniques using motorized boats, canoes and logs. Said battalion enjoyed it so much they never returned; two men have just field-tested our Escape and Evasion Course; ten cases of inedible C-Rations; and 5,000 pop-up, shoot-back targets of various calibers. If you ask me for an inventory again you skinny son of a bitch, I promise you, I will kick your ass all the way back to Okinawa, if I survive this damn fiasco. Hank sends."

We got no more silly requests from Captain Lukow after that. The same day, Captain Hank made what is commonly referred to in the Green Machine as a "command decision." He sent our interpreters to Thailand with all the money that we had to buy food. Our interpreters were Thai, not US. So, that night we finally ate. I don't remember what we ate, and I'll be honest with you; at the time, it didn't really matter very much what it was.

A Chinese Wedding
by Don "Val" Valentine

Our Chinese Battalion Sergeant Major married a beautiful Chinese lady while our A-Team was stationed with MACV-SOG of Command and Control North Forward Operational Base in Danang. All of the SF assigned to the Hatchet Force at CCN on China Beach and my entire platoon were invited to their reception. Maybe my platoon was invited because they were the only parachute unit in the battalion and had just finished all of their training. I really do not know why my entire platoon was invited because they were the newest recruits and almost all teenagers.

At any rate, the reception was held at a restaurant in downtown Danang. Schofield and I took our platoon down in 2 ½ ton trucks. Danang was off limits to U.S. personnel at the time except for official business. How this party qualified as official business, I didn't know.

Anyway, things in that restaurant got mighty drunk and mighty loud. One of my little Nungs filled a small plastic glass, about 3-4 ounces I guess, and a tall 12 ounce glass with whiskey and handed the large one to me. He toasted the couple, downed the whiskey in the smaller glass, and told me to toast and drink up. However, I toasted and only sipped.

The little soldier said, "Oh, no Sargie, I drank all, you drink all." They all had a good laugh when I told him, "F--k you, you little shit. I'm not that much bigger than you."

It was very late by the time I finally got my troops out of that restaurant. Maybe I was drunk, but I wasn't nearly as drunk as they were. Most of them had to be drug out and tossed on the truck; but while I was back inside getting some more, at least one of those little dudes that I had already put in the truck would wake up and crawl back off the truck. What a damn mess that was and loud, boy were those little shits loud. They were loud enough to cause someone to call the White Mice (Vietnamese Police) down on my noisy, little drunk Chinese.

The Viets and the Nungs hated each other. The Viets also hated all of the mountain natives, and I know the feeling was mutual in both cases. My boys were not armed. The White Mice were armed with clubs, pistols and M-16s. They bad-mouthed and threatened my China-boys. A White Mice poked one of my China-boys in the stomach with the muzzle of his rifle. My little Nung quickly disarmed him and threw his rifle away. Maybe his daddy had taught him that trick, I didn't recall teaching it. I thought for sure he was going to blow that cop away and get us all slaughtered.

Suddenly a miracle happened. I finally got all of my China-boys on those trucks without anyone getting shot, and off to camp we went. Of course, I was unaware of it at the time, but the White Mice had arrested our Chinese Battalion Commander, who was also at the party, and had taken him to jail. As I lay on my bunk, I felt very proud of myself, even though I was as drunk as a skunk, my common sense and military bearing had prevailed. My little Nungs had followed their great white leader home.

Shortly after I hopped into bed, I heard my loud, drunk little Nungs chattering and the trucks cranking up again. My little Nungs were in full battle garb with, grenades, machine guns, M-16 rifles and M-79 grenade launchers; and I staggered to the door just in time to wave goodbye to them as they headed back downtown to settle their dispute with the White Mice. My brain just wouldn't believe what my eyes were seeing. My little devils were armed to the teeth and grinning from ear-to-ear. The only reason my little devils had returned to camp with me was to get their weapons; so much for my inspirational leadership.

The next morning I found out what happened. Our troops had gone straight to the source of the problem, the Police Chief. How they knew where he lived, I do not know. They surrounded his home and demanded the release of their Battalion Commander and immunity from prosecution. Apparently negotiations did not proceed fast enough to suit them, so they fired an M-79 grenade through the window of the house to speed things up. The grenade blew off the leg of the Police Chief's wife. The two sides quickly reached an agreement.

Our Nungs got their commander back, but they could never again enter downtown Danang. The White Mice erected a sign on the bridge between the beaches and the mainland that warned our Nungs that they would be shot on sight, if they were found downtown. White Mice also manned a roadblock at this bridge from then on, just to enforce this new law.

Famous Jump School Cadre
by Don "Val" Valentine

I remember two cadre from the 82d AA's Pre-BAC (Mar-April '55), Cpl Kirk, my platoon cadre, and SSG Jones, who I believe was NCOIC of Pre-BAC and also another platoon's cadre. I believe we had a platoon from each regiment and maybe a fourth platoon that was composed from the other units, but I'm not sure.

Jones was the pushup king and Kirk was the runner. I remember one day we were in mass formation at close interval just prior to PT (or just after), and we didn't react fast enough to please Cpl Kirk. He ordered us all to drop for ten and we were all over each other in a cluster fuck trying to do pushups.

Just then, a staff car drove up and out hopped what turned out to be our Div Cmdr (you know better than ask me the frigging name). He ordered Cpl Kirk to get us back on our feet and then he commenced chewing Cpl Kirk's ass right there in front of everyone. I recall something about we don't treat them like animals and don't repeat this incident again. Anywhoo, when he had finally
blown off his head of steam, off he went in his shiny little OD car and we were left with one pissed off corporal.

Kirk said, "The damn general ain't in charge of this class, I am. Drop!" And here we went back to the cluster fuck right where we were before the general arrived except we caught even more hell the rest of that day.

Pre-BAC was hell. The Basic Abn Crse was a piece of cake. Hard to believe anybody dropped out of it. My BAC platoon's cadre appeared to be the oldest cadre there. He actually had gray hair. He never harassed us, he was just there. I can not recall his name.

It seems that I remember a big black guy running one of the doors in the tower, but I wouldn't swear to that. I think Duke was another platoon's cadre, he wasn't ours and you could hear his mouth from one end of jump school area to the other.

After Pre-BAC, jump school really didn't impress me very much except for the tower and the actual jumps.

The Raid
Don "Val" Valentine

RVN - last half of 1965:
Project Delta was assigned the job of raiding a North Vietnamese Army Division Headquarters, killing everyone we could find, and capturing all of their electronic equipment intact. The main job was to capture that main bunker and all of their equipment and records. This Headquarters was supposed to be in a large bunker complex on a knoll in the middle of a large valley. The US Air Force was supposed to provide fighter cover for our raid and they were also supposed to bomb the target to soften it up before we attacked. This raid was all based on photo interpretations of aerial photos.

While rehearsing our plan for landing and clearing the landing zone, Major Charles Beckwith said, "Men, don't just put your heads down, your asses up, and charge. Stop and think before you act."

For some unknown reason, Charging Charlie seemed to love to have me near him which thrilled me to no end since I thought the man was suicidal. So naturally I was picked to be "his" damn radio operator on that operation. That meant that I had to go in on the first wave of choppers with him. La-De-Damn-Da!

While flying enroute to the target I became extremely anxious, regular soldiers might use the term "scared." Until we came within sight of the target, I couldn't figure out why I was so concerned. When I saw there were no fresh bomb craters anywhere near our objective the answer came to me in a flash. How can they bomb the command bunkers and still expect us to capture the electronic equipment intact for our intelligence people to analyze? They can't! They had lied! Aw shit, they're not going to bomb anywhere near those damn bunkers. If they do, they'll destroy the electronic equipment.

When that thought hit me, my asshole puckered up so tight, I thought that I would suck my canvass seat right up inside of me. We were all supposed to land within about 50 meters of the knoll where the main bunker was supposed to be located.

The LZ was so small the only way we could put our force down on it was three choppers at a time, so they approached and landed in a trail of "V"s. There were three choppers to a "V" with Charging Charlie, his trusty radioman, meaning me, and some LRRP guys going in on the first three choppers. Our RVN Ranger Battalion and the rest of the LRRP guys followed them. When I hit the ground, I immediately got tangled up in the elephant grass and fell flat on my kisser. The next wave of choppers roared in with machine guns blazing and one of them damn near sat down on me. The terrified door gunner was spraying bullets all over the damn place. I figured I was about to find out how friendly 'friendly' fire really was. As soon as they lifted off, I jumped up and raced past everyone: I was the first man to reach our assembly area. (That's odd because I was the slowest member of my high school football squad.) Those damn choppers weren't getting a second chance to land on my ass. The Vietnamese ranger battalion with us was the one that served as Delta's "Hatchet Force."

Each wave of choppers landed less than 100 yards from the enemy-held knoll in an open field covered with elephant grass. As soon as we regrouped at a pre-designated point at the foot of the enemy-held knoll, we headed uphill. Somehow, I ended up being point-man with everyone else in single file behind me and I was carrying the only damn radio in the assault force. Those LRRP guys were smarter than I had thought. That knoll was almost straight up and the underbrush was as thick as pea soup, consisting mostly of vines that had very long and very sharp thorns. We respectfully referred to these vines as "wait-a-minute vines."

Breaking trail under such circumstances is not easy, especially when you are also toting a damn field radio with antenna; consequently I was slowed up considerably.

Major Beckwith was about six men back and finally about half way up the hill he yelled, "Move it out up there, move it out!"

I replied over my shoulder, "My ass is ahead of your ass."

To which I heard the response, "Charge, men! Charge!"

I yelled, "What the hell happened to that stop-and-think shit?"

In response to which I heard, "Shut up and charge damn it! Charge!"

Some of the LRRP men finally passed me up, snickering as they went by, and took the point; we eventually reached the summit.

There were no enemy troops anywhere near that knoll. The huge "bunkers" proved to be very old bomb craters. The "eight foot high stone wall" or "aqueduct" proved to be a two foot high stone farm fence just like back home in the Smoky Mountains. The "radar antenna" was a reed basket hung upside down on a stake in the field.

There were absolutely no bad guys there, and that made me very happy. If there had actually been a division headquarters on that knoll there would have been hundreds, maybe thousands, of troops in the immediate vicinity for security; we would have all been slaughtered and as a radio operator on point, I would probably have got it first. However, I was still pissed at the stupid photo interpreters for scaring the hell out of me like that. That is one reason that Charging Charlie got his nickname. Knowing Charging Charlie, I'm sure there are plenty of other reasons.

Delta's tactics changed when we changed commanders. Before Charging Charlie arrived, the RTs concentrated on traveling light so they could travel as quiet as possible and had a better chance of out-running the enemy and escaping, if spotted. After Charging Charlie arrived, the RTs concentrated on being heavily armed because they knew that they might not be exfiltrated when they got into trouble. Before Charging Charlie came to Delta, I wanted to serve on an RT-after Charlie came to Delta. I was damn glad that I was not on one of our RTs, and I made a mental note to never again volunteer for LRRP duty. And that's one promise that I kept.

My experience with Delta taught me a very valuable lesson about special operations and LRRPs in particular. In order to efficiently perform such duty and have a decent chance of survival, it must have de-centralized control. If it is a SF unit, it must be a 100% SF operation; all the US ground troops had to be SF, SF planning, and SF control. Control had to be de-centralized down to the lowest level within SF as possible. Indigenous personnel could not be informed of any mission details until after the operation had already begun.

The White Rose
by Don "Val" Valentine

While in Laos, and shortly after, I located and destroyed Mimi's 'mechanized dandruff', we received a couple of cases of brand new green berets. They were our newly authorized headgear. After trying mine on, I stuck that funny looking thing in my footlocker and left it there. My camouflage-colored, Australian-style bush hat was much better. That was a real hat and it had only cost me about a buck-fifty.

We were each allotted three days R&R to Bangkok during our tour, so I put a little extra money aside and went on R&R. The guys going on R&R had to be processed out at our C Team in Vientiane. The C Team Sergeant Major, Curtis C., informed me that my flight to Bangkok would depart from the local airfield at 0900 hours the next morning and he highly recommended that I be on it. Until then, I was on my own, so I rented a samloy, which is really a rickshaw; except the cabbie doesn't walk he rides a bike. They are called by various names in the orient. He took me to the hotel the Sergeant Major recommended.

Before I left Luang Prabang (LP), an A Team that was due to leave Laos was staying with us, and their commander asked me, "If you see our radioman, Bill B., tell him to get his ass back to LP pronto. He left for a weekend in Vientiane three weeks ago and we haven't heard a peep out of him since."

Shortly after I got a room at the hotel, I ran into my next door neighbor. He was none other than the infamous Bill B. Bill was drunk, naturally, and very glad to see me, because he had ran out of money and everyone he knew had just left. I did my duty and informed him that he was three weeks AWOL and his Team CO dearly wanted to see his ass; then he informed me of the most wonderful restaurant in the whole wide world that he had discovered right there in Vientiane. The name of it was the "White Rose."

"Well, why not," I thought. "I'm hungry. First things first." We toasted the White Rose a couple of times and then hailed down a couple of cabbies. As I recall, we decided the cabbies were not moving fast enough to suit us. The White Rose really was a great restaurant and we were in a hurry, at least I was, so we had the cabbie stop.

Bill and I hopped out, put our cabbies in the back seat and we pedaled those damn contraptions - that was our first mistake. Bill and I got into a race - that was our second mistake. Be 'ye warned. It is very difficult to negotiate a ninety degree corner with one of those stupid tricycles. Mine hit the ditch at the first intersection; I did a double front flip over the handlebars and bent the front wheel double in the process. My cabbie was about to have a heart attack until I gave him a handful of Kip, and told him I was sorry and jumped into Bill's cab. Apparently, I gave him enough to replace the whole contraption because he just stood there grinning like a well-fed bear. Hell, maybe he was going to retire.

We finally arrived at the White Rose. As I just typed the words "White Rose," it brought back a warm feeling after all of these years, but I can't remember exactly why. All I know is that Bill was right; that was, and still is, the best damn restaurant in the whole wide world. It was a restaurant, bar, dance hall, hotel, steam bath, massage parlor, and whore house all rolled up into one. All of the women who worked there were imported from Bangkok and Thailand is famous for beautiful women. To the best of my memory, the food was great also.

It took us three days to run through my money, and I dimly remember a lovely lass taking us by the arm and escorting Bill and me outside and bidding us farewell.
When we finally found our way back to the C Team, I had to face Sergeant Major C., who was somewhat pissed-off because I had missed my R&R flight to Bangkok - three days ago.

Try as I might to explain to him that I didn't have to go to Bangkok because it had came to me, it didn't seem to come out right. My head was at least three times as large as the normal human head and all of his screaming and threats really hurt. He yelled,
"You will go directly to the airport and catch the next plane back to LP which will be leaving in about an hour. You will never return to Vientiane again and I don't care how damn long you are in Laos. You will stay in the damn jungle."

It all seemed a bit harsh to me; after all I had been sent on R&R and I had found R&R, so what if there were a few hundred miles difference between my intended destination and my final destination? Oh well, Sergeant Majors tend to be a picky lot anyway. There's just no pleasing them. Besides, my head really did hurt something fierce.

Bill never let the Sergeant Major see him; he hid outside in the hall until I came out. Bill returned with me I think, but I'm not sure. Bill was a real chickenshit tour guide, if I ever saw one, hiding from the sergeant major like that. Maybe he found another SF enroute to R&R and gave him the White Rose tour also. Bill's expenses were minimal, well worth the tour and he didn't eat much.

If it is still there, I highly recommend the White Rose. It must be tourist favorite - male tourists, that is. In fact, all male chauvinist pigs in the world should unite and fund the construction of a 100' marble monument to honor the White Rose. Better yet, let's buy the damn place.

Moc Hoa
by John Blevins

I spent the bulk of Tet '68 in Can Tho getting hit about every night. Talk about a clusterf--k, this was the first time the C Team in Can Tho had ever gotten hit, and the whole place was going nuts.

Paul Newbold, our medic in Tuyen Nhon, was there on some mission; we stayed pretty close to each other because we felt we were the only two people in the whole world we could depend on. They had closed the NCO Club, and we had not had a drink for a couple of days; Paul got a bottle of Scotch from somewhere. Ever try to drink warm scotch without any ice or mix?

After a few days, I got a ride to Moc Hoa with my load of chow, with the 1/Lt who I rescued from downtown Can Tho. I ran into Tom Elr. and Sebastian De, two of my former team mates from Tuyen Nhon. They were laughing about the rockets that knocked them down; but they were unhurt because there was no shrapnel to them. But an E-7 Mills got hit in the head with an AK-47 round. I saw him back at Bragg about a year later and asked him if he remembered us being in VN. He told me he could not remember anything about VN. I heard that later he lost everything.

While at Moc Hoa, they stuck me on guard one night. This other guy and I were peering out thru the arch over the main gate when this Lt. came up behind us unheard and fired one of those hand held rockets between us and through the gate. I turned around, not to see who it was, but to shoot somebody. I was already tightening up on the trigger when I saw it was an American. I don't know who was the most scared: him or me, but if he survived the war, that is about as close as he ever came to being killed, I'm sure.

Got out of bed one morning and my web gear was gone. Who did I but this Lt. that I had rescued in Can Tho wearing my web gear It was a BAR belt and the pockets held 3 M-16 mags in each pocket standing up and one across the top. In addition, it had my compass, knife, canteen, etc.

"Prove it's yours." says he.

I went in the orderly room and asked to speak to the CO. SGM Bow'r asks why and I tell him, "I am planning to shoot a Lt."

After I explained what happened, Bow'r told me, "Wait here." He came back in about five minutes later with my gear. I finally got an aircraft to take me down to Tuyen Nhon, but had to leave the load of chow at Moc Hoa.

When I got back to Tuyen Nhon all was quiet on the western front. Nevertheless, every night for about a week, some one would hear something and sound the alarm, and everyone would run to their posts. Nothing happened. Each night, just before it got dark, I would shoot off a few rounds from the .50 cal we had mounted on top of the Commo bunker to make sure it was OK.

One night while I was out there, it would not function, so I took it down and put it in the supply room. Before I went to bed I got to thinking about it, went and got an M-60, took it up there, linked two 720 round belts together and loaded it. Sometime in the night the alarm went off again and everyone manned their posts. I told my radio operator to go inside the commo bunker, and I crawled on top and picked up the M-60. There I was standing like a fool silhouetted against the sky, not thinking there was a VC for miles, when right in front of me and where I was pointing the M-60 all the green tracers in the world came up in my face. They saw me, assumed I saw them and opened up on me. I didn't have sense enough to get down and stood there like Rambo, giving them all 1440 rounds. Those poor bastards; if they had not sabotaged the .50 cal by the time we saw them, they were so close I could not have lowered it enough to use on them anyway.

Sharing MRE's
By "Yukon Don" Shipman

I went into a little village/hamlet along the coast of Hondo one time called San Francisco. We probably pulled close to nearly every tooth in the village (they were rotten as could be from a lifetime of sugar cane and not fluoride; poor hygiene). They didn't have a pot to piss in, but absolutely insisted on feeding us polo, plantains, etc. Sure didn't want to eat their chow up, but didn't want to insult them either. Beng the SF guys we were, we whipped put our MRE's started sharing with everyone (especially the kids), and had a feast.

105mm Cannons
by Ben Roberts

It was early August 1967, and my last mission in Vietnam. I was sent (for two weeks) TDY as a Medic 91B4S, across the river from Bong Son A-227 to a new camp which replaced Bon Son A-227 called "Ha Tay". This camp was located about two miles across from a large river that separated our old camp at Bong Son which was recently taken over by the First Calvary division.

This new camp was located near the head of the Anlo Valley where a large river ran from the mountains of the central highlands into the ocean several miles away.

Ha Tay was the new camp known as A-227. It was being built in a terrible location. I questioned the location of the camp because it was on the side of a small hill located very close to a large river flowing to the ocean several miles away. This was a main supply route for the delivery of ammunitions and food for the NVA who controlled the area by boat and by mountain trail. Surrounding the camp were many hills higher than the camp itself.

To insure the safety of the camp, we were supported by a temporary battery reaching up to 15 miles away while all of the defenses were being built into the camp. One only had to look at "Ha Tay" to understand that it was surrounded by hills higher than the camp making it an easy target for the NVA mortars and rockets. Its location was truly a big mistake. It was built in the wrong place, with an A-Team of dedicated people waiting for disaster.

On the third day, I was sent out on a search and destroy mission five to six miles from our new camp. The majority of the Vietnamese forces were conscripts from Vietnamese jails who were given the opportunity to fight for Vietnam or be forced to live in the jails. These Vietnamese would rather run away at the first fire fight, never to be seen again, than stand and defend themselves, their countrymen, and their two Special Forces advisors controlling the mission.

We depended on the few, very trustworthy Montagnards in camp who would die rather than run away, leaving their SF American counterparts behind. They knew the Special Forces were totally committed to saving the Montagnards from the NVA communists. These were the indigenous people Special Forces depended on to protect the 12 American members of the A-Teams, rather than the 400 Vietnamese conscripts who were for the most part worthless and uncaring rogues...

Every day before a mission, 50 to 75 DG (conscripts) would fall out for sick call just before participating in a one day mission, delaying it for hours before I could sort out their bullshit sick claims from the truly sick, and force them back into the ranks for duty. We knew we were surrounded by hostile forces on that side of the river.

On my successful last mission where we killed several NVA carrying automatic weapons (AK-47's), we returned with half of our forces. The other half disappeared... never to be seen again.

Upon returning to camp and being debriefed, I was sitting under a newly- built bamboo patio cover of the team house watching the US Army Artillery people (20-40) manning 105 mm. cannons discharging their weapons miles away, directed by other military spotters calling in for fire support. The noise was loud, and the smell of the cordite permeated the air. The 105 crews fired their loud cannons as fast as they could, adjusting their fire at new coordinates sent to them by radio, adjusting fire on the enemy positions...

I sat under the bamboo partially built patio cover of the team house trying to unwind after a less than enthusiastic mission. Suddenly, a white-hot flaming round was fired from one of the mountain tops, landing in the middle of the 105 mm. rounds stacked in a large pile of artillery ammunition stored above ground. Our team house was less than 50 yards from the stacked ammunition. If the whole pile of ammunition went off from a cooked off round, we would have been toast. I lay down in the trench waiting sixty seconds while all of the SF camp personnel jumped into a shallow, three foot deep trench, built for the camp's basic protection.
They flattened themselves to the ground as best they could.

If the ammunition stock pile of 105 mm ammunition had gone off, the shallow trench on the side of the hill 50 yards away would have been vaporized, including our 12 man A-Team. I waited a minute for the shell to explode and whatever consequences followed. It seemed a lot longer. Even though the errant round had not exploded causing all of the stacked boxes of ammunition to explode, I was not going to wait around for the burning round to ignite all of the boxes of ammo rounds, killing all of us.

I ran down to the ammo dump and found a pried 2 X 4 from a pallet where the large 105 shells and boxes of other ammo were stored. I knocked the intensely flaming round that lay burning through the boxes, from one box to another trying to prevent the round from igniting the entire ammunition stock pile, and blowing the entire camp to hell. I felt it would explode each time I touched it; but I kept moving it to keep it from burning through the 105 mm cannon shells, and setting off the entire ammo dump. The shell eventually burned out.

"Shit!" I thought. I was never trained for this! But I had already committed myself. It didn't mater if I walked away or not. I was probably going to die!

Finally, the shell stopped burning, and I nudged it to the ground hoping it was dead each time I moved it. I know of no US military program that teaches how to do this... Normally, the damn shell would explode and kill everyone around after it, igniting the entire ammo dump. It was just sheer stupidity on my part, but if I was going to die it was going to be with courage! It was just my lucky day!

Ten minutes later, I returned to camp where all of the team members were still seeking out the (false) safety of the shallow trenches in front of the camp. It was my last official mission and I thought I had "done good", only to have some Jackass Captain of the new A-Team of "Ha Tay (A-227)" chew my ass up one side and down the other as I laughed at him.

He said, "I might have been killed." He had no concept of what 500 each 105 mm shells would do to him and the crappy camp after one shell caused an entire ammo dump to explode at once.

I simply told him, "Fuck you! I didn't see your ass trying to help."

Did I get a medal for this? No! Only an ass chewing from someone who was only two years older then me, never even been in a fire fight, sought the false protection in a trench that was way to close to an ammo dump, and praying to a God who would have let the entire area be blown to hell! Shit! I was just damn glad to be alive! F--k some worthless person who had been made a Captain, who hid rather than try to save his team. You don't need a stupid medal to know you either risk your life immediately to try and save your team and yourself, or you hunker down in a three foot trench, waiting for everything to explode and rip you to pieces. It was my lucky day! Thirty-five years later, I remain a Lucky Son of a Bitch!! That Captain is probably working for some rent-a-car business. I really don't care!

Never Say Quit
by Ben Roberts

I remember running for what felt like several hours in the morning runs at jump school in Ft. Benning, GA. That was in Feb of 1965. If you fell out to puke and did not catch up you were history, a.k.a. LEG! I planned my entry into the service for late summer and got to jump school in winter, so I could survive. If it had been summer, the runs would have been a real killer and I wonder if I would have made it.

I only fell out and puked once. When I looked up and saw my future running away from me, I ran as fast as I could, and caught up. From then on I always tried to run behind an officer or a person most likely to quit (I am not officer bashing here). Each time the person in front of me would drop out; it felt like a shot of adrenaline. After that, I had no problem keeping up the pace. If the fellow in front of me did not drop out it made the course seem very long. No matter how long it was, if the other guys could do it, and so could I. Someone would have to kill me to drop me from the course because I would never say, "I quit".

A-Team in the Dark
by Ben Roberts

One night, my clunky PRC 25 reached all the way to our B-Team 40-50 miles away. Mortar rounds were landing, and exploding on top of the hill, and we were always out of support range from our A-Team A-223. I was trying to get Ivan Bomark to describe how to get one of the Yards' M-60s MGs to work in the dark. We could not see that a piece of link had dropped onto part of the track. I wasn't about to turn on a flash light to take a peek at it.

The B-Team came at Qui Nhon and tried to give us help, wanting to know if we were requesting a Mike Force. I told them, "No. We would just wait things out." Then I got my ass chewed out by Maj D. or some officer for not using proper language on the radio while we were in a fire fight. I'm glad he didn't make me stand at attention on top of the hill. It made for an interesting night. Any other day, you could not even reach the A-team.

M-2 Carbine
by Ben Roberts

I chose to carry an M-2 carbine over an M-16 piece of shit. All my yards carried the M-1 or M-2 carbines. Our ammunition was always interchangeable, however I also carried an M-79 because I could not convince them not to fire through the tree tops overhead. Most of our targets were less than 100 yards, and I rarely had a WIA NVA from carbine rounds. Almost all were KIA's.

Great little round.

Tiger Patches
by Ben Roberts

I am reminded of a couple of incidents we had with the Korean Tiger division located about 15 miles from our camp at A-223 in II Corps down an untraveled road which was frequently booby trapped and ambushed. I was driving a duce and a half full of supplies down the road to our camp. We had to drive through the Korean Tiger Division area. As we passed a bunch of Koreans, one of the twenty or so CIDG tossed a tear gas grenade at them and we almost got our asses shot off.

I slammed on the truck's brakes, and went back to apologize to the Koreans, as they were breaking out their weapons. I ordered all of the CIDG off the truck and sent them marching towards our camp. When the Korean soldiers saw the CIDG lose their ride, they started laughing. That broke up the tension, and we averted a nasty situation. I drove the truck back to camp, the supplies unloaded; then had to drive back and pick up the CIDG who were faced with a long walk home.

Another time our jeep broke down along that road and we had no radio or means of getting any communication to our camp for help. As we stood there looking at our situation we saw a Korean Tiger division jeep coming towards us. Although we were waving our hands indicating for them to stop and help us, they sped up as if to pass us. Not wanting to be left on the lonely road, Ivan Bomark and I decided to aim our rifles directly at the jeep and stand in the middle of the road to make the jeep stop. Things could have gone either way, but the jeep, full of very surpassed Koreans, came to a stop and picked up a couple of armed hitchhikers.

We made them drive past their camp and deliver us miles on down the road to our camp.

Worthless Chaplain's Assistant
by Ben Roberts

In 1967, we had a chaplain's assistant on A-223. Had I known, I would never have gone out on the mission. He could not read a map, or find our position. I ran with the Yard recon for several days while an NVA company tracked us. He got a lot of good Yard killed while we ran to where he should have been setting up a large ambush. He wasn't even close to where he was supposed to be. When we got back to the team house, I stomped him into the floor and stuck a .38 special into his mouth. I was ready to kill him. He cost me some dear friends.

He was not allowed out of his quarters for a week until our captain decided he had learned to read a map. His name was "dog shit" as long as I was in camp. As soon as I left, he took an AK-47 right through the hip. That was when our Commo man Eric Muller was killed and several other SF was wounded. Herman B, wherever you are, you are still on my list of worthless people.

Pistol Packing in Vietnam
by Ben Roberts

I pondered over the following issue during my 30 days of leave before going off to Viet Nam (1966-1967). I wanted to take a small 25.Cal Beretta and a box of ammunition with me into Vietnam. The regulations were unclear to me. I figured if I asked the question, I was not going to like the answer. Therefore, I followed my instincts pertaining to the carrying of a personal side arm into Vietnam, and packed my auto 25.cal Beretta and a 100 rd box of ammo in the bottom of a large can of smoking tobacco in my luggage along with several pipes for the trip to Vietnam

We circled the city of Saigon to land. There were no signs of war. Just a beautiful aging city. However, we all hunkered down in our seats expecting a communist rocket or mortar shell with our names on it to come flying at us out of nowhere and explode next to our plane. The weary stewardesses had each earned at least the equivalent of two purple hearts on that flight, by being exposed to so many young GI 19 year old psychos at once for 15-20 hours while defending themselves from the GI's crude jokes and wandering hands. They were really good sports and wished us all good luck, personally kissing a few of us as we were about to leave the plane.

I observed lines of GIs walking down the stairs of their plane, and standing around waiting while their duffel bags were being thrown in a pile on the tarmac. The young soldiers sorted through the mound of olive drab duffel bags trying to find their bags among the others and then began to drag them over to the long Customs line. Other planes continued to land. When the crew opened our plane's door, we were instantly hit in the face by the extreme heat, humidity and perpetual smell of incense and tiger balm that would remain in our nostrils from the time we set our feet on the tarmac of the air strip in Saigon until the day we left for home in the good old USA.

The cargo door of our plane opened and a couple of guys jumped up and began to throw our duffel bags on to the concrete tarmac. As we found our bags, two Green Beret SFCs appeared, reached out and shook our hands telling us Special Forces did not go through customs. You should have seen the grin on my face as I threw my bag into the jeep and climbed in. The SFC saluted the customs officer as we drove around him and smiled. We were suddenly being driven down the streets of Saigon, inching through thousands of people on bicycles, Pedi cabs, and rickshaws. Other military vehicles honked their horns and cut folks off while everyone tried to peacefully move along as quickly as possible in every possible direction.

We drove 10 or so miles with our mouths open looking at all the pretty Asian girls in their long straight black hair; but we also noticed the chicken wire nailed over open patio ceilings and walls of outdoor clubs and restaurants as deterrents to terrorists' hand grenades - our first sign that the city was not quite as peaceful as it looked. Finally, our jeep turned down a quieter street and drove into what seemed to be an old French compound with 15 foot high walls completely surrounding the compound. The walls had two very large heavy gates, encircled in concertina wire barrier and guarded by Vietnamese soldiers who opened and closed the massive gates as we drove into the compound and parked the jeep.

The Special Forces Saigon detachment commander welcomed us to Vietnam. Then they gave us our first bad news. Apparently Special Forces were not civilized enough to be allowed out of the Compound, and on the orders of some great commander in Saigon, the city was suddenly off limits till further notice to all Special Forces personnel. Talk about bad timing. Great! We had been thrown out of town before even going into it. I think they were losing too many MPs to SF encounters. We spent the next three or four days getting drunk on our asses, drinking 5 cent highballs and playing the many 10 cent slots along the bar walls. Hanging around the bar's walls were 16" X 20" pictures of all Special Forces camps in Viet Nam taken from the air. These camps were armed to the teeth and heavily defended, giving us some clue that we were not just here for the cheap booze and gambling. Things were going to get tough. People were going to die.

Our next flight to Na Trang was bumpy in the small overpowered airplane because of the hot weather, and our clothes were soaked in sweat from the humidity in no time at all. This was a condition we learned to live with. If the heat, humidity and mild daily rain showers couldn't be avoided, the other 6 months of the monsoon season kept you even wetter. From the air we could see the countryside literally pockmarked with thousands of 500 pound bomb craters from B-52 air strikes. You could even see the concussion rings from each of the bomb creators that reached out several hundred meters around the bomb craters, destroying taller trees and laying the brush and vegetation flat in larger circles.

After an hour and a half, our small plane descended into Na Trang which was one of the larger cities in Vietnam. Half of the area was walled off with military bases and airports. The war began to assume a more realistic face as we saw all of the familiar signs of a number of well-organized American military units and hundreds of military aircraft loaded with bombs and helicopters. They came and went in large numbers while actively fighting war miles away.

We were met by a large military open duce and a half. We threw our duffel bags up into the back of the truck and climbed aboard with the Special Forces people while other passengers went their separate ways. Next, we were driven to a large headquarters as the tires of the large duce and a half kicked up perpetual red dust from unpaved roads. We pulled up to the 5th SFG HQ where several gate guards raised long poles preventing unauthorized vehicles. This was a much larger compound, and was connected to other compounds like a true military encampment. High walls of protective razor sharp concertina wire intended to prevent intruders and the enemy from entering the area surrounded everything. They did not, however, protect anyone from incoming mortar rounds.

We dismounted the duce and a half and jumped down with our duffel bags while being processed into the base. There, we were again assigned temporary bedding. We handed over our records to the administration Sgt who gave us a brief introduction on the do's and don'ts. Then they told us we were free to come and go into the city, but to remember there was a 9pm curfew. We were advised not to carry firearms into town. Hell, no firearms had even been issued to us yet.

The first night in camp at Na Trang around 10 PM, bells and signals went off; and we were told we were under attack by a couple of VC platoons on a large mountain that ran down to the level of the entrance of our camp. Then, they told us to run over to the arms room to be issued an M-16 and one full 30 round magazine of 223.cal ammo. Afterwards, we were told to report back to the edge of the sandbag walls at the entrance of the camp. Mortar pits began lightening up the sky with 10 -20 illumination rounds at a time.

We sat there behind the sandbagged walls and sand filled fifty gallon barrels along the camp's perimeter. The camp's large mortar pits began firing high explosive rounds into the mountain side 500 meters away, giving off a great light show of explosions in the darkness. There was no returned fire and no targets for us to aim at. In true Vietnamese fashion, we just sat smoking cigarettes and wondering if we were going to face any enemy charges.

After an hour, the all clear signal was given and we reported back to the arms room, reluctantly clearing and returning our weapons, plus the one magazine that had issued. The camp was under lock down for the night. We went to one of the many SF bars and proceeded to get drunk, noticing many other SF soldiers who had obviously spent a good amount of time in A Team camps drinking alone. Many were armed to the teeth, and had that "1000 yard" stare. Not wanting to look like the newbies we were, we left them to themselves feeling we did not deserve the honor to drink with them; and they more then likely didn't want a bunch of new guys hanging out with them anyway.

A guy trucked me over to the informal small airport on the base. There, other GI's sat outside on a cement patio trying to stay in the shade rather than the 110 degree sun, until they were assigned a seat to a small airplane that would deliver them to their various destinations. Much to my relief, before leaving Head Quarters Company in Na Trang, they finally issued me an M-16 and a bunch of full ammo magazines.

Soon, a small plane arrived and I was flown to our B team in Qui Nohn where another Special Forces soldier met me.

He drove me to another old French compound which also had high walls and was located next to the MACV building across the street from the beach.

This B team supported approximately ten other A-Team camps and coordinated all missions, intelligence and supplies as well as transportation. This was a small but highly effective management team, and all Special Forces were accepted as brothers as soon as they entered the compound. This team was also known for serving the best steaks and French fries to A-team members who did not enjoy the same luxuries. This was because A-Team food was either scrounged from oversupplied hospitals, purchased on the local economy, or composed of K rations. Not only was the food plentiful but it was unlimited, free, and delicious.

This B Team, known as B-22, had a large bar that still had the five cent drinks and the ten cent slot machines. At night the bar was almost like a night club with many other officers and nurses wanting the privilege of hanging out in a Special Forces bar even though they were associating with enlisted men .They were there as guests only.

The first day I was there I met an SF soldier who was packing up and returning to the USA. He offered to sell me his 38 cal. special snub nose Colt revolver for $20.00 with a shoulder holster. I could not pass it up. Unfortunately, the gun came with a history. For the last three consecutive days, three different Special Forces soldiers had been caught after curfew with that gun in their pocket. It had been passed around from friend to friend for protection. Fortunately this was back in the days when all Special Forces people looked out for each other, and were seldom disciplined for anything other then murder. For the next three nights the unlucky Special Forces soldiers, who just happened to be carrying the same gun, were picked up by an M.P. They were taken to the Provost Marshall whose duty was to call their team Sgt at the B team to come and collect their prisoner as well as his gun. In the regular army this would have been unheard of. This continued for three straight nights. As soon as the SF guys were out of sight the gun was returned to the pocket of the owner, and the team Sgt gave them a lecture on escape and evasion. Upon return to the compound they went to the bar and had a couple of drinks together, and that was it.

I was now the fourth owner of the gun. Probably the greatest thing about our B-team was it had no accommodations to put any A-Team soldiers up for the night. When you came into town in a convoy or by chopper, you reported to the Team Sgt. Depending on how many days you were staying in town you were given $20.00 a day per diem and directions to one of the many whorehouses within two blocks of the B team. The only restriction was you had to return for roll call at 9am the following day. In Qui Nhon the curfew was 7pm, and anyone unlucky enough to be caught in public was picked up by the MP's; then the B-22 Team Sgt had to come and retrieve his soldiers. Other GI soldiers could get into big trouble, but in those days we were immune from the chicken shit stuff - no article 15's etc.

I lost track of time. It was dark and I decided I had better try to find another whorehouse to spend the night in. It was a little past 7pm when I was walking down the street very close to my destination when another f--king jeep with a couple of M.P.'s spotted me. I turned and ran down a very dark alley that any other day I would not have even considered walking down in the daylight. The M.P.'s had a reputation for thumping you good if you were caught; so I made it as difficult as I could for a couple of big young buck

M.P's to stop, jump out and try to follow me down the pitch black alley. I ran a hundred yards or so and ducked into the home of some Vietnamese family, not really carrying who the hell they were. There was an old woman who began to scream and draw attention to my location. I pulled out my 38 and stuck it up to her head. In the universal language, I whispered "Shush" into her ear and made the rest of her family turn out the single light in the hut. I think the 38 special to her head translated better than the "Shush", but at least the light went out and things got real quiet. I could hear the two M.P.s coming my way, but they only walked half way down the alley before I heard them say, "Hey! F--k this. I am not going down there for nothing." Then I heard them return to their jeep and drive away.

After ten minutes, I removed the gun from the old lady's head, gave her $10.00, apologized and slipped out their front door. I made my way back to the street, staying in the shadows till I was sure the police were gone; then ran like hell for a block and a half. I made it to the location of one of the preferred whorehouses and slipped inside where I spent the rest of the night under the protection of a mosquito net with a cute young thing named My Linn while her mother washed my uniform and spit shined my muddy boots for the next morning.

I figured the reason they didn't want guns carried in town was because they didn't want you to shoot back I carried the 30. snub nose revolver in my shoulder holster in camp and for the rest of the war when I went on missions. After roll call I was told to get my shit together (I always had my shit together) and be ready to fly out to A-Team A-227 in Bong Son before noon in a little two-seat overpowered little observation aircraft. The flight took us about 45 minutes to fly over a lot of unfriendly mountain ranges without roads or signs of civilization. We came to the wide mouth of a large river and flew inland several miles where I spotted a small heavily defended A-Team camp. The plane dove sharply and landed on a red dirt runway, stopping about one hundred feet beside the camp; I strained to retain my breakfast and not blow chunks all over the cowboy pilot in front of me.

I was deposited unceremoniously at my new team A-227 Bong Son, let into the locked front gate, met the members who seemed like a good selection of Special Forces soldiers. They showed me to my underground bunker / bunkhouse and gave me a bed and a small footlocker to unpack my gear in. I was anxious to see how my large tin of Pipe tobacco had survived containing the little 25 cal. auto Beretta and concealed ammunition. Hot damn! There wasn't even a dent in the can as I removed the small pistol, removed the plastic covering and placed it in my pocket. It seamed real insignificant compared to the 38 special I carried, but better to have a back up piece than nothing at all.

Several months later I switched A-teams and opted to go to a free fire zone, meaning there were few farmers and a whole hell of a lot of North Vietnamese. Be careful what you wish for; you might get it. I joined A-223 at Van Canh about 60 miles inland from my former camp, located in a small valley surrounded by several large mountain ranges on either side. That was a great A- team with more freedom then I had ever had before. There was no where to go because there was no town, but there was always something to do to improve the camp defenses. . There were always seven to ten "search and destroy" missions to go on. As the junior medic in the camp, I chose to work with the Montagnard recon platoon of thirty jungle people and one other American. We humped heavy packs of food, ammunition and whatever it took to live off of the land for up to ten days at a time. We walked up and down thousands of mountain trails in 110 degree heat and high humidity, enjoying the cool water of the mountain streams crossed each day while searching for North Vietnamese supply routes and enemy soldiers.

I enjoyed traveling with the Yards as their medic and advisor, and we worked very well together for the 9 months I stayed in that camp before returning to the USA. It was like being an anthropologist with a gun.

I carried my little 38 snub nose, an M-2 carbine and an M-79 grenade launcher which I still to this day consider the perfect weapon through the entire war. When it came time for me to leave the team, I decided to pass my precious 38 colt on to a Montagnard Lt. from the recon platoon that I respected and trusted. The Recon Yard Lt. and we worked well together and always completed our missions. Neither of us spoke much of each other's language, but we were friends and managed to communicate between ourselves. We saved each others' lives and had a common bond as brothers.

I gave my 38 cal. sub nose to the recon Lt knowing that as soon as I left, the LLDB commander would probably take it away from him .Before leaving I wrote out a "will" for the pistol, stating that I was giving it to my Recon Lt. and friend with the stipulation that the gun was U.S. property and could be possessed only by the LT. or my Captain at the time. If the gun was taken away from the Lt., it was to be returned to our American CO who I left the note with.

However, I did ask the LLDB commander if he might be interested in trading something for my little 25.cal Beretta and its box of 90 shells. His eyes lit up when I slowly unwrapped it from the oily cloth with the ninety rounds of ammunition. The LLDB commander had never seen one before, and immediately became interested in trading anything to own it. I decided on a fully automatic AK-47 that I had captured which sat in the corner of his office. I had him write up a few words personally awarding me with the captured gun and I handed him my smuggled Beretta and remaining ammo. He was extremely proud of that little gun, and carried it all over camp, showing it off to his friends. I shipped my AK-47 home, had it decommissioned as a war trophy and still have it today.

I learned several days after leaving camp that he had slyly confiscated the 38 snub nose from the Recon Lt., however my commanding officer retrieved it showing the pissed off red faced LLDB commander the "will " I had left behind with him. It served me faithfully up until the end of my tour and proved to be one of the finest tricks I ever pulled on the Vietnamese LLDB commander…. and it only cost me $20.00.

So You Wanna Be a Medic
by Ben Roberts

I was a Sgt and a Special Forces medic located in a free fire zone in 1966-67 in the central highlands.

There were two medics on our 12-man A-team. My responsibilities included pulling sick call for the Vietnamese and Montangards Civilian Defense Group, a private army working exclusively in a heavily infested enemy area and running missions with the Montangnard recon platoon. Their families lived outside of the camp, and the soldiers lived inside the heavily armed perimeter surrounded by several other perimeters of concertina wire and clay more mines.
I was responsible for ordering all desired medications in quantity for 5,000 people a month. Naturally, that included a few cases of Dexedrine (to be used as vitamins for myself and night guard.) No one questioned my pharmaceutical orders.

I was twenty-three at the time, and this was my first and only hitch with Special Forces and the military. Upon graduating from Dog lab, I initially was assigned to the 3rd Co of the 7th SFG with only 11 months remaining on my enlistment. My assignment was to teach National Guardsmen in basic, because I was considered to have too little time to be sent to Vietnam.
The day after I found this out, I went to the Pentagon requesting reassignment as a 91B4S Medic on an A team in Vietnam. There was a lovely woman named Mrs. Alexander in charge of Special Forces assignments,
and more than happy to amend my orders to the 5th SFG in Vietnam. Thirty days later, I arrived in Vietnam with a wealth of medical knowledge learned over the forty-four

week SF Medical Course that I was not going to waste on National Guard folks.

While in Vietnam, I was assigned to two different teams. After one and one-half months on an a-team with too many civilians by day, and enemy by night, I requested assignment to a team in a free fire zone. I didn't want to kill any civilians by accident.

This decision to move was partially brought about by an ineffective chicken SF Captain who never went out of the camp after we were ambushed outside, and many people were killed. I also lost my best friend that month in another part of the country and wanted some revenge without killing any civilians. We acted more like the Mafia than any other branch of the military because we did what we wanted, traded outside of military channels command, and stole the rest which could not be traced to Special Forces Civilian armies.

Many of our drug supplies at the time came through CIA channels as did the payroll, and just about anything else requested. Our troop's old guns were not accountable. The B-teams and HQ did a fine job of supplying us, but I have no doubts where my stuff came from.

I was the Jr. Medic because another Medic outranked me by five days. I chose to spend the majority of my
time taking other team members' missions with my own, on 7 to 10 day missions; many of them back to back because I liked working with
the Montagnard Reconnaissance Platoon of 30 Montagnards and one other trusted friend and A-team member. At that time, many of the more senior and older SF people were more than happy to stay behind in camp while I took their places.

I liked working the highlands, and the jungle trails because we always made contact with NVA, and I sent home many foot lockers of souvenirs and objects of the Montana culture. I did as much fighting as I did being a medic, and have a Silver Star to show for it, an elephant tusk, crossbows and poison arrows, and many relics.

Here are some suggestions I can pass on to you although I am sure not what the military position is today on SF Medics. Remember you are cross-trained as a medic and hopefully a weapons and commo man. If you are just starting SF Medical School, the following is the most important thing I can pass on to you if you want to be an SF Medic. Learn the very first glossary of words from the very first textbook given to you and all subsequent books including the Merck Manual. The Merck Manual is like your bible. Read it and quiz each other. Make flash cards of all the words and their definitions at the end of the medical books. Pick a good study partner. If he is not willing to do this, dump him and find another because he will fail. Carry these cards with you, and every five minutes or any spare time you get for breaks, quiz each other on the meaning of these words. Put the definitions on the back of the cards. You will be surprised how fast you will learn them. This is the only way you will pass the course. If you know what the medical terms on test questions mean, then you can correctly answer the question. If you do not study extremely hard, you will not graduate. Flash cards are the best way because you carry them with you always; and as I remember it, in the Army you are always in line somewhere.

When you are transferred to another hospital and get a chance to work the emergency room, get the Dr.'s permission to take the place of any of the regular night emergency room people who would like to take off for four to five weeks. Work double shifts. Get as much emergency room time as you possibly can, and NEVER drink while you are in Medical school. Ask a doctor to prescribe some weight loss diet pills at one of the hospitals you will work in. Save them for when you are really soft and get to dog lab. Take one of the pills half an hour before they get you up in the early mornings for PT. You will enjoy the early morning runs while wearing out the instructors.

Taking care of you:
Always carry a large caliber gun with at least a 6" bbl. I recommend 357.mag wheel guns in a shoulder holster and a pistol belt full of h/p rounds. Respect and fear of an armed medic is crucial. Never take it off - even when in camp.
Always have a compass, fire, map, water, C-4, lots of ammo, and a medical kit. Always carry the same rifle that matches everyone else's ammunition. Always zero your rifle before each mission.

I always carried a couple of sticks of C-4. A piece of C-4 the size of a small marble can always be placed beneath a metal coffee cup to boil water instantly. Light it with a foot long fire brand or it will burn your fingers off. It is that quick. If you like to blow stuff up make sure that someone else carries the blasting caps.

Never leave camp without some form of communication and extra batteries. Cell phones sound great these days, or civilian walkie-talkies. Have something to communicate with others including a whistle and field glasses, smoke and a translator.

Your patients:

Make up a bunch of laminated small flash cards
hooked together with a small chain or thong that
has pictures of bees, centipedes, scorpions, snakes, spiders
and other pictures that a patient or their relative can point to
and immediately indicate what is wrong with them. Many
times, there are so many dialects the interpreter can not
properly translate quickly. If you can get your hands on
a big bag of cheap candy, it goes a long way
towards goodwill with the local children...
Medevac anyone that you possibly can, and keep a log of
where they went - American or indigenous. Don't try to
play doctor if you can get you patient to a real one. Just
stabilize your patient. I know from experience, as I
temporarily lost the village chief's four year old son for two
weeks, when I sent him out very sick, requiring life saving
facial surgery. (We found him in an American hospital,
and in such great shape he didn't want to return to the
village chief.) If children are dying of dehydration
and malnutrition, expect Cholera, and request an
infectious disease control unit ASAP.
Triage is something that is not talked about much in medical
school; however, the objective is to sort out the ones you
can save from the hopeless ones who have no future (no
eyes, faces or hands and legs. Although this will never
be taught in the Army, an overdose of morphine two to
three rapid injections is the most humane path. Just don't pin
all of the seretts on the patient.

When treating indigenous people for a venereal disease,
make sure that the man and woman are treated at
the same time. Appoint someone responsible for
insuring their return for future treatments on time, or you
will never see them again; and they will continue to re-
infect each other as well as others. When in doubt,
give them each a massive dose after making sure they
are not allergic to penicillin.

I have found that in Asia, many of the Asians were allergic to the anti-venom made from horse serums. Watch the patient closely, even after you have skin tested him. I have had to yank out lots of IV's injected with anti-venom within 2-3 minutes because the patient's skin test did read as allergic.
Order more medicine than you need. It is good trading material. Some outfits in the military give repeat offenders of sexual diseases, such as the clap, article 15's. Make some good contacts with other outfits; and let it be known that for favors you will treat them on the QT so they will not get into trouble.

When you make Medical patrols, always inquire from other indigenous people around to see if anyone they know who is sick, because half of them will not show up for sick call or medcaps. You have to make house calls. Cortisone can do wonders on people. It is also good to have a good working knowledge of wound blocks by injecting lidocaine, and stopping bleeding by topical application of Epinephrine or adrenaline.

Your team:
Spread out the contents of a large medical kit among those you know; and know who is caring what, and where they are. The team should always be near you. If you are hit, the others will have medical supplies. Cross train your team at regular intervals, being sure they know how to apply pressure dressings and know the use of a three way air stopcock for sucking chest wounds. Make sure they carry lots of water and water purification pills or filters.
After each mission make sure you have all morphine injectables returned for you. Depending on what country you're in, a few of the basic rules for Team health are administer Tetracycline or a similar stomach sterilizing

antibiotic several hours before drinking or eating food prepared by your counterparts. This will help keep your misery to a minimum. The same includes going into towns. It is better to get drugs into your team-mates before they come down with something and prevent something, rather than trying to nurse sick team-mates, which could jeopardize your mission. It is also wise to carry a full bottle of Dexedrine for those times when your team must continue for long hours.

If you are going to walk long distances, it is important to bandage up everyone's feet before blisters and sores occur. Check these daily. Keep your feet dry and carry extra socks. When Team mates are required to take drugs that have unpleasant side effects such as malarial pills it is better to have your CO watch each team member to insure they take that pill. Otherwise, you will certainly lose team members to illness and also get them pissed off at you.

Scrounging:
It is very important that you be introduced to any medic's contacts for trading, before that medic leaves the team. A good source of trading is with hospital mess Sergeants. Hospitals are required to stock enough food per day to serve four meals a day to the maximum number of people in that hospital. A lot of that food goes to waste. Most hospitals' mess Sergeants are non-combatants. They are not issued weapons, and have little chance to get souvenirs. In the past, I have traded one or two WWII grease guns for an entire duce and a half full of food.

Always be sure to take several goodwill gifts of your sincerity to the first meeting. When you go to town, always take your syringes and antibiotics with you.

You are one of the key people on your team, and only one other medic on your team can do this.

Leaving people behind in fire fights:
One of the first things you hear is we never leave our people behind. One of the things you don't hear are the agreements team-mates privately make amongst themselves. If you are outnumbered and all hope is abandoned, the most severely injured team members will ask you to put a bullet behind their ear. If you have a severely wounded team-mate out in the open and you try to retrieve him without any cover, you will join him in death. A dead hero serves no one. Our forces will come back and get the bodies later. You are not just a medic, but you are a fighting medic. Try to stay alive and fight another day. Leave no team-mates behind to be tortured alive. Shoot and kill him from a distance.

Traveling in country:
Traveling in country can mean long waits of up to several days. This can be overcome by going to your commo man, have him place a newspaper in a government envelope and stamp it SECRET COURIER. Strap on a side arm and you are guaranteed to bump anyone off a plane (except a Col.) and leave on the first plane. No one may open or take the envelope from you except the commo man at your destination. At that point, you tear it up.

There are many medics that are more qualified then me on the Special Forces list, and I can honestly say we are all high quality. This is all I was able to glean from my tour in Vietnam, and I am not qualified to speak on other areas other than the generalities I have mentioned which are useful anywhere. However, it has been thirty-five years since I left the Army.

SF Medics are the best, and many go on to make fine doctors.

Out of Ammunition
by Ben Roberts

There are times when you become low on ammunition, and it is nice to have any sharp pointed thing. In April 1967, we overran an NVA outpost on top of a bare mountain earlier in the day with our "Montagnard recon platoon". That night the NVA mortared us, and a platoon sized unit tried to retake the outpost. We were out of parachute flares.
We tried to direct a Spooky Gunship in on our position by crawling out into the open and throwing trip flares to show the way. Let me tell you now, that don't work. You can only throw those little flares about five feet. The powerful springs that release the trip flare's spoon negates the throw. This was real bad. Ivan Bomark and I both laid out in the open in a fire fight and played dead, illuminated by the intensity of the burning flares. We lay still and waited for the illuminated trip flares to go out. I pumped all my last two M-79 rounds into the brush about 150 feet ahead, trying to hold off a charge..
Ivan was almost out of ammunition, and I crawled back about 30 feet to our packs behind some rocks, grabbed the ammo bag and returned back to Ivan just in time for him to snap in a fresh magazine in his M-16 and drop an NVA charging our position with a fixed bayonet on his SKS. The NVA died ten feet from our position thinking he was going to make sure we weren't just lying in the open, wounded. Surprise! I thought I was going to have to use a spear I had found earlier in the day. That's how low on ammunition we were.

The gun ship never found us. We could see him overhead, so we had him shoot the hell out of the jungle as a show of force (more, just to make us feel good).
We turned down an offer to have additional support troops parachute into the area as they would have been spread all over hell.

The next morning the helicopter resupplied us with ammunition. There was so much we had to blow half of it because it was shotgun shells and we weren't using shotguns. We didn't want to leave it behind for the enemy to use. We had to shoot our wounded horse and beat the hell out of the area. We changed our return direction plan, and waded a narrow river bottom for about six miles, and avoided running into a company size ambush planed for us. Unfortunately, our X/O and a platoon of CIDG coming from our camp ran into the ambush that had been set for us. We cut across country a mile to help rescue his platoon and saw the NVA's green tracers from their 50 cal machine guns firing at the air support above him, before they retreated back into the jungle.

Studies and Observation Group
by Jim Stewart

It was early 1966. I was in "B" Company of the 3rd Grp at the time. Had just returned from Camp Drum, where I had been a member of the Ski Training Committee along with the NCOIC, "Ranger" Roy, Charlie Telfair (RIP) and some other FOGs from the 10th.

On our first day back for duty, we started hearing about this list of names that had started circulating around 3rd Grp while we had been at Camp Drum. It seems that Billie Alexander (RIP) had contacted CSM Leal (RIP), the 3rd Grp CSM at the time, and asked him to send her a list of names - volunteers for a Top Secret assignment in Vietnam. No other information was forthcoming except that MOS didn't matter as long as you were "S" qualified. Oh, not to worry, CSM Leal says this is a "Good Deal". You might guess that CSM Carlos Leal was known then as "Good Deal" Leal.

BTW, this list wasn't one that was posted on the company Bulletin board to put your name on. Leal contacted Senior NCOs in companies he knew were dependable; they in turn, added names that they knew. Most of the volunteers came from the 3rd Grp, but there were some on the List from the 7th and 6th Grp as well. IIRC it was John Roy who contacted me.

Well, you might expect it to be difficult getting a list of folks to volunteer, for a Top Secret assignment to Vietnam, where no other information would be forthcoming until you arrived in Country; but you would be wrong. Access to the list was closed before some of the guys even knew it was being circulated.

In the latter part of May 1966, all the guys on the "Good Deal" list gathered in San Francisco for a Commercial "Champagne" flight on a 707 bound for Hawaii and then on to Saigon. There were a few E-6s, but most were E-7s & E-8s. The NCOIC, of course, was CSM "Good Deal" Leal. It was like old home week, and I think that the Stewardess on that flight will probably be telling stories about those crazy guys in the funny green hats for the rest of their lives.

There are some stories that could be told about that "Champagne" Flight out of San Francisco, but suffice to say that we all made it to Saigon without being threatened with a Court Martial - even with the newly assigned Provost Martial of Saigon on board.

We arrived in Nha Trang for a couple of days' in-processing and right away started getting bits of information about our assignment. Seems every clerk in 5th Group HQs knew what we were going to be doing, and as soon as they looked at our orders would give us the old smug "all knowing" smile.

As soon as they turned us loose that first evening, we all headed to the best place to get a Top Secret briefing - the NCO Club. I was sitting at a table with "Crash" Whalen (RIP), and one of the guys that we had known in the 10th was telling us about another friend that we had served with in the 10th, "Slats" P. Seems that "Slats", a couple of months earlier, had been awarded a Silver Star for the work he was doing with a unit that people were calling SOG. Of course every clerk in Nha Trang knew this was an acronym for Special Operations Group. Not until we got to Danang were we to find out it actually was short for something much more benign sounding - Studies and Observation Group. Anyway, that was the night that we found out that we were all going to get a Silver Star. NOT!!

After finishing the In-Processing through the fifth, we were flown to Danang for a Top Secret, no holds barred assignment briefing. First, most operations would be conducted in areas across the DMZ in Laos or Cambodia, "Across the fence". Second, we would not be wearing uniforms or carrying weapons that might identify us as US Military. Third, if we were KIA, or captured, the US would deny any knowledge of our activity and we would be carried as Missing - not as a result of hostile action.

The Officer conducting the briefing paused a couple of minutes, then before continuing the briefing, he told us that anyone who did not want to remain should leave for a debriefing and would be sent back to the 5th Grp for another assignment. I saw only some small movement among the group - maybe it was just me - but no one left. Although, I did find out later that there were a couple of guys who declined the assignment after the briefing was over.

We were split into two groups, one group assigned to Kham Duc and the other to Kontum. My first stroke of luck... I was assigned to Kontum. I didn't realize how lucky I was until I looked out at the Camp as we made our approach to land at Kham Duc. The first Group left the Aircraft including two of my friends "Ranger" Roy and "Crash" Whalen. We were then off to Kontum where I would once again be a NFG replacing the FOGs who were TDY from the 1st Grp; and to begin what would prove to be a very interesting if not unbelievable Special Forces assignment: FOB-2 of Studies and Observation Group.

Mess/Bar
by Jim Stewart

Our Recon Team from FOB-2, Kontum, along with some Teams from Kham Duc, built and opened FOB-1 at Phu Bai. We didn't even have water to bathe (hauled in Sea water and used salt water soap), but we had good chow from the 'git-go'. We each kicked in $50 to start the mess/bar and found a scrounger whose only job was to keep us supplied with chow and booze.

It was written in stone that every weekend we had steak barbecued on the grill. It was a real incentive to get through those hairy missions knowing that cold beer and good chow was waiting for your return. We were all being paid for RNA, but except for the initial $50, no one paid a penny for food. When you left Phu Bai, your $50 was refunded and you were given one of the SOG knives - alas, didn't get those last two items -since my departure from Phu Bai was routed thru the USS Repose.

Situation Resolved
by Jim Stewart

During my almost 20 years in SF, 1955-75, I was on every detail including Ash & Trash, Fireman for those coal burning furnaces, policing pine cones on Gruber, policing up the parking lot at the main PX, stocking shelves at the commissary & cutting grass with all of the tools mentioned except for the power mower. My E-8 time in SF was spent as a Bn Opns SGT in the 7th - exempt from those details, so never qualified for a power mower. I accepted all that stuff as necessary, in order to serve with the best MoFo's that ever hooked up, checked their static line and jumped out of a perfectly good airplane.

One time, I did refuse to comply. In 1966, a bunch of E-6s & 7s were sent from B Co of the 3rd to a COSCOM Warehouse on Gruber. Since I was the ranking guy, I was given the responsibility of making sure that everyone got there. Considering the NCOs we had in SF that was quite a responsibility. Anyway, I managed to get them there and found the civilian that I had been told to report to. That ass hole then called in a Leg PFC, told the PFC that we were his detail and would be working for him the rest of the day. I almost lost my cool, thought better of it and just told the guys to load the vehicles and go back to the company. Then I went back to B Company and told CSM H. what I had done. He just smiled and told me to go back to the Team Room. I guess he squared it with Charlie F. at Group Hqs because I never heard anymore about it.

Hatchet Force- SOG- FOB-2
by Jim Stewart

In the latter part of May 1966, I was one of the PCS FNGs that was assigned to FOB-2 in Kontum to replace the TDY FOGs from Oki. There was a period of overlap between them and us, and the guys from Oki were assigned to the Recon Teams; so most of us new guys were assigned to and given the mission of organizing and training a new unit to be called a Hatchet Force.

As the SOG Recon Team operations had grown in number, so had the incidence of contact with large units of enemy forces, many of them being well equipped NVA. The Recon Teams lacked sufficient personnel and weaponry to handle these contacts. To help the Recon Teams break contact so that they might be extricated, someone in the higher pay grades came up with the concept of a Reaction Force - called a Hatchet Force. The initial Hatchet Force at FOB-2 was designated the "First Raider Company". We were even issued a shoulder patch (never sewed it on). The patch was a white skull with gleaming red eyes resting on green crossed arrows on a black background. There was a black tab over the top with red lettering that read - 1st Raider Company. (Side note: I found this patch in one of my trash/treasures boxes a few years ago. I was looking for something to sew on my "I was there" vest, that Ed Sprague(RIP) had convinced our group of FOGs to wear to the Convention in Boston. From the first day that I wore that vest, Scott K. followed me around trying to get it from me. Scott is from Plano TX and is a collector of SF/SOG Memorabilia - seems that patch is now a collector's item. I told Scott, not only no, but hell no! BTW, if you would like to see that patch, Scott usually has his table set up at all the SFA Conventions and at SOAR.)

Anyway, my first operation out of Kontum was with the Hatchet Force. We had only been organized about two weeks, and the mission was not typical for the Hatchet Force.

Early one morning we were told that COL "Bull" Simons(RIP) wanted four U.S. and a Platoon from the Hatchet Force to meet him at the air strip in Danang ASAP. Al Fontez(RIP), Don Fawcett(RIP), Jerry L. and I were told to get our equipment and troops, and get on the choppers. When we arrived in Danang, "Bull" was waiting for us on the airstrip with his tripod, complete with map and some drawing paper with which he started to brief us on the operation. Seems we were going in to secure Camp Ashau so that "Bull" could make an onsite inspection. Well, I noticed that the Huey pilots' eyes got a little bigger and there was a look of disbelief on their faces. I'm sure they saw the same reaction from me. For those who may not be familiar with Camp Ashau, it was an A Team camp located in the Ashau Valley, and had been overrun/lost in March 1966, (just over two months earlier) to the NVA. Some of the A Team members had to E&E (escape and evade) for two or three days to escape. It was well known that those same NVA were still in the hills surrounding the camp.

Well, the questions were few, the operation was simple. Our Hueys would land and our Nungs - actually most were Cholon Cowboys - would establish security around the camp, after our Hueys had left us there; then "Bull"s command ship would drop him off to make his inspection. I don't think anyone there believed it was going to be that simple. I know the Nungs didn't. They had so many incense sticks burning in their rifle barrels that I thought I was going to suffocate in route.

Well, to make a too long story shorter, everything was simple. We landed and put our Nungs in a very loose perimeter around the camp. It looked as if no one had been there since the camp was over run. The KIAs were still lying everywhere - just skeletons, the rats had gotten all the meat. Weapons were lying all over the camp - even had huge stacks of unfired LAWs that hadn't been touched. Bull made his inspection - probably on the ground less than a half hour. He was picked up, and we didn't take any fire from the bad guys until the choppers came in to pick up the Hatchet Force. I still think the only reason we weren't put in a real hurt on that operation was because the NVA were probably dumfounded at the audacity of four slicks coming in to Ashau (without a gun ship). They probably couldn't believe their eyes.

I heard later that "Bull" was considering reopening Ashau as a SOG FOB/Launch Site. I don't know if he decided against it or if it was vetoed by someone higher, but I was certainly glad that it didn't happen.

Well, that was my first and last operation with the Hatchet Force. About a week later I was asked by the 1-0 of RT Dakota to come aboard as his 1-1. Assignment to a Recon Team was what I would have preferred anyway. The Recon Team Leader pulled the right strings; I was transferred to RT Dakota, and began another phase of service with "Studies and Observation Group".

Gunny
by John Cleckner

I was up to my butt in major alligators and "Did Not Want to Leave My Team" - especially for a "C Team Commanders Conference". LTC R. gave me a direct order to attend, so I caught a bird back to Da Nang. I figured I could beg, borrow and steal enough material to help us rebuild some of the massive destruction we had sustained during two months of rocket and mortar attacks.

The arrival was routine. As soon as I got my bunk and put my gear away, I made a beeline for the Mike Force Bar. (Some guys might remember the big fish tank behind the bar.)

A marine had just "Bought One of the Fish". The bar made more money out of selling raw fish to idiots who wanted to demonstrate their manhood and guts more than they did with booze. He ate it and immediately puked on the bar. He left with the help of one of the Biggest Active Duty Polynesian Special Forces Soldiers I had ever laid my eyes on. When the Polynesian winked at me saying, "Hi, Sir", I felt pretty safe. I never opened my mouth when I drank, and I was there to drink. I was really ragged out from the weeks of attacks during the siege, and also pissed that I had to leave the guys on the Team for this Mickey Mouse bullshit commanders' conference.

Before the night was over SGM H. was knocked through the "C Team" bar door (which I never patronized) in front of me. He went down big time with a tall thin black marine playing the Marine Corps hymn on his jaw. The Marine looked at me as I approached the action on my way to the Mike Force Bar, just stepped back and let me pass. I didn't fight; it wasn't in my mindset, and I think the kid knew I would have killed him in place if he had looked at me sideways. By the way, this was a lance corporal fighting a SF E-9. Something was very wrong with that picture.

The Bar at the Mike Force was much better. I sat at it in an out of the way place and just watched the action out of the corner of my eye. I had to turn in my M-16, but had my 45 and two grenades just in case. The problems I saw that night and the next day were a direct result in poor leadership, and the fact that the powers that be allowed Marines into the C Team area for the "bucks" they spent there. It made for a very dangerous situation in my opinion. I raised this issue the next day at the Conference, but was whistling in the wind. I told R. that men could not be brought directly out of a combat situation and exposed to this bullshit. I had had it with Marines at that point, and told the Old Man my men would never come to Da Nang.

I cannot remember how long this turkey conference lasted, but I did anticipate that the Command would have something substantial for us to do other than get smashed every night we were there. Da Nang was off limits and had a helluva curfew because it was "a Navy/Marine town with all the baggage that goes along with that scenario". At some point in time, a C Team First Lt. (Engineer type) who had been there a long long time and had a major problem with Whores and Venereal Diseases, talked everyone into going "Down Town" to meet and greet our VN "counterparts". I honestly believed this was something that the C Team had arranged.

We piled into jeeps and had all of the appropriate paperwork in hand to justify our trip and dispel any improprieties as far as breaking "Curfew" was concerned, should the Shore Patrol (SP) show up.

Our convoy ended up in an alley someplace in down town Da Nang. I was sitting in a jeep, like a dumb ass waiting for the fog to lift so we could get to our destination. This muscle bound 1st Lt. Marine type walked up to me, and flexed his muscles and his mouth.

Little did I know this dipshit Lt. from the C Team had made arrangements for all of us to get laid at this multi-level whorehouse someplace in Da Nang, and the "counterpart" story was just a cover. I also remember seeing at least two whores in every window screaming, "I love you, G.I!" and waving at us frantically to come in.

The smart ass SP came up to me and asked if I was Captain Cleckner and I said yes. It appears I was the ranking man present and I was being arrested along with everyone else. I told him he was full of shit we had authorization to visit our Counterparts. He told me I was full of shit and that I and the others were at a whore house which was off limits, in violation of Curfew, and rattled off a list of other violations. He stated that multiple SP Jeeps surrounded us and that we "would" follow him to the Brig.

Mind you now, the entire command structure of every/all the "A" Teams in I Corps was being arrested at the same time.

When we arrived at the Shore Patrol Station, I refused to allow our Officers to be put in the "Pen", a holding area with all the drunken marines - puke and all. I ordered all of the SF Officers to sit on the benches that lined the walls of this very big room. At this time the marine Lt. disappeared.

I directed my attention at the Gunny, who was sitting in this elevated seat behind an enormous wooden wall. I told the

Gunny to call our C Team CQ and relate to him our situation.

Sometime later the Marine Lt. came out of the door behind me and I could hear his heavy breathing and feel his presence. He had taken off his blouse and was just wearing a skin tight White T-Shirt with his name stenciled on the front. He flexed and made one too many disrespectful remarks to me, along with what I considered an aggressive move. As I said, I had had it with Marines, up to my ass. I hit him with everything I had, right on the button. He went down and I immediately looked at the Gunny. He shook his head and didn't say a word.

Shortly thereafter, the old man arrived with the Cavalry. He was wearing LBE and had his M-16 as did the others. After busting through the door, he looked around and told the Gunny he was taking his men. The Gunny said that was all right with him.

We went back to the C Team and I never heard another word about the event, although I heard the Lt. really caught hell.

A Seabee Story
From John Cleckner

This is about a Navy Sea Bee who came to our Camp and really saved our bacon. Many of us had these fine folks helping us through hard times and I am sure you all feel the way I do. These guys were magnificent.

Gary Dalton asked me to send this story to a buddy of his who headed up the Retired Sea Bee Association. He put it in his newsletter years ago. It has not been copyrighted and no one has any claim to it but me, God, and Godfrey, where ever he is.

I have a Seabee Story from Special Forces Camp Tien Phuoc A-102 in I Corps Tactical Zone, South Vietnam 1968-69.

Intelligence was telling us that there was a huge build up of North Vietnamese Soldiers in and around our Special Forces "A" Team (late 1968, early 1969). I kept calling DaNang (C1 our C Team and Higher Hqrs) asking for Engineer support to fix my C-123 dirt runway. Call after call went in, and finally I threatened to call my Higher Headquarters in Nha Trang for help if they did not respond to our plea for help.

The Combat activity was really picking up and everyone knew something was about to hit the fan. Alerts were called on a nightly basis.

In early 1969, a huge Sikorsky crane flew in with Engineer Equipment dangling underneath it. The crane let down and placed each piece of equipment on the runway; then it landed and a man got out. The crane took off and the man began moving the equipment to the south side of the runway.

I was looking through binoculars and the rest of my team kept asking, "Who is this guy?" and commenting, that he was going to get his butt killed. We hopped in our jeeps and 3/4-ton trucks, locked and loaded the 30 caliber machine guns and proceeded to the runway as fast as we could. This guy was just getting out of a dump truck, and I noticed he had on a uniform with some kind of odd rank on it.

I asked him who he was and he said, "I'm Godfrey." from some unit that I couldn't understand. I asked him what the heck he thought he was doing, and he told me he was there to fix our runway. I asked him when the rest of the guys were going to show up and he told me he was it.

Years before, I had an "A" team in II Corps, A-222 Dong Tre. We were kicking Charlie's butt and racking up a high kill count each month. Well, General Westmoreland flew in to check us out. After he was satisfied with our briefings, he asked what he could do for us to help us continue to kill enemy soldiers.

The first thing out of my mouth was, "We need a runway, Sir." We got it (a C-130 runway) and the Army brought in an Engineer "Company" and a mine sweeping platoon and lots of security. I later found out it takes a platoon to build a runway, but I wasn't complaining.

So, here I had "one" guy with three pieces of equipment to repair a C-123 dirt runway, full of mortar and rocket holes and surrounded by bad guys.

I finally got around to asking Godfrey what unit he was with. I knew he wasn't Army. He said he was a Seabee and

I said, "No kidding. My father told me you guys could build anything." My father (A Navy Guy) spent 8 1/2 years in the Pacific, during and after WWII. Get him started and all he could talk about were the Seabees and how great they were during the War.

So I asked him his rank. He told me, and I didn't know anymore than I did before I asked him. I asked him what that was in "E" ranks. (For example, E3, E4 etc.) He said he was an E4. I then asked him if he was sure he could handle the job by himself. He laughed and said it was a piece of cake. I told him how dangerous it was around there, and informed him that a Special Forces "A" Team had two Engineers assigned to them. He accepted that, and I immediately assigned both guys to him even though they both outranked him. I also put a platoon of my "Strikers" (Mercenaries) around the runway for security.

He worked from daylight to dark everyday, and his coming and going got pretty routine. I had forgotten about him until the night and morning of 22-23 February 1969.

Just after 2AM the proverbial crap hit the fan. We didn't know it at the time but we had come under siege by an NVA Heavy Weapons Regiment. We fought all night and into the morning.

After a very bad rocket attack just after dawn (my XO and Senior Medic were both seriously wounded), Godfrey came up to me and asked what he could do to help. He told me his equipment had been destroyed and he wanted to help fight. I asked him what else he could do besides drive heavy equipment. He told me that Seabees were all trained on 50 Caliber Machine Guns. I was ecstatic. I put him and my Team Sergeant, MSG Ramon M. (who was supposed to have left for the US but couldn't get out of the Camp because of the intense rocket and mortar fire) on the East Side of the TOC covering the high-speed approaches from the East. They had a well-constructed bunker and tons of ammo and extra Barrels for the 50 Cal.

Both of them fought independently as needed for nine days. I finally realized that I hadn't seen or heard from them for a long time. At first I remembered hearing the 50 Cal. going off all the time outside my Tactical Operation Center; then the firing became routine.

The Siege continued until 15 July 1969. Godfrey was medevaced around the fifth or sixth of March after I found out he had been wounded and continued to fight. We had 784 defenders at Tien Phuoc and took on 3 NVA Divisions. The Americal Division and the 101st Airborne came in and saved our bacon, as did TAC Air from all the Services, but our Special Forces Team took hundreds of the enemy with us and Godfrey was a big, big part of that effort.

I was so impressed with what my Team Sergeant told me Godfrey had done in defense of our Camp that I contacted his Headquarters in Da Nang and recommended him for the Silver Star and a Battle Field Promotion. He received a Purple Heart for his Wounds, the Bronze Star w/V for his heroism, and he was promoted to E5. I was at the dinner when his Commanding Officer pinned everything on.

That is my Seabee Story about a guy named Godfrey. I never did know his first name, but he was one helluva Engineer. He fixed our Runway well enough for us to get our resupplies in during a 5-month siege of our "A" Team (Special Forces Camp).

Hamburger Hill
by John Cleckner

The Weather was great; the 101st Tactics were horrible in this situation. The Air, mortar and Arty support killed more of them than the VC/NVA did. It reminded me of typical Marine tactics. This action was across the mountain range from me (west). It was rare that the 101 blew it.

I was hit the 15th of May and put in Chu Lai (American Hosp) in intensive care for 30 days. During this time most of the casualties from Hamburger Hill came into the same Huge Quonset at the Americal Hospital in Chu Lai. I thought that these guys were from the reinforced 101st Brigade fighting in my camp and in relief of the Americal.

When the powers that be sent in all of the PAOs and Senior Officers and Celebrities to talk to these guys, because it was on National TV in the US, I again stepped on my dick.

All of the of the 101st. guys had neat name plates on the end of their beds identifying them as members of the 101st w/decal

The first guy through the door was Ricardo Montalban. He talked to several guys and then keyed on me. Maybe it was because I was dark complected with black wavy hair, Italian, and had NO NAME TAG on the end of my bed.

http://teamhouse.tni.net/scrapbook/Cleckner/montalban.htm

He came over and asked who I was and why I didn't have a TAG on the end of my bed.

As the cameras rolled and the REMF packed in behind him, I told him who I was, the unit I represented, all about Tien Phuoc and the siege, and the fact that these kids were from my Camp, wounded and fighting for their lives against incredible odds.

Little did I know that HH was going on. I had no idea of the situation in that battle or that they were taking casualties. After this experience I listened to what was going on in the Intensive care ward, and realized that at least two of the guys across from me had been put in for the MOH. It was a real education for a SF NCO/Officer to hear what goes on in an Infantry Unit. (Another story)

Anyway, Ricardo and I had a great talk and he sent an autographed picture to my wife. The Senior Officers behind him all threatened my ass, and I could have cared less.

Military Chaplains
Men of God, Men of Great Courage
by John Cleckner

I heard our Country's Vice President tell the story of the New York City Fire Chaplain giving last rights to a dead fireman when one of the WTC towers came down and killed him on 9-11-01. The story was so profound that I want to tell all of you of my experiences with Military Chaplains, especially during my War Time service.

I felt obligated to tell all of you of these incredibly brave men of the cloth that served Special Forces after hearing what VP Cheney said about New York's Fire Chaplain. We didn't see them during the battles like the American Units did. It was after everything had settled down a little. Then out of the Jungle they would come; out of the Fog, the mist, or the Smoke.

I would be there, bloodied, mad, confused, scared, sick, and sometimes wounded, and he would come up to me and say, "John, how are you, lets talk". Sometimes he and I would have a drink together, sometimes he would ask me questions, sometimes he would try to repair my wounded body, BUT ALWAYS, always, "HE" was there with me after these horrendous events had occurred. Always there to give me new direction and comfort.

At one time I thought it almost spooky, how every time I got into a big fight, or after we took a lot of causalities, or when we had been under siege for a long time, that these men of GOD would appear and proceed to calm and reassure us. I cannot speak for ANYONE else. I can only tell you what happened to me, what I saw and experienced. I can tell you that these men helped me through the Horrors of War and they helped me cope with Death of a magnitude that would stun your average American Citizen.

The most profound Chaplain Story came on a day when everyone was sitting around the "Team House" licking their wounds and resting up for the next battle. It was like every other day to us.

Out of nowhere a man came walking toward us. When he was close enough I recognized him as a Chaplain. He said good morning to us and asked me if I knew what day it was. I told him I had no idea. He said it was Thanksgiving. No one on the "A Team" had any idea that it was Thanksgiving; we were too busy fighting for our lives.

He asked if we would pray with him and we did. It gave all of us great comfort and peace. Then he said there is something on the runway for you. We all piled into our jeeps and 3/4 tons and proceeded down to our runway. There we found a C-123 with two Full Bull Air Force Colonels on the ramp waiting to give us a big Turkey dinner for Thanksgiving. I lost it when I saw what they had brought us. I will never forget that Thanksgiving, the Air Force or that Army Chaplain.

30 Cal Carbine Round Bullet
by John Cleckner

Our Team at Dong Tre had the very early version of the M-16 and all of our strikers had M-1 and M-2 carbines. Intelligence told us that there was a lot of movement about 10 klicks north of us, so we planned a short 3 day op to see if we could find anyone moving around. This was daylight "start" operation, which was very rare. By early afternoon we found some movement after entering a Vil and finding massive defensive positions.

All of a sudden all hell broke loose. We had a hundred or so guys in black PJs in front of us (caught in the open). I called "District" to see if they had RF-PF out on any kind of op. The replay was NO.

Within minutes I had no ammo left. The other American was also out of ammo. The little people were not about to give us their guns. It was one helluva lesson. I built web gear to give me the firepower I needed. That shit NEVER happened again.

(Got shot in the leg with a carbine; don't like the little pricks, no punch, but mine hurt).

POW-EandE
by John Cleckner

For whatever reason, the Camps I commanded in VN all had strong Intel that mobile POW Camps were in our AO. Without getting melodramatic, I can tell you that every operation I ran in VN had a POW rescue element in it. Unfortunately I was always a couple of hours short of finding them. They were definitely there, but apparently they had better Intel on us than we had on them. Our Intel did result in a number of recoveries (by American Units because we shared this info with them) and nothing short of killing the enemy gave me more pleasure than knowing we had a part in rescuing a young American soldier.

Later, when I was assigned to the 82nd, Bad Eye R. tried to recruit me for a mission. I knew it was to get those 5 jumbo jets back from the Libyan Desert. I had committed myself to DA. I swore I would not go back to SF as an Officer, because I had five straight tours as an Infantry Officer with them, and under no circumstance would I dishonor that commitment. Well, little did I know it was not Libya, but rather the Son Tay Raid that Robby was asking me to volunteer for. I honor those that went, especially our own George P. and also a friend and neighbor named "Dick", who is no longer with us.

I can tell you that certain schools I attended had POW camps and E&E courses that were the hardest part of a very extended field training program, both in the pure Infantry concept sense and the Special Forces Concept; and were schools that made it mandatory to go through extensive POW interrogation and E & E Programs until you could escape. These were far in advance of the SERE programs that were later part of the Air Force and SF. The programs taught to us during my time were the hardest I ever participated in.

Nick R. (Five Years to Freedom) as I understand, individually took it to another level and perfected it. I know that Danny P. (he was captured with Nick and let go after 4 1/2 years) and I talked about what Nick was doing, and Danny worked with him on the concept. Guys like Jimmy J. didn't participate but addressed it in their Special Forces MOS Classes at the Dog/Goat Lab.

I had the honor of putting them all out on their first jumps after returning from POW status in RVN. For whatever reason, we all became social friends in the 70s (except for Rowe). I learned more than I ever wanted to know about the horrors of POW status from them.

These training experiences were real world to me. My mindset had to accept what was coming. We were never captured. We were always incarcerated, tortured, questioned, starved, and encouraged to be clever and bold enough to escape if we could. That was my quest. I had to escape and of course never revealed one ounce of information. I witnessed many men who sustained broken bones and more minor injuries under the circumstances we were tested in.

When I was able to rewrite the training program for the 2/6 Infantry in Berlin, which we executed in West Germany, I incorporated a POW Camp and an escape and evasion exercise to test our troops' will to survive. It was only a 5K escape and evasion exercise, and it turned into the biggest cluster fuck I have ever seen.

Obviously, troops taught to march and not to fight had a problems shooting an Azimuth and negotiating very easy German wooded terrain.

Our POW camp was very elaborate and a fabulous teaching point, but the E&E part of the program was a piece of cake. Well, in my mind it was.

As the S3 of the 2/6 Inf., I knew this was the right thing to do. Gentleman, this was my only LEG assignment in 22 years. It was magnificent from the stand point of "let me help you accomplish your mission and get your shit together", especially after the anti-war/black power take over of the Berlin Bde in '69 & '70.

Being a Zero tolerance and "I will kill you in place" kind of guy, I did not fit into the new concept of *Pro Life.*

I survived with the help of Det A and especially the SGMs over there at the time. One other guy that helped out was the Berlin Brigade Provost Marshall (an LTC in the USA). He was an officer and Berliner in the German Army during WWII. Why we connected is only speculation. Maybe it had to do with something SF, but I did survive.

This POW/E&E Program set the stage for me to be able to rewrite the concept of training for the Berlin Bde when they went to the "Zone". I loved every minute of it, as did the "Plans" NCOs assisting me.

Whiskey Joe, Skydiving, Subdued Patches, and Vietnam
by Joe Cleckner

Here is a story some would find fascinating and other would call bullshit. But it is all true, I was there. I dare anyone to challenge this story.

My next door neighbor was Specialist 6 Ray O. He was a great guy and a good friend and neighbor. Ray was also a first class Helicopter Crew Chief. CIRCA 1964-68 Special Warfare Center before his heart attack.

Ray was part of the effort by Brigadier General Whiskey Joe S. to set the World Record Freefall attempts in a 24-hour period. This effort by BG S. had to have been sometime in 64-65 (CRS). One day Ray banged on my door and told me that his chopper and several others along with a large support group had been a part of BG S.'s effort to set this World Skydiving Record and when the General left Ray's A/C he streamered in. Ray said he was dead. He had to be!

I went to OCS in April 1965 and was reassigned back to Special Forces in January 1966.

Sometime in the late spring of 1966, I was sent to the Special Warfare Center Headquarters to be interviewed for the position of Aide-de-Camp to General S., the Commander of Special Forces.

For any of you who ever met him, he can only be described as "profane" (every other word was a curse word), fearless, somewhat of a bully, smart, very similar in approach to enlisted men as Mike Healy was and strikingly similar about telling WAR STORIES, and "Just a Little Unorthodox", not to mention the fact that he survived that parachuting accident! The Doctors designed "Feet" that were not really feet but more an extension of his legs in a kind of semi-circular design, if that makes any sense. It was pretty gross to see, but he did his thing and was still on active duty, kicking ass, and taking names.

Needless to say, with absolutely NO qualifications at all, he chose me as his new Aide. General Stillwell controlled his Command from his desk and very seldom rose from behind it.

I became his legs, and he ordered me around in situations that were bizarre to say the least. He constantly told war stories and when a thought came to his mind, he called in his C of S and others in his staff to respond to his requests. He told me I was NEVER to answer to anyone but him. He chose me because I was an old enlisted man and he liked Mustangs. I really never understood him or what he was all about. To be around him was to be in a constant state of terror and confusion. (I am stating this now reflecting back on a 2nd Lieutenant's mindset and what I was into up to my earlobes).

I recall trying to understand what he was trying to accomplish and how I could be a true aide to him. I became too protective, and he immediately assured me that he was no cripple, and he didn't need any sympathy. I fired back at him with a comment and just knew he would pull out a 45 and kill me for being disrespectful. He mellowed out a little after that exchange, but I never patronized him again.

Then one day, he said, "John, I want you to help me make a decision." He wanted me to help him decide what to do with an Army Directive. "Every" senior Commander in

Special Forces was called to his office to discuss whether Special Forces would agree to go with the new idea of converting all of our cloth name tags, badges, patches to subdued or stay with what we had.

A Colonel came in with all of his nametags, badges and patches sewn on and subdued. I want to say his name was Welch or something like that. He was a big guy, very sophisticated, and unlike the others, not the least bit intimidated by BG S.

BG S. made the Colonel stand against one wall in his office and then I had to stand against the furthest wall and read his name, tell everyone what his badges and patches were or said, and describe everything on his uniform. BG S. shut the blinds and turned off the lights in his office. The Colonel and I continued with this drill for at least 30 minutes. I told the Old Man I could read everything he had on his uniform. Stillwell went with the "Subdued" even though the majority of his Commanders thought it was a bad idea and would create enormous ID problems.

This whole assignment was very short. I was not a happy camper. I had orders for the 5th in VN and could not understand why I would be tasked to do this Bull Shit duty. BG S. asked why I did not want to be his Aide, or why I was unhappy with this assignment.

I told him that being chosen as his Aide was a great honor, but I wanted to go to VN and had orders assigning me to the 5th Special Forces Group.

He blew up. "What asshole sent you down here when you were on orders for Combat? I will never keep a man from Combat!" He said a hell of a lot more, but you get the picture.

BG S. ordered me back to Training Group and told me a couple of War Stories I will never forget. One at least helped me later on in the War. He was an experience beyond description, but a very very interesting man to be around.

Supply Smith
by John Cleckner

When I took over the Company they had just failed an IG. I told our Supply Sgt. in A Company, SFTG Smith, the future of the company was on his shoulders.

I did my initial inventory and accounted for every blanket and pillow case, every sheet and pillow. I told him that the same count had better be there when the next IG came around and when I left for another assignment. If it wasn't, I was sending him to Leavenworth. You see, we had a little problem with "The Guys" taking their stuff downtown. They didn't have very much doe-rae-me, so the blankets ended up at their trailers or in some pawnshop. Yes you could pawn a blanket back in those days.

Anyway, Smith got the message. Every time I saw him, he was hustling someplace to con, steal, what ever he had to do to make up for those "lost and stolen" bedding items.

I was so impressed with his tenacity that I sent him to OCS before I left. When I was assigned to Berlin years later he was there as the Berlin Bde official greeter. Kinda like the unofficial American Mayor of Berlin and the head of the Tourist Bureau all rolled into one. If you were just coming in to town and needed to learn the lay of the land, he was the "Man".

We renewed old friendships and he took me to every "Neat" place in town, not to mention the best whorehouses and gambling joints (The Cherry Hotel). He had truly come into his own.

That's my Supply Sgt. Story, and I'm sticking with it.

Visit with Rudolf Hess
by John Cleckner

As I grow older, I reflect back on my life & times. Because I was a professional Soldier, and in particular a Paratrooper and a Special Forces Non-Commissioned & Commissioned Officer, I think of Historical events that I was either involved in, or asked to be involved with.

I was assigned to Berlin Germany and had the great Honor and distinct Pleasure to serve as the Senior Aide de Camp to the United States Commander of Berlin.

As stated in General H. Norman Schwarzkopf's Biography, his selection as an Aide-de-Camp to the Berlin Brigade Commander (A one star General) was described as one of the most significant assignments in his Career: "He was aide-de-camp to the Berlin Command in 1960 and 1961, a crucial time in the history of that divided city", and further in his Autobiography, "It Doesn't Take A Hero". General Schwarzkopf stated that this assignment was a trip into the Military-Diplomatic World with great involvement in the international arena dealing with International Relations that involved the Germans in West Berlin, and the Quadripartite which involved the British, French and Soviet governments and armed forces.

As the Senior Aide-de-Camp to the United States Commander of Berlin (USCOB), my involvement and duties were at least one hundred times more critical and demanding than those of the aide to the Berlin Brigade Commander who was subordinate to the USCOB.

The United States Commander of Berlin was always a very senior Major General, usually with great international and combat experience. Major General William W. Cobb was the USCOB and my boss, and his experience was having fought in WWII, Korea, Vietnam and having served for over 38 years in the Military. As I reflect back on this military assignment I can say it was one of the most demanding and satisfying of my Professional Military Career. I was involved with too many events to list them all here with the exception of this event.

The event that I most remember of the thousands I was involved with in Berlin during this fascinating assignment was my encounter with the **Reich Chancellor of Nazi Germany himself, Rudolf Hess**. I was one of only a handful of individuals who had ever been allowed inside his cell and within inches of him since his incarceration after the Nuremberg Trials. This event occurred in 1973 while I served as Senior Aide-de-Camp to General Cobb. The story below is the reason "I" was allowed into Hess's cell. I will mention now that he was tall, lean, his hair was dark, he had a protruding brow and his eyebrows were enormous and he had the most piercing eyes I have ever looked into. He looked almost exactly like he did in the pictures I saw of him at Nuremberg.

This story starts out shortly after my assignment to Berlin Germany as the Operations Officer (S3), 2nd Battalion, 6th Infantry, Berlin Brigade. Each member of the **Quadripartite**, American, British, Soviet, and French forces were required, on a rotating basis, to Guard **SPANDAU PRISON.** All of the WWII prisoners from the Nuremberg Trials had been executed, died while in prison, or had been released. The only prisoner in Spandau Prison was **Rudolf Hess**.

An Infantry Company from each Battalion was responsible for this duty 365 days a year. The Soviets hated Hess so much that they told us that after he died he would be buried in the Prison courtyard and then the guard responsibility would continue over his grave, because he would be buried there and never leave.

The Prison also had a "GOVERNOR" from each of the Quadripartite Governments that managed the Prison. Each of the 4 COBs also had a hand in what was going on from time to time. Especially if Hess was asking for something, which was usually medical care. The Soviets refused to treat him and at some point in time the US secretly moved him to a British Hospital close by to treat him for urinary problems. Somehow the Soviets got wind of what we had done and the whole damn town went on alert until Hess was returned to the Prison.

On the 1st of January 1972 the $2/6^{th}$ Infantry's turn came up for Spandau Prison Support. (This was my baby, my first time, and the demands were unbelievable).

I learned that it was customary, especially when there was a holiday involved, to have a very large elaborate lunch provided by the Spandau Prison staff for the out going and incoming Military units.

In attendance that day were the 4 Governors of Spandau, the outgoing Unit representatives (British) and the incoming Unit Officers (Americans). We were initially taken around and introduced to the Prison and briefed on our responsibilities.

When the briefings had concluded, the day's festivities started with the usual European Cocktail time with Champagne, Gin & Tonic, Scotch & Soda, & Beer. During this time it became very evident to me that no one gave a darn whether you spoke his or her language or not. Interactions were attempted even though the other individual could not understand your language.

No one could understand the French Governor and he refused to speak anything but French, and obviously no one could understand the "NEW Soviet Governor, because his German was lousy and he spoke no French, no one spoke Russian and those that tried to speak to him in German had less acuity than he did. What I witnessed was a disgusting attempt by everyone present, excluding my Battalion Commander and myself, to kiss up to the New Soviet Governor.

My Bn Cmdr and I did not drink, and noticed that everyone in the room was getting a little tipsy, loose - whatever you want to call it. Actually he and I did not even participate in the intercourse going on in the lounge area and viewed most of this activity from the dining room.

When we retired into the dining room and looked for our seating positions, (and believe me these were very well planned), I found that the individual sitting to my left was the NEW Soviet Governor of Spandau Prison.

In Europe, especially in a place like Berlin and even more so under the multi-nation environment we were experiencing, everything related to this "Lunch" was perfectly planned and orchestrated; no one was offended, left in need, or catered to. They ultimately experienced the finest "Lunch" they had ever eaten.

Everyone was seated as the outgoing British Commander expressed his thanks. My Battalion Commander greeted everyone and stated that we were prepared to accept the task at hand and meet our obligation. The Americans were taking over and the American Governor was in charge.

He introduced everyone at the very long table. The Soviet just smiled and nodded his head during these proceedings.

As soon as this was over with and everyone had settled down I turned to the Soviet Governor and asked him, (In English) "How are you doing today?" He turned to me and replied that he was doing great, and his response was IN PERFECT ENGLISH…Everyone within ear shot almost fell off of their chairs. NO ONE had even tried to speak to him in English. No one knew what his linguistic capabilities were. Shame on someone in the intelligence field.

After our first exchange he looked at me and said, "You have many medals, more than anyone at this table. You also have a Special Forces Combat Patch and that tells me you are a very experienced Combat Veteran. (We were required to be in full dress with all awards and decorations on display, that was what Berlin was all about, "Presence")

My answer to the remark about my Military Decorations was, (and this is as I looked at his three rows of ribbons, the two on the top with 3 each and the one on the bottom with 2 each), "You are also decorated. You must have fought hard against the Chinese Horde on the Sino-Soviet Boarder". (I was being a Smart A--).

He laughed and said, "No, No, these are medals for doing a good job", and I replied, "Oh, for meritorious service". The Soviet stated he had never been in combat, but that he did recently command an Artillery Battalion in Potsdam, a suburb of Berlin.

As I stated, everyone within earshot almost fell off their chairs including my CO who was to my right front across the table; and directly across from me sat two British majors whose eyes were as big as silver dollars as they listened to this verbal exchange between the Soviet and me.

No one could believe that this guy spoke fluent English. No one could believe he was telling me who and what he was, and holding a discussion like this, especially in Berlin.

Then the Soviet Governor said, "You have had to have fought many battles and been away from your wife and family for a very long time. How did your wife handle you being away so long"?

I thought for a moment and said, "She is an Army Wife and she would never say anything, no matter how long I was gone. She would always support me, no matter what. He told me I was very lucky. He said his wife was always mad when he had to leave home, even for a short period of time.

We toasted and ate. He shook my hand and hugged me and asked me many more questions that were easily answered and did not disclose anything of an Intelligence nature about me. What I got out of him filled pages of intelligence files after the Americans debriefed me.

Now, fast forward to the day I stood beside Rudolf Hess. The old man was having terrible medical problems, and the Americans were in charge of the prison. General Cobb made a decision to go and personally visit Hess along with the American Surgeon General to see if he could help. As the General's Aide, I of course was beside the General and took his lead.

After entering the Prison and greeting each Governor, the Soviet walked over to me and said, "Hi. Good to see you again."

General Cobb almost fell over. He leaned over to me and told me that the Soviets did not allow anyone in Hess's cell except the Governors and very rarely the COBS when they came to visit. General Cobb told me to stick to him like glue, with my pad and pencil in hand, and to follow him right into the cell. He said, "If the Soviet steps in front of you, back off".

As the whole entourage came to the door of the cell, the Soviet Governor stopped everyone but General Cobb and me from going in. Even the American Governor and Surgeon General had to stop at the cell door. The General spent over 10 minutes talking to Hess as my eyes took in Hess's presence, his cell and the four walls filled with books from floor to ceiling, the meager bed and table and chair in his cell.

I honestly believe that I was allowed to go into Hess's cell only because of the chance meeting I had with the "New" Soviet Governor years before when we first met at Spandau Prison.

That is the end of that story, and for me it was truly a historic experience and one that I will never forget.

Bloodshot
by John Delavan

Sometime in mid 1967 I was an MP at Flint Kaserne, Bad Toelz, Germany - home of 10th Special Forces Group and the hated 7th Army NCO Academy. Late one swing shift my partner Sp/4 Alan F. and I were sent out to a gasthaus near Lenggries right on the main road to Bad Toelz. There had been some complaint and we were to pick up a Special Forces guy and take him back to his company up in Lenggries. Seems he had been pretty much living at the gasthaus and humping the owner's wife and the owner was beginning to take exception. No problem; glad to help out.

We arrived at said gasthaus and spoke with the owner. The Special Forces Troop in question was a young Staff Sergeant and was in his car parked right out front. We looked and found him passed out in the front seat. Alan went around to the passenger's side, and I to the driver's side. The car was open so we tried to wake him up. We fully intended to either tell him to go on back to Lenggries or, if he was too drunk to drive, we'd give him a ride. That would have been situation solved and no paperwork - paperwork always happened in typical USAREUR double quadruplicate.

After two or three attempts we managed to get this guy more or less into a sitting position behind the wheel. This is where we figured we made the first big mistake.

While attempting to get our passed out friend into a sitting position, I noted he was only a few years older than I (I was 20 at the time) and a huge pile of rock hard muscle. As I was noting this, I saw him open one very bloodshot eye with which he more or less looked me over. The next thing

I knew I had my head on sideways and I was lying on the roof of the next car over. I have never been hit that hard before - or since.

Old bloodshot came out of that car after me, grabbed me by the feet, pulled me down off that car and was about to hit me again when good old Alan came leaping over bloodshot's car like Superman. It didn't help a whole lot though. After Alan landed on this guy's shoulders, I got tossed back up on top of the car again and Alan landed out past the middle line on the highway.

Ingrown Toenails
by John Delavan

I've had considerable experience in the subject of having to remove many ingrown toenails on others and on myself; and having observed quite a number of M.D.s and Podiatrists perform the procedure. Please allow me to shed a little light here.

There are a number of different ways to remove ingrown toenails. I've seen some real butchers go at it and their patients in considerable pain for a long time after. I've also been fortunate enough to learn the procedure from a couple of really quality docs whose patients experience far less pain post operatively and almost none a couple of days down the road.

There's also something to be said for repetitiveness. Even though the nails on my big toes are a total mess and naturally grow back in an ingrown condition, I've never bothered to permanently remove them by excising the nail bed and root. I've done the simple removal procedure so often on both my own great toes that I no longer use anesthetics - I just grab the toe tightly enough to cut off circulation. Doing this in just the right way also blocks nearly all pain. Then just shove one jaw of a Kelley hemostat all the way back under the ingrown section, clamp it down and twist it back until the ingrown portion is pulled up and free. Then it's a simple matter to cut the offending portion of nail free with a one-point sharps, put a snug band-aid on it and drive on. It's a good idea to have the area and instruments clean, but any procedure with the toes needn't be totally aseptic. I've never had a patient (or myself) suffer any sort of infection when properly done.

Removing the entire nail is almost the same procedure, and if you don't want the nail to grow back at all just excise the nail bed and all of the root along with the nail. Healing time is somewhat longer, and any of the above performed on a patient requires blocking the nerves to the toe.

How well the patient tolerates any procedure depends on his/her motivation - both to undergo the procedure and get on with it after. I went through 300F1 and my 8 week hospital rotation phase at FLWAH with a broken right heel. Damned if I was going to be recycled! I was too old and didn't have time for that shit. It's clear a buddy referred to as "Ratman" had a similar incentive. We've all driven on through pain when we've had to. That's part of what it took for all of us to earn that S qualifier or 18 series MOS.

About this time two German Policemen appeared out of the night and the four of us pounced on that young Staff Sergeant like a pack of lions. I do believe we managed to wrestle him to the ground two or maybe even three times. The second time we got him down, Alan was on his back and got his nightstick across bloodshot's throat. I remember that both German Policemen were on his legs and

I was trying to hold one arm while attempting to get my handcuffs out. Old Alan was rearing back on that nightstick for all he was worth trying to choke that young Special Forces Staff Sergeant out. I think that pissed him off because with the one hand I didn't have hold of, he was pulling that club away from his throat. In fact he pulled Alan right on over his head and landed him out in the street again.

Well, we ended up starting all over and finally managed to get him face down on the ground with his hands behind his back and I got my genuine military issue Smith & Wesson handcuffs on him.

Whew! Was I glad that was over! We stood him up with Alan hanging on one of his gigantic arms and me hanging on the other. The two German Police were standing in front of him, so naturally old bloodshot snapped out a kick and left a great big size 12 boot print on that German Policeman's pretty white shirt. Now it was the German Policeman's turn to sit out in the middle of the street.

His partner didn't miss a beat and snapped that young Special Forces Staff Sergeant right across the face with his nasty little hard rubber spring baton. POW!

Now I reckon that young Special Forces Staff Sergeant really got pissed off this time because he BROKE my genuine military issue Smith & Wesson handcuffs, tossed me back up on top of that damned car again and sent Alan and that German Policeman with the nasty little hard rubber spring baton out to join the other German Policeman in the middle of road - all in a heap.

About now it appeared to everyone that the young Special Forces Staff Sergeant decided he didn't want to play anymore because he took off for the gasthaus. It is important to note at this time that the gasthaus owner had already decided he didn't like the games we all were playing, and had run back inside and locked the massive double wooden front doors that adorned the front of his gasthaus.

Our hero didn't seem to understand that these were massive double wooden front doors or that they had been locked. He hit them running and they exploded into the gasthaus like they'd been hit by freight train. Hinges, doorknobs and splinters were flying everywhere. He continued on out of sight and upstairs as the gasthaus owner and a few other people came running out like the place had been set on fire.

As the two German Police officers, Alan and myself regrouped, the 10th Special Forces Group Commander COL Isler, SMG Childress and a few other important type people showed up. As the senior Military Po-damn-lice Sp/4 in-charge, I told (more like mumbled) to COL Isler that my partner Alan and I would go up there and get him. At the same time I drew my trusty M-1911, 45 Caliber, Semi-Automatic Pistol and jacked one of my five issued bullets into the chamber.

SGM Childress stepped up and told me to "Put that damn thing away. I'll go up there and get him and I want all of you to stand back out of the way when we come down. Then we're going to get into that car and leave." He was pointing at the car I assume they arrived in. I looked at COL Isler and he nodded to me, so Alan and I went and stood over by our Jeep. Vastly relieved I might add.

SGM Childress went into the gasthaus, stomped up the stairs and we heard a terrible row going on up there for what seemed like half an hour. I'm sure it was only a couple of minutes but you know how time flies when someone is having fun.

Pretty soon here comes SGM Childress with our huge Special Forces Staff Sergeant in tow. Out the door and into the car and never a look in our direction. With nothing else to do, the rest of the party broke up and we all went our separate ways.

The following evening Alan and I were sitting in the Provost Marshal's Office inside the main gate at Flint Kaserne (Bad Toelz) writing up all the stinking reports on this incident in the customary USAREUR double quadruplicate fashion. Who should appear but our favorite Special Forces Staff Sergeant in Class A uniform and spit shined glory. He apologized profusely for the previous night's donnybrook and excused himself because he had to catch transportation back to the States to attend OCS.

I distinctly recall shaking his hand but I don't think I had much to say. I know my mouth wasn't hanging open like Alan's was. I'd lost one tooth, had two others rebuilt and my jaw was wired shut because it had been broken the night before by a Special Forces Staff Sergeant who looked mighty like this one .

That very minute I decided that someday, some way, somehow I would earn one of those silly green hats all us legs made so much fun of. I wanted to be one of those guys! It took me about ten years, but I did it.

The Grader
by John Delavan

Sometime around 1983, our team, ODA 335 was on a graded FTX to determine our deploy ability. The grader assigned was a young, skinny SFC from the 7th who was obviously raised "back in the hills" of Tennessee and spoke with a most unmistakable accent. His protruding Adams Apple bobbing up and down and copious amounts of tobacco spitting accompanied his accent. Time would show that he was sharp and knew his job.

We did our isolation in the old barracks area of Camp McCord, Wisconsin, breezing through and into the midnight jump in Arkansas without a hitch. As is usual, after 'chute turn in at trucks always parked as far from the drop zone as possible, we humped rucks all night and through most of the next day before RON just short or our objective. Just before nightfall we formed our defensive circle and prepared to chow down and rest up a little.

Now you have to understand that our team was made up of a bunch of hard chargers from the Southern California area and, as Reservists, we got very little equipment that was worth a shit. So, as hard chargers will, we all bought our own stuff to make up the difference. That night each man on the team broke out a Therma-Rest air mattress (which at the time was one of the newest high speed/low drag things on the market), opened the little valve and tossed the things out on the ground where each one proceeded to unroll itself and inflate with air.

One of those new fangled Therma-Rest air mattresses landed at the feet of the Grader and began doing it's thing. Now, being a worldly kind of SF Troop who isn't surprised by anything on earth, the SFC Grader stood there looking at it like a pig looking at a Cray computer. After a minute or two his mouth opened - then clamped shut again. He looked around at the team, and then looked back at the mattress, which was almost fully inflated by now. He then blinked a few times, moved his large chew of tobacco around in his mouth, spat, and quizzically gazed up at our Team Leader, CPT Morrow. With a most confused look on his face and one bushy eyebrow arched high on his bony forehead, this Ichabod Crane of a Special Forces SFC pointed at the mattress and with his Adams Apple bobbing up and down said in a trembling voice, "But, how do it know?"

Maybe you had to be there, but at the time it was funny as hell. After a successful mission, exfil and brief-back, we packed up and headed for Little Rock Airport. But before we left we stashed one of those new Therma-Rest air mattresses in the Grader's gear. Maybe the cold ground in Sleepy Hollow won't put the ague in his bones now.

The Iron Triangle
by John Hauck

As II Field Force troop strength built up in 1966 and became more capable of attacking the enemy in longtime havens, General Seaman's headquarters was considering the possibility of a powerful strike into the Iron Triangle. The Iron Triangle is generally defined on the southwest by the Saigon River, on the east by the Thi Tinh River, and on the north by a line running west from Ben Cat to the town of Ben Suc on the Saigon River. To the north lies the Thanh Dien Forestry Reserve. The Iron Triangle has been characterized as a dagger pointed at Saigon; being only twenty kilometers away, it was the enemy's closest large haven.

The area was heavily fortified and known to contain the Viet Cong headquarters for Military Region IV which directed military, political, and terrorist activities in the Saigon-Gia Dinh capital region complex. Viet Cong's control of the Iron Triangle permitted the enemy forces to dominate key transportation routes in the surrounding area. This important center for controlling and supporting enemy operations had to be attacked decisively and in force if the attack were to succeed in rupturing and neutralizing the control structure.

Sky Spot
by John Hauck

We had Sky Spot on Nui Ba Den. Normally, the weather was so bad up there, air support was impossible. Usually, about 18:00 hours, a little cloud would descend on the tiptop of the mountain and remain there until late the next morning. Once it stayed there for two weeks, no mail, chow, or shuttle of troops/CIDG got on or off the mountain. Usually, there would be a torrential rainstorm accompanying the cloud. Visibility on the mountain, when the cloud was in place, was practically zero. Strange place. Normally quiet. It was about 10 degrees cooler up there than down in Tay Ninh.

Marine Ordinance
by John Hauck

I was stationed at Lift Master Pad, Phu Bai, west of Hwy 1, flying Cobras. We had just about run out of rockets in the supply chain, to the point we were having a difficult time supporting missions. I was Co Ops Officer at the time. I stuck the Co Cdr in the front seat and we flew down to see the Marines at Da Nang. They had plenty 2.75's. We scored. Scrounging mission complete, we walked back out on the ramp to get our Cobra and go home. Parked right next to the Marine Cobras, our Army Cobra had some new stenciling done while we were inside. Stenciled in gold was, "Fly Marine Corps". No sweat. It was worth it to get the needed ordinance. Course we both got ribbed when we got back to the Hawk's Nest.

Choppers and Leeches
by Larry Sellers

I landed at Mang Buk about 13 March 1963. The team from Oki we replaced jumped on the choppers as we got off of them. That was our introduction to II corp. As we were moving into the house two Mohawks flew over and buzzed us. Minutes later we got a May Day; one of the Mohawks lost power and the pilots elected to bail out. It was about 15 K's away to the east. I was the chosen one along with Duane J., a demo man, were elected to for the hunt. First day in the area, new to the country, hung over from the night before Marecheck did not want to go. We took off, along with 15 Yards from the Ranger Co.(Viet) across the runway, an interpreter and dry rations. It seemed none of the others on the team or the Rangers ever been over that way. Off we went looking for bodies and a plane. It took us two days to get close to the site. Meanwhile, a chopper went down while we were looking for the people. They inserted two young LT's that had come in on some other choppers consisting of Marines and Army. While inserting a couple of the Rangers, a Marine chopper snagged a tree with a repelling rope and was pulled down. One Viet Ranger and the pilot, a Marine Major were killed. The crew chief broke a leg. The 3 young Lts stayed with the site for two days while we were trying to get there. To make it short, we got all survivors out and evaced the bodies. We blew up and burned all the parts we could pile up, walked about 5 klicks downstream and were evaced back to Mang Buk.
Now for the leeches... Alison, our medic, took me outside the hooch and bared my poor old body. He found leeches on every part of my body. My hemorrhoids were acting up, and those little bastards were the size of apples. My jewels and toy were also being worked on. As it was, everything came out okay.

B52 Strikes
by Joe Waskas

Proximity to B52 strikes made me wonder when the thunder would stop.

Our Hvy Wpns man and I were out doing a little recon with a couple of Yards and watching the 4th ID take on the 66th NVA Regt(I think it was called Opn Wayne Gray). They were using A241 (Polei Kleng) for a storage base, and we went out to try to help with locating some of the bad guys (somewhere in the Plei Trap). We were told to get the hell out of the area because the 4th was bringing in an ARC light within one click of our present position. It didn't take us long to put a few more clicks in between us and the first boom. The most startling thing was the dead silence after the last boom. I thought I had gone deaf until my partner said "let's go home".

One other question I have. I heard talk about planes using a weed killer and what was left was set on fire. That couldn't have been Agent Orange. The stuff they used around Kontum and Polei Kleng made the leaves and plants turn black, soft, slimy and mushy. There wasn't any vegetation that you could burn after that stuff took hold. I wonder if I was looking at another type of herbicide being used.

Circle U and Red Dot
by Leamon Ratterree

The "Circle U" preceded the "Red Dot" by a few years. The dots arrived with BG K.C. L. when he took over the 193rd Inf Bde. I recall seeing the "U" painted on a man-hole cover at Gulick prior to L.'s arrival. I thought it might be related to the "Circle Trigon" or some such non-sense.

The red dot caused quite a ruckus amongst the 3/7 SFG which suffered collectively from "oppositional defiant disorder" (That really is a diagnosis). As long as LTC Chuck F. was there, we didn't play. However, when LTC R. came on board and brought CSM I. with him, the CSM's main function was to make random watch inspections. Oh yeah, we had to have our black earplug cases hanging from the top button of our OG 107s. (According to fairly reliable sources, R., who was Asst G-3 at 5th Mech with KC L., was hand picked by L. to come and straighten up 3/7 SFG) We lived in turbulent times. As the 3/7 was becoming the most tasked battalion in the world, the Commander and his CSM were more concerned with appearance and kissing up to KC L. than mission proficiency/capability. The CG 193rd, fired all our San Blas Indians who had worked for us for who knows how many generations, and had us cleaning our own barracks, shining our own boots, etc. He set up standards of appearance for the barracks which said we were to have a bunk, a wall locker, and only one authorized picture on the wall which must be framed. He sent his DCO to Ft. Gulick for an impromptu inspection.

F. was still the CDR at 3/7 when the inspection was conducted. Needless to say, the SF barracks was quite distinct from the rest of the 193rd. We had waterbeds in some rooms. Several of the guys had well stocked bars. We had all sorts of posters on the walls, and even a black guy with a confederate flag.

The DCO, 193rd was not pleased. LTC F. diplomatically told the DCO to go pound sand, and to the effect: "My soldiers work hard and train hard. They deserve to live anyway they want, and have the right to party hard."

I didn't like my AST haircut.
Ratman - I still have my black earplug case.

Toe Troubles
by Lee Ratterree

I had a bone spur in the top of my "great toe" left foot since I went through SFQC. I had it removed once, but was told it had a 50 percent chance of growing back. It did. I also had two ingrown toenails removed. One was done in Phase II, when I was exfilled from Pisgah to a MD who removed it. My FAC (SFC Batton?) wanted to recycle me, and I convinced him otherwise.

SSG C. in Panama removed the other ingrown from the right foot. He used Jack Daniels to anesthetize himself and lidocaine for me. He also used the JD to sterilize the wound. He did a better job than the MD.

E-tools
by Leamon Ratterree

They have been issued to guards for years. Unlike billy-clubs, they tend to not break as easily. In basic training, due to shortage of axe handles, we showed up for guard mount with, "tool, entrenching, 1 each, O.D. Green." Well, "the trigger went off again."

In basic, we had this one SP4 94B cook, who gave all the "trainees" a hard time when we entered "his" mess hall. It wasn't his; it "belonged" to an SFC. This cook lived in the Company area (C-10-2, Ft Jackson). He had himself a nice little "cadre room" in one of the open bay barracks. One Saturday night, he entered the company area quite intoxicated, and was met by a 5 ft 2 Puerto Rican guy from New Joisy. (BTW, the cook was Messican American, but we weren't PC in those days.) Well, S. pulling his shift, challenged R. the intoxicated belligerent cook. R. refused to properly respond to the challenge, and approached S. in a hostile manner. S. then exercised proper use of force by slamming the flat side of the e-tool against the flat side of cook's head. The 94B went down; the DI/Sgt of the Guard on duty heard the uproar and arrived on scene.

DI got the reports, filled out the paperwork, and called an ambulance (in that order). The cook was never seen again in the company area.

The next day, the Company Commander, Captain G., a Messican American with a 173rd SSI-FWS (AKA Combat Patch) arrived at the morning formation and cited Sanchez for a job well done. PVT Sanchez had thoroughly complied with his general orders, and applied necessary force only as a last resort and for self defense.

It was later confided that the CDR had been looking for a reason to get rid of said cook, and finally this incident took care of that. My PLT DI was SFC B., spoke a strange dialect of English and had a 1st Cav SSI.

Worst Team Leader
by Leamon Ratterree

We took a whole company down to Equitos, Peru in 84 for a major JTX, and all had a good time. We had a Company Commander and our Team Leader vying for this Chinese-Peruvian girl. So, when time came to deploy on the FTX portion, we were sent to a remote site in the jungle, next to the Amazon River with the Peruvian 6th Commandos. We were supposed to train with them in their camp, along with a Recon Platoon from the 193rd Inf. Bde. The USAF SOS out of Hurlburt Field, Florida, provided helicopter Support flying UH-1N helicopters. The team leader wanted to get back in so he could get some of this Peru-China before the Company Commander got a chance to "occupy by force."

We finished our interoperability training, and were supposed to deploy the entire grouping back to the town, and redeploy on the FTX portion back in the jungle. The team leader was plotting his moves, howsomever, the Co Cdr had all the cards.

The first few lifts came in and extracted the Recon Platoon. The following lifts took the Commando Company. We waited for the longest time, and things were getting WAY behind schedule. The team leader wanted me to get on the radio and try to figure out what the delay was. So, I got on the radio and got the B-Tm commo to give me an update. Shortly afterwards, ONE each UH-1N was overhead, orbiting around. I came up on his FM and right after hearing my call-sign, the pilot answered (before I could ask) "I have been instructed to leave your team here and pick you up for redeployment in two days to the FTX area."

I laughed (no problem for me), and relayed word for word to the now-anxious team leader. The helicopter flew away, and the team leader stewed. Team medic said "Sounds like the movie Wild Geese." (After that we called ourselves Wild Geese Team II.)

Around noon the following day, I, being the "commo guru" was tasked by the team leader to figure out a way to get to town and rent a truck for exfil. So, I found a trash truck full of civilians and rode for two hours to Iquitos. I felt real comfortable on that truck, the only one in uniform, and fully armed, locked and loaded. "No sir, ain't no one gonna rob this garbage truck."

Upon arrival at the B-Tm, I was met by the angry Company Commander. "I figured he'd try to pull this! Sergeant, I am sending you back out there tomorrow morning. When you get there, tell that young captain that I am ordering him to stay put until further instructions." I wasn't about to argue with the CO.

The next morning, I went out to meet the grinning AFSO helicopter to fly me out to the base camp. There was a thick ground fog, and navigation was nearly impossible flying across miles and miles of swamp. As we were approaching where we thought the camp was, we were fortunate enough to have a slight break in the fog over the camp. We could at least see the LZ. WELL, the brightest team leader in the world had somehow been brainwashed to throw smoke when he heard helicopters approaching. Everyone on the team had warned him about this practice in the past, and the team sergeant told me afterward that he told the team leader to abstain from said practice this time, too.

So, what color smoke did the world's best team leader use? If you guessed WHITE, you are correct. Blends in well with the fog. I had on the headphones and had been talking with the chopper crew. Suddenly the pilot (the AF Det Cdr) yells "Who is the f___in' idiot who threw smoke?!"

Says I, "that would likely be our team leader, Sir."

"If I get hold of him, I'll break his f_____ing arm!" replies the AF Major.

We sat there for another day and a half till we were flown to the FTX area, and finished our missions in the jungle. The next time we saw Iquitos, was the evening before redeployment to Panama. That's when the whole puzzle fell into place. It was all about a love-triangle in which our ODA (783) was ensnared. Names have been deliberately omitted to protect the idiots.

Three Medics and an MP
by Leamon Ratterree

I lived on Ft. Davis and of course, everything was walking distance. I walked to the snack bar/ post office / PX / Library and classroom complex every evening and usually would bump into guys who weren't deployed. We would get caught up on who was where in what country, and what they were doing, or who was in deep kimshee, or who died.

Well, I was on the railed walkway around 1700 hours at said complex, and standing directly in front of the post office were three SF medics, and an MP. All were leaning against the rail, looking at someone out in a car with the door open and their feet out on the ground. Another MP was walking toward the car. Both MPs were ready to go on the evening shift. A postal worker came out and asked "Is he still out there? He said he wasn't feeling well and was going home and that was a little after four." The inquiring postal worker then departed for home.

The conversation was slowly and casually moving along. First medic says, "Yeah, I checked him, and he is dead."

Second medic replies, "I can verify that, and I already called the ambulance."

Third medic says, "I'll take their word for it. You wanna go check Sergeant Ratterree?"

"No thanks," says I, "I'm a commo guy, and can only offer electric shock."

Medic one offers, "I think rigor mortis is setting in already. We told that young MP that it is too late, but I reckon he wants to be a hero."

The MP standing with us leaning against the rail adds, "I told him to listen to you guys but he is gonna try CPR anyway."

Sure enough, we watch this 150 pound MP pull this 300 pound dead weight out of the car and start attempting CPR.

A lady goes in to check her mail, comes out, sees what is transpiring and asks, "Is he gonna be OK?"

Senior medic present answers, "He's dead."

Woman looks shocked and walks away quickly. Forty five minutes have transpired. We watch the MP trying to revive the corpse. Corpse vomits on MP. We all know the rules. Once you start CPR, you continue until relieved by proper authority. I figured 3 SF medics to be proper authority. Therefore, we continued to wait for the meat wagon to arrive. It finally arrives, nearly an hour since it was first summoned. The EMTs check the body and verify to the puked-on MP that the man has indeed expired. They thank him for his efforts and then get statements from the SF medics. They zip the corpse into a body bag for further disposition.

That evening, as I am going for an evening run, I see the MP who had attempted CPR on the post office corpse. He was on duty at the Ft Davis main gate. If I were his supervisor, I would have given him the evening off and maybe a 3 day pass. Nevertheless, he was there, on duty, and they didn't even give him a chance to go clean up. He still smelled of vomit. I imagine the 549th MP Company to be a demoralized bunch with that sort of leadership. (This series of events took place circa May 1986.)

Intercept Operator
by Leamon Ratterree

I had a special role in 1982 in the final FTX. Maj. J. (the one who looked like a bulldog) requested me to play the role of a "G" intercept operator. When he asked me to do that, he also asked what kind of equipment I needed. I requested two steno pads, a couple of pens and a PRC-77. I told the Belloso guys in their Sig Plt that I'd find their command freq in 30 minutes. I lied. I found it in 18. For the next 24 hours, I copied all their coms and broke their primitive code. We had taught them our system and gave them opscode books. Their CDR didn't like our stuff. So he made them use theirs. He changed his mind after I showed him that I had broken all their codes, and could locate their units. The one thing they did correctly was use the Letter Figure Letter call-sign system. (ex: R3Q22)

JD D. was with their Recon Plt. They were really good, except I had compromised them, too. I had two guys attached to me from the 82nd. They were to be my security. On the third day, I was supposed to get captured. I was searching the freqs and came upon some guys who were using bird names for call signs. I noted in the journal that "this is obviously a distinct element of the Belloso Bn, and probably the Recon Plt."

As I monitored the frequency, the chatter on the radio turned to whispers, I informed my security that we were about to get hit. Within a minute we were overrun, the Salvos "killed" my security and took me prisoner so I could get transported back for interrogation. I axed the soldier why he capped my security while they were surrendering. He told me that their instructions were to take me prisoner. So much for "implied tasks."

When I got back to the interrogation center, Cpt V. and Pete Roman were there as observers/advisors. Two guys from the 82nd were captured and singing like canaries. They weren't being tortured, in my view, but not necessarily in a comfortable position. I wasn't interrogated, but was able to brief the Commander, S2, S3, and Sig Officer. I had my steno pads and showed them their piss poor comsec. One pad was completely filled, and the other was about half-way.

Small, Sanchez and Sterns
by Lonnie Shoultz

Burt Small was my replacement when I left A-108 in December 1966. He was knocked down and went missing while on patrol with a guy named Roth (Jake?). Roth made it back and Burt went missing. Stearns and Sanchez were part of a reaction force that went to the ambush site. They were ambushed also, but well after the first action. So, Burt was not actually with Stearns and Sanchez, although they probably all died the same day.

I talked with "Doc" Paul Whitehead, our Senior Medic on the team, later while he was the Sergeant Major for SOCOM's Medical component who went to the ambush site after the shooting stopped. He told me there was no doubt in his mind that Burt died when hit or from loss of blood. Roth knew exactly where they were jumped and Paul said that Burt would have never survived the loss of blood that he saw. But, the Army carries him as a POW so I guess we will also.

I'm not certain about their MOSs and ranks. Most POWs continue to be promoted while they are captive. The last site I saw had Burt as a SSGT. My situation might be instructive for you in trying to piece this together. I went on-site as a PFC 11C2P. However, we already had a heavy weapons guy who flat KNEW how to run a 4.2 mortar (and I didn't cut charges as quickly); so I handled small arms (in addition to being the leader of the CRP, being the Assistant Intel Sergeant, signing for the CA money that we used for intelligence agents, and running a battery of three 81mm mortars and our ten 60mm mortars as my NDP).

Like everyone else in 1966, when we had the big "A" Team camp built, we were authorized fourteen officers and men. We never got over nine at any one time. We usually had seven. I'm not bitching about wearing three or four hats – we all had to. It's just the way things were. After two months onsite I got a set of orders promoting me to Spec-4 (it really didn't matter because we all wore "brevet" Sergeant Chevrons anyway because the LLDB would not work with anyone of a lesser rank than them). After about five or six months onsite, I got a set of orders changing my MOS to 11F4S that awarded my "S." I don't know what kind of hocus pocus they used to figure out those MOSs. The only intelligence background test I ever took was briefing Colonel Kelly when he stopped in unannounced one day and the Intel NCO was at a meeting in Quang Ngai. I had to give the Intelrep to him.

The last time I saw them, Burt took my place with the Yards and their guns. He was a Spec-4 at that time as was I. Mike Stearns was a Spec-5 and our Demo man/Engineer/Supply Clerk/Store Keeper and like that. Sanchez had just taken over the team as I was leaving. Bob Price was the Team Sergeant from May, when I arrived, until about mid-November. Then Price got a slot on a Mobile Guerilla Force (MGF) going into the Ashau Valley and left the Team's camp. That brought in Sanchez. I'm almost sure that Sanchez was an E-8 because I don't really remember anything unusual about him. Since Team Sergeants were supposed to be E-8s, I would have remembered if we had gotten one that was out of place. When Sanchez arrived we were patrolling aggressively trying to keep the NVA off the front doorstep.

In I Corps, we had no rice paddy Charlies and damn few Viet Cong. We had main force units trying to come by our camp in order to get to the rice lands to the east of us around

Mo Duc. They could run over us anytime they wanted, but when they bottled us up it gave us a chance to call the Marines and tell them, "Here they come." That would enable the mud Marines to get a unit large enough to handle an NVA Regiment in place to stop them. We had nine Americans and about four hundred strikers. All we could do was slow them down.

Therefore, to give us some warning, we were working the CRP to death. Since I always went with the CRP team looking at the Intel sighting with the best chance of hitting a unit on the move, I wasn't around Sanchez very much. I doubt that I spent over four or five nights with him in the Team House. In addition, we put one company of strikers outside of the wire after dark every night and one of us was always gone. I just didn't know the man very well.

Welcome/ Mike Force
by Mark Atchison

June 8-9, 1967: There was a big operation for MPT, 14-16 clicks west of XS600200 or was it XS200600? It meant big trouble for 263rd VC Battalion (Main Force); the two companies from A-411 had them just where we wanted them...on three sides. The principals were John T, Woody, Cary C. (RIP), and the SP5IC.

As Reg would say..."Well, we commenced to fightin' and....". Our incursion into their base camp was around noon. By 1400 we were in very deep kimchi, well, water buffalo shit, anyway. On came the gun ships, on came the dust offs, and then, and then, along came the IV Corps Mike Force. Damn glad that they did too. At one point, we had a full company of CIDG with two very pissed SF pinned down in a ditch running perpendicular to the tree line that housed the Sons of Ho, or was it Son of Hos? I fergit. About three p.m. (1500 hours), the first gunship went down; fortunately for all, they came in on top of us. Everyone survived.

Next came the CH-47 Sheeitnook to bring baby brother home. I don't think so. There musta been, and this ain't no shit, several hundred muzzle flashes from those Sons of Ho's guns. Exit big bird. Enter little birds - many, many helicopopters from Chau Duc, Moc Hoa (?). Mike Force had arrived. We had some contact during the night, and at first light here came A-411, bolstered with a company of Mikeys & the USAF. These fooking F-100s were screaming right over our heads and dropping 250s or 500s in the tree line as we assaulted. Whoa, dudes! Better than any 4th of July that I could remember. Well, those chicken-shit, lily-livered, mother-fooking, commie fags were gone. Imagine that! They slipped away from the fight like a slimy anti-American sucker.

BTW, there was a black officer with them. He had a mortar frag ding on his CAR-15.

Sanctuary
by Mel Thornton

Back in 1967, it seemed like the club at DaNang was the only place at the C-team where a young smart ass SP/4, trying to get a little R&R, was safe from SGM H. I never quite understand why, but if you could get inside the club before he knew you were off your A site, you like claimed Sanctuary, and no one would bother you, till you left the club proper. The most Harmon might do is come in the club, ask you how you were doing, and politely inquire when you might be going back to your camp. Then as he left, he might slyly ask you to drop by his office, when you had a chance. If you were foolish enough to go there, you were meat.

The trick was getting from the club to the dispensary to sign out an ambulance, so you could get into Da Nang and get drunk for a few days. However, never stay in one of the nice transit rooms or go near the dining hall (which I heard served world class food). Because, if he could find you outside of the club, you were sent right back to your camp, on the first chopper.

Now the only explanation for this situation, that I could think of, was that some kind of unspoken rule existed (since all the ranks were drinking together in the same club), and no Army business was conducted inside. I don't think that the SMG really hated SP/4's. However, I think it did offend his sensibilities that one could serve as the Senior Medic on an A-site.

Sp/5's In Charge
by Mel Thornton

There was an extremely inept, paranoid, ring-knocker Det. CO at A-104. He was quite comatose, but for some reason he could talk and walk around. When the Team Sgt. had seen enough of the Capt., he slowly sent the team back to Danang one by one on the mail slicks.

After a few days, the whole team was sitting in the club in Danang. The C-team commander walked into the club and wanted to know what the hell was going on. Basically, the Team Sgt. explained that the team was staying in the club until such time as they saw the Capt. getting off a chopper in Danang. After a quick trip to Ha Thanh, and a quicker talk with the Det. CO, the Col. returned to Danang with the Capt. And the team, complete with a new Det.CO, was on the next bird back to camp.

No High Ground
by Mike Rhode

I slept in a hammock for two nights while on an operation out of Tra Cu. After that I slept ON THE GROUND! I had visions of tracer rounds going under my hammock in the middle of the night. I preferred sleeping on the ground. I do remember, on an op with Thires P., out of Katum, sleeping sitting down, leaning against a tree and Pick, because if we laid down we would have been underwater. It was during the monsoons and there wasn't any high ground anywhere. I also remember sharing a poncho with Pick and taking 40-60 rounds of incoming at 0500 and breaking our RON faster than I ever thought possible. The CIDG radio bearer took a mortar round in his back while he was still asleep, and virtually disappeared.

Dirty Dick
by Paul Whitmore

I've never knew of a guy some call "Dirty Dick Dandeneau", but I am aquatinted with a "Dirty Dick" Dalley (sp.) a 10 from CCN. In fact, once on an insertion of his team we had an immediate abort and everyone came away with a "pucker factor" of about minus 10.

As we were coming into our third LZ site, following two false insertions, both with "night-in-gale" devices, a real sweet Vietnamese female came up on our frequency and transmitted the following:

"Come on down 'dirty dick' we are awaiting your arrival. We are ready to show you a real (emphasis on the real) good time."

We surmised that the transmission was a little premature since they were just beginning their final approach not 300 yards from their LZ. When we got back to the launch site Dalley was visibly shaken as was his 11. Needless to say, from that time forward there were no Vietnamese allowed in the TOC briefing area back at CCN when the teams were receiving their assignments or when they were briefing the Col. and S3 on their plan, nor were any allowed in the TOC at the launch site.

Following that transmission, Mike Smith, the covey rider, ordered the entire standby "Sandies" and a few fast movers to unload all of their ordnance on that LZ and the area around it for 100 meters. It was quite a show as there were numerous secondary explosions. A couple of days later they sent in a "Bright Light" team to conduct a BDA, but I don't know what, if anything, they found as I never read their report.

Ax Handles
by Randy Cesani

When I was in the 2ID in Korea and we pulled one of our two tours of duty on the DMZ, we were given a briefing by someone or another. The briefing consisted primarily about the "Tree cutting incident" that resulted in the deaths of two Army officers. Besides all the support on standby, B52's in orbit, fighter bombers, and all the helicopter gunships in Korea, etc, they had a Battalion from the 9th Inf Manchu just out of site on standby also. They were in Bn Mass formation and every man had an ax handle at port arms. They moved them forward at a shuffle, and every time their left foot hit the ground they hollered Manchu. It must have been an impressive sight. In addition, the video showed a North Korean chasing an American MP with an upraised ax. The MP kept backing up and finally was able to get away. He never drew his gun. The narrator said it was discipline, and I said to myself "bullshit" - the kid was scared about using a firearm. Maybe they should have given that MP an ax handle.

Cold Beer
by Ray Flaherty

Forty-one years ago, our half team was coming in from a walk in the woods with the 11th B.P. W had been out a bit over a week and were coming in to return to the parachute center at Seano. Trucks were supposed to meet us just North of a village on Route 13. Unfortunately, the bad people blew a bridge South of the village.

It had to be well over a hundred degrees in the shade. The unit was out of food and water but still had some ammo left. Highway 13 was not a highway, as we know it. It was nothing more than a two-lane dirt road, and the powdery dirt clouded with every step to further irritate our already parched throats.

Whenever events would be beyond our control, James, our medic would ask his rhetorical question, "What are you gonna do?"

With the situation being as I described above, he said it for probably the fifteenth time. I turned toward him and through my dry throat, further irritated by the road dust clouding the air, told him if he asked that question one more f--king time I was going to kill his ass.

Well, to make a short story longer, the situation improved somewhat as the troops found a water source, and nothing could stop them from drinking their fill. We, the American team, well disciplined as we were, and aware of the dangers lurking in the untreated waters of Southeast Asia, plodded on toward the village where we found a place selling COLD Tiger beer. How they got and kept it cold I have no idea, nor did we give a shit. It was there that we drank our fill. None of that tainted water for us.

We stayed in that village a day or two until contact with vehicles was made, and we rode safely to Seano where we were welcomed by "Sam" Bass's half team. But… that's another story.

Seat Taken
by Ray Flaherty

There were three guys from different A Teams who became very good friends. Whenever they were back on island they would be seen hoisting a beer or three at one club or the other. One of them was killed in an unfortunate accident but the other two didn't forget him.

When we moved to Machinato, we kind of took over the NCO club, and you'd sometimes see one of the surviving members of the trio at the bar. He'd order two drinks - one for him and one in front of the empty chair on his left or right. When asked if the seat was taken he'd simply say it was. If one of the uninitiated tried to sit there, he'd be told nicely, at first, the seat was taken.

Woe would befall the stupid shit who insisted upon sitting in that seat.

Now I'll have to find the other book back so that I can search through both of them to make sure the story isn't in either.

Fayetteville Days of Old
by Ray Flaherty

After the paper napkin places of Bragg and Benning, we felt that we were shitting in tall cotton when we went to Ft Carson for mountain training where the downtown establishments had linen table cloths and napkins. Now that was class!

Damn! Names of bars on "combat alley" are coming back: The Brown Derby, and another one down the street with a big circular bar. I can't remember the name of that one, but a woman who would occasionally pull the plug on the jukebox and sing owned it. That woman had a voice that many a first sergeant would have been proud of. People would be yelling for her to shut the hell up and plug the juke box back in, but she'd sing merrily along. Now that was entertainment until the fights would break out and the MPs called.

The 82nd had some MPs that would take their pistol belt with weapon off, hand it to their partner and duke it out in an alley with a wise ass talking tough. The division MPs didn't carry clubs because some time before, or so I've been told, General Gavin forbade the use of clubs on his troopers. If you couldn't take him with your hands, he walked. Those were the days when promotions were scarce as hen's teeth, and we had 2x1/2 ton trucks transporting drunks, etc. back to their units so that a D/R wouldn't screw them up.

Those were the days when everybody wore uniforms into town, and it was fairly easy to tell the players.

That is a no shit story

Ammo "Forced Issue?"
by Reggie Manning

At Katum in early '69, every time we turned around we had yet another C-130 arriving with three speed pallets of 4.2" ammo. We had every bunker full; CONEXes full; storerooms full; and ammo stacked in the open for lack of anyplace to put it under cover. That created a real hazard as we soon learned to our dismay.

For about a month, I'd go out every evening after what passed for "supper" and shoot up as much as I could manage. Fired on "likely avenues of approach" and H&I fires. Also fired on any place where I'd seen any signs of activity during my most recent wiggle-waggle out and about in our AO.

No clue as to the dollar value of all that ammo I shot up, but it had to have been a bunch. Seems someone told me a 4.2" round cost about $105 dollars. Dunno if that's even close or not.

Speaking of shooting the 4.2", we had a Caribou which got shot up on a long final approach and lost an engine. He immediately pulled back up and headed home to Bien Hoa or TSN. The loadmaster kicked a couple of small pallets of 105HE out the back door to lighten the load. The FAC marked where one of the pallets landed but couldn't see the other. (Anytime a fixed wing aircraft landed at our house we had to have 3 things: a FAC overhead; fighters on station; and our arty firing on "likely mortar positions".)

So the FAC cranked up our 105's to shoot the ammo pallet out there in the boonies. One gun firing and they boomed and banged all day long. Shot down a whole bunch of trees and came real close but never did hit it.

After "supper", I decided to try my luck with the 4-deuce. Did the little map and compass thing out to where the pallet was sitting. The FAC came back from his almost nightfall patrol, so I called him on the radio and asked if he'd spot for me. I gave him the max ord of the round. He asked WTF I was shooting for the round to go up that high. Therefore, he moved off to the side and told me to Fire One.
Directly he came back on the radio and gave me a correction: "Ten meters left."
"Pard, I ain't got no ten meter correction that I know of."

I never did hit it either. The next morning, the FAC reported that the ammo boxes were still there but the ammo was gone.

Intentional Discharge Wounds
by Reggie Manning

Saw more than my fair share of "intentional" discharge wounds at Katum. The CIDG we had (2 companies of Cambodes and 3 companies of Saigon Cowboys) would do anything to get the hell outta Katum. Not the Cambodes, but the others.
Had quite a number of "foot-shooters" until I put out the word that "If you shoot yourself, I'm gonna operate on you without the benefit of Lidocaine.... no pain pills, no nothing except severe pain. And no MEDEVAC."
Two of the little nutz made a pact to shoot themselves at the same time with the same bullet. One put his hand over the muzzle of his M-16 and the other put his hand on top of the other guy's hand. Holy crap! The hand on the bottom didn't

fare too badly. It got a helluva flash burn and a nice hole through the palm. The one on top, however, was upgefuched to the max. You could have dropped a golf ball through the hole in his palm and never touched the sides of the wound.

Another intentional shooting was while I had the hospital at Fort (yuk! ptooie!) Dix. I got the word that a basic trainee had been brought in to the Emergency Room with a gunshot wound. So, I walked around the corner to see what was going on. Trainee was on the table with a shot-off right-hand trigger finger. The room was fulla MP's and CID's and everybody 'cept the Coast Guard. Even the Post Chief of Staff was there getting in the way.

The MP MMFIC was there and was making notes about what happened, so I axt him what he'd found out thus far. He said that the shootee had told him that he was in the foxhole on the firing line and was ready to shoot, had reached forward to get some grass or something off the muzzle, and the rifle went off. I asked the MP if the trainee was left-handed or right-handed. He didn't know so I went and axt the patient.

He allowed as how he was right-handed. I asked him, "Why did you shoot yourself in the finger?" Well, he started crying and blubbering about how "hard" it was and "how he couldn't take it".

No way is a right-handed shooter who is leaning forward in a foxhole going to reach out with his RIGHT hand to clear something off the muzzle of the rifle while holding the pistol grip of his M-16 with his left hand.

Artillery Playing Games
by Reggie Manning

While at A-323 in early '69, the redlegs there used to "play" with their guns every evening after supper. They had very little else to do with all their ammo during that period.

They'd do all the calculations and fire three rounds attempting to get three WP airbursts in the exact same point in the sky at exactly the same time. First round was fired at a very high angle, 2d a little flatter, and the third at Charge 7 so it would hurry and get there.

I never saw them quite pull it off but they came very close on a number of occasions. I know that there was one of them boys could sho' crank that elevation hand wheel in a big hurry. It was fun to watch.

Moreover, speaking of Commo Men at 323.... I was sent back over there to relieve somebody or other for about 10 days in late June. I considered it R&R after having been at ka-BOOM for months. That was when COL Rheault came to visit. Next thing we heard, he was in LBJ.

Anyhooooo, one night the camp started getting mortared. 82mm's landed out on the turn around point. I automatically started counting the incoming. Everybody else is running around like headless chickens. I figgered I must have missed something.

Finally, the mortars stopped. None came anywhere close to the camp. I wandered by the commo bunker just in time to hear the message: "Rec'd xxx number of 82mm rounds. All landed 300 meters west of the camp. No damage; no injuries."

Want to guess where the next ones landed? A couple of them blew the tin roof off the kitchen/mess hall, one on the teamhouse roof, etc.

The Speaker
by Reggie Manning

At A-322 at Katum, The Vietnamese SF Team (the LLDB) decided they needed a public address system for the camp. Supposedly it was to be used for essential announcements to the Camp's defenders and as a morale builder in their nonexistent PsyOps Program. Soon afterwards, a PA system was flown in and put in service so they could make their announcements to the camp. The principal use of that system, however, was to play music (?) every evening after what we laughingly called "supper". That alleged music was absolutely the worst racket I'd ever heard. Moreover, the one and only speaker was about 40 feet away from my dispensary bunker and pointed right at it. I got the full effect.

I decided that I'd had enough of that noise. So, one night in the dark I sneaked over to their bunker, climbed up on the roof, and put a primed 1-pound block of C-4 in the speaker horn. Spliced together enough Claymore wire to reach back across to my bunker and attached a Claymore clacker.

The next time we started getting mortared, I ran thru the mortar bursts to get back to my house so I could "make" one of the incoming mortar shells "land on" their speaker. Blew it all to hell and gone. Vaporized it. "So sorry. We'll see what we can do about getting y'all a replacement." (Never did.)

Hiding
by Reggie Manning

I was out at the turnaround point at the north end of the airstrip at Katum one day directing traffic and trying to move some 463L pallets out of the way for the next C-130 or C-123. Airplane traffic of any sort caused the bad guys to start lobbing in 82mm mortars. Some of them started landing a little closer to me than was comfortable, so I started looking around for some overhead cover. There was none because that was prior to my building a sandbagged bunker covered over with a speed pallet and more sandbags.

Then some of the mortars started getting really close. I went for the only thing that provided some cover. One of the just offloaded 463L's was a pallet of concertina wire. I crawled inside one of the doughnut holes. Got eat' up with the stickers.

After getting inside, and upon further review, I quickly came to the realization that hiding inside multiple rolls of concertina wire during a mortar attack was probably one of the damndest, dumbest things I'd ever done. I figgered if one of the 82's landed on top of my stack of wire, the end result would be similar to being inside a hand grenade when it went off.

I decided to take my chances out in the open so I crawled back out of my tunnel and assumed a fetal position out in the middle of nothing, well away from that pallet of wire. Fortunately, everything missed me that day.

The Generator
by Reggie Manning

At A-322, Katum Special Forces Camp (aka: ka-BOOOM), the Vietnamese Special Forces (LLDB) were too sorry to even go put gas in their own generator. Consequently, they sat around in the dark a lot, twiddling their thumbs. This was also their daytime occupation. Eventually, in order to see what we were doing, they tapped into our power line which ran about 40 feet from the generator bunker to the Teamhouse and Commo bunker. Not being very astute about electricity (or anything else which I was ever able to discover) they plugged into our system with a variety of WD-1 field wire, extension cords, and whatever else would carry electricity without melting. Their tapping into our poor lil' ol' 5KW generator meant that it did not only have to carry the load of our essential radios but the LLDB's Teamhouse and every CIDG bunker in the camp.

This situation caused all sorts of problems in trying to power the things which absolutely had to run. The generator was really struggling with the massive overload. The voltage, supposedly 110 volts, would sometimes dip to 80 or 85 volts depending on how many light bulbs, TV sets, stereos, radios, refrigerators, and freezers were on at any point in time.

Being a self-styled electronic genius, I decided to grab the bull by the horns and fix the problem at least temporarily. So, one evening just after dark, I turned everything of ours off and told our folks what was going on, went out to our generator and turned it off for just a minute. The whole camp went dark. I flipped the generator's "Output" switch to 220 volts and cranked the generator back up. Everything in the camp which wasn't unplugged blew up or burned out

I turned the generator off, flipped the switch back to 110, and then went back and plugged all our stuff back in.

"Your refrigerator / stereo / TV / radio / light bulbs all blew up? Sorry 'bout that. No idea what happened. Must have been "aliens" at work."

Jordan SF B-team
by Richard "Dick" Cooper

Our company had deployed to Jordan back in April or May '85. I was Ops Sgt then. We were deployed in the Desert Mountains; it was me, then Capt. M., SGM F., our medic W. and the commo guy. We were with the Jordan SF B team. In the morning, all of a sudden we heard the unmistakable sound of M16's locking and loading. We all looked at each other, SGM F. said, "Feet inside.", and we had a wagon wheel us behind our rucks with our 45s out. I had flashbacks of how it must have been in the Wild West. Once the Co Commader defused the situation, we found out that the U.S. had just bombed Libya, and some of the Jordanians wanted to show their displeasure by shooting at us.

Well, of course we got up and said, "Hey, we didn't do the bombing. We are here training you. You know the Air Force; who knows what they'll do?"

They just looked at each other and said, "Yes, you're right. Damn Air Force."

But it still was an uneasy feeling.

Spider Holes
by Robert Stepanian

In September of 1968, after a pretty good fire fight with the NVA Northeast of the village of Ha Thanh, I realized what you don't do around a spider hole.

Then, SFC Bill Abe (Now retired SGM in Ontario CA) and I had taken a small group of Yards against an entrenched NVA force.

(Sparing you the detail of the fire fight I jump right to the spider hole part of the story.)

I walked past a Yard longhouse, and stood directly over this spider hole. I called over to one of the Yards , "Lam ta Ko" (I think "Come here." in Hre) While I stood there with my CAR15 in hand (round in the chamber and safety off), an AK47 appears from the spider hole. I froze for a split second as the AK was readied to take me out nuts first. The Yard, Ha Lang, instantly pushed me aside took my CAR15, and emptied the clip into the hole. We each in turn pulled the pins on grenades, and tossed them into the spider hole. There, we found five dead NVA.

The AK47 along with three grenades (I defused) were later given to Martha Raye. Lance L. was at Ha Thanh when we gave her those goodies. Maggie said they hung in her Team House. I never did get to see that AK again.

Experiences
by Steve McAuley

In National forest in Penn, in 77 or 78, I was appointed Guerilla Chief for an A-team from the 20th SFG. Immediately after the team jumped in, the team sergeant asked me where the nearest bar was, and at the same time pitched a fit as his bottle of Jack Daniels had broken in the jump. I was pretty serious at the time and it took us a couple of days to realize that the Artep was (at least for me) serious. We got along okay, and the team passed the Artep.

As a drill instructor at Ft Knox in 75-76, I worked with members of the 100th Reserve Division, many from Kentucky. They were tasked to take over the DI duties at Knox in the event of war to relieve the active duty guys to fill units.

Most of the guys were competent tankers; the DI's were a bunch of drunken sots! Much too heavy to do the PT, they did a lot of griping and drinking and not much else.

As a medevac helicopter pilot in Alaska in 83-84, a medevac company from Michigan for the Brim Frost exercise augmented my unit. Those guys were some of the craziest pilots I ever met! They would fly in any weather, especially when AC commanders grounded us. Not much for military disciplines, but definitely had a can-do attitude.

During Desert Shield, about twenty percent of the civilian workforces teaching at the Ft Rucker flight school were either Guard or Reserve. One out of the forty or fifty guys actually volunteered to go active to fill out AC units, even when asked at unit formations for volunteers. In addition, most of these guys were highly experienced; Vietnam era veterans with thousands of hours under their belts.

Of course most of above stories are of leg units and non-SF guys. My point is, even if a SF RC/NG unit isn't up to the same standards and readiness as an active SF unit, they are still a giant step above the readiness of a regular army straight leg outfit.

I say, bring em' on. Let them get into the fight, too.

Jerry M. Weaver (KIA)
by Steve Shanahan

ref: 1970 07 16 E-6 SSG Jerry M. Weaver 12B4S KIA SVN; CCN, FOB3, or A-236, Bu Prang, Quang Duc Prov.

This happened while Bu Prang #3, the last A camp to be built in SVN, was still under construction. I was next-door at Duc Lap at the time and cannot speak from first hand knowledge. I heard about it at the time.

At the Convention, I got to see Rans Potter again, after 32 years. Rans was Team Leader of A-236 at the time Jerry Weaver as sent to Bu Prang. He had been XO of A-236 at BP #2 when I was there. He is a very smart man and a fine gentleman. (You might have seen him at the convention. He's got MS and wears arm-brace crutches to help him ambulate.) I also spoke with Skip Shelley who was the 91C at Bu Prang # 3. Shelley came to BP #3 after I went to A-239.

At dinner we talked about this incident. Shelley was there and said it happened like this: SSG Weaver was on duty at night, maintaining radio watch and camp security. While checking the perimeter, he woke a sleeping CIDG and the startled youngster let go a burst that caught SSG weaver across the chest.

A & D
by Terry Dahling

My SF bud, Comini said, "My roomy in Lenngries, George Allen, used to tell me you won't get anywhere unless you screw-up so your name will be known."

One night my car got drunk and ran off of the road on the way to Munich. The car was totaled, as was I, almost. I got an AR. 15 and lost my license for six months. A while later, my bike got drunk and got me written up on the Lenngries Bridge.

Not too long after, I got a GCM and was promoted. Maybe Allen was right.

A-Team vs. Recon
by Terry Dahling

I can't much speak for life in an A camp in RVN. I spent a little time at A-244 as commo for the launch site but went home every night. The camp was practically shut down. They were putting the finishing touches on a new camp at Ben Het. The most excitement I saw was a VC/NVA soldier with brass balls walk to the end of the airstrip and raise a VC flag. We were so flabbergasted at his ballsie action that no one even took a shot at him.

As for C&C, you have to take the bad with the good. The missions sucked. There was minimal immediate support. I was on Leghorn at the beginning of Tet, and had to transmit a message to all deployed teams to "find a hole and start no shit" since all assets were committed in country.

On the other hand, there was the good. Normally we got a one-day stand down for each day on the ground. The chow was good - especially at Phu Bai. If I stayed there I would have needed a Chinook to insert. We had a real good camaraderie between Tm members, as close as or closer than on an A-Tm. I said the missions sucked, but they had their good points. I enjoyed working in small units. There was a time I had a five-man team, which may have been fatal with a full team. Small units can snoop and poop and disappear. I was never in a company sized action or larger, and probably would not have liked it.

I took what I was given and made the best of it. I see no competition or conflict between the two - other than friendly.

James Sweeney
by Terry Dahling

We were in Scotland on an FTX and Jim was captured by the SAS. They were going through their interrogation bit and he says, "Look I know it's your job to make me talk. It's my job not to talk. You can make me as uncomfortable as you want but you can't kill me so let's knock off the bull shit and go have breakfast." That's just what they did.

One payday morning we had "Mandatory Training" on the Code of Conduct. Jim, having been a POW for around thirty months was asked to give a talk on how to conduct oneself if captured. Jim goes to the podium and says," If you are ever in a PW camp keep an eye on the "yes men" and ass kissers. If they are that way in garrison, imagine how they'll act under real pressure."

End of class and Sweeney departed the stage to the accompaniment of silence and gaping mouths. Sweeny always told it like it was.

Close Call
by Terry Dahling

Once, while returning from a VR in a King Bee, a couple of Hueys met us as we crossed the border. They pulled alongside and we waved at each other. I thought they were being friendly. When I got back I found out how close we were to being shot up/down. They were a little jumpy in the tri-border region about sightings of un-identified choppers and aircraft. Here we were in an unmarked CH-47 being flown by a VNAF pilot who didn't file a flight plan and didn't answer the radio. Our waving saved our asses.

Leghorn
by Terry Dahling

Leghorn was the call sign of a radio relay site in Laos. Our recon teams were unable to reach the launch site at Dak-To or the FOB located at Kontum. Leghorn was located atop a very steep mountain and was the highest point in the area. It was so high I could fire an M79 round at 45 deg elevation and have time to take a drag or two off of a cigarette before I heard it explode.

In January of 1968, I took a tour on Leghorn. There were two U.S. and a platoon of Yards from the Hatchet Force. Having only two Americans, my partner and I didn't see each other except at shift changes. We did talk some, but after about three days of each other we were no longer on speaking terms.

For amusement I used to shoot grenade rounds at a tree limb about 100 meters down the hill. That wood was so hard I barely put a mark on it. I named it "Iron wood tree". One day I got thoroughly bored and fired over a half case of rounds at that limb. I don't remember ever knocking it off. As an aside, this reminds me of a man who was going to clear a LZ with his M79. He was too close to the tree, took frags and was med-evaced. I didn't realize it at the time but after a while my shoulder started to get sore. The next day I could barely move my arm.

I heard some interesting things on the radio. If a team was close enough, I could pick up their traffic on their squad radios. One night there was a team preparing to ambush a convoy. After dark I heard one say:" Did you just walk behind me?"

"Nope, I ain't moving."

"I just saw a wrist watch go by. Was that you?"

"Nope. Mine is covered with tape."

It went on and on and the only thing that went through my mind was "Oh Shit! This is going to be a long night!"

Another night we got a message from the FOB to all teams. The gist was "Find a hole and don't start any shit. All of the assets are busy in country." This was the beginning of Tet. I missed it. I was safe on my mountain. We had to stay over, and got resupplied twice before being relieved. Some of the teams had to be re-supplied rather than extracted.

I learned a lot listening and relaying traffic. Some teams just couldn't get the proper info to the Staff. The staff will always ask what was the kind of fire; and ask if you have tried all possible solutions before declaring an emergency - so don't make them pry it out of you. One day I heard a quote I'll never forget. There was a 10 by the name of Pappy on the ground.

He called and said: "I have a company of NVA surrounded from the inside. I gave them three minutes to surrender or we are going to attack."

The reply was: "Alright Pappy, get your panels out. We are on the way!"

Working on Leghorn was boring, but I learned a lot that benefited me later as a 10 on the ground.

Mean SGM
by Terry Dahling

Childress was a man you either loved or hated. I probably did both at one time or another. He spoke his peace and didn't care who heard him.

I once overheard him briefing a new company commander. He said that he was the "Big Daddy Rabbit" in the company, and all the commander had to do was stop by three times a day to sign the papers on his desk. I didn't feel too sorry for young officers, because those who had the balls to explain the rank structure to him usually gained his respect.

The last time I saw him I had just gotten off of a flight from Khe Sahn to Danang to Nha Trang. I was a mess. Everything I had on, including myself, was the color of red clay. A young officer stopped me, and started reading me the riot act about my appearance. I was a disgrace to Special Forces, yadda, yadda, yadda! Luckily I had no magazine in my weapon. Childress saw us and came over to see what was up. I explained I had just gotten off a chopper direct from Khe Sahn. My bunker had taken a direct hit; luckily no one was home but I was wearing everything I owned. The SGM told me to report to the supply room, get some new uniforms and go clean up. As I was walking away I could see Childress had that young officer braced up against the wall and was telling him the facts of life. I thought of him as a soldier's 1SG and SGM even though I never knew of him in anything other than a headquarters position.

At night he carried a little miniature ball bat to keep the riggers under control in HHC 10th SFGA.

My Longest Day
by Terry Dahling

This was my first mission with FOB-2 (or any other combat unit for that matter). For personal reasons I choose to not name my 10. His wife and family may still be alive and I do this in deference to them. I had just left the commo section. The 10 was also an O5B as were a generous proportion of the other recon personnel. It had something to do with the fact that most would rather be active participants rather than spectators. Our team consisted of the 1O, 9 indig and me.

We had one day to prepare formations, movement, VERY etc. On the evening before launch the 1O took me to his hooch and showed me a drawer full of letters from his girl friend. He asked that in the event he was medevaced or killed I destroy the letters. He didn't want them to get to his wife. This will become relevant later.

In the morning we attended the air briefing, collected our commo gear and SOI's and were flown to the PF launch site at Dak To - A-244. We were inserted about 2 PM and set up a listening perimeter near the LZ. After a time, we moved a short distance and waited. It appeared to be safe and we released the assets.

Just before dusk, we came upon trail (beeeg one) and snooped around. The indig got water. While snooping around, I spotted some rabbit holes dug into the side of the riverbank. These holes were squared off and man made. Not long after, we heard a group of people joking and BS'ing quite loud, coming down the trail. One of my indig planted a "toe-popper" and we moved into the woods. Within five minutes the mine went off, and thus began my longest day.

One of the NVA (in uniform) came into sight. Just like slow motion, I saw him raise his weapon to his shoulder. He never got a round off; the tail gunner cut him down. We withdrew as deeply into the jungle as we could until it was too dark to move.

All night the bad guys would throw sticks and stones trying to flush us out. Thank god for well-disciplined troops.

At the crack of dawn they had us surrounded on three sides and were pushing us to the river. The 10 and I decided to try to slip through one of the flanks, and we were successful. We broke contact and appeared to be in the clear.

The 10 wanted to return to the trail and take pictures. I was dead set against it. Somewhere I learned that it wasn't a good idea to return to a site of contact. I told the 10 that if the staff wanted pictures I'd draw them. However, the 10 was adamant and was the boss.

We hadn't been at the trail site for three minutes when all hell broke loose. The 10 took a hit over his left eye during the initial burst of fire. As I feared, they were waiting for us. He had a scratch over his left eye, and appeared to be conscious. Being a good trooper, I took out my first aid compress, intending to tend to the wound. I reached to lift his head and the back felt like a cellophane bag of popcorn. I immediately panicked and started hollering on the radio, to no avail. I collected my wits and realized that the radio and antenna were lying on the ground. I righted the radio, and made contact. I spent some time on the Leghorn RR site and realized that if you don't explain everything you know about the situation, time would be wasted while HQ pried the info out of you. We got a PF emergency declared and the covey was overhead immediately. We were at the edge of a very large field, about the size of two ball fields. I got the yards together and we moved to the middle of the field and the yards set up a perimeter around me and more important the radio. They knew we were their ticket out of there. The closest distance to any tree line was about 200 feet. At least they weren't going to sneak up on us.

Another thing I learned was to explain your position in detail to the FAC. I described the tree lines, and the river. Luckily I did so, because when I started giving compass directions they were 180 deg. off. The FAC (I think it was Dallas Long) realized what was happening and put fire support right where I needed it. He never said a thing to me. A few days later I realized what I had done and said so to Long. He said he knew but there was no need to mention it and get me more upset than I already was. Our Covey Riders were extremely professional and responsible for saving many of our lives.

When things settled down a little I went back to get the 10. He was about 20 M away. He was a big man and the only way I could move him was to grab his feet and drag him back. I thought I may have killed him, but later the medics said he had died instantly.

The yards conducted themselves admirably with little leadership on my part.
Finally we got two F-100's for support. I described where I wanted the ordinance (Long made sure the pilots got the correct info). When they said to get our heads down they meant it. The napalm was close enough and hot to suck the air out of our lungs. They asked where I wanted the next run and I said "The same place but on the other side." When they expended their entire ordinance, they asked if they could make a couple of strafing runs. I said:"What5 the hell, any thing is better than nothing." I had no idea what effect that Vulcan 20 mm or 40-mm cannon would have.

They made three attempts to extract us but were shot off each time. Finally a slick came in. He wouldn't set down on the ground. Anyone who has handled a DB knows the problem. The adrenalin kicked in and I literally threw the 10's body into the chopper. I then commenced to grab the yards by the ass and collar and throw them into the chopper. I'm surprised I didn't throw a couple in one door and out the other.

Got them on their way, and then I got the rest of the team on the second chopper. Just as we were reaching altitude I said, "Whew!" The crew chief asked who was on the other ship. I told him and asked why. He said that the first chopper had gone down. You can imagine what went through my mind. I explained, as best I could to the yards, and we prepared to recover the rest of our team. In a few minutes the crew chief explained that everything was OK. One of the yards had snagged the fire extinguisher entering the chopper and the crew thought they had been hit. They set down, un-assed it and then realized what had happened and took off again.

We went directly to Kontum. Everyone including the FOB commander and SGM met us at the pad. The Commander reached for my gear and the adrenalin ran out and I dropped everything on his feet. I also saw that the entire camp was preparing for a "bright-lite" mission. It was great to know that everyone will do everything possible to get you back.

I had one beer and they put me on a chopper to Pleiku. This mission was for the four ID. Upon approach to Pleiku the crew chief said we had lost hydraulics and we were going in "hot". We must have made a trail of sparks a quarter mile ling. I believe we hit the PSP at around 70 kts.

At the debriefing, I explained the "airshafts" and the hostility of the locals, and told them that IMHO we had run upon an underground cache. On my word an arc light was retargeted to this area. Three days later there were still secondary explosions coming from that site. Kind of reminds me of CSM Edge's writing. Where else could a SSG command so much clout?

When I got back, I went directly to the 10's hooch, and found it had been pad-locked. The S-1 informed me that, according to regulation, all of his effects would be shipped to his NOK. I said Bull Shit - there was no need for his family to know anything about the letters. I raised so much of a fuss that the other recon members went to the SGM. He came down and broke the lock off of the door, and let me get the letters.

Klaxon
by Terry Dahling

In '68, in FOB-2, a couple of guys set off a "nightingale device" outside the O Club. Lots O fun!!

The signal for ground attack was any automatic fire. One night about 0200 we all woke up to auto fire. We grabbed our shit and ran to the wall. About a half hour later we were wondering where the attack was. Then we heard "Pappy" W. asking what was up. We told him and he sheepishly said he was test firing the machine gun in the tower -- at 0200!

Lesson One
by Terry Dahling

I had just arrived in country and was staying at the Safehouse in Danang, waiting for a flight to FOB-2 in Kontum. I was a true "cherry", and very impressionable. That evening there was a group of us sitting around a table listening to 'combat stories.' I didn't know any better, so I was all ears and really lapping it up. This one guy "knew it all."

All of a sudden, a wiry little dude picked up a steel pot and calmly walked up to the table and cold cocked the "warrior" with the helmet. He never said a word and went back to the bar. After I recovered from my shock, I went up to the bar and asked the wiry dude why he had done that. He said that the "warrior" was a com-center clerk who hadn't ever been out of his air-conditioned com-center. He had access to all of the after-action reports, and as a result, knew all of the "good stories."

The wiry dude was SSG Fred Z. He later earned a CMH. I had seen him do many things deserving of the CMH, but he was awarded this one because the pilot he rescued submitted him. C&C was notoriously stingy with their awards. I guess extraordinary heroism was expected of us.

The one thing I learned from this was that the true heroes tend to be quiet about their accomplishments.

"Sarge" Scuba Dog
by Terry Dahling

In 1970, I was assigned to A-21 (UWO) in the Canal Zone. Being single, I opted to live in a room at the abandoned seaplane hangar, which was our team area. I inherited a mutt from a previous member. He was ugly brindled and weighed about twenty pounds. He was a true member of the team.

Every morning he was outside waiting for PT. If it was a holiday or some other event, he wanted to know what was going on. Sarge made the runs with us everyday. He really pissed us off sometimes because he always stopped a couple of dozen times along the route to mark his territory and take a dump. Then he caught up with the huffing and puffing bunch without even breathing hard.

I had a FIAT convertible and he went everywhere, sitting in "His Seat". If I had a passenger, they had to get in back. One day, outside the PX at Ft. Gulick I called: "Hey Sarge, get your sorry ass over here!" I noticed the shocked looks on some faces and realized the fun I could have with his name.

He went everywhere the team went. When we went somewhere on the LCM he was always the first off of the ramp when they dropped it - testing the current and wildlife. When we went sport diving for dinner, no shortage of lobster in Limon Bay, he would follow me everywhere I went. He followed the exhaust bubbles. The first thing I saw when I surfaced after exhausting a single tank of air was Sarge's smiling face.

He had the proper attitude and ability to express what we didn't dare. One morning, we were in formation and our new TL was telling us how things were going to be different now that he was Boss. Sarge strolled up to the CPT and very nonchalantly barfed all over the CPT's shoes. We couldn't suppress all of the snickers.

Sarge knew the entire SP's at Coco Solo. There was a leash law on post but he didn't think it applied to him. Every once in a while someone would call the SP's and complain. They would pick him up and put him in their lock-up overnight. The next morning they would usually deliver him to us or call us to pick him up. They liked him, too.

He got to where he recognized a pick-up truck with lights on the roof as trouble. One afternoon we were at the deep-water pier preparing for an operation. I looked around and didn't see Sarge. After a few minutes I remembered that a SP vehicle had gone by a little while earlier. Just on a hunch I looked in the water and there was Sarge swimming around in circles. It was about a fifteen-foot drop to the water. I presume he saw the truck and decided to un-ass the area.

When I DEROS'ed, I wanted to bring Sarge home, but because of rabies I couldn't bring him in my car. The team was going to ship him home but they sent a letter stating between the quarantine time in Panama, and upon arrival at LAX, I would probably already be on my way to Thailand.

I wonder what ever happened to that old mutt.

Waiting for Training
by Terry Dahling

I arrived at SFTG in August 1963. We were bussed from Ft. Benning after BAC and were dropped off at Smoke Bomb Hill prior to the busses continuing on to the 82 Abn. We arrived late at light and issued bedding and bunks for the night. The next morning we processed in, and were tested and assigned to our respective "career" fields. Most PFC's like me were assigned to 05b training. Prior service personnel had a greater choice. We were then assigned to a training company in SFTG. I was assigned to A Company. In addition to the three training companies there was a "quitters' barracks." They caught most of the shit like KP until they received reassignment orders.

Depending upon the MOS one was to be trained in and the availability of classes, we waited for classes by doing details. Since we weren't the f--k ups and quitters, we got relatively easy details. If we were good and so inclined it was possible to disappear during police call and before detail selection. (Evasion and Escape Training) If there weren't enough details to pull or we finished early, we waited in the barracks for more work. This is where ghosting became an art.

As different MOS's required different times, there was always a period of waiting unless one was extremely fortunate. In my case, I waited a few weeks for MOI, the start of Branch Training, because a 05b class was already in session. We didn't go on the FTX, but waited for 05b Training and went to the field as 05Bs after MOS training.

Only after the completion of all training did we receive our orders and assignments to various groups.

I'm sure things changed, but that's my story and I'm sticking to it.

Sergeant Major Childress
by Terry Dahling

We could probably write a book on him, but I would like to relate two short ones episodes.

When new troops came into the group they would go to town and get completely wasted on German Beer to which they were unaccustomed. If they barfed in the company area instead of the latrine, and Childress caught them, he made them pitch their shelter halves outside and live there until they learned to live inside.

One night the CQ called and said the riggers were fighting in the barracks. Childress came in with his miniature bat and calmed things down in short order. He then called the CQ aside and said if his sleeves were too heavy, he'd take a couple of stripes to make them lighter.

He was the last of the hard core "Old Army" first sergeants I ever met. "Hard But Fair".

Still Alive and Kicking
by Toby Todd

12 Feb '71 is an important date for me.

On this date, 32 years ago, RT California, SOA, CCC, 5th SFGA, was on day three of a seven day mission. Our target designator was OSCAR-50. The area was in the Plei-Trap Valley, close to the NE part of Cambodia.

That day, RT California consisted of 1-0, SSG Chuck C., 1-1 SSG Galen L. M.(aka "MotorPool"), 1-3 CPT Bob C., and yours truly, 1-2 SGT Toby Todd. Four US Special Forces soldiers, plus ten Montagnards, total of 14.

About 1030, we came upon an abandoned enemy camp that had recently been inhabited. We spent approximately 20-30 minutes gathering intelligence, taking intel photos, measuring depths of foxholes, etc. We then moved off a couple hundred meters to a small hilltop. Since it was close to time for lunch, we arranged ourselves into a defensive perimeter, and took turns eating our lunch. We wanted to record our recent findings on paper, as to a man. We felt enemy contact was imminent.

I was situated so I could observe past the "tail gunner" section of RT California; i.e., over the shoulders of CPT C., armed with M-60 MG, and one of our 'Yard tail gunners, who had a CAR-15. They could observe down our back trail. All of a sudden, I saw the 'Yard's eyes get big as ashtrays and he opened up. I also observed Bob getting hit in the right arm. He began returning fire with his MG, yelling for us to "lay down a base of fire." I fired the B-40 rocket that was in my RPG-2 tube and tossed Bob one of my Field dressings. It was on!!!!

Everyone on RT California immediately started firing. I quickly reloaded and got off another round. "Sir Charles", who we determined later to be a heavily reinforced squad of hard-core NVA, was getting worked up as well, but I felt we were in control, until...

An enemy grenade, or rocket (to this day, we're still not sure) detonated in our midst. Chuck said: "Toby, you asshole, was that you?" 'Tweren't me, as it got me, too. Everyone was hit, but we continued firing aggressively. The guys were throwing hand grenades, shooting, and calling S/C a bunch sorry mo-fos.

I had fired four of my six rockets, and was loading the fifth into my tube when Chuck ordered a withdrawal off of the backside of the hill top toward an extraction LZ that FAC was gonna lead us to. I think the Covey rider was Larry "Six-pack" W., but CRS. As we were withdrawing from the battle scene, Chuck and Bob noticed an enemy soldier in a khaki uniform coming towards us, and they stitched him.

We encountered no further resistance on our march to the extract LZ, and were extracted by ladder without incident. We RTB'd back to Kontum, where Chuck, Bob and I were treated then medevaced to the General Hospital in Pleiku (CRS the numerical designation) for more definitive care, to include wound debridement, cleaning us up, and general TLC. I have met a retired LTC Nurse, S L A., on a military discussion board, who tells me she was stationed there at that time, though not part of the Surgical Team who cared for us. Thanks again to you and your people, ma'am. She's prolly tiring of hearing this, but I'll never tire of saying it!!).

We stayed a week, and then Chuck and Bob were further medevaced to Quin Nhon. I hooked up with a convoy heading back to Kontum. Chuck and Bob returned a couple of days later, and we once again reassembled RT California.

Chuck, Bob, and I have stayed in contact through the years. I lost track of MTP in the early '80s, about the time 1st SFGA was re-activated. Recently, I have had telephonic conversations with him, so I can now say that the USSF on RT California that day, are still alive and kicking.

Not so for some of our valiant 'Yards. Our point man, Ngron, was killed on my first mission, Sep '70. And Wit (pronounced "Weet") died on 21 Dec 2001, in Kirkland, WA.

It was a great day in our lives, because in spite of our wounds, we survived because of strenuous training, and because we believed in each other, and our courageous 'Yards. I'm extremely proud to have been a part of RT California, Special Forces, and the US Army.

This story, plus pics of RT California, then and now, can be found at my website that my kids set up for me.

Four-holer View
by Tom Long

When I arrived as a replacement at Plei Me, the fighting at the camp was over and the Cav. was having all the fun just west of the camp. All the buildings had been knocked down by bad guy mortars and good guy bombs and we just put them back up with what ever was left as it was a while before any materials could be brought in.

The USSF latrine was a four-holer made of tin. You could sit in the latrine and watch everything in camp through the holes in the tin. Lucky it was the dry season as the only thing the tin roofs did was keep the sun out. Before I left, they built a new team house out of teak. Imagine what that would cost here.

Tug of War
by Tom Long

Bob G. and Dan S. triggered a little ambush killing some NVA and capturing either five or six. They sent Nick W. and I out in a Cav slick to pick up POW's who were quickly loaded on board as the LZ was taking some fire. (Nick and I discussed this later at Bragg, but we don't remember if the bird got hit lifting off or hit something.) In either case, we were told to get rid of the cargo, which we immediately set about. The POW's would not cooperate and started clinging to the quilted insulation, wiring and whatever else they could get their tied up hands on which set the crew chief off.

While the chopper was topping out a few trees, Nick got frustrated and whipped out his .45 thinking if the NVA were shot, they would be easier to throw out. This set the whole crew to yelling which just added to the confusion. The pilot finally calmed everyone down, got the bird out of the LZ, and limped back to camp where we discovered all the POW's were tied together with a rope. Nick and I had been playing some sort of tug of war trying to throw them out opposite doors. I wish there was some sort of video of that whole cluster f--k.

Supply Sergeants
by Tom Schultz

While on Oki in the 400th SOD, the detachment had teams in Vietnam, Thailand, Korea, and Taiwan all at the same time. The only people left on the Island were the XO, SGM, clerk, and me. Before the CO left he designated me the Supply Sergeant. Uh-huh, a SP5, 98C, with 11C secondary and 11B additional MOS's. I bet you see the fun and games already. The CO did comment he realized putting Schultz in a supply room was like putting a blind dog in a butcher shop.

I told him I would give it my best shot, get the teams what they needed and wanted, if he in turn would keep me out of jail. He thought that was a fair deal, and so the games began.

About a week into my stint the SGM told me that the CO wanted a RCF-15 requisitioned, and as soon as we got it, to send it to Thailand. Ooooooookay. I checked the equipment authorized and found out we were only authorized one, and that one was in VN. When I informed the SGM of this, he was not impressed with my sudden knowledge and repeated," The old man wants a RCF-15 for Thailand."

I, of course responded as any good young troop would. "Yes Sarmajor."

Oh, by the way, the RCF-15 was an AN/GRC 19 mounted on a jeep, with a jeep trailer, and all the associated antennas, etc.

This was in the days of the punch cards that you filled out in pencil and submitted to the Supply Depot. So ignorant type that I was, I started filling out cards. First Card-RCF-15, Next Card- M38A1 4x4, Next card-transmitter, next-receiver, etc. etc. ad nauseum.

Very proud of myself, I galloped down to Machinato and submitted the requisitions. I got a call in a couple of days from the depot and was informed that it would take a couple of extra weeks to get the stuff because I specified M38A1s, which had been replaced by the M-151s. I told the depot that was okay because the rig could not be handled by the 151.

About two more weeks go by and I got a call from the Supply Depot. "Send two drivers down to pick up your two RCF-15s". "Whoa!", says I,"I only ordered one." Supply says "We don't need any guff; you got two, come pick up two."

Now, at this time I am thinking that I just got over like a fat rat. Ordered one, got two, now the det has a total of three with only one authorized.

Should I tell the SGM? Naaaaaah, I'll let it be a nice surprise to him. So, anyhow the clerk and I get the XO to drive us to the Supply Depot and we pick up and drive two nice new shiny RCF-15s back to the Det and I get one shipped out to Thailand.

So far so good. In another couple of weeks comes the IG inspection from HQ Ryukyu Islands. A crusty old E8 that was Supply Sergeant who must have been with the Roman Centurions inspects me. I failed the IG inspection miserably. Crusty old E8 tells me "If you had ever had a supply MOS, or even heard of a Supply MOS, I'd have your sorry ass under the jail. But you don't need punishment, you need help". He came back the next week and spent a couple of days with me teaching me enough about property books and such so I could survive until most of the det returned to the island. That's when I stopped worrying and started to love Supply Sergeants.

Oh, by the way, I also found out that all I had to do was fill out the one card that said "RCF-15" and that included aaaaaaall the stuff.

That's my story, and I'm sticking to it. How the 400th managed to keep the two extra RCF-15s, I don't know and ain't tellin'.

Free Beer
by Bill Coombs

John's reference to the anti-war/black power take-over in Berlin brought back a memory. One day, a bunch of black soldiers were demonstrating right outside the Berlin Brigade Headquarters. Hard to believe but it is true. They were raising hell and using nasty language.

The Deputy Brigade Commander was a black full colonel. I cannot recall his name. He came out and called the ringleaders into the building. From what I heard, he really chewed them out. That ended the demonstration.

The colonel used to come over to visit us in Det A once in awhile. He was a Master jumper and I asked him if he wanted to jump with us. He said he wanted to but he had some physical problem that prevented him from doing it. He was a nice guy.

About a half mile from Andrews Barracks was a gasthaus that I had never been to before. One night I went in, and one of the first things I saw was a large poster depicting an American soldier bayoneting a Vietnamese baby. I realized quickly that I was in a place I should not be and started to leave when the bartender came up and shook my hand. His name was Richie and he was from Chicago.

The place was covered with anti-war and pro-communist crap. Richie gave me a beer. I knew the place was not off limits and the beer was free, so I decided to see what it was all about. Richie told me that he was not a communist but a socialist. I looked at one of the pamphlets that were obviously locally produced on a Xerox machine. It was called UP AGAINST THE WALL, MOTHERFUCKER.

Richie told me that they catered to black soldiers although there were none in there then.

I picked up some of the propaganda and left. When I got home, I read through the UP AGAINST THE WALL and noticed that they had a column titled PIG OF THE MONTH. In it, the writer excoriated a captain who was stationed with the 6th Infantry at McNair Kaserne. I had picked up two issues and the other one took off on a First Sergeant.

I brought them over to a friend of mine, Mr. McKee, who worked at the G-2 at Brigade Headquarters. He was reading it when the G-2 himself, a full colonel, came in and Mac let him read it. He asked me where I got it and I told him. He asked me if I thought they should put the bar off limits and told him it would better to leave it open so it could be watched. If it were closed, they would just go underground.

It was sort of funny. I was in my Det A uniform, civvies, and the colonel thought I was a spook who worked for him. He started to chew me out for not doing something or other. Mac set him straight and the colonel apologized to me.

They left the place open but I never went back. I did talk to a black soldier one time and he told me that the blacks went there because the beer was free. He did not know of any of them who believed the crap that Richie and his commie friends were putting out.

Running Beer
by Bill Coombs

Those of you who had been stationed in Bavaria know how good the beer was. I fall into that category. I guess I was naive because I thought all German beer was that good.

I learned differently when I got assigned to Detachment A in Berlin. The two main beers in Berlin are Schultheis and Berliner Kindl. I thought they both were lousy.

My job took me to Bad Toelz from time to time. I do not mean when we made jumps there but when I had to drive down there for supply business.

I opened an account with the Lowenbrau Bier Depot on the Marktstrasse and carried two cases of beer back with me. My trips to Bad Toelz usually coincided with my beer supply running low. Over three years, I must have resupplied my Lowenbrau stock about ten times.

I recall having to pay a deposit on the cases and on my last trip to Toelz; I would turn in the two cases and get my deposit back. The owner of the place knew that I was from Berlin and said I was his only long-distance customer.

I never tried to hide the beer and often wondered what the Russians thought when they looked into my Volkswagen and saw the two cases of beer or empties, depending on which way I was going.

Ah memories.

SFOB Officer's Club
by Bill Coombs

There was a very nice officers club at the Special Forces Operational Base in Nha Trang, Vietnam.

One evening I had to go to the "O" Club to get someone. Of course, as I was an enlisted swine, I was politely asked to wait downstairs while someone went looking.

I thought about all of the officers that used to come to the NCO Club. They would hide their rank by turning the collars of their shirts inside. Like no one would guess what that was all about. We were glad they came to our club, especially the officers from the teams who wanted to drink with their guys.

Anyway, while I was waiting, the Club Manager, a Master Sergeant whose name I have long forgotten, showed me a small bar on the first floor that had some type of thatched roof nailed to the ceiling and along the walls. I asked him about it and he said very loudly, "This is my team house." That got the attention of some of the officers who were inside drinking.

I asked him why he called it that and he said, again a very loud voice, "This is as close as some of these sons-of-bitches will ever get to a real team house but now they can write their wives and girlfriends and tell them that they had been in a team house."

Everything went quiet and you could have heard a dime drop on the floor. I don't think he cared too much for HHC types.

He asked me what I was doing and when I told him that a lieutenant was looking for someone for me, he said, "Bullshit." He then brought me upstairs to do my own looking. To my knowledge, he stayed on as the Club Manager. This happened around '68 or '69.

8th SFG IG Inspection by Bill Coombs

I was the Supply Sergeant of Co E (Signal) of the 8th in 1965-1966. During that time, we were very short of troops because almost everyone was being sent to Vietnam. We got to the point that we had less than 30 guys in the company. If you were familiar with the Signal Company of a SF group at that time, then you know that we had a lot of vehicles. For maintenance, one soldier would be responsible for three trucks.

The group had an IG inspection coming up and the Group Commander wanted all of the buildings painted on the outsides. My company commander did not agree. He told the commander that he did not have the troops to do that.

Lucas B. III was my CO. He told me that we were not going to paint the building but everything inside would be straight. I went through the building and put in job orders for everything that needed work. The Post Engineers came and fixed cracks in the walls and the showerheads and all of that other stuff. I heard that Captain B. and the commander were having words over painting the building. Guys, if you have never been to Fort Guluck, these were not little one story jobs. They were three or four story high stucco buildings.

Well, the IG comes through and looks us over.

Fast-forward to the IG's exit report where he said and I paraphrase, "Notably, Company E's building was the best in the group because they repaired problems, they did not paint over them." That did not go over too well with the Group Commander. I cannot recall if Bull was the boss then or not.

I wondered why Captain B. did not seem to worry about things. He was a big guy and I understand he played football for West Point.

I was working on some report that the HQ on the other side of the isthmus wanted. I did it two or three times and they kept sending it back for changes. Captain B. got tired of signing them and made arrangements for he and I to meet with a major in the G-4 of USARSO.

The major was very polite and explained that DA was dropping changes on them and they just had to pass them down to us; but they finally got it figured out and he explained it to us. When he finished, Captain B. asked me if I completely understood it and I told him I did. Then he said to the major, "This is the last fucking time we are going to do it. If you want anything else done on it, you will do it yourself." I couldn't believe my ears. The major asked me to step outside.

A few minutes later, B. comes out, we get into his convertible, and head back to Fort Guluck. He knew I had a question and he answered for me before I asked.

He said he was visiting an officer's club one time. It was in the afternoon and he was sitting at the bar. He went to the john and when he returned, some guy in civvies was in his seat. B. told him that he wanted his seat back. The guy said, "This is MY seat." B. said, "No it is not. That is my drink right there."

He leaned towards the guy to get his drink and the guy pushed him away. So B. decked him. I guess I should stop referring to the guy as "the guy" and start calling him the "general".

B. told me as soon as had decked the general, the bartender came over and apologized for not telling him that the chair in question was always the general's after 4:00 PM, and he thought that B. had left.

Captain B. knew that he had only one more year to go in the Army and they would not let him stay in after that. He did come over to the 5th SFG and I think he commanded Signal Company there also.

He was a terrific guy who looked after his people, but should have kept his fists to himself.

"Recon Rex"
by Bob Jack

Here is the recipe for at least one of the best-or worst- drinks in the world. (From Volume three of the Hippy's SOG history, pages 401-402)

Recon Rex wasn't a man, a secret codeword, or radio call sign; it was a most creative concoction of various mashed and distilled grain spirits, formulated, like a science project, in a large glass beaker of perhaps at least, quart sized proportions. It was prepared for the initiation of newly assigned recon volunteers at Command and Control, North (CCN, da Nang); and was in no way analogous to an after dinner cocktail.

The key advertisement and appeal of the project was in the knowledge that if a man could drink a Recon Rex, stand, and walk away (unaided) -- the volatile mixture was free of charge.

At times, in the absence or unavailability of a glazed beaker, a combat boot would suffice. Containment of the liquid was not as crucial as the leaking-to-drinking ratio. The final test was proven in the scientific theory of Sir Isaac Newton hypothesis, *"For every action there is an equal and opposite reaction."*

The secret assemblage consisted of, at least, a jigger from every available liquor bottle on the back bar. (There were a lot of them) At times, other flavorings, such as pungent socks, found their way into the glass pitcher. The containers for Recon Rex were usually in short supply since the men opted to throw the glass vials against the wall, in a salutatory fashion, after it was devoid of fluid. As a result of the concoction, accompanying vociferous commotions normally erupted from the newly assigned volunteers. In describing a morning-after hangover, it was more comparable to a dinosaur than some minute reptilian lizard. Experienced recon men at CCN **NEVER** purposefully returned for "seconds.""

I don't remember finishing mine, let alone if I walked away, but I don't think I paid for it, since I was almost broke when I got to CCN. I could have paid for it by club chit but I don't remember. I never had the nerve to try another one.

I wouldn't even drink one made from the stuff Ben has in his home bar! The bar at SOAR doesn't have enough different types to make a "true" Recon Rex.

A SF qualified Captain, who was in Walter Wonderful with me, tried to come close on one of our R&R trips away from the hospital to Trinidad when he got promoted from 1LT to Captain. (N. was pulled from his SF assignment when he got to Vietnam.) I told him the legend of the Recon Rex, but we had not been able to talk a bartender into making one.

There we were in Trinidad; he was on crutches and I had an early peg. This was at Hilton Hotel built down a hillside; you enter at the top and went down to the rest of the hotel rooms - really a neat place. The actual bar was set below the floor level of Trader Vic's; you could lean back from your chair and rest your elbows on the floor. Like all Trader Vic's, this one had an exotic drink menu. I remember it being in an accordion form with a total of about eight drinks one to a page. Jim and I got three menus, one each for him, the bartender, and I. We had a grease pencil to check off each drink as it was consumed. Four of the Texas oil men working there (WWII and Korea veterans) found out what we were doing and picked up the tab. At least we didn't pay for them. The last drink we finished off with at the promotion party was a Zombie.

We have all seen, "normies" (that's what us amps called people that have all four limbs in relatively good working order) stagger down the street or hallway weaving from side to side bouncing off the walls; but it's even funnier when it's an amputee doing it down a hotel hallway on hands and knee's while I was bringing up the rear as crutches bearer.

Collecting Beer
by John Blevins

I saw a whole pallet of Coors in those soft aluminum cans streamer in at Tuyen Nhon. You should have seen the CIDG digging trenches to collect all the beer flowing out of the busted cans. The pallet was reduced from about five feet high to about two feet.

Wrong Place, Wrong Time
by David Stafford

One evening a bunch of buddies and I were "libating" in the late night shadows of Breckenridge Park in San Antonio. Due to the reality of boozing until the wee hours of the morning (~2), we fell out into the streets and realized that any liquor store we required was closed.

After stumbling around in search of a welcoming tavern, my 20-20 vision noticed three masculine forms entering a darkened building with what appeared to have some form of subdued illumination. Shrieking at the delight of discovering a heretofore unexplored watering hole, my chums and I made our way through the heavy, wooden doorway into a boozery that offered some relief from our parched, insatiated conditions.

Because of the lateness of the hour, we weren't originally taken aback by the absence of the lonely hearted female skunks usually frequenting such a fine establishment, but suffice it to say, some of the animated smirks and apparent warmth of the clientele certainly made us feel immediately welcomed.

When we entered, we passed by a long bar and took a left into a small room with about five or six small tables. Through the fog of my sedation, I sat down and noticed the dark blue walls were accented with nice petite, original paintings of lilies, lilacs, and a rose or two. I looked at the paintings and then into the eyes of one of my companions... "What the fuck is this?" said I puzzled by the decor.

"Who gives a shit?" my companion said. "They've got beer!"

I took my eyes from his, scanned the walls again, and then my eyes rested on the two brass bars which usually mark the boundaries where a waitress receives her orders from a bartender.

My eyes were greeted with the movement of a little pair of stylish designer jeans whose mustached wearer stopped between the brass bars and attempted to gain the attention of the sweet, accommodating bartender.
I looked back to my companion...

"Where are all the Texas babes at?" I asked.

"Dave," he said with really wide eyes. "LOOK!"

I turned my head back to the designer jeans and noticed a hairy forearm, and a hairy hand, gripping the mustached guy's ass.

"Jesus Christ," I spewed trying to cover my mouth. "We're in a homo bar!"

What happened?
A four minute mile gentlemen...maybe less.

The 'Original' Delta Club
by Don Valentine

Because of the Bien Hoa incident, Major S. was being transferred out of Delta. We decided to give him a going away party. At Bien Hoa, he had won my eternal respect when he went against the orders of some idiot in MACV-S3 and saved SSG Peter G. M.'s recon team. The team had been ambushed on their first day. Morley was wounded and he and the Vietnamese Special Forces [LLDB] medic had become separated from the rest of the team and was MIA. Meanwhile, they were all very busy evading the enemy. Hauling ass!

When the team radioed for extraction, the idiot in MACV-S3 told Major Strange to leave them in because they still had 7 days of patrolling scheduled. Major Strange went ahead and picked up the main body of the team and continued searching for the MIA for the next two or three days. I can't recall the exact number.

About a month before the party, the Delta enlisted men had decided to rent a former French restaurant, home, and hotel that was on Beach Boulevard in Nha Trang. Vietnam is literally covered from one end to the other with beautiful sandy beaches. This was where Major Strange's going away party was held.

In order to make our club legal, we had to establish written by-laws. One man from each section was selected to represent his people in the club committee. John Miller represented the Recon Section, Sergeant Dunbar represented Supply, I represented the Commo-Section and that's the only guys that I can still remember. That's how I know the following details.

Here are some of the actual rules we put into the by-laws:

"Uniform Regulation: Something on your feet and something on your ass. Shower shoes and jock straps shall suffice.

Guests: Any female is to be allowed entrance whether accompanied or not but no female shall be allowed to exit the club without permission of a club member.

Associate members: Any member of any branch of service will be allowed to join as an associate member."

All of the tiny motel units were rented the very first day, all to Delta members. The restaurant was open 24 hours and served food and booze of any kind at any time but Delta Members ate regularly scheduled Breakfast, Dinner, and Supper meals there. Our little "business" thrived and the Delta Club quickly became the most popular watering hole in Nha Trang.

To get food for Major Strange's party, we organized fishing and hunting expeditions. I volunteered for both. Delta had its own air force of a sort. As I recall, we had two C-47s and four H-34 Choppers, all manned by Vietnamese crews. They were all hotshot pilots, the best the Vietnam Air Force had. We got two choppers for the hunting expedition and they flew us to an area that used to be strictly reserved for hunting by their former King. That was before the French colonized Southeast Asia, screwed everything up and caused that damn war.

Both choppers were filled with game when we returned. We also spotted a tiger chasing a deer that we were after and shot it. Not me, I couldn't shoot it. It was just too beautiful and I knew we weren't going to eat it; besides it was just doing what we were doing, looking for a meal. When we hit the tiger we landed to pick it up. The deer it had been chasing was long gone. The tiger was still thrashing about in the elephant grass the last we saw just before we sat down about 30 yards away. We discussed who was going to wade through that thick grass to finish off the tiger.

I asked, "Who thinks that they shot it?"

Sergeant Keating said, "I did." He was stationed in Alaska and had taken up big game hunting while there.

I said, "I didn't even shoot at the poor dumb bastard so I suggest you go finish it off."

He eagerly accepted the job and hopped out of the chopper armed only with his .45 pistol. That elephant grass was so thick; he stepped on that damn tiger before he saw it. Keating jumped straight up about three feet and fired two or three rounds into it almost before he hit the ground. If that damn thing had not already been dead, it would have had him for breakfast. It was about nine feet long from nose to tail. I don't know how much it weighed, but it took five of us to load it into the chopper.

We also got a huge Mule Deer. It took everyone from both choppers to get that mule deer in a chopper. That was the first time that I had seen a mule deer; we only have whitetails in East Tennessee. All the way back to Nha Trang, I stared at that damn big-ass deer. It was difficult to believe it was just a deer.

That was in the morning; in the afternoon some of us went fishing. We took an outboard motorboat, our swimming suits or PT shorts and a case of grenades out into the Nha Trang Harbor. We wreaked havoc on the fish all that afternoon, but not one damn fish floated to the surface.

We were out near an island that was just offshore from Nha Trang beach. They later used that island to train recon students and newbies on their first tour in-country. It was also the same island where Senator Kerrey [then a SEAL] won the MOH for his actions during a fierce firefight with VC. I don't know how there could have been that many VC on that tiny island with all the training going on all around them.

The water was crystal clear and we could see all kinds of fish that were killed from the blast, but they were on the bottom. We tried and tried, but none of us could reach the bottom. If I had brought some large rocks with us, I might have been able to do it. [I had used that trick when I was a kid to reach the bottom of a shallow part of Norris Lake, just to see what was down there.] A boat of Vietnamese fishermen came along and a couple of them were spear fishing. We called them over, pointed down below us and to our grenades and with hand and arm signals we finally struck a deal. We would split the catch, if they could bring them up. This deal worked great because those little shits brought all of the stunned fish up. We really had a great feast.

Hell, nobody ever had a better person responsible for their life in any military anywhere and that was the best party anybody ever got under such circumstances. Maybe the best party anywhere for anybody period! SF lived like animals when in the field, but they believed in living as good as possible when they weren't.

Delta made it their mission to set the example for both field duty and camp life. Many of the SF guys stopped wearing skivvies, especially those that had served on SOG or Delta LURPs [long range recon patrol]. Underwear and socks tended to restrict air circulation and were always soaking wet, all of which encouraged jungle rot. Some guys put sand in their jungle boots while in camp and wore them that way without socks to toughen up their feet.

The most comfortable clothing in the world is loose fitting, light weight jungle fatigues with no skivvies under them. It can't be beat. The original Delta Club was only operational for about 45 days, then the Inspector General shut us down at the request of the 5th Group Commander. It seems that one of our extra-curricular recreational activities attracted the attention of a local reporter, Master Sergeant Donald Duncan, who found our sense of fun both newsworthy and repulsing. His news article concerned the antics of two members of Delta, whom I shall merely refer to as "Hewey" and "Dewey."

It seems that these two yahoos decided, while dead drunk, to have a contest to settle an argument between themselves as to which one was the best "pussy eater." One of the two, I honestly don't recall which, sold tickets to any and all interested spectators. Apparently the reporter bought a ticket. According to a Delta member who supposedly witnessed the contest, Dewey won! Dewey reportedly didn't come up for air for an hour. That part's hearsay because I was not present for the contest. Honest!

As I recall, Duncan had been Dewey's recon patrol leader. Duncan quit recon and
Delta after his team blundered into a couple of unarmed villagers while on his last patrol. The team took them as prisoners because they were afraid they were either VC or

would tell the VC about seeing them. Duncan reported it by radio. According to Duncan, Delta's Headquarters ordered him to kill the villagers and continue the mission, and he refused. Duncan wanted exfiltration along with the villagers. I am almost positive that this happened while Major Strange was still commanding Delta.

Duncan always carried a pair of "utility pole climbers" with him so if he found a suitable tree, he could have a good observation post and would also be better able to determine where the hell he was. Duncan impressed me as being a very good soldier. He was a very young Master Sergeant. Duncan, like many others; he just did not have a stomach for that stupid war. (The last that I heard about Duncan, he quit the army and took a job as a reporter with some "liberal" west coast magazine that specialized in bad-mouthing the US and our involvement in that war. He later wrote a book, I believe it was called, The New Legions, and I think he also had articles published in Life Magazine.)

In the short period of time that the original Delta Club existed, it made enough profit to pay the civilian labor and buy enough material to build the most beautiful club in Vietnam. They built it on our new campsite. Our club didn't cost the taxpayers one red cent. Most club managers skimmed money off the top and left their club in debt. Some never paid a single beer company the entire time they were manager. Our camp was classified Secret and no reporters were allowed inside.

The Delta Club became famous throughout SF and units that Delta worked with. It was the place to go for fun, good drinks and food at reasonable prices, unless you were a non-SF officer or a reporter that is.

It became a "Class Act."

Teamroom Story
by Terry Dahling

In 1966-67, while assigned to CoA 10SFGA, we were at a promotion party at the Lenngries NCO club. Jimmy H., a black medic by the name of R., and I were at the bar drinking. Someone spilled a beer down my leg, and being the shy quiet trooper I was, I shouted: "Damn H., put your dick back in your pants and stop peeing on everyone!" R. took up the cry. A few minutes later, the MA came over and told us it was time to leave. We asked why, and he explained that we were seen peeing all over the bar. We told him we were just playing and he said that the bartender, an SP4 who shouldn't have been working there anyway, had "seen us."

The next morning we were before the Co SMG. We told him our story, which he didn't believe. He bought the story of the bartender. For our penance we were to clear the snow and ice from the company quadrangle - after work. That night we got our little shovels, and started scraping and shoveling. After a couple of hours we looked at each other, and then looked towards the downstairs latrine. I was the only barracks rat, but knew there was a hose and hot water hook-up in the latrine. Three light bulbs went off at once. We got the hose and cleared off the quadrangle in no time and had the SDO approve our work.

About 12 o'clock the fun started. It was very, very cold and the wind was blowing across the parade field. The water soon turned to glare ice. It was so thin it was impossible to see. The lot looked clear. The troops started to return from the club and as soon as they stepped on the lot they went feet up and ass down. We stood there for almost an hour busting our guts.

As the bartender was an SP4 and subject to bed check, the first time I had CQ I was standing outside his room at 2400 sharp. He got an article 15 and lost his job. Served him right. He wasn't assigned to us, just billeted in the company. I think he belonged to the 402 d ASA det.

Bulla's Fantails
by Tom Long

There was some old black lady in St. Croix who made a concoction called Bulla's Fantails. They only made them for really special occasions, and nobody ever had more than one. In fact, I think she would only give you one.

Some people opened a new restaurant and bar there in 1987 and asked Bulla to make Fantails on opening night. I hired three guys from Texas who went to the grand opening and somehow finagled themselves a bunch of these things. When I came in the next day, these guys were in the office floor moaning and were turning a shade lighter than haze gray. That condition lasted pretty much the whole day.

These things contained dark "151" rum, some spices, some sort of tree bark and belladonna. Someone told me she ground up Valium in them. One would make you a mellow fellow.

Bangkok…Ahhhh Bangkok
by Bill Pelletier

Bangkok…for those who have been there in the '60s and '70s, (and I just know…it is still a great experience for a GI of today) just the word brings back sensual memories hard to put down on paper. The many different activities that once experienced, can never be forgotten. A few of the more memorable times follow.

I had been in VN for 30+ months when I got the orders for 1st Gp on Okinawa. It was great, as the only other choice as the 10th Gp, and I hated snow.

After only a couple of months on Oki, I was told to use up some accrued leave time…or lose it. Never one to give the government something that did not belong to them, I chose to go to Bangkok (again).

There was this 1st Lt. on Oki who had become a close friend by the name of Mark. Well, since Mark had never been to BK, and said he wanted to come along (and back-up is always a safe option). A short hop from Oki, and we were there. BK…the place where dreams come true.

I made arrangements with my old driver, Bill Vatoon, to pick me up and to have my latest Thai dream girl with him. I knew she had remained 'true' to me, as she was far too pretty to be a liar (right!).

Mark was ready, more than ready, for some treats of the Orient. In as much as Mark was a "Newby", I figured he was ready for some good old fun, courtesy of yours truly. My normal schedule while in BK was to get up early, pick up my latest 'true love'. Then it was off to the snake/mongoose flights, the Palace or some other tourist trap. Always spent at least one afternoon at a local jewelry store to restock goodies for my 'true love' back in VN, After a pleasant morning it was time to knock off a little with my new love in BK. I had a quick snack at the restaurant and then off to my room, the one with the stirrups.

Mark was new and needed to let his hair down a bit, so I had the driver, Bill fix him up with a local Katoy. It was all set up for the morning after a late breakfast, Vitoon show up with our escorts. Mine was good-looking, but Mark's was gorgeous even for Katoy. Anyway, we all had coffee and left for our typical morning tour. We went to an early Thai kickboxing match which always got everyone in the mood to exercise. A quick stop after the match at a local soup shop, and the fun was ready to begin. Of course, all the way through the matches and the soup our dates held us in great esteem, or at least held us somewhere. We were into some heavy spit swapping when we got back to the opera. Mark was ready, more than ready. If there had been a mongoose in heat, Mark would have bred it right in the taxi.

Back at the Opera, word had spread about what I had done and, by the time, we got a seat at the windows facing the pool and the rooms, it was almost SRO. All four of us sat down to make the evening plans on how to outspend our last trip. We decided to play with our new 'girlfriends'.
Knowing that Mark could not stand it any longer, I dutifully ordered another drink so I could watch the eruption. We all started our stopwatches as he entered his love nest for an afternoon of sexual sport. Hand in hand, they climbed the stairs with the Katoy's hand firmly gripping Mark's butt. Mark was just as hot, giving the 'thing' lots of hugs and lots more tongue. The groping up to then had been kept above the waist as 'she' had what looked like a great pair of stand-

up titties, and Mark kept them busy. The time had come…the moment was near, they entered the love den, the door shut closed, but not before Mark looked back at the club, where a dozen SF guys were hanging out at the windows. I'm sure he wondered why, but he turned and gave us all the 'thumbs up'.

One minute…two minutes…three minutes…all the way to the five minute barrier…when up from above came the most blood curdling scream I had ever heard. The door exploded open and a small petite body came hurling out like a spear headed for the pool 20 feet below. Luckily for Mark, the Katoy hit the rail instead. Mark, in his white boxers launched himself after the Katoy, who was half in terror for his life and half laughing his ass off. He was still in his bra and panties, no shoes, skirt, or top. The crowd at the bar was screaming with eager delight (not unlike the Romans watching an event at the Coliseum), awaiting the soon to come slaughter of the innocent.

Just as Mark got close to the tranny, he saw us laughing our asses off; he turned his fury toward us. At this time, I figured that discretion is the better part of valor, and I fled up the alley to possible safety. Jumped into the first taxi and told him to get me the hell out of there…and fast. He did (obviously, as I am still here to tell the story).

A couple of hours later, I decided it was safe to return to the Opera. It wasn't. I ended up in the pool with a few extra knots on my head, but came away with a life long friend who would remain in contact through many worldwide assignments for both of us.

Throughout the years, I always gave Mark hell about the five minutes alone with the queer tranny from BK.

"WHAT TOOK SO LONG!?" I would always ask. It took three years before he admitted the truth (or so he claims). Seems Mark had to take a monumental shit when he got to the room, and told the Katoy to get in bed and wait. The Katoy stripped down to the bra and undies and turned out the lights. That's when Mark jumped into bed and immediately found the extra appendage. The rest is history.

It is all the truth, so help me.

Big Bar Manager
by Ben Roberts

I remember walking into one of the clubs in Na Trang in the 5th compound and saw a seven foot tall Sgt/Maj running one of the clubs. This fellow was wearing fifteen metal yard bracelets on one arm. He might have been a great bar manager but was a definite liability clanking along with all those bracelets...In addition, it would have taken a fork lift to raise him if he ever got hit, although I seriously doubt that he could have made it through those brush tunnels and narrow mountain trails. Still he looked like someone nobody had any interest in messing with, and the bar was probably the best use for him due to his size.

Land Leeches
by William Foxworth

There were/are leeches in the second Corps Area of VN, due west of Kontum. These were not like the leeches in the Africa Queen; these were LAND leeches, usually about an inch long before feeding. The vibration of your walking would wake the little suckers up.

Sometimes there were pools of water in the areas that would stand for awhile and then dry up close to rivers and streams. This is where you could find them or perhaps they would find you.

Gecko
Steve (nofault) Andres

Small, about six inches that scurry around the walls eating bugs...supposed to be good luck.

Friendly Trench Spiders
By Ben Roberts

I was ambushed by a VC coming out of a trap door in the ground on a trail to a VC Village. We had just finished stepping over a dozen trip wires connected to blue Air Force bouncing Betty anti- personal mines stolen by the VC. I was the first to hear the VC begin to open the trap door - totally inexperienced. However, having been a bird hunter, you listen for noises on the ground. I pointed to where the sound was coming from.

The lead Montagnards looked in the direction for a minute and waved to us to continue. I took about five steps and the little f--ker in the tunnel popped up, and had me in his sights as he unloaded an AK-47 in my direction. I could hear the pops of his bullets going past my ears before hearing the gun firing. Thank God I was out of the minefield, or I might have thrown myself on the ground setting off a disastrous chain of mines wounding a lot of folks on the trail. Thank God there was a trench left over from France's attempt to control Vietnam in the 1950's near me. I dove into the black trench filled with a foot or so of water because it was only about ten feet from the river bank. There were spiders all over the place the size of your fist. Considering that my choice was to have my brains spread all over the place or getting bit by a big ass spider I sought comfort in the trench with my spider friends, who left me alone. I was a lucky son of a bitch.

Sikkim Leeches
by Buck

The worst leeches I have ever encountered were in the high-altitude rain forests of Sikkim. Damned things would drop out of the trees and brush. We used salt to sprinkle on the leeches causing them to drop off and turn into a gooey mess.

Pain – Long and Short
by Charlie Noyes

MSG Jim S. and I went on patrol with two of our counterparts and about sixty CIDG in early 1970. We set up a RON and ambush along a well traveled trail Northeast of Bu Dop and just below the Cambodian border - L-shaped ambush along the trail, half circle perimeter behind the L, and us in the center.

We were in bamboo. I scraped up a nice soft mat of dried bamboo leaves, laid down my poncho and turned in, only to find an old dried up bamboo root cluster under my back. I got up and drug the poncho a few feet away and turned in again.

I was rudely awakened about 0200 when I rolled over and placed my bare left arm on top of something that didn't care for the personal contact. Whatever it was, it stung the crap out of the inside aspect of my left forearm. When I woke and sat up, clutching the offended extremity, the creature could be heard skittering across the poncho. It sounded like someone thrumming their five fingers across a kitchen table top. It reached the edge of the poncho and went into the bush.

I crawled under the poncho to look at my arm with a flashlight. There was a huge red whelp about three inches in diameter and getting bigger. The center was white, raised and looked like Mount Rainier to me.

The rest of the night, I spent looking at my arm, taking my pulse and blood pressure, both of which went sky high; and talking to someone on the radio at Bu Dop (I do not recall who), trying to figure out if we really needed to do a nighttime extraction.

We did not. Blood pressure and pulse and respiratory rate all returned to normal by daybreak.

CIDG cranked off an ambush about that same time, blowing the top off the head of an NVA solo walker. Funny thing was when the claymores took the top of his head off; it cleaned all the brain matter out with it. The inside of his skull looked like the inside of a yellow Tupperware bowl.

Apparently, when he was first hit, he reached up with his left hand. Postmortem, he grabbed the front of his forehead and wrapped all four fingers over the edge of his skull and laid them along the inside of his head. That's exactly how he hit the ground and didn't let go.

Strange stuff. Have to wonder.

His head only hurt for a moment; my left arm stayed sore for a week.

Centipedes
by Charlie Noyes

We were sitting in the TeamHouse at Bu Dop one evening when one of those giant centipedes went skittering across the floor. Sergeant Gifford was the only one wearing boots. Everybody else put their bare feet under our asses while we watched Gifford jump up and down on that thing. I swear, every time Gif landed on it, it carried him a few inches across the TeamRoom.

Gecko Sounds
by Charlie Noyes

I don't really know the maximum size a gecko can obtain, but we saw some that were definitely greater than six inches running around in the tree canopy around Bu Dop. They could be heard taking in big gasping breaths of air; and would then expel it repeating, F—k Youuu! F—k Youuu! Until they ran out of air. The last sound was usually just a croak.

I'm sure they didn't reach ten pounds, though.

Leeches in Vietnam
by John Blevins

I only remember one leech getting on me in the IV Corps area. I was at the FOB at Tuyen Nhon during monsoon when the water was up. Inside the camp, I was walking around barefoot and cut my toe on something. I put my foot in the water to wash the blood off and this leech came for it like a bullet; all I saw was a blur. Before I could jerk my foot back, this sucker (no pun intended) was firmly attached. Don't believe that I have ever seen anything move in the water that fast.

Lizards and Loincloth
by Bruce "Hardcore" Koch

I saw several of those FU lizards in N.E. Thailand at Nam Pung Dam when we were building our B team camp. (B4610) They weren't any bigger than about a foot long and about two pounds. There were some walking sticks, some as long as 14 inches, plus scorpions like small lobsters. (Centipedes were about 6" long.)

We were carving that camp out of the jungle and living in hammocks; each A team had one side of the perimeter, and we had foxholes dug just in case.

One night, Whiskey Webber was half shit faced (as usual) and sitting in his hammock next to mine. One of those lizards let loose with a f--k you; and I said, "Well f--k you too, you sonofabitch!" Well, ole Whiskey thought that was the funniest thing he had heard lately, and laughed so hard he went over backwards out of his hammock, and headfirst into his foxhole. He was too drunk to get out by himself, so Skeeba and Augustin each grabbed a leg and hauled his ass out of there. They thought it was so funny that they drug his bony ass another twenty feet or so across the ground. Whiskey was only wearing a Thai loincloth (Pakama) so his bony ass was rubbed raw for a while.

Leeches and other Vermin
by Jack Moroney

Mang Buk had leeches all year round. On the high ridge lines, we had large nasty black leeches and an incredible number of centipedes. In the river valleys, we had all sorts of leeches. In the rainy season, there were so many that they looked like thick waving pieces of grass reaching upwards towards the body heat we were putting out. We used that thick jelly leech repellent on our boots which often picked up flecks of gold dust after we waded some of the mountain streams. Also had our share of bamboo vipers and an assortment of other nasties which the yards would kill as they saw them but only on the right side of any trail we happened to be using. Always wondered why I would only see mangled snakes that had been hacked to death hanging from vegetation only on the right side of any particular route we were using. The yards explained that those on the right side of the trail were bad luck but those on the left were not.

Blood Suckers
by Jack Carey

We had several very nice leeches at A-231 Teiu Atar. Some in the water, like normal civilized ones, and some of those real nasty super small 'tree' leeches. Loved them.

Up North, we called them 'Blood Suckers'. In the 10th in Tolz, in the Glockenspeil at the Rathaus, they used to sell leeches at the drug store across from the clock. They were as ugly in those jars as they were in VN. In the 60's, the Germans would use them to suck out the 'bad' blood after you got a bad black and blue.

Bloody Leeches
by John Cleckner

I only remember two types of leeches in VN. The huge buffalo leeches that I can't remember ever getting on anyone and the mountain leeches, as we called them. They were everywhere in I & II Corps. Especially in I Corps. The little bastards would get all over you when walking through the "woods" or when lying, counting and trying to figure out how to blow them to hell and back.

I got up one time after lying in a pappy area for over two hours, and my uniform was covered with blood. I can't remember how many leaches they took off me, but it was more than I ever want to remember.

Bamboo Viper
by John Hauck

I remember sitting down on a large fallen log in the jungle to take a smoke break. I was looking down between my feet when a beautiful florescent lime green bamboo viper crawled between my feet. In a normal situation I would have had heart failure. This particular time I don't remember having much reaction at all. Amazing what the jungle, heat, and fatigue will do to you.

Hammocks
by John Hauck

I slept in a VC hammock that was handed down to me from Benny Stafford when I got his job as XO of A312, Xom Cat. I also had a lightweight poncho. I strung the hammock a couple of inches off the ground to stay out of range of the leeches. If it was raining or going to rain, I strung the poncho over the hammock. I had to sleep in the hammock with knees bent. A jungle sweater had to be worn at night to stay warm. I wore one pair of socks and kept a dry pair in my rucksack. In the morning I put on dry socks, not necessarily clean. Psychologically it was a boost putting on dry socks in the morning. They only stayed dry but a few minutes after we started moving out. There always was a stream to cross, but such is life in the jungle.

I only slept leaning up against a stump I shared with Glossup one night. By daylight I was eaten up pretty good with leeches. Suckers got me in the neck and on the side of my head. It was 17 Oct 1966. We were on a search and recovery mission to find our two teammates that had been killed. By the time we found out about the attack, it was too late to get to their area. They were found the next morning. Helicopters could not get in to extract the bodies; no LZ's. The CIDG put them in ponchos and strung them on tiger poles. I walked behind either Lennon or Jackson; don't know which one it was all the way back to Xom Cat. The toughest operation I ever went on. I had just gotten in off an op the evening before; quick turn around.

The VC got my VC hammock back. The night before, Lennon asked to borrow mine because he could not find his. War is strange at times.

Shit On by a F—k You Lizard
by John Hauck

The F--k You Lizards I saw around III Corps were about the size a blue runner or racer, as some folks down here in the SE call them.

One evening, after recent arrival at my new team, temporarily located with an RF/PF company in the little village of Phuong Lam, Hwy 20 just south of the II Corps/III Corps border, I was sitting at the table in the temporary team house writing a letter home with the aid of the light of a gasoline lantern. I wasn't feeling on top of the world, had been in country about 4 months, didn't know my new team, nor what we were gonna get into when we replaced the team at Xom Cat - just did not feel red hot.

I jotted away at the lined pad trying to make it interesting, none the less. The F--k You lizards loved the rafters of the thatch roof. They were busy talking their shit. Suddenly, something hit me on the back of my hand and stuck there. I looked down at it, then up in the roof. There he was. I had gotten shit on by a f--k you lizard. I went to bed.

The Earth Moved
by Jon Comini

On the last op on the Chu Pong and in the Ia Drang, during which I admitted to sometimes sleeping on a pneumatic appetence (btw, carefully prepared web gear neither makes noise nor punches holes in anything), I had a most unfortunate incident. Remember, this was the last day of my last operation and I just knew deep in my heart that there was a golden BB out there with my name on it. I consciously had to remind myself that I had to remain alert and cool, and to be just aggressive enough to overcome my natural reticence.

Hence, I was employing every bit of my hard-earned Southeast Asian wood lore to make sure that my wards and I performed every aspect of our assigned mission in the most professional manner, while still making it to the relative safety of Du Co. Coming to an obstacle, I would pause, check it out, pick the spot where my next footfall would be and commit. I was operating in the best tradition... virtually moving across all those deadfalls like warm honey.

Until the last one! I checked it out, stepped across putting my left foot down and just as I was transferring my weight to it and beginning to lift my right foot, the earth moved. I looked down and saw that I had stepped on the biggest effing python that ever lived. I did not excrete, my sphincter was not tight -- it had grafted closed-- but I did emit a long, gassy girlish scream and went straight up in the air. My Yards began to giggle (they could do that at the most inopportune times) and the python just shrugged in annoyance.

I was proud of that op. We got some very good intel and there were no injuries (to my guys, anyway) save for the massive trauma to my dignity and to the python which was elegantly served for dinner that night along the runway at Du Co. I ate my share sitting on my air mattress and contemplating my impending nuptials, which were several weeks away, and wondering about the science employed in calculating PCODs.

Vermin
by Lance Lollini

I had the good fortune to have been on operations in each Corps area. Some of the vermin I encountered were as follows. In I Corps, leeches were relatively common but not present in every location. I wonder if there were distribution differences in general, or whether there were seasonal population differences. I remember watching one small black leech with an orange stripe as it made its way up over the toe of my boot. I tried to stomp my foot and shake it off but the little bugger kept on coming. Finally, he met his demise at the tip of my knife. Often you were alerted that a leech had visited a part of your body because the wound bled after the leech departed. I don't remember any leech encounters in II or III corps but they were probably there.

The biggest leech I have ever seen was in Cambodia. It was on an operation out of BTT in IV Corps during the dry season. We were going to try a snatch in a part of Cambodia that was considered a NVA strong hold. At twilight we moved to and across the border via dugout canoes and proceeded on foot from there. Mr. Charles had observed our insertion, and the obligatory signal shots were fired. We moved out in the darkness and lost our tail by swimming a relatively wide river (at least the map called it a river) and moved along on what could only be defined as supertrails (hard packed with evidence of heavy traffic). The ground was flat and dry, and a lot of the area was burned off; so cover was a problem. However, there were trails going every which way, which would have made it hard to figure out where we were going. Just before daylight we got to a huge grassy area, probably the remains of a large swamp with scattered clumps of low bushes, and set up a day location.

During the day we saw several large, company sized groups searching for us. Needless to say we kept our heads down and hoped they wouldn't find us because we were too few and too unprotected to be able to survive a fight. It was really hot during the day and we didn't have much shade; consequently we were running low on water. All that was available to us was a shallow (2 to 3 inches) puddle of water that was the remnant of a small pond. Most of the ponds that were drying up were slimy, shiny, mucoid, blue-green water. This one was no exception. I had to tilt my canteen cup and let the water slide, not flow, in. While filling my cup with the slime a huge, at least 6" long and 3/4" wide, leech came slithering by. It made my skin crawl. Later, while waiting for the two iodine tablets to kill what ever was living in the water, a thought popped in my mind that those huge leeches were probably in the river that we swam through. I figured they were so big that we would have felt them crawling and gnawing on us before they could attach and feed. The funny thing was, for a moment, my attention was completely diverted to the leeches rather than concentrating on the more pressing situation of being in close proximity to a large hostile force that was searching for us. We didn't have any more leech encounters, and we played hide and seek for a couple of days before returning to SVN on foot. No, we didn't snatch anybody; probably just as well because we didn't have any arty, helicopter or air support to back us up or get us out of Dodge.

The other vermin I encountered, excluding mosquitoes which were everywhere, were ants and snakes. Chris McClure, a list member on TDY, and I were in the field phase of the COC course on Hon Tre Island when the point man encountered a very large python. Yep, I mean really large - lots bigger than the largest of the boas at the JOTC in Panama. The Yards killed the snake and we took it out the following day when we were extracted. The snake made fine grub for a lot of Yards. At the time I wondered what was big enough on Hon Tre to serve as prey for that snake.

Another snake encounter occurred during a Mike Force operation in I Corps. We had inserted at the edge of rice paddies just outside of a VC village west of Nong Son (SP?). We were looking for some 50 cal machine guns that the NVA were supposed to have set up in the area. Air strikes heavily prepped the LZ and surrounding area, and we landed unopposed. After moving out of the LZ and into the jungle for awhile, we took a break.

The strikers were composed of Hoi Chans and Yards who were loosely scattered in the break area. I was sitting next to another USSF when I noticed movement on a twig above and to the left of my head, just between me and the other American. It was a bamboo viper that was moving down to the ground. For those who have not seen a bamboo viper, they are bright green relatively slender snakes. This snake was relatively small, only about a foot and a half long. I didn't want to scare the snake or anyone else so I signaled the other American to be quiet and we waited to see what would happen. The snake moved along slowly, passed right next to my foot, and it continued until it came close to one of the Yards. The Yard was carrying one of those hooked beak rice knives (L shape with the short leg at the front of the blade). He spotted that snake, whipped that knife out, and took a mighty swing at the snake. Fortunately for the snake, the tip of the hook hit the ground but did not penetrate. The blade was arrested just above the snake's head. The poor snake was, however, scared shitless and it took off like a missile, flying through our strikers and into the safety of the jungle. Nobody was injured, not even the snake; the operation continued and that, my friends, is another story.

I saved the ant story for last but certainly not least, as far as I am concerned. During the Nui Coto operation in 69 I wound up with a company that formed part of the blocking force around the knoll that was the target of the operation. The first thing we did was to recon our area as it extended from the main part of the Mt. out along the SE portion of the knoll. During one of the recon patrols I happened to rub against the branches of a small but very thorny tree. All of a sudden ants covered me, and my body felt like it was on fire. Those little bastards were biting me with great enthusiasm. I had to strip off all of my clothes and the strikers beat my attackers off of my clothing and my body. Seems that the thorns were hollow and ants lived within them. That day my enemy turned out to be very small, but fierce, and their unrelenting ambush was a success; fortunately, only my pride was wounded and I lived to fight another day.

Garrobo
by Leamon Ratterree

This ain't no S****. Down in Hound-ur-ass, there are Iguanas and Garrobos. The difference is Iguanas are quiet, slow, and docile. The Garrobos are very fast, and fight back.

Well Mike Stangle -as many of you know- is well known as a guy who collects all sorts of exotic "animules". (Could have had his own TV show on Animal Planet, but that hadn't been invented yet.) He (sometimes, WE) caught iguanas, boas, snakes of all shapes and sizes, turtles, piranhas, caimans, scorpions, tarantulas, ad nauseam.

Well, he caught a garrobo approximately 18 inch long, and had it bound, gagged and strapped to the top of his rucksack. When we stopped to rest, he would un-gag it so it could drink. One late afternoon, we settled down in some bushes to chow down on C-rats, and he decided to feed and water his garrobo. Except for the string around its neck, the garrobo was free to move about the rucksack. Mike was feeding his garrobo, whilst I faced the opposite direction, leaning against the tree, chowin' down on spaghetti and meatballs (not my favorite C, BTW) as I was opening my pound-cake (my favorite) I heard "OW, he bit me."

I turned to look, and blood was squirting through the air. The little bugger had ripped Mike's skin all the way to the bone, which was very visible. "I guess I'll have to go back and get stitches."

"Reckon so" says I, "and as soon as I finish my dessert, I'll call a MedEvac."

Nobody is excited. We are both tawkin' "matter of factly", and I was about to break into laughter. I finished my pound cake. Grabbed the radio operator and dragged him up the hill, switched his radio from their command freq, to our Medevac freq, and gave one quick call. Got an immediate response from our own, John Raybon (RIP) who said he had just passed over the ridgeline departing Palmerola. That is about 150 miles north of where we were. (I was talkin to him on a PRC-77.) I gave him the sitrep, got out my signal mirror, VS-17 panel and spread it on the ground, and started scanning the western sky with the mirror.

At 35 miles out, Raybon saw the mirror. I couldn't see nor

hear him, but he told me to keep scanning with the mirror. I could finally see him - a dot in the distance - and he could see my panel. Mike made his way up the hill and we were now looking for a better LZ but couldn't find one. Raybon set one skid on the side of the hill and we had to crawl (real low) under the rotor blades, dragging Mike's rucksack (which now had the garrobo stowed inside). After the "two" passengers got onboard and were secured, I stayed flat on the ground while the UH-1 lifted straight up and flew took Mike to the hospital (SEA Hut, One Each).

But wait! The story doesn't end there.

While Mike was en route to the hospital, the other "passenger" died. Mike had been giving it some of our chlorinated water, and it had bloated when it reached higher altitude. Our guess was that garrobos don't fart.

Mike showed his wound to the high-speed US Army Medical personnel who allegedly knew all there was about wild ani-mules, cuz they watched "Wild Kingdom" when they were growing up. They want to give him a Rabies shot.
  Mike tells Medic #1 that he don't need no stinkin' Rabies shot cuz garrobos are cold-blooded reptiles and do not carry Rabies. Along comes Medic#2 - same discussion. US Army Doctor-expert-of-all-he-purveys arrives and the same discussion ensues.

While these four are standing there arguing, a crusty old CWO medical type arrives on scene and says "You idiots, Sarge here is right. Reptiles are cold blooded and don't carry Rabies. Stitch him up and send him on his way." Mike hugs the Warrant Officer, gets his stitches and takes the garrobo to the morgue.

And that ain't no (feces).

Lizards, Commies, Fire Ants and Such
by Mark Atchison

I think the fire ants dropping out of trees in a firefight were a huge challenge, but God Damn It, there was nothing like a Vietnam centipede to scare the living fook out of you. These boogers, if they bit, they'd put a most serious hurt on you. They were 8-10 inches long & each segment was as large as or larger than your thumbnail. This is no shit! I'd be exaggerating if I said that rocket/mortar attacks were preferable, but the really big bugs flat scared me shitless.

Fauna
by Merlyn Eckles

The recon unit I was assigned to in '66/'67 did most of our work out in War Zone C and D. As we were in the snooping, and pooping mode, we were able to view some of the local flora and fauna, up close, and personal.

Ants:
Those little critters loved to live in bushes and trees. On one patrol, I heard this commotion behind me. It was my one-one trying to get out of his rucksack, LBE, and shirt. Seems he had brushed up against a bush that was loaded with ants, and they were proceeding to bite him, frequently, and viciously. After a few minutes we were able to remove all the ants. He had a lot of angry looking bite marks, but refused any anti-histamine, as he didn't want to dull his senses. It took all the rest of the day for the bites to disappear.

Bees:
During Black Jack 33, my one-one had the misfortune to get stung by a bee, on the back of his neck. It really caused him

a lot of pain. I gave him some antihistamine to help. The patrol spent a couple of hours, putting cool compresses on his head. This delay caused the patrol to miss getting to its assigned point, to spend the night, observing a road for a chance to check out an armored car known to be traveling along that road. As luck would have it, we heard the vehicle, saw the tracks the next day, but no sign of the car.

Pigs:
On more than one occasion we surprised a sleeping pig that startled us by it's noise and movement. We almost compromised our location by shooting the damned thing.

Squirrels:
One time, when the team was eating lunch, we attracted the attention of a red squirrel. It came down this sapling, stopped about four feet away, and proceeded to give us hell. When I would throw a stick at it, it would only run up the tree about six feet, then come back down and continue to chatter at us. After about a dozen times playing this game, it got tired, and moved on which allowed us to continue with our "pak "time.

Chicken:
As the team was moving along, we heard this funny "erk" sound coming towards us. We dropped down on one knee, and turned to face the noise, as it drew closer. Out of the jungle burst this dirty, white chicken, running hell bent for leather. Every time it squawked, it flapped it's wings. When it saw us, it let out several squawks, started trying to fly past us, and disappeared into the jungle. It took us a few minutes to let things quiet down, before we could continue the patrol.

Gibbon:

Once we attracted the attention of a black simian, with white fur around its face. We were so startled when we first saw it; we thought it was a V.C. sniper in the tree. This guy was upset with us; and kept pace with us as we traveled through the jungle. It would break off small branches, and throw them at us. We stopped to let him go away, but he stopped also, and continued to throw branches at us. After two or three starts and stops, he tired of the game, and took off. We were worried that all the commotion would attract the attention of the V.C.

Leeches:
The Cambodes were really afraid of those things. If leeches were around, they would not kneel or lie down, when stopping for breaks, or to listen. They would only squat down, and their heads and eyes were going around, a mile a minute, to check out the surrounding area for leeches. No amount of instruction by me would get them to keep a sharp eye out for the V.C. They were too busy with the leech patrol.

Unknown Animal:
One night, after the team made its commo check, ate the evening meal and settled in, a small rodent type animal (I thought it was a Kangaroo Rat) jumped into the middle of our night position. The team's night position was with our heads together like the hub of a wheel with our bodies out like spokes. Well this critter jumped into the midst of us, and we commenced to whale on the little guy with our hats. It was squeaking and jumping. We were whaling, and trying to keep the noise down to a low roar. Eventually, the animal moved on, things quieted down, and we could get back to sweet dreams. No harm, no foul. I never saw any snakes on patrol except for one cobra at the F.O.B. at Quan Loi. The strikers chased it all around the area, before chopping it's head off with an E-tool.

Leech Repellant
by Merle Eckles

In B-56, in '67, we were given some plastic bottles of leech repellent to test. Bottles were same as mosquito repellent, but did not have the plug with the hole in it. The repellent was yellow goo, similar to Vaseline, and smelled like nicotine. I only used it one time because of the odor. I put it around the tops of my boots. Worked real good.

I was only bitten once. It fell out of a tree, and attached itself to my earlobe. After it drank its fill, it fell off, and then I felt the blood running down my neck. It took a couple of weeks to heal.

The leeches were fully alert to my body heat, since I was the third person in line during the patrol; and they moved towards me, from all sides. They looked like those 'Schmoos" creatures out of the Lil Abner Comic strip, with the heads of their bowling pin bodies waving around, trying to get a good fix on my position. Also, when we would stop the patrol for any reason, the indig, would only squat down, not lie down. They would also be so busy checking out the surrounding area for leeches, they wouldn't have time to keep a lookout for the VC. Sometimes when we took the troops down to the river to bath, we would see these big leeches in the water, three to four inches long. A lot of our indig had scars on their bodies from leech bites that got infected when they were children.

Dinosaurs
by Mike Parks

There was some dinosaur looking things around Budop that weighed probably 20 pounds or more. I only saw two of them. Yards caught them on a couple of our camping trips, tied them to their packs and brought them home for supper after ripening for a couple of days. They were black, over six feet long, had big back legs and little bitty front ones. Sure looked like dinosaurs. Glad we never found their mother. They had a lot of big teeth. Saw a tiger track the size of a pie pan.

Tookaas
by Randy Cesani

The leeches in Thailand were called Tookaas. Like their brothers in Vietnam, you never saw them - just heard them. The Thai's caught one in Lopbur, and they were mean little buggers. They had sharp little teeth that slanted back so they locked when they bit down. We put a pencil in its mouth and then couldn't get it out. The little ones were called chinchoks and they were silent and harmless except they wiggled in your mouth when you got drunk and ate one.

I saw a Tiger south of Ben Het. He was down the hill from us maybe 50 yards or more. He looked skinny and bounded away when he saw, smelled us. I didn't sleep too well that night.

One BIG Lizard
by Robert Pryor

My first encounter with the dreaded "F--k You" lizard was at Vung Tau. Nobody had warned me about them. It was my first night there. I was staying on the second floor of the "Grand Hotel". Nice room with French doors that opened out onto a small veranda. I was in the room when some communist mofo out on the veranda yells "F--K YOOU!" Like Reg, I too went for the grease gun. Not all that good of a weapon, but intimidating as all Hell. Besides, I could sweep those French doors as those VC hordes came charging through.

Here I am at the ready, but nothing. Then another "F--K YOU!" then another. Okay, I figured it out; Charlie has an ambush set up for my young ass on the veranda. With the best defense being a strong offense, I slowly start making my way to the French doors, ready to open up with my weapon. A couple more fuck you's as I make my way. I cautiously check the veranda, including the blind spots, and nothing. No VC were visible.

I got tired of this coward shit and did a John Wayne through the double doors. There he was, on the outside wall of my room. My first up close and personal look at a f--k you lizard. Thank goodness I didn't start shooting. I felt like a fucking idiot, and when I got back to Bunard I never mentioned a word about it. I didn't want to spend the rest of my tour in Viet Nam having to hear about it from my teammates.

By the way, that f--king lizard weighed every ounce of ten pounds. Well, maybe not, but he was one big mofo. I have read here on the SF-List comments from guys that say it was those small geckos. Well, if that's the case, they sure grow up to be some big assed lizards.

F—k You Lizards
by Reggie Manning

The first one of those critters I ever heard was during radio watch at about 0200 at Katum.

The commo bunker/CONEX box had an air vent pipe behind the radio stack. Prolly a 12-inch diameter pipe to let some of that infernal heat out. The pipe outlet had screen wire (to keep the bugs out) and rat wire (to keep grenades out) over the interior opening.

The lizard was ensconced therein.

I was sitting there trying to stay awake and somebody or something said "F—k you!" I went straight up in the air. It was all I could do to keep from emptying my .45 and the commo bunker's M-3 grease gun into the air vent opening.

Everybody had a good laugh when they looked in the log book the next morning, and read, "Somebody said 'F--k You' at 0218."

Leeches and Mosquitoes
by Steve Shanahan

I am reminded of the hoards of small, dark forest leeches in Western Quang Duc Prov. Rainy weather or dry, they were always waiting for a warm body to pass by and French kiss. Since not wearing socks or underwear was my habit, I got them critters on my nuts and in my boots, down between my toes, as well as everywhere else. I couldn't feel them until they got to the dessert portion of their meal, all tight and full. If they were a food source for some higher animal, that critter group was more than well fed. If birds ate them, then there weren't enough birds.

Leeches were a nuisance, but not as bad as the damn mosquitoes. Those babies will drive you insane. The GI insect repellent worked pretty well, but humping and sweating like a mule would dilute it and wash it off, allowing for periods of free feeding for these little diseased blood-suckers. I got myself a nice case of falciparal (plasmodium falciparum?) malaria from them. Leeches are pests but mosquitoes will kill you.

Abalone
by Terry Dahling

We were on an FTX with Thai SF at Kanchanaburi. At a party for the end of the exercise I was offered a roasted lizard. I had already had my share of cobra blood and Mekong. I popped the lizard into my mouth and swallowed. When I saw the look on the Thai SF faces I realized I was supposed to pull off the legs and eat them.

Flesh Eating Fables
by Terry Dahling

While waiting for the school bus we used to have crawdad fights. We'd face two off and bet on whose would be pushed off the bridge rail into the water. Not being too bright, I looked those crawdads over real good and decided that those little tiny pincers weren't too dangerous. Sooo, I stuck my finger into one to make a point. Mistake! That sucker wouldn't let go even after I separated him from his claw. Had to totally destroy the claw to get loose.

Leech Valley
by Wil Wiltgen

I spent a year or two one month in I Corps. The NVA was supposed to overrun DaNang. We launched 3 MF companies from B-55. No way were we going to let a couple NVA divisions fuck with DaNang! The Marines inserted us in the vicinity of Thung Duc A Camp. We ran ops in their AO looking for the big build up. Two places that stick with me very vividly were two valleys on the map...one named Happy Valley (which wasn't) and Leech Valley (which was). Leech Valley has to be the most appropriately named spot on the planet. Every leaf on every bush had a leech doing their little "search dance". I was a veteran of the leech campaigns in III Corps. I learned to live with it. Leeches were one of the reasons we slept in jungle hammocks instead of the ground. When setting up our RON position I'd do a final check for leeches on the body, switch into dry black PJs and squirt some insect repellant on the hammock strings to keep the SOBs from flanking me at night. Of all the shit that walked, crawled, swam and flew in there I place leeches waaaay down on the list of hazards. I actually liked leeches...they taste a lot like worms.

A "Santa Out"
by Jerry Braudrick

I arrived in Alameda, Calif. for an honorable discharge from the Army. What a culture shock that was. Just twenty-four hours or so earlier, I had been drinking beer at the Da Nang SF club. I was listening to the radio in the commo room about the patrol from Ba To (sp) that had been overrun.

The team Capt. was telling Da Nang, that he was taking everyone out of camp to go find his people. Sgt. Logan, the other demo man from Ha Thanh, had been sent in with me for a Santa Out. We both volunteered to go out with the Nungs to help find the patrol. They told us that there was no way they would take a chance on getting either of us shot this close to going home.

Seemed like just a few hours later an army dentist was telling me that I would have to stay in the Army for a few days so he could fix my teeth. Told him, "No, Sir. Thank you anyway. I'll worry about my teeth after Christmas." An army doctor tells me about the same thing when I tell him about my stomach problems and the fact that I didn't shit anymore. Just squirted like a fire hose. I told him I would be fine as soon as I got the VN water out of my system. With that done, Logan and I took a taxi ride to San Fran.

We told the driver to find a nice but cheap hotel and drop us off. As soon as we had our room and put our duffle bags away, we were off. I stopped in the lobby and got two match books. One was for Logan, who looked at me kind of funny and said, "After a year together, don't you know I don't smoke? Told him they were not for smokin'. "This will be your E&E map if we get separated." Back then all hotels put their name and address on the match book covers.

I don't recall paying for dinner or drinks all night long. Everywhere we went, we were the center of attention. It was a good thing. About 0130 hrs, we got a cab to a liquor store and picked up two bottles of booze. No idea what the hell I was drinking; probably bourbon and water. The California drinking laws used to be "no service after 0200". Maybe it still is. The cab driver took us to an after hours place where there were about two or three single women to every guy! Set ups to go with your booze were $1.00 for coke/water.

My memory gets real fuzzy from here on out. I just remember drinkin' till I could drink no more. The match book must have worked because I woke up in the hotel room. Logan came in around noon. He said he never would have found me if not for the match book in his pocket. Two young ladies had taken him home to their apt, and he woke up on the floor wearing nothing but a smile and a sheet. He said he must have had a ball, but damned if he could remember what or if he had done. I asked him what the ladies had to say before he left. He said while they were in the kitchen fixing him breakfast, he found the match book and sneaked out to catch a cab to come check on me. Now he couldn't remember where the hell their apt was. He wanted to know if I had been as lucky as he thought he might have been. Got no idea what I did? Sure hope if I did, that I performed as only a good SFer can.

I was my mother's Christmas present Dec. 1965.

BBQ Master
by Terry Dahling

We roasted a pig in Thailand and I was elected the spit man. Between the heat, beer and Mekong, I just made it until the pig was done before passing out. When I came to, the pig was all gone and I was in Ed Foushee's room. His son drowned some time ago in a pond in Lop Buri and his wife kept his ashes in the bed room. Some how I managed to knock the urn onto the floor. You should have seen Ed and me scrambling to get the ashes back into the urn.

I've had better luck roasting a pig in a closed barbeque and with a thermometer.

Must be a Thailand thing. Charlie Gray and I bought and cooked a pig overnight at what I think was eventually called Camp Pine, to Hell and gone at the north end of the country. We cooked that thing all night long, accompanied by a whole lot of beer. When it was done the next morning, so were we. We did manage to stay on our feet long enough to bring in a load of the local beauties for a party that day. Charlie, being from NC, controlled the recipe, so we did East Coast style. It was tasty.

I don't know how it happened but we roasted a pig in Panama and when they went to check it, it was a mass of worms.

Strange Supply Requests
by Bill Coombs

When I was with the 10th SFG, we used to go to France each year on a Fall Maneuver. The teams would go into isolation at the SFOB and then fly out all over Europe, jump in and do their thing.

Like all Special Forces units overseas, we worked for the Joint Unconventional Warfare Task Force (JUWTF). It was pronounced JUTFA, but of course, we would call them JUT FUCK. The real name of the office was the Support Operational Task Force - Europe (SOTFE). It was located just outside of Paris in a building called the blockhouse. It was a joint command, and the J-4 at the time was U.S. Marine Corps Full Colonel K. (I am not sure of the spelling). What a gruff old son of gun he was.

About a week before we were to leave for France, I answered the phone in the S-4 and it was Colonel K. calling from Paris. The Major and NCOIC were not there so I took the message. He said, "When you come to France next week, bring the following things with you: 1,000 lined tablets, 1,000 pencils, 1,000 erasers, a working model of a steam engine and 5,000 balloons." I said, "Yes Sir" and he hung up.

We had no problems with the lined tablets and pencils and erasers but the working model of a steam engine presented a challenge. Then, there were the balloons. As this was in September of 1961 or 1962 (I don't recall which but naturally, it was before DeGaulle threw us out of France), the summer season was over and the PX's had no more balloons. We placed the order with our supply point in

Munich and told them to ship the balloons to us at Dreaux Air Force Base near St Andre in France.

A week or so later, I was unloading my truck in the hanger at the AF base when the field phone we just hooked up rang. I answered it and it was, you guessed it, Colonel K. Again, no Major and no NCOIC were there. He asked, "Coombs, do you have that stuff I told you to bring?" I told him we had the lined tablets, the pencils, and the erasers but we could not find a working model of a steam engine. He then said that he thought that would be a problem and that it was OK.

Then he asked, "Did you bring the Mickey Mouse head balloons??" MICKEY MOUSE HEADS?? What the hell was he talking about? He never mentioned Mickey Mouse to me. I saw my SP4 stripes fluttering away.

I was trying to figure out what we needed balloons for. I knew that we sometimes used balloons on the rifle range as targets. No doubt if you hit them. So now the Spec Four in Charge made what he thought was a good suggestion to the Colonel. I told him that we were not able to get the balloons but how about using condoms as the targets. There was a pause and then he asked, "What are you talking about, Coombs? What targets? I want Mickey Mouse head balloons." I asked him if Yogi Bear head balloons would work and he said they had to be Mickey Mouse heads.

About that time, Major B., my boss, came in. I told him that the colonel was on the phone and what he said. He was laughing so hard he could hardly talk. When he finally composed himself, he took the phone and talked to Col. K. What this was all about was we were sending teams into several countries on this maneuver. The balloons were not going to be used as targets but as gifts to the local kids.

Mickey Mouse automatically meant the USA. Those kids would have no idea who Yogi Bear was.

To make a long story even longer, I called my contact in Munich, sat back and listened to him laugh about the Mickey Mouse head balloons for awhile. What happened was an "emergency" request went from Germany to the USA for the balloons. When they came in, we had to convert dollars to marks to francs to pay for them. It was a Finance Department nightmare but we accomplished the mission, and the teams went into battle with all of their combat equipment ...and the Mickey Mouse head balloons.

VC C-rations
by Bill Adams

There I was. Weapon in hand, a nicely blued S&W .38 revolver, five-inch barrel. T'was a purty piece, and, although a little old, still good in the tunnels.

I was taking aim when I decided to rest my shooting arm a spell, and as I was bringing it back down with muzzle pointed toward the earth, my thumb slipped off the hammer. I was in the process of lowering the hammer as I was lowering the weapon. I was standing on a good patch of concrete at the time and the slug dug a small hole to the right of my right foot, spraying concrete up against the right side of my foot.

Did it hurt? Well, if had been from WBG, Virginia I'd say no, it didn't hurt. But the truth is I ain't from WBG, Virginia and it hurt like hell!! On top of that, that damn VC C-ration can I was shooting at got away!

The Dance of the Flaming Assholes
by Bill Coombs

The first time I saw this was when guys of the 22nd SAS from Hereford, UK were in Bad Toelz in 1962 or 1963. They were in the club, suggested the guys do the "Dance of the Flaming Assholes" and the loser would buy the drinks.

Two of them demonstrated it by rolling up some newspapers, dropping their drawers, putting newspapers between their legs from the rear, and lighting them on fire. The first one to open his legs and drop the burning newspaper had to buy the round.

I don't know how the winners could stand it. The losers either for that matter. Being the chicken that I was, I did not volunteer.

The Girls of Bad Toelz
by Bill Coombs

I recall a guy in the 10th who came to Toelz unaccompanied. His wife would join him later. He went to the Weinhaus, other places and mingled with the gals. He did not wear his wedding ring and told the girls that he was a bachelor. About two weeks before his wife arrived, he stopped going to town. Guess he figured the girls would forget him. Then his wife arrived.

He was walking down the Marktstrasse (the main street in town) showing her around. I don't think he planned to take her to Weinhaus or the Knockerstuebl. Anyhow, as he is walking his bride through town, a couple of the lovelies see him; they spot the wedding ring and his wife. I think one of them was Big-Titted Erica, but I don't recall. Then they played a nasty trick on him.

They crossed over the street, pretending that they thought his wife was German, started kissing him and hugging him and speaking to the wife in German. Then, all of sudden, it dawned on them (wink wink) that she was an American and must be his wife. They apologized to him and continued on down the street.

Of course this guy must have told his wife that he was a straight arrow all the time he was waiting for her. After that little demonstration, she knew better. She ended up going back to CONUS and I think they got divorced.

If he had only told the girls while he was waiting for his frau that he was married, probably none of this would have happened. He brought it on himself.

Honesty is the best policy so they say. They also say a hard dick has no conscience.

Fetch
by Charlie Fraley

I am reminded of a friend who a few years back was having a New Years party. He lived a ways off the beaten path and decided that to greet the New Year he would set off some dynamite for our enjoyment. He lit a 1/4 stick and tossed it out into the backyard where his dog promptly retrieved it and started running towards us! People scattered everywhere; my friend, my brother-in-law and I proceeded to chase the damned mutt attempting to catch him before it blew. Fortunately it had a long fuse and we were able to get it before everyone was covered in dog.

Needless to say, my friend's LYB no longer allows him to "play with fireworks".

Moose Turd Pie
by Bob Smith

When I was at DLI, I used to sleep with the radio tuned to KFAT out of Gilmore, CA. They always had some crazy shit on there. One morning...about 4:00 am I awoke to a story about a guy who once worked, in his younger years, as a track repairman for the Union Pacific.

The UP...being cheap...would provide a boxcar with extra rail, crossties, spikes, etc....a sleeping car and a cook car for the maintenance crew. They were too cheap to even hire a cook for the cook car. So.....the last guy to complain about the chow became the cook...the lowest job you could have!

Story goes....said new guy one day complains about the lousy chow and ends up being the cook. It being summer...and the car being hotter than hammering rails...he decides to get his ass out of his current position.

So....he goes out into the prairie and gets him a fresh moose turd. He then proceeds to cook the best meal he ever has.

....steak, mashed potatoes, green beans, corn.....pie.

For the pie he makes a delicious crust....places it in the pie pan and dumps the moose turd into it. He then makes those nice little lattice crosses on it and cooks it.

When the dinner is served, everyone sits down and consumes, with relish, the dinner. The biggest, meanest, ugliest S.O.B. on the crew finished first. He then asked for the dessert. The cook sliced him up a piece of the "special" pie.

When the brute took a bite of the pie he jumped up and yelled "God Damn....this tastes like Moose Turd Pie...but it's GOOD!"

Bourboned Chivalry
by David Stafford

I once went on a booze cruise in Boston Harbor. Northeastern University ran the show. They had a band, three full levels of plenty of room, and a dance floor where my imbalances caused me to burn a hole in a bonecrusher's nice aligatored, upturned collared, costly (I guess) shirt.

The thing that stands out the most was the fact that with hundreds of early twentyish flesh bumping and grinding into one another; on a good sized boat with three levels of potential and active romantic chaos. Only two restrooms were provided on this sizeable craft.

Halfway through the evening the angriest female bladders split their long line and broke off into the men's room. Some of those sphincter stressed faces weren't so appealing then, regardless of how well they painted themselves up for a dose of masculine attention.

Going as heavy on the sauce as we did, many of the classiest guys (me included) opted to climb to the highest, less consolidated level, force our way along the rail between the masses swapping spit and grinding pelvic regions, and urinated off the back to the dismay of anyone caught in a wind receiving position below. I had about five giggling belligerents there with me. I might have hit a Rolex or two with my jetting stream.

Made a lot of good friends that night.

Didn't give that crusher one slim dime for that shirt he used to knock the head off my cigarette with, either. That crusher ended up taking a shine to me though. I offered to replace the garment and tried to pass him my leather jacket for collateral. He didn't go for it. Therefore, my bourboned chivalry impressed a few people, and his gorgeous girlfriend ended up leaving with me.

Nice guys finish first. Always have in my book. Texas Jim is one such example.

En Route to Dinner
by Gary Lamberty

On one of my trips up to Nha Trang, a few of us were invited to have dinner with Ko Jea Duk, the Korean Tae Kwon Do instructor at the SFOB. On the road, right before we got to the ROK compound, our Jeep was stopped by some White Mouse/QC (Vietnamese MP) at a roadblock with those A-frame, sawhorse-type things on the ends. Ko had a few words with the guard; even though I couldn't understand what they were saying, they both started getting pissed.

It looked like the guy wasn't gonna let us pass, but Ko finally got out of the jeep (he was driving), walked over to the roadblock, and commenced to smash the shit out of it with his hands and feet. The guard just stood there with a dumb look on his face as Ko got back in the jeep and drove over the wooden remains. Dinner was almost as exciting. I think it was the first time I ate pulgogi, pindetto, and kimchi (sp for all 3?).

Chad
by Greg Hoisington

When I was a cop, I worked for a short time for a Patrol Sgt who was a clean patrol car fanatic. He had pulled something on me, and it was time to strike back. I went into the Records section, where they used paper tape machines to record info, and retrieved a couple of handfuls of the little chad thingies that were punched out and fell into a collection box in the bottom of the machine. Took them out to his favorite Sgt's car and dumped them down the defrosters, set the controls on defrost and put the fan switch to the max.

Just to add a little over-kill, I collected all the butts from other cars and filled his ashtray, another thing he hated. For the finale, knowing that he had allergies, I squirted just a tiny bit of Mace on his sun visor. This would be just enough to make eyes water a little, and maybe a little nose-running, but subtly.

After briefing, I grabbed my shotgun, got my car and hit the road, visualizing him climbing in, turning the key, and thousands of little "holes" flying out of the defrosters. After the shock and cleaning up, he would get on the road and discover that not only was his ashtray full (oh, my!), but his allergies were also acting up. Keeping a straight face when the subject was brought up was a supreme effort.

Aahhh yes, law enforcement was serious business... Right there in Ben Roberts' very own Goleta.

Cold C's
by Greg Hoisington

I could handle eating cold C's (after scrapping the congealed grease off the top) because I was always hungry. What would piss me off during training was to have to dump my favorite concoction, made of things I had saved up for days, because we got hit.

I remember running through at least a hundred yards of saw grass in Panama, determined to get away and to the rally point, WITH my freshly brewed and un-tasted hot cup of mocha (2 coffees, 1 cocoa, 3 sugars and all the creamers available). That would have made a great video... ruck over one shoulder, rifle in one hand, hot canteen cup in the other, attempting to run through waist-high saw grass that was trying to rip my jungles off <BG>. Hated to dump that cup.

Also remembering slugging down packets of coffee with a sip of water to stay awake... yuk.

Broken Leg
anonymous from Don Valentine

This is a true story about Carlos P. He lost a leg in VN and stayed in SF on jump status. One night on a jump he broke his artificial leg. A female medic came over to check him out and asked what happened. He answered, "Broke my leg"; then pulled the broken end of his prosthesis out of his trousers leg. The female medic fainted.

Hang Fire
by Greg Hoisington

I've got a pretty good pain tolerance and don't usually take pain meds after I get hurt or repaired, but I was a hurtin' puppy after hernia surgery. Two on one side and one on the other. The doc had given me a prescription for Percodan or Percocet, and I was taking them according to the instructions. It didn't help any that I could tell, so I doubled up on the dose. Still didn't help, but I became terminally constipated. Well, says I, it will be time when it is time...

A day or so later, I noticed it was getting difficult to urinate, and I felt like I had to go all the time. Then I couldn't. I must have been so packed that it was putting pressure on something. Got scared and called the doc, who said to have the LYB go get a bottle of magnesium citrate, drink it and don't get too far from the toilet.

Well, I gots to tell you that that little innocent looking green bottle contains some nuclear grade blockage bursting power. F--k a bunch of SADM; two bottles of magnesium citrate would take out the Hoover Dam.

Within minutes, I was looking for a seatbelt, riding my throne like an astronaut, wondering at the power of the rocket force beneath me, and hoping I could reach the flush handle before the second stage took over.

Bottom line (no pun), with such assistance there will be no hang fires. You could effortlessly give birth to sea lions or manatees - all for the small price of that little green bottle.

Therapy for Skip
by Bruce "Hardcore" Koch

Somewhere around 1980, I ran in a distance race at Ft. Bragg. IIRC, it was the Jingle Bell Jog sponsored by 7th Group. My buddy and arguably one of the fastest runners at Bragg, Lonnie "Skip" P. was also a participant.

Being an experienced runner, he should never have made such a dumb mistake. Most people who participate in long distance events eschew wearing a jock strap because it is too easy to acquire galled balls. Good quality running shorts have a support built-in, and are made of synthetic fabric, usually a blend of nylon and other things. However, they have a drawback in that in cold weather, they will wick the moisture from your body and the heat also. When running at temperatures in the 40's and below, one should wear underwear beneath.

Skip was so pumped up over his impending duel with Marlin C., a lanky finance clerk from the 82d that he forgot to properly prepare.

He won the race, and had an exhausted, happy, painful smile on his face. I asked, "WTF?", and he relied that the end of his dick was hurting like hell. I advised him to check in at Womack ASAP.

I saw him in my office later that afternoon. He had a big shit eating grin on his face, and said that there would be no permanent damage. He also stated that the therapy the nurse gave him was great.

The Prized Rooster
by Hugh Johnson

Zebediah was in the fertilized egg business. He had several hundred young layers, called pullets, and eight or ten roosters, whose job was to fertilize the eggs. Zeb kept records, and any rooster that didn't perform well went into the soup pot and, was replaced. That took an awful lot of Zeb's time; so, Zeb got a set of tiny bells, and attached them to his roosters. Each bell had a different tone so that Zeb could tell, from a distance, which rooster was performing.

Now he could sit on the porch and fill out an efficiency report simply by listening to the bells. Zeb's favorite rooster was Old Brewster. A very fine specimen he was, too. However, on this particular morning, Zeb noticed that Brewster's bell had not rung at all!! Zeb went to investigate.

The other roosters were chasing pullets, bells a-ringing! The pullets, hearing the roosters coming, would run for cover; but, to Zeb's amazement, Brewster had his bell in his beak, so it couldn't ring. He'd sneak up on a pullet, do his job and walk on to the next one.

Zeb was so proud of Brewster that he entered him in the County fair. Brewster was an overnight sensation!

The judges not only awarded him the No Bell Piece Prize but also the Pulletsurprise.

Sorry...but a good pun is refreshing every now and then!

PSP
by James Lewis

While at A-432 on the Mekong, someone showed up with a couple of 40 ft Navy boats. We decided to use them as a helicopter pad. Built a wooded frame and I went into the C team in Canto to get some PSP. There were two piles in the yard. When I found out that one was for Ma'cek and the other for whatever, I went for the other. Loaded it on a truck and took it down to the airfield to get a C-123 to haul it out to the camp. Didn't think I would get away with taking it as Ma'cek and the Company Supply SGT were watching me from a balcony. I am sure that each was thinking that I was taking the other's PSP.

Talked the AF into hauling it out to my camp and within a couple of days, had a floating helicopter pad. Meanwhile, the S-4 missed the PSP and found out that I had it. He sent me a message to return it ASAP. Sent him a message back that, "possession was nine tenths of the law" and didn't hear anything for a couple of days.

The first helicopter that landed on it was carrying the Company Commander, LTC Hass'ger. When he got out, he looked around, complimented me on having such a fine landing zone and asked me where I got the materials to build it. I was sure that he already knew, so I just laughed and said," Sir, if I told you I might get court martialed"…hoping the CID isn't looking for me or that the statue of limitations has run out.

Col. Orderly
by James Savell

It was early '69, and I was assigned to 6th group. In those days guard duty was not duty rostered but assigned for the month. Guard Mount was at Bronze Bruce. It was a ritual and nothing like in regular units. You tried not to be "Colonels Orderly" because that "man" didn't pull duty that night but had to report to the "Puzzle Palace" the next day and be a "gopher" for the SGM and Col all day while everyone else was off. Seems there was a lot of rank, so E-6 and below were sentinels.

We formed up this particular guard mount, and the OD (Officer of the Day) was a scrawny, pimple faced, 2LT; and he was wearing a pistol that hung down because he was too thin to fit the belt. Usually the OD would go through a ritual, and in short order would finish but not this 2LT. He would ask the SGT of the Guard all kinds of questions. Next was the Commander of the relief (we had 4 ranks). When he got to the 2nd guard that was armed with an M-16, the 2LT asked him for one of the General Orders. The guard reached in his pocket, pulled out a card and read the General Order to him. The 2lt asked him if he knew his General Orders, and he said he had them right there on the card.

The 2Lt didn't know what to say...but he had to say something. "Well, what if it is dark?"

"Well, sir, I got this heah' flashlight. See how I can read this card," and he demonstrated.

The 2LT gave him his rifle back and came in front of me. I didn't do anything except normal stuff. Then he went to the next guard. He snatched the M-16 to inspect it and you next guard. He snatched the M-16 to inspect it and you could hear the bolt close as he took it. I really don't believe this 2LT had much knowledge of an M-16. Well, he looked it over real good as he asked all sorts of questions. He then presented the rifle back to the guard, who just stood at attention. The 2LT then inspected the rifle some more and turned it around (I figure he thought he had it backwards). The guard just stood there. Then, he inspected it some more, and when he presented it he said "Take this rifle."

"No sir, I gave you the rifle with the bolt open", said the guard.

The 2LT looked at the bolt and finally got it opened, but closed the dust cover. He then presented it and the guard just stood there. By now there was some snickering in the other ranks. The 2LT was red as a "beet". Very quietly he said, "SGT,pease take this rifle".

"No sir, when I gave you my rifle the dust cover was open", said the guard very loudly.

Now there was loud laughter in the other ranks. The 2LT then tried to pry open the dust cover with his fingernail. The SGT of the Guard snatched the rifle, opened the bolt and told the guard to take this rifle. The 2LT almost ran the rest of the way through the inspection, and in about a minute was departing the area. I was sure thankful someone in the 4th rank was selected as Col Orderly.

"Fowler went across today. He forgot his Swedish K..."
by Jim Stewart

Those were the first two lines of a not so famous song - set to the tune of Ballad of the Green Berets. The guys from FOB-2 composed it on very short notice, in July 1966 while waiting for the Members of RT Dakota to return from a mission. That mission and the 1-0 of RT Dakota are still remembered and retold by the FOGs of FOB-2 every year at SOAR when we have our "Last Man Standing" reunion, open a bottle of cognac and toast our comrades who opened SOG's FOB-2 in 1966.

I had been assigned to Kontum's Hatchet Force a little over a month when asked by the 1-0 of RT Dakota to take the job as his 1-1. I had been trying to get this assignment since my arrival in Kontum, and it didn't take me long to accept the offer.

About a week later, RT Dakota was alerted for what would be my first trip "across the fence" into Laos. After the alert, the 1-0, Don Fowler(RIP), flew a VR of the target area to view the area and to pick an LZ for insertion. The next day we were flown to Dak To for our final operational briefing at the TOC located on the airstrip, and boarded the Chopper for the flight and insertion into the target area.

We didn't suffer any casualties on that mission, but that outcome was in doubt right up to the moment we finally arrived back to Dak To five days later. So, as not to alert the "bad guys" in the target Area, we inserted two days walk from the target. Everything went well until we moved into the vicinity on the second day. We had secured some high ground, were preparing for a RON, had just made our evening contact with the FAC and would not have another contact until the next morning, when all hell broke loose from the security positions we had posted.

The security was in contact with a company sized unit of bad guys. Luckily we were able to contact the Airborne CP and get two A1Es into the area to help us break contact. Then we spent that night going back down the mountain that had taken us two days to climb. We had hoped to get an extraction the next morning after our scheduled contact with the FAC, but as usual when you think that things can't get any worse, they do. We made our morning contact with the FAC, but couldn't see him. The whole area was socked in tight; no way could we get a chopper in for extraction. So, we ran all that day and night and were greeted by our FAC and broken clouds the next morning.

We used our survival saws to cut an LZ for the Kingbee that we knew was on the way - NOT! Unknown to us, one of the KingBees returning RT Nevada had crashed killing all aboard and all the VN Pilots were in mourning - not flying. When we heard the sound of the approaching chopper it was a sweet sound but at the same time it was a disturbing sound. Even before we saw the chopper, we knew from the sound that it was a HU1E. We had cleared for a Kingbee that could lift straight up. Not so for the HU1E. He got in all right, but on lift off the main rotor hit a piece of bamboo near the edge of the LZ. It took a piece of the rotor off and the Pilot told us later that he know how we managed to get back to Dak To.

Soooo, what does all this have to do with the title of my story? Well, I skipped the part about my 1-0 talking to the Pilot on the intercom about 10 - 15 minutes out from the insertion point. A couple of minutes later the Crew Chief brought an M-16 and a bandolier of ammunition over to my 1-0. It seems that Fowler had left his Swedish "K" in the briefing tent on the airstrip at Dak To. Don Fowler would become the first member of SOG to carry a US weapon across the fence into Laos and have the dubious honor of hearing his name in the song that was sang regularly in the bar by the guys at FOB-2 in Kontum.

When we landed back at Kontum and the Team was headed to the bar to get the traditional "Cold One" after a mission, the FOB-2 Singers greeted us - "Fowler went Across today. He forgot his Swedish K." and our resident artist had already drawn a picture which was displayed behind the bar, unmistakably our 1-0, straddling a barbed wire fence with his pants down around his ankles. RT Dakota would be inserted many more times on missions into Laos, but the mission most remembered was the one when the 1-0 left his "SK" in the TOC at Dak To.

Sentry's Challenge
by Jack Nesmith

3rd Tng. Reg't Ft Gordon, Ga., across the street from A Co. and C Co. 7th Bn. was a POV parking lot. We had a lot of young officers right out of ROTC and IOBC. The OG one night was checking guards and approached the sentry, tall slender black guy "Halt Who Goes There?"

The OG said, "Cpt. Midnight," the sentry replied, "Advance MOFO and meet Superman"!

The OG didn't get laughed off post, but he took a lot of heat.

Light Sleeping Bags
by Jim Stewart

In the summer of '63, our A Team (A-10) jumped into Greece with a mission to train some members of the Greek Raiding Forces.

Before we deployed, John Southworth, Dave Boyd –RIP, and I, thought we would be smart and make a light sleeping bag. We bought some summer sleeping bags from the Alabama Depot in Munich (actually just a GI blanket folded with a zipper); then we lined them with parachute material. Those things were compact and weighed hardly anything.

We were the envy of every other guy on the team - at least until the first night after we arrived in the training area, the highest mountains in Greece. Long story shortened, the three of us froze our butts off for three weeks, and Ed Sprague (RIP) never let us forget it.

The Average Summer Temperatures that were in the study of the area must have been taken from the lowlands, because they sure as hell weren't correct for the area we were in.

Boots for Ba Kev
by Jack Nesmith

I was sitting in the rear with a beer one morning and the radio keyed up.

"NOVEMBER" this is "WHISKEY". Great OPSEC on our net! Billy W. called and wanted 100 pair of jungle boots, size 4, 5 and 6. I went to see a big fat assleg Arty officer S-4 hooked up with the CWO PBO at Bn. S-4 and the horse trading began! I offered him 55 gals. 30Wt. Motor oil.

The old Chief said," There ain't 55gals. of 30 Wt. in all of the Pleiku area."

Then I proceeded to do what any good SF NCO is capable of, borrowed the Chiefs ¾ ton and went and got a barrel of oil. I traded the barrel of oil for 99 pair of boots. Summer of '70 there was a shortage of 30 wt. in Pleiku.

Gorgeous Turd
by Bruce "Hardcore" Koch

That is what happened to me on R & R in Australia. Me and my buddy were sharing a suite in a hotel with adjoining bathrooms and bedrooms. We had been there about three days eating steak and eggs three times a day, and scarfing up all the fresh dairy products and cheese and baked goods that we could hold, not to mention copious quantities of Aussie beer.

Well, late one morning I sat down to do my duty; and instead of the usual wet fizzy result, I felt a vaguely remembered sensation. Here came this long, round, firm thing - the most gorgeous turd that I had seen in months. I walked out of the bathroom after admiring it for a few minutes and then yelled at my buddy, to come and see what I had wrought. He was flabbergasted. He ran and got his camera and took several pictures; then ran out in the hallway and got the two maids and showed them what I had accomplished.

Their response was a fit of giggles, and "Oh, you Yanks!"

Worst Team Leader
by John Blevins

Det A 415, Tuyen Nhon in 1967 had probably the worst officer ever assigned as a commander to an A camp. This officer believed in leadership by intimidation, browbeating and insults. He was a Sp/5 before he going to OCS, and frequently bragged that he was the only OCS grad that had also served stockade time. I envy the guys who talk about what a great team they had in Viet-Nam, because our team was just about split in two by those who wanted to suck up to the commander and those who hated his guts. I have good memories of some of the guys that I served with, Tom Elr., Mervin Moats (RIP), Paul New., Tom Wal., Richard Camp., James Thom. and others, but on the whole, it was not a very close team.

Our camp cook had an attractive, well, maybe sorta cute daughter, and soon Dai was in love. I can still see them strolling through the camp hand in hand gazing deeply into each others eyes. Of course, since she was the Capt's girl, she could not be required to do the duties she was hired to do - mainly Kp and hootch cleaning.

The Capt went on R&R to Thailand and was gone a week while the whole camp rejoiced; but upon his return who should step off the aircraft with him but Mama San's daughter. The Capt. announced to one and all that this was now his wife, and would be accorded all the respect due an officer's wife. From now on, everyone in camp had to be in complete uniform at all times to include the Green Beret, all boots spit shined everyday and all the rest of the negatives associated with garrison life.

We had TV at Tuyen Nhon and one long couch where about half the team could sit and watch TV. This became a love seat for the two love birds. He would sit on one end and she would lay down on the rest of the couch with her head in his lap; and they would feed each other popcorn. I still laugh when I think about this scene with the rest of the team standing around in full uniform behind them to watch TV.

The honey moon only lasted until the first people got off site and reported what was going on. I gladly copied the message that informed him a chopper would be there for him in thirty minutes; and be on the airstrip with bag and baggage, minus a wife. I could not help grinning as I gave him the message and still had the grin on my face when I drove him out to the chopper pad. He had tears running down his face when he left.

Dirty Ole Bitch
by Larry McMillin

When I was in the 505 Abn in Mainz, Germany, I was shopping at the PX in Wiesbaden on one of my rare days off. I was in a Renault Dolphin, and the way the parking lot was arranged, you could pull into a parking place from right or left.

Well, I saw this lady coming out of the PX, and I scooted my car to where she was going to back out. She took forever to back out, but when she did I had to back up to let her out. (Small parking lot there in 1961). As soon as she backed out, in whipped a woman in a big new Ford. I pulled up behind her, snatched my door handle off and called her a dirty old bitch.

Well I was called to my Company Commanders office a few days later. Lt. Anthony B. He. said after I reported, "What's this about you calling the Col.'s wife a 'Dirty old Bitch?''

I said, "Sir, I never did that."

He asked, "Do you remember being at the PX two Sat. ago in Wiesbaden?"

I thought and said, "Yes" and told him what happened.

He said, "Well she was a dirty old Bitch, but you can't call the commander of the HQ of the AF wife a 'Dirty old bitch.' You have been counseled, so keep up the good work Sgt." RHIP

Moral: Don't buy frog autos with plastic door handles.

Toe-nail-ectomy
by Leamon Ratterree

We had a platoon of Honduran soldiers as the guard force on Tiger Island. One of the soldiers was into malingering so he didn't have to do any shit-burning, nor guard duty, nor police call, nor K.P. He always came up with something.

One day he says he cannot pull his night shift cuz his foot is bothering him. Therefore, his LT tells him to take off his boot in the presence of our medic, Doug W. Doug notices the beginning of an ingrown toenail and requests the LT bring the soldier to the clinic and have him sit on the table for a closer look. Well, with grins all around, and four healthy SF troops and the LT, Sgt W. decides that a toe-nail-ectomy is necessary in order to save the foot, and put this solder back to duty status.

When the soldier caught on to what was about to take place, he tried to put his boot on, and yelled that he felt fine. His LT ordered him to get back on the table and whilst we held him down, Doug did the nerve blocks and removed the offending toenail. The soldier was given 24 hours quarters, and never again shirked his duties during the rest of his tour on Ti.

Two-man Party
by Leamon Ratterree

During the upcoming holiday of December 20 - 5 January at Mott Lake, in 83-84, we had a conex of Demo to be done away with because the paperwork was too much of a problem and we didn't want to have to post guards on them. Therefore, when asked for volunteers, a guy and I decided we wanted to play. We took the manuals and gave each other classes. We even did our own "abatis". We daisy chained, det corded, and even launched 55 gallon drums. It was a two-man party, but at least WE got good training out of it.

"No comprende"
by Larry McMillin

I've been to Camp Kilmer NJ and will never forget that trip. About fifty of us were trying to get a flying $20. While we had to wait, there was a large number of Spanish speaking guy's there. They were all laying around in the shade and doing nothing. Not one word of English could they speak or supposedly understand. The Cadre would attempt getting a police call together and no-go. This great big Ugly M/sgt walked out and shouted "Information!" I have never in all my life seen at least 500 people assemble so fast. The Ugly M/sgt called out some names and they came forward. Then he said" Let's eat CHOW."

Those guys stampeded the one small mess hall, and most ate outside. They had enough food on a tray to feed five people. I don't remember what town it was near, but I know it was not far from Brooklyn Army terminal. I had just gotten off the Rose, or the Patch troop carrier (those were Army Ships)

Tenn-shuttt!
by Lewis "Cargo Drop" Pace

I never will forget this one bull session I was eavesdropping in on while on CQ during an alert one night. One of the team sgts and a visiting Sgt Major (both married) were comparing notes on who had the most "liberated" household. The Sgt. Major said something like, "Walllll, SHEEE-yutttt, Sarge. If the EYE-GEE wuz to step thru my front door and holler 'Tennn-shuttt!' purt'near ever' damn stick of furniture inna house'd stand up and present arms!"

I thought I was gonna CHOKE, I laughed so hard!

Turd Length Competition
by Leamon Ratterree

Mike Stangle was on an MTT and along with his teammates, was obviously quite bored. They had a contest on who could create the longest turd. They even had a tape measure brought in for the competition. IIRC the medic won with a 24 incher. Stangle's second place masterpiece was a distant 18.

The other competition they had was "the most corn found in the turd." Thaaaaaaaaat's right. They ate a lot of corn, and counted the residue in their turds.

Things we do when bored.

Getting Even
by Mel Thornton

When I was working at Mare Island in 1972 as an outside machinist in the test section, I had many run-ins with the XO of a Boomer. The sub was still in dry-dock, but some of the crew were living aboard.

My job consisted of isolating different ships systems and to a large part, pressure testing them. Over a period of months I was getting real tired of this XO and getting very familiar with the tag out and lockout procedures for valves and switches. Of special interest to me was the way they flushed the heads on a submarine. This had to be done, at times, at very high pressure (at deeper depths) to blow it out of the hull.

So each head had a large ball valve at its base to isolate it from the holding system, when it was being pressurized. I had watched a sailor on occasion go into the XO's cabin, close the ball valve, put a red tag on the handle, and followed by the system being flushed. So one day after the sailor left, I opened the valve. Even though at sea level they don't use much pressure to flush the system, there was shit, piss and toilet paper, over every sq. inch of the XO's cabin.

There was one hell of an investigation, but he was so hated by all the sailors, that no blame could be found. Moreover, civilian workers were not even suspected. It did result in a new policy. Moreover, in the future the valves were always locked out with chain and key.

Guarding the Hen House
by Mel Thornton

The post made the mistake in 1966, of they putting a group of medics, waiting to start Dog-Lab, on a detail moving pharmacy supplies from one building into trucks and then into a new building. Among the supplies were 5gal metal cans of 100% alcohol, cases of quart bottles of liquid Phenobarbital and little bottles of flavored syrup. For the next few months, the cough syrup going into the field from Training Group, used the following recipe: 80% alcohol 19% phenibarb and 1% flavoring. There just wasn't room in those tiny little bottles for any water.

Igloo Tents
by Mike Rhode

In July '67, the 3rd Herd went to Alaska for river boat, glacier and mountain training. While on Gunnysack Mountain we had an overnighter. We were issued these polar type tents that had an entranceway that could roll out similar to an igloo, if I remember correctly. At any rate they had sides and a floor. We were also issued air mattresses. That's a good thing.

We pitched our tents on the side of the mountain and my tent mate, I forget who it was, slept on the down hill side of the tent. During the night we had a pretty good rain storm. We awakened in the AM to find that our tent leaked and his air mattress was floating in about two inches of water; that's my story and I'm sticking to it.

Hard Hat
by Merlyn Eckles

When I was an apprentice excavating engineer (read laborer) for the local utility, we had an equipment operator who was a real pain in the ass. No sense of humor and a disposition like a bear with a sore tit.

He made life miserable for us hard working folk. Yeah, a great big horses ass. Did I mention nobody liked him? Anyway, one day he went to the storeroom and received the first hardhat, with attached ear muffs, in the district. He was strutting around the yard as if he was some kind of royal person. He laid the hardhat down in the crew room, along with his brand new pair of gloves. When the whistle blew at 1630, he busted his ass to get into his pickup, and lead the race out to the first traffic signal.

After I finished my shower (using the company's water), I saw the hardhat and gloves. Payback time! I got a big tube of Silicon Lubricant and greased the inside of the ear muffs, headband, and fingers of the gloves.

The next morning, when he put on his new hardhat, it almost fell off his head. His face got cherry red, and we thought he was going to bust a blood vessel. He threw it into the dumpster, and stormed off to his truck. When he got to the job, and started to put on the gloves, he really went berserk. Ranting and raving, he was jumping around and swearing. The foreman tried to calm him down to find out what was wrong, while "hardhat" was spitting, and yelling. The foreman finally got him cooled down, and had him delivered back to the office. He took a couple of vacation days and transferred to a different district.

Nobody found out it was me that was the perp, until after he retired.

Not getting mad; just getting even.

Kissing a Bunker
by Patrick McTamany

Anybody ever miss Gatun DZ and kiss a black palm? Ouch!!

As I recall there were some double and triple canopy trees down thar'. Some guys would land in the French canal. As I recall all jumps down there were with LPU's. We had guys in plastic assault boats armed with M-16's; somebody must have imagined the possibility of Camen, crocs, sharks or somethin'.

There used to be a bunker in the middle of Gatun which got kissed several times before they destroyed it. As memory serves me, SGM. M. did the job on the bunker. Mac might remember all this stuff. What say you, Mac?

Burning Down Vietnam
by Reggie Manning

Gotta tell one on my own self, about how I just about, single-handedly, blew up and burned down Katum.

During the wet season, the grass grew up 'waaay too tall in the wire and the surrounding minefields. CIDG wasn't about to go out there and cut it. Me either, because nobody knew where the mines and trip wires were anymore. But the tall grass was a real danger.

So, one day a spray-equipped Huey came and flew circles around the camp for awhile and sprayed weed killer (AO???) on all of it from the berm out about 300 meters or so. Not long after that, all the grass was dead but it was still standing so we still couldn't see squat.

I, in a stroke of pure genius, decided that a 60mm mortar and a whole bunch of WP rounds should cause dead grass to catch fire, burn up, and not block our vision. Before too long, I had the entire camp surrounded by 360 degrees of a conflagration of magnificent proportions because the wind was blowing like crazy. Sparks and burning embers were showering down. Everybody said "Ooooooh!".

Then the fires started cooking off the antipersonnel mines, the antitank mines, booby trapped hand grenades, all the duds out in the grass, and some of the Claymores. Everybody then said, "Where's that dumb sumbitch who started this crap?"

I hid for awhile.

About three or four days before I was moved from the nice, neat, quiet camp at Thien Ngon (pronounced TIN yon) over to ka-BOOM, an incoming mortar round hit a stack of their 4.2 ammo which was sitting out in the open. During that time period, "higher" was force feeding ammo out to Katum whether they needed it or not. They ran out of places to put it; so a big stack of ammo got hit and it started going off. That set off the main 4.2" ammo bunker which set off etc and etc and etc.

We heard them on the radio telling B-32 that everybody had gone to ground while the place self-destructed. We went up on our Teamhouse roof to look to the East over in their direction. Sure enough, all the smoke in the world was going up. They asked what it looked like.

I asked, "Didja ever see a garbage dump burning?"

Dunno why, but they took offense at what I thought was a rather innocuous remark.

PCOD
by Randy Cesani

I am reminded me of the time John Martin and I went on pass in Ubon, Thailand. John was going to PCS, so he had himself on a PCOD date. Me, I was single and not going home, so I just wallowed in it. At the Hotel John got up early and was in the lobby most of the morning just hanging and reading the paper or whatever, but he could see my room door. I was just running the girls in and out of my room in some cases two at a time. John came down to my room, called me all kinds of names, and said I was being cruel to him. Still have to laugh at that memory.

The Speaker
by Reggie Manning

At A-322 at Katum, The Vietnamese SF Team (the LLDB) decided they needed a public address system for the camp. Supposedly it was to be used for essential announcements to the Camp's defenders and as a morale builder in their nonexistent PsyOps Program. Soon afterwards, a PA system was flown in and put in service so they could make their announcements to the camp. The principal use of that system, however, was to play music (?) every evening after what we laughingly called "supper". That alleged music was absolutely the worst racket I'd ever heard. Moreover, the one and only speaker was about 40 feet away from my dispensary bunker and pointed right at it. I got the full effect.

I decided that I'd had enough of that noise. So, one night in the dark I sneaked over to their bunker, climbed up on the roof, and put a primed 1-pound block of C-4 in the speaker horn. Spliced together enough Claymore wire to reach back across to my bunker and attached a Claymore clacker.

The next time we started getting mortared, I ran thru the mortar bursts to get back to my house so I could "make" one of the incoming mortar shells "land on" their speaker. Blew it all to hell and gone. Vaporized it. "So sorry. We'll see what we can do about getting y'all a replacement." (Never did.)

Tu Do Street
by Robert Pryor

I was down in Saigon with my team sergeant. We were in a bar having a few brews when he suggested we venture over to a nearby steam and cream on Tu Do Street. I "reluctantly" agreed and nearly ran him over charging out the door.

We entered this place with a rather large lobby. No sooner had we cleared the door when the mama-san comes charging across the lobby loudly exclaiming, "Johnny, Johnny, where you been? Me no see you long time. You no love me no more?" Then she throws her arms around Top and plants a big old kiss on him.

Hey, I like whorehouses as much as the next guy. Hell, maybe more! However, I have never become such a regular customer that I was on first name basis with the madam.

Okay, fast forward 33 plus years:

Top meets one of my daughters for the first time and proceeds to tell her that he has some tales about me to share. To which she responded, "Hey, I've heard a few things about you as well."

Top gets all defensive and exclaims, "That's a lie! I've never been on Tu Do Street." Hey, I'm not one to gossip so you ain't heard anything from me.

By the way: I recall the sign at the steam and cream located at the "A" Company compound there at Bien Hoa. It said, "Special Forces comes first". I still don't know if that meant that we had head of the line privileges or it was some kind of a shot...

Berserk Staff Sergeant
by Terry Dahling

I am reminded of something that happened while in school. I was working in an "Oscars" Restaurant in Sherman Oaks, CA. One night a drunk passed out at the counter. We called the police and they showed up with four or five squad cars- two cops in each. After they got the man up and out I asked one of them why so many people to wake up one little sleeping drunk? They replied that you can never tell how a drunk will react when woken up. Some just go completely berserk like your Special Forces Staff Sergeant.

The Great Escape
by Terry Dahling

The news has been making a big deal lately of using rock music to break down EPW's in Iraq. That's nothing new. I remember them doing that in Lenngries. The MI set up across the street from CoA, by the 402d and used to keep me awake at night with their noise.

Thinking of this reminds me of an escape I saw take place. They had one of our guys, the name Lawhon comes to mind; anyway, all of a sudden this sucker bursts out of the door (bare assed naked) out the gate and down the hill. They say he didn't stop until he got to his maedchen's house. The Colonel saw this and the SFC got a letter of commendation. The MP's tried to say that they would have shot him but the Colonel said that he was gone by the time they got their jaws off the ground.

When I first got to Lenggries I was introduced to the team, and after the noon formation we went to the field. While down by "B" Garden we got captured and were taken to the Prince Heinrich Kaserne Jail. I had no idea where I was but we broke out of the jail one day after being in there. We all left with our clothes in our hand and didn't stop to put our boots on until we hit the snow line up on the Brunneck (sic). And then, only because our feet were bloody, and we were leaving a trail of red blood in the white snow.

After two days of freedom, they flew overhead in choppers and begged us to surrender because they were afraid that we would freeze to death in the mountains and they could not find us. We were comfortable hiding in a Jagerhutt on one of the mountains in Lenggries and they could not see us. We waited another four days, until the field problem was over and then turned ourselves in.

Claxton Theft
by Toby Todd

Sometime early '71, a couple of us CCC Recon guys were hanging in the NCO Club at FOB 2, when all of a sudden, COL Maggie enters with a flourish, followed by her entourage, which included LTC "Browse", the US Compound CO (or was it LTC Scalise, his successor-CRS) and SGM Joseph, among others. She sang "The Ballad ...", called SGT Steve K. an asshole for not standing, and bellied up to the bar.

After a few minutes, Maggie was spirited off to the "Country Covey Club, which was sorta the center piece of teamrooms. A couple of us young bucks took umbrage with the fact that the upper crust wanted to spirit "our Maggie" away. Mike Bentley and I went to the Security shack at the gate and stole the claxton device.

We snuck over to vicinity of The "Covey" teamroom, gave the c-device a couple of turns, and ran away laughing. We repaired back to the Security shack to return the c-device to its rightful place, and stood back to watch what calamity we had wrought. Sure enuff, SGM Joseph came flying out of the "Covey" TR, trying to find out WTF. Bentley and I were ROTFLOAO. Moreover, all would have been ok, 'cept...

Bentley wanted to do it again. Try as I might, I couldn't talk that dumb f--k out of it, so we go back and steal the claxton again; but with Bentley on point with the claxton, I'm able to hang back a bit. As he turns a corner, SGM Joseph nabs him, and I'm able to walk on by, kinda innocent-like and not get caught. SGM Joseph calls him a buncha dumb mofos, and I think his RT ended up in Juliet Nine about a week later.

Years later, when I was an Instructor at Mott Lake, Maggie paid us a visit. Though small and frail then, when I reminded her of that visit to CCC so many years earlier, she remembered this incident, and said, "Man, Joseph sure had a case of the red ass at Bentley, didn't he?"

Yes, he did.

For just a second, that sparkle was back in her eyes.

Figure It Out
by Art Hines

This was one of those mass jumps over Yomitan, and 1st Group seemed to have a LOT of newbie jumpers who had never jumped an MC-1 before. I think half the group was there that day, and we were jumping from slicks - something none of the newbies had ever done before.

Add to that the fact that somebody was obviously not thinking clearly and put that lunatic Major from Camp Hardy in charge; and this was a recipe for disaster. For those of you who don't know this Major, it was his habit to throw his steel pot up in the air, and if the wind didn't blow it off the ledge into the rock quarry, he'd say "Jump 'em!" Any time he was OIC of anything, it was always entertaining - at least interesting.

Anyhow, I had already jumped, and not being seriously injured or bleeding too badly, was waiting around with the other "walking wounded" to see if I rated an ambulance. Here comes this young Cpt pulling a full forward slip with his MC-1 to get close to the trucks, and it seems he didn't realize the wind was blowing WAAAY higher than normal. The MC-1 added about 7MPH speed to that; and that Yomitan wasn't really all that big a DZ to be worrying about walking to the equipment turn-in trucks. When he discovered this fact, it was too late to do anything but scream. Here he came, like a bat out of hell. Both legs were sticking straight out ahead of him, his eyes as big a pie plates, and his mouth wide open and screaming. You could actually HEAR it when he ran into the door of the deuce and a half. He left in the ambulance with what I heard were 2 broken legs. Never saw him again.

1st Group had over 70 people injured that day bad enough to require medical care, and this included the Group Chaplin. He broke his neck trying to do a PLF into the side of one of the hangers. I didn't rate a ambulance; so what happened with me is somebody started my motorcycle for me, and two guys picked me up and sat me on it so I could ride it to the dispensary. I couldn't raise either leg to get off it, so I just drove it into the curb and let it fall over so I could get off of it.

BTW, was I the only guy in the 1st whose training class with the MC-1 consisted of,"Here it is. You'll figure it out on your way down."

Night Drop
by Bo the Japanese Polack

After a month of hard Scout Swim school in Kongsore, Denmark, we made a night drop outskirt of Aalborg; and we got little scuffle with Homeguards and their dogs at DZ.

I got a nasty gash on my leg. They took me to local hospital where they found out I had broken bones; so they kept me in hospital for few days, which became a torture chamber for me.

These round eyed nurses clad in skimpy white gowns got my two inches of Japanese delight going 24 hours; and buddies, that was hell.

50,000 volts
by Ben Fenske

Not me but Francis B., newly qualified free faller, was asked to go along on a demonstration jump in Virginia. (Sep 1961) He went, and they asked if he wanted to jump with them. He volunteered, and not knowing too much about canopy control was told to follow the other jumpers and stay close so he would land on the DZ.

I believe the DZ was a baseball diamond. Being a hot day, all jumpers wore nothing but bathing suits covered by coveralls, helmets & boots. Bushong landed short on intended drop zone and almost cleared high power lines, raised his ass and sat right on them. 50,000 volts jumped through his ass and blew out a chunk of meat where the tops of his boots were tied at the calf of the legs. It burned the chute clear through and B. hit the ground - not from a long distance.

He woke up in the hospital none the worse for wear, and was able to ride back to Ft Bragg with the other jumpers. He was later promoted to E8 and then E9 on the C Team of 5th SF in VN as Group cameraman and picture developer. He died shortly after his last promotion of cardiac arrest.

Standing Landing
by Ben Fenske

At 3d Gp at Bragg, out in the boonies for a week, behind barbed wire. Load in 2 1/2 ton trucks, transport to Pope Field, load, take off, fly due north in a C130 that is flown by computer. Armed AF guards up forward, computer behind canvas so that we cannot see it. Fly several hours, get ready to jump, DZ lights lit up and suddenly all lights are extinguished.

Winds too high. Fly back to Pope Field, back to boonies, try again next night, same sequence. I am JM, DZ ahead, lights in correct "L" configuration, out we go. Helmet ripped off of head immediately, must have been going 200 knots and forgot to slow down or computer drinking antifreeze. Darkest night in 100 years, no stars, no moon, can barely see trees below whistling along about 30-40 mph. We have steerable T-10s (MCI?). Hold into wind and prepare for backward landing w/no helmet. Do not drop rucksack.

BLAM! Swinging like a kid on a swing in the park. Just missed hitting my right elbow against the main tree trunk. Rucksack upside down, hit trunk, ripped off side pocket with mess kit and flashlight inside.

Stopped swinging. Feel with legs, hit a large branch, pull myself over to it with legs. Get on it and still cannot see anything but pitch-blackness. Flashlight and mess kit are somewhere below. Standing on branch, I get out of harness, pull quick releases and drop rucksack. It reaches end of drop line and bounces. Still, don't know what is below or how far.

I carefully lower myself onto the prcht harness, slide down the drop line until I am standing on rucksack. I slowly lower my self over rucksack, hanging by my fingers, tensing my legs for a fall and PLF to follow. I let go............

I fall about 1 foot. Standing on solid ground, I thank my lucky stars, then "Sonofabitch! I left my fucking M-16 tied to the main lift web. I climb up the drop line, secure rifle and slide back down. Feel around for mess kit and flashlight, and don't find anything.

Put my rucksack on, rifle in hand and head down the mountain. DZ party is in a small group on DZ about 1 km upwind, smoking as I guide on the cigarettes. People are coming from all directions, fellow team-members. We assemble and are all accounted for, are taken for a 1 km walk to a civilian truck and taken about 10 miles and put up in a barn.

Discussing jump while in transit, I find out that those who landed on the DZ were about 100 feet from ground, when the wind stopped and they landed softly. I and whoever else was near me landed on the side of a mountain where the wind is probably still blowing.

Location was in Coleman, NH 30 June 1968

Note: please note that I made a standing landing, professional that I am!

Airborne Pigs
by Bill Coombs

I am reminded about the delivery we used to make of cattle to camps in II Corps. Sometimes the cows, pigs, ducks, etc. were flown to the camps and other times, they were air-dropped in. We had no big problems with the cows but the pigs presented a little one.

For some reason, the pigs did not like going airborne and got all excited and many of them died from fright. Many times, the pigs were drugged so that they were alive after they landed.

That, of course, was the idea. The camps did not have large refrigeration units so the animals were delivered alive and later butchered. Someone gave it the name "Live Refrigeration".

We had some very talented riggers at the SFOB who could even package eggs that would survive an air drop.

Clean Boots
by Bill Coombs

I have been reading all of these stories about the nasty jumps that some of you have experienced. I have one that is just the opposite.

I was a young tiger in Recon Platoon, 502nd Airborne Battle Group at Fort Campbell. This jump happened in 1959. It had rained before the jump and the drop zone was pure mud.

Without any planning, I landed on the parachute of a guy who had just landed before me. As the guys were lining up to turn in their chutes, they looked like mud balls. I, on the other hand had a little mud on my boots. A Captain asked me whose chute I was turning in and when I told him it was mine, he did not believe me and he got angry and accused me of lying. It took the jumpmaster to convince him that I had indeed made the jump.

Power Lines
by Ben Fenske

I made my fourth jump with the 101st after just having left what was left of the 11th /24th ID in Germany. The wind was very windy and blowing approximately 28 mph on a day jump. The wind carried me north over Yamoto DZ, headed right for power lines followed closely with RR tracks. I landed under the wires with the canopy over the top. The wind pulled me up tight like a banjo string and pulled so hard that my reserve was at my throat. The first cable was biting into the back of my neck and the wind was strong enough to very soon break my neck. A tall 1LT from BN S4 drove up in a jeep to the nearest telephone pole, threw a switch turning off the power; then he drove up to my canopy which was still trying to break my neck. If I had pulled my reserve, I would probably have been decapitated. He reached up, grabbed the skirt of the canopy and pulled it down letting the air spill out. I was lowered to the ground for another standing landing. I thanked the LT profusely and went on my way. My first, last and only wire landing.
28 Feb 1959 ... C119...

Wind in My Face
by William E. Edge CSM (ret)

As a kid during WWII, I got hooked watching newsreels of Paratroopers. As soon as I graduated from high school I went off to join the US Army. The Korean War was somewhat of a distraction, but my destiny had already been sealed. The events that followed in my life only confirmed that I had taken the correct path.

I soon discovered that a lot of people in the Famous 82nd Division at Ft Bragg wanted the Wings and extra pay of a paratrooper, but very few actually wanted to jump. One of the reasons was the old T7 chute was quite painful. Thus, many units were always short of personnel when it came to be "jump time". That allowed me to "scrounge" jumps with other units. In a very short period of time I accumulated enough jumps to be rated a Senior Parachutist, which oddly enough was in short supply. Even more rare were Master Parachutists, the highest rank. Scores had as many as ten years service, but were still wearing basic Novice wings. There were many men who wore up to five GOLD stars on their wings, denoting combat jumps. These were my heroes.

A small firestorm was set off when I applied for Master wings after having piled up the required number of jumps in only three years. (Now you must have three years active airborne duty before getting Master wings.). Some of the older big wigs at Headquarters were further upset by the fact that I had only two years and two months service at Division; but, short of a new rule there was no way to prevent me from getting my Master wings.

I managed to land a job as an Instructor at the Division Jump School and remained there for 4 and half years, working up from "go-pher " to Committee Chief and Senior Jumpmaster. After being sent to Germany in May of 1959 I became chief and the only instructor in a freefall club. I discovered that I was the only American with a real license to teach in Germany at the time. Some people in the 10th Special Forces Group were just experimenting with freefall at the time, but were not rated as instructors. While in Germany I a member of the highest altitude jump in Europe - 21, 000 feet. This excluded Russia, which was going full out with a freefall program. After losing a coin flip with Don Cunningham, the officer who was head of the freefall club, I was assigned German license number *two* and had to do all the paper work.

Traveling all over Germany and putting on exhibitions at Fests and German holidays only added to my good fortune. I racked up enough jumps to qualify for a class "D" License, the highest class awarded. Today there are over 21, 000 class "D" holders, and my number is D-23. This makes me somewhat of a relic in parachute circles these days, but not the oldest by far.

Upon my return to the United States I was reassigned again to the 82nd and selected to be a member of the now-official Army Parachute Demonstration team, the Golden Knights. They were touring the nation at air shows and events such as the Daytona Five Hundred auto race to promote Army recruiting. In only two years, I was able to tour all 50 states as a member of their team.

The war in Asia was warming up, and I was feeling the call for Special Forces - the only unit sending men to Asia at that time. Consequently, I arranged for a transfer to the new 5th Special Forces Group. I was assigned Special Duty to the Training Group to set up and lead the new skill of free fall parachuting. The Army was now taking a keen interest in this skill. We started from scratch - inventing as we went.

Eventually we were turning out qualified jumpers every 6 weeks. Our program began at 6000 feet and progressed as high as we could get. We routinely achieved heights above 35,000 feet, and, once at 41,000 feet after the Air force stripped everything they could off a 130 aircraft. That jump was a "honey", as it was 62 degrees below zero at 41,000 feet and 92 degrees on the ground at Ft Bragg. That record held until the HALO group went to Yuma Arizona and made a 43,000 foot drop without any problems. This proved once and for all to the naysayers that insertion of Army troops behind enemy lines was viable. Today, the HALO school at Yuma is a combined services operation showing excellent results, and turning out highly qualified personnel from all services.

As for me, I still enjoy jumping - almost every weekend, weather permitting. At the age of 71, I am a fun jumper who still manages to keep up with some of the youngsters. I have had my ups and downs including a quadruple heart by-pass, removal of eighteen inches of intestine, a few other medical procedures and five Purple Hearts for wounds in Korea and Vietnam. But I figure that if you love any activity, you should do it until you die and still enjoy it. I entered the Army as a Recruit and left as Command Sergeant Major in Special Forces, so I have had a good trip. Now that I am retired I have to pack for all my jumps just like all the other civilians - a fact that bothers my frugal soul. I have made slightly over 7,000 parachute jumps, 1,284 of which were Army troop jumps. The rest are freefalls ranging from a low of 500 to a maximum of 42,000 feet. They include both water and land jumps. One of my knees was ruined from a night jump exercise in the mountains of Montana, but it healed well.

Thirty-five of my jumps have been parachute malfunctions. These are critical situations where the reserve chute must be pulled when the main chute does not open properly. Once close call was when a crashing C- 119 at Fr Bragg ran me over in the air. Eighteen other troops were killed in this tragic accident that occurred on my birthday in 1954. I have lost several friends due to parachute accidents. But overall, I consider myself fortunate to have been able to serve my country in time of war, and still be able to do what I enjoy. In my book, you just can't beat that.

So that's it, and I still like the wind in my face. People come up to me all the time and ask why I am still jumping, I answer, "Because I like it."

Jumping in Africa
by "Yukon Don" Shipman

My first trip OCONUS with 5th was to Kenya. At one point, we were doing a jump with the 20th Para. American 130, chutes, and JMs (Thank God!). Kenyans were jumping their own stick and us our own (Thank, thank God!). Kenyans were jumpin' first, so all we had to do was watch them go for the first pass. Twenty minutes out they are chanting to beat the band. At Stand Up, they start chanting even faster and kinda dancin' around (just like in frekin Zulu Dawn). As # 2 jumper in the SF stick, I am thinkin', "These guys are alright...they are really into this jumpin' shit!"

THEN, CW2 Ward (PJM) screwed up and said sumfin like, STAND IN THE DOOR! That first dude sat his happy ass right down on the floor of the A/C! Chief says "GO" Kunta Kinta says "NO!" Ward promptly kicks him in the back of the head, and that's the last we saw of him. The rest of the Kenyans fought every step of the way and I kid you NOT...Chief had to literally throw every one of them basstuds out of the bird! No lie, G.I. Never did figure out why they stopped singin'.

Shaking Chutes
by John Gilgren from Don Valentine

Around the 1972-3 time frame, I was jump master on one of the normal Hollywood jumps at Yomitan. The last jumper in the last stick had to go -- I mean really bad and couldn't wait to go around one more time so I moved him up to the last man in the stick before. Well as things went, everyone jumped and when I got to the ground I found the man and asked if he made it.

"Yes, but just barely. When I got to the ground I covered up with the chute and took this massive dump, rolled up the chute and went back to the trucks." No problem, right? Well that afternoon we were detailed to shake the chutes at the rigger shed. The rigger was a jerk, yelling and screaming at everyone; well, he was the one demonstrating how to shake the chutes properly. He pulled this chute up and low and behold a pile of smelly, fecal material materialized from the chute and landed on his shoulder. This guy was not a happy rigger. The next day SGM Mc. said in formation that if anyone had to take a dump, to do it before jumping. The WO who ran the rigger shed threatened everyone and demanded to know who pooped in his parachute. I have never told anyone else this before. You had to see the look on the riggers face when the poop dropped down and landed solidly on his shoulder. It was priceless.

Wild Geese
by Bob Smith

While assigned to ODA-581, we were always searching for HALO jumps. We had a hot team and could put 10 of 12 jumpers into the pit out on Sicily....on 10 jumpers because there was no more room. Back when Col. Palmer was 7th Group Commander he decided (I guess after seeing the movie "Wild Geese") to attempt a 100 man night, combat equipment, oxygen jump out of a C-141. Every swinging richard who had ever been to HALO school was ordered to jump.

Well, a few practice jumps were made. Us Hawgs out of 5th Group were given permission to do the deed with them on a jump at Sicily DZ. Because we didn't really want to get tied up with a lot of inexperienced jumpers, we boarded the aircraft first in order to be the last off. There we were, tightly packed in, good body position, breathing good clean oxygen....then we left the plane. Everything looked like it had turned to shit. No formations...just a bunch of guys whirling around. Some trying to get out of the way of the spinners, others just spinning and tumbling. Reminded me of a bunch of flies buzzing around a moose turd. Our jumpmaster flew around in front of us and motioned to follow him. We all tracked over in the area of Falcon airfield and waited for deployment. Palmer's "Wild Geese" were to allow their timers to fire to open their chutes, but we were going to hand-deploy ours. Then chutes started popping around 3500 feet. We watched as the inevitable happened. Someone fell right through another guys chute.... destroying it. He managed to get his reserved opened though. We deployed our chutes around 3000 feet and lined up in trail. We watched as the guy in the reserve did the most fugged up landing imaginable and lay still.

Our low man started steering toward the hurt man and our team landed in a circle around him, doing standing landings with the ParaCommanders.

Our medic began doing his stuff and I ran to get the ambulance.

Not a bad jump...but we never volunteered to play with Palmer's boys again. BTW, the hurt guy ended up with a broken pelvis.

Hot Wire DZ
by Greg Hoisington

I was still in the air when it occurred, so I didn't see it happen, but we had a wire landing. Several teams were jumping a C-130 into El Centro, Mirror Lake or some other desert place in CA. It was a day time drop. The entire desert was the DZ; and the only obstacle within 20 miles was a huge power transmission line running across the desert, way over to one side of the actual DZ.

A guy named P., an FNG on another team, went right into the wires. The DZ folks said he hit, bounced and slipped between the layers of wires, caused a few sparks; then he and the 'chute fell to the ground, deader than shit.

I thought he'd look like a piece of fried bacon, but he had only two pretty bad burn marks; one was on his shoulder and the other on his lower leg. No kind of CPR would bring him back. If the juice didn't kill him, the fall probably would have. I don't remember the height of those big metal supports, but they were fairly high.

Hanging in the air, with nothing to look at except the smoke and the beer truck (I mean parachute turn in point) in one direction, and the transmission lines in the other, you wonder HTF could something like that happen. My guess is he fixated on the lines, turned his 'chute to keep an eye on them, and sailed right in.

I won't mention anything about the Edison Award, out of respect.

Rude DZ Introduction
by Greg Hoisington

A bunch of teams jumped onto the same DZ one night to begin a desert FTX. Either someone needed a night/equipment/mass-tactical, or it was during the Peanut years when support was difficult to find. Can't remember if it was CA or NM, but the plan was, after turn-in, each team would head for its own AO.

It was a clear night, with enough moonlight to see the ground and differentiate between sand and dark patches. Turns out that the dark patches were cactus patches; the type cactus that looks like a bunch of green pancakes growing together, with thorns on both sides. Las tunas might be the name.

Anyway, the first couple of teams out landed in an area where the patches were thicker, and there were many cactus injuries. Several guys medevaced, including one who landed right in the middle of a mess of it. I can't even begin to imagine how bad it would be to land and roll in a dense patch of three foot cactus plants, when we were rudely introduced to black palm, saw grass, prickly pear, locust, Joshua tree and some cactus; many of which would break off and be stuck in a dense patch of three-foot cactus plants.

Wounded in a Nanosecond
by Greg Hoisington

Part of 12th Gp did a PR jump onto the main ski slope at Squaw Valley, right in the middle of the season. The "DZ" was a hundred or so yards from the lodge (and bar). I think we had two C-130's.

On the command "Stand Up", I found that some piece of my equipment was caught in the nylon strap of the seat, and I couldn't get up. Therefore, I pulled out my trusty knife and began operating behind my back to free whatever was caught. Naturally, I cut the crap out of my thumb in the process and was bleeding like a stuck pig.

Out we go. It was a little chilly in jungle fatigues, but everything looked great from the air. Snow all over the place, dark green pine trees every where, happy skiers on the slopes... and the trees kept getting larger. When I got down to being even with some of the ridges, I realized that some of these trees over a hundred feet tall, had no lower branches; and were too big to get your arms anywhere near half way around, unless you were Mighty Joe Young. It was time to pay attention.

Missed all the skiers and did my first snow PLF. I guess you call it that; it was different. All my guys landed OK. My thumb was still bleeding and the blood in the snow looked quite impressive. It attracted the immediate attention of several snow bunnies, who insisted on helping me with my 'chute. It was a PR jump, so of course I let them. Got that steel pot off, the beret on, and became wounded SFC Profile in a nanosecond.

Meanwhile, the second pass came over and looked like it was a little off course. Sure as shit, they missed the slope and headed for the trees. All were OK except for one. A guy named Miranda got hung in the top of one of the big pines. He managed to get out of the harness and climb a little way down, but he was stuck in that tree for several hours, scared and freezing his ass off. The Forest Service finally showed up with a monster ladder and got him down.

While this was going on, my team was in the bar, drinking to his memory and getting into condition to attack the baby slopes. I don't remember the rest...

Rear PLF
by Greg Hoisington

It was Aug '64 - jump week for 46th Co students. There I was, after two weeks of harassment, because of being one of the very few USAF students, and because I showed up with nothing but tailored fatigues (hey, we were supposed to look pretty, not get dirty). I was jumping and closing in on those coveted wings. The first three jumps were great. Nothing to it. Number four was the "equipment" jump.

After unassing the plane, checking my cantaloupe and enjoying the moment of silence, I was brought back to reality by the sound of the Cadre yelling at us. What a bunch of assholes, ruining a perfectly good thing. Watching the ground, I saw I was going to have to do a rear PLF. No sweat... contacts! Heels...canteen...pain. The old metal canteens did not have a lot of give to them, and I thought I had crushed mine. However, I had mastered the PFL in only four jumps, and made the first of several slow exits from a DZ. ... and a cool breeze blew across Friar Drop Zone.

DZ Wires
by Jack Tobin

In '82, I had A331, 11th SFGA. We jumped into Berlin NH, 10th GP DZ. Our party got there late, threw down an inverted L. 150 meters into a 3700 meter DZ with power lines on two sides of active road. Since I had a static JM, I led the team out, and headed toward the base of the L - team SOP. My light weapons guy went past me to provide security for the roll up; wires came out of nowhere, his ruck hit bounced, he hit bounced and both landed on both sides. He took out the wires and got a pretty bad shock. The next guy in the stick pulled low slip to avoid the live wires, and broke both legs when he hit in a ditch.

Avoiding SDO
by James Lewis

Most of C Company was on a jump in Saudi in early '63, and the GP CO and SGM were on the DZ when we were landing. I had picked up on a camera man and was making sure I was in his sights when I made my typical 3 pt landing and went ass over head in one second. Piolitti saw me and walked over to see if I was ok. I was up, still smiling into the lens and didn't know that he had stopped and was looking away. The heel of my boot landed on the toe of his and he landed on his ass. When I looked and saw who it was, I made some remark that was sure to land me on SDO for the rest of my tour. He never mentioned it, and I must be one of the few that never pulled SDO at Tolz… remembering Tom Udall landing on a VW Bug that day and knocking the fender off.

Spilt Coffee
by James Savell

I was DZSO, and MSG B. was medical coverage jumping in a Phase I class to MacKall. The C-130 came in, the sky filled with chutes, and then one white chute appeared. We jumped in the jeep and went racing across the DZ. B. held on to a cup of coffee while driving. We arrived and found the jumper lying on the ground with the chute over him.

Bumgardner went running over, shouting "Are you O K?"

A weak voice replied, "I think so".

Then Bumgardner started kicking the jumper and yelling, "You stupid S.O.B. I almost spilt my coffee coming over here". The jumper must have been OK because he immediately jumped up, rolled his chutes and double timed off.

DZ - Tree
by John Cleckner

We jumped on Fryer DZ (Benning) in '58. It was a night jump with equipment as I recall.

I hit a tree and could not see anyone else. No lights. Released everything and deployed my reserve.

I slowly started down my risers, hand over hand, and after about four or five hand over hands, my knees hit the ground. As I was lowering myself I must have bent my legs or something because that is what touched the ground first. Thank God it was dark and no one saw me. I couldn't have been more that 4 feet off of the ground when all this started.

Empty Harness
by John Cleckner

The 325th Airborne Battle Group was tasked with a 6-month TDY to Ft Benning Ga. and elsewhere to do multiple tasks in 1958. Being a new guy, I had no idea whether it had ever been done before. We left Ft. Bragg on April 1, 1958 and convoyed to Ft Benning.

While there, we supported the National Rifle and Pistol Matches that year at Benning as opposed to Camp Perry Ohio. We trained College ROTC Students during their Summer Camp commitment and put a Platoon of Marine Force Recon through jump school. We also kicked ass and took every Post Sporting Event on Ft. Benning for a 6-month period.

I experienced my first Prop Blast as an enlisted man taking care of Drunken Officers.

For you old heads, Col G. (Later to Command the Americal Division in VN) was the 325 ABG CO. JJ C. (RIP) was XO of HQ&HQ, Cpt. S. was CO, and the most famous of all was, Cpt. Sa. (the baddest-ass Company Commander in the 82 Abn Division) Commanded B Company. Blood B., by the way, was a Corporal in the 82nd Jump School with Bill Edge.

While at Benning, one of our Companies, "B" Company, Riggers, and Hqrs & Hqrs Commo personnel and other action guys went into English AFB La. We jumped into a combined operation as a separate Airborne Company and I was the guy with the 2niner2 and radio, first in the door with a GP bag bigger than I was, and a fucking reserve that was choking my Adams apple. (By the way, back in those days a good Commo man could put up the antenna all by himself.) I had been selected as B Company CO's radio operator.

We had not been at Ft Polk 24 hours when we got into one helluva fight with a Battalion of Tankers out of Ft. Hood. (We had just watched a movie called "From Here To Eternity")

The first punches were thrown by the Tankers, then a guy in Mess Whites, who happened to be a "Spoon" and also the Middle Weight Champion of the 82nd Abn Div. knocked out 6 guys with six punches. We kicked their asses, and the next day Cpt. Sa. had us all in formation ready to rip our heads off, telling us that our little Company with it's Hqrs augmentation kicked the shit out of a Battalion of TANKERS and put over 20 of them in the Hospital.

We did our thing the next day and jumped a couple of times transitioning from fixed wing to helicopters for the first time in my short life. I was scared to death, but I was beside the Company CO all the time and watched his every move.

Then, we were off to Panama for a continuation of the exercise. Thank god I was not the first guy in the door going into that part of the exercise.

As SGM Edge said, this poor devil went out and all they found were some harnesses. Lots of very big fish with very sharp teeth in those Pacific waters. We jumped on an Air Force runway (CRS) on the Pacific side. More than one hit the water, but there were shark nets for the rest. Thanks, SGM, for the Deja vu all over again.

PLF over Pine Trees
by John Cleckner

Jeeem and Guys, PLF's in any manner or fashion was a rarity when jumping into Uwharrie or Pisgah when I was jumping. It didn't have anything to do with skill, it was Luck and usually none of us had that.

The farmers' fields we jumped into (ALL Night Jumps) were to small for any of the sticks we had aboard the A/C we used to make it on them, then there were the Ponds, but mostly "trees", pine trees. I remember 123s mostly, once in a while a 130, & C47s, no Caribous (sp) as I recall. We would jump team at a time mostly. Then Drop Zones we got were NOT...

Anyway to the PLF issue. All the jumps were tree landings for me. Around 30 or 40. This finally culminated in a SFOC Jump. When I made my SFOC jump my canopy landed over four monster pine trees.

I was dangling right in the middle of all four of them. No way to get down from my perspective in total darkness. I thought about pulling my knife and cutting my way out of the harness, and then I thought about releasing the reserve. Then the Gs showed up with flash lights and I really knew I was in trouble. I could see at least two canopies below me. Had to have been 70 to 90 feet up.

The Gs yelled for me to jump, and I replied, "Kiss my Ass". Remember, full gear, weapon, ruck etc. I finally released my harness and hung with my underarms and started to swing. Somehow I managed to reach on of these monster loplolys (sp) or whatever they were and I hugged that sucker liked I loved it. Somehow I managed to release the harness without pulling me off the tree and the harness sprung back like a bullet. There hung all my gear, ruck, rifle, water, sleeping gear. I was in deep shit and then I had to persuade myself that I could shinny down that pine tree. Obviously, I had a death grip on the tree which I could only get my arms half way around. Somehow I made it and spent the night moving to our RON and then freezing my ass off until dawn.

LTC Longfellow (a totally worthless piece of shit) was my grader. He didn't like me and I didn't like him. To add insult to injury he had to hire a farmer to cut the trees down to retrieve all of my gear. Cost a bundle according to him. He never stopped dogging me the entire exercise. I ended up with him as my B Team Cmdr in VN for a couple of months in B22. (another story)

This was the famous SFOC jump were no one landed on the DZ and many were lost until daylight and a Marine Major jumped, (having never attended jump school), and was MIA for a day and finally walked all the way back to Bragg and reported in.

What a mess. Of course, as I said, I was the only one who got his ass kicked, (a second lieutenant with master wings is expected to be better than the rest: right).

Smoking, a Tranquilizer
by John Cleckner

Guys, I was the Jump Master on Colonel R's first jump after Liver Surgery. He called me over and informed me he was jumping a double L and therefore had to go out first; besides, he wanted to be as close to the turn in point as possible. I agreed and walked away.

Then I found out about his recent surgery. I went to him, concerned, that it was too soon to jump after surgery. He showed me his purple scar. He told me he was OK and needed the Jump Pay.

Just before we loaded up, he lit up a huge cigar; as he boarded the A/C when we took off, he notified me that he would smoke it. He said he would go out the door with it as he had done on every jump in his career. I told him he would not smoke on board the A/C as long as I was the Jump Master. Several senior officers called me aside and asked that I reconsider. I said, "No."

Then the A/F Crew Chief walked by and said, "If the Colonel wants to smoke a cigar on my A/C that's OK with me." Rowe smoked it. When I put him out, he looked at me and smiled, all the while puffing like a fool on that stogie. He later told me at the turn in point that Jumping made him nervous and that is why he had to smoke.

Just Popped In
by Leamon Ratterree

I never missed Gatun DZ. I did however miss Venado DZ - three times.

First time, I went into the trees and landed so high up, that even after lowering the reserve, still had to play Tarzan to get down. Apex of the reserve was still about 25 ft off the ground. Later, I jumped and slid straight down through the trees and while hanging there, my toes could touch the ground. 3rd Jump I landed inside their ASP between the first and second concertina -topped chain link fence. Rolled up my gear, started walking toward the gate. I came up behind the AF Security guy with his loaded M-16. "Excuse me, Sire, but can 'ya tell me howta get outa here?"

The lad spun around. "Who are you, and how the hell did you get in here?"

"I just sorta dropped in ya might say."

"But who are you?" I then 'splained to him who I was, what my unit was, and WTF/HTF I got inside his wire.

"Do you do this very often?" he axed.

"I certainly hope not." says I. With that, the fine lad unlocked the gate to let me out. I actually heard him at the AF chow hall early that morning (24 hour chow hall) tellin' his buddies about wa-happend. I went over to the table of AFSPs, and introduced mice-elf, then told the assembled lads that their entire colleague said was true and correct. He wore one of those "See, I told ya so" expressions.

Toelz DZ
by Larry Sellers

Some people were needed to drop to help the halo pilots I think. There were only a couple of us, and when we went up to jump, somebody wasn't paying attention. I was the last man; and when I went out, the wind picked up, blew me over the runway, and stopped. I heard a noise and turned to look what it was. It was a f--king L19 coming right at me. I saw the pilot working like hell. I started to pull lines and silk, and had an armload when I hit the ground. Just lucky I guess. No broken back after landing on it.

Earning Wings
by Mark Sprague

Hope Mills NC, 1957:
Somewhere my father acquired and gave me one of those spring loaded pilot parachutes used to open large cargo load. I was nine years old at the time and to my thinking I thought that the pilot chute could hold my weight. The next Saturday morning, I climbed up on the roof of our house, and tied that chute to the back of my belt and promptly jumped off the roof of the house. The problem is, at the age of nine, I did not understand physics, nor the fulcrum principal. Since the body is top heavy the spring loaded chute flipped me 180 degrees and I plowed into the ground head first. I think that one eight of a second passed from the time my feet left the roof and my lips kissing the ground.

I must have laid there for several minutes before getting up and shaking it off. I never did tell my dad about that dumb-assed attempt at earning my wings. It turns out my first jump at Benning was marginally better. I made a 3-point landing - heals, ass and the back of my head. It got better after that. Really!

Honey Wagon
by Marvin Crist

Our team Sgt, Bill T., had arranged a trip to Toelz for ski training. He had a honey at Toelz he wanted to see again. Before we left, he took the job of 1SGT out at Recondo School. Herbie O. then took over as Tm Sgt.

We were to fly from Bragg to Karen DZ at Toelz with a stop in the Azores. When we got out of the C-130 over the DZ, we all steered for the nice dark brown areas. We knew this would provide the softest landing possible. The team had seven guys on it at that time. 6 of us had been raised on farms at one time or another. I got about 100 ft off the ground, took a deep breath thru my nose and yelled "SHIT!!!" and it was. The farmer had just sprayed the field with the honey wagon. Only one of us hit that shit. You guessed it, the city boy. He didn't recognize it, knew the smell, but couldn't place the color.

Jumpin' in Africa
by Marvin Crist

My jump with the 20th paras was much fun. We were jumping on Archer Post, about 10 of them per stick, c-130 taligate. I was safeting; I think there about 4 safeties. They stood up and shuffled to the ramp. Number 4 jumper dropped to his ass and started to crab walk to the ramp. Number 5 jumper went around him and beat him off the edge of the ramp.

I watched this in amazement. I was not going out on that ramp with those idiots. On the next jump we were going to bring a video camera. We wanted the guys at Benning to see this shit.

Kenyan Jumpers
by Marvin Matteson, Jr.

In 1979, while in A/3/5 I went to Kenya with Capt Hy R. Company Co, Capt Dan A. Tm Ldr, and Lt Victor B. Tm Xo. We were the first American SF unit to go there, so you can imagine some of the things that went on. We were on an FTX After a train-up period with the Kenyan Abn Company.

Initially, the Kenyans were going to jump from a MC-130 but that was canceled when the plane became stuck in the mud after landing at a dirt strip near our base camp. Therefore, everyone ended up jumping the Kenyan Airforce C-115 Buffalo with Israeli made MC1-B parachutes. I don't remember very much about the Kenyan jumpers during the actual jump, but I do remember that over there, the Airforce controls the jump, not the jumpmasters. In addition, the aircraft had to do a low-level pass to chase the zebras, giraffes, wildebeests off of the DZ. It was a very rewarding cultural experience.

Feet Peekchurs
by Mike Rhode

We had a guy named W. who went through Jump School with K., P., P. and me. On the 4th jump he "knew" it all and was experienced. He took his Kodak instamatic along to snap some good aerial shots. He was taking pictures of his feet and forgot that everything was smaller, thus a long way away. Fryer Field, with that hard dirt runway in the middle, jumped up and nailed him. He had the imprint of the camera in his forehead and was knocked out like a light.

Swift Strike
by Randy Cesani

In '61, when I was in the 101st, we jumped on Swift Strike; and as I was coming down onto a farmer's field I saw a shack and a well below me. Having seen the movie "The Longest Day" where a guy goes in a well, I started concentrating real hard on that well and slipping away from it. I landed okay, got up, looked for my chute and realized it was draped over wires leading to that shack. I was concentrating so hard on the well and shack that I missed seeing the wires. I Left my chute in place, reported it and went on to whip the 82nd in mock war.

Carlos Parker
by Reggie Manning

Carlos was in the first of the 5th at the same time I was. During that time we made several trips to Colorado, Montana, Greece, and other lovely spots. For some reason, he and I were always on the Advance Party of these fly-aways.

After flying for what seemed forever, the AF Weenie In the back would tell us we were about an hour or so out.

Everybody on the entire airplane would shout, "Carlos, DROP YOUR PANTS!"

In order to keep his prosthesis from departing in midair, he'd drilled a hole in the upper rim of it. He'd drop trou, tie a piece of 550 cord through the hole, pull his pants back up and tic the other end of the cord to his belt.

Hey, whatever works.

Cattle Truck DZ
Reggie Manning

During one of the Fort Bragg phases of the Medic training, our class was scheduled for one of those late afternoon / early evening pay jumps.

"Somebody" was trying to get really close to the turn-in point and actually landed in the back of one of the open topped cattle trucks. Seems that he and those benches had quite a go-round there for awhile.

Blacktop River
by Reggie Manning

Let's look at these jump stories from a different angle.... looking from the ground up while mentally rehearsing what to do and waiting for somebody to do a bust-ass.

I can't recall where this happened... whether it was in Pisgah or Uwharrie or WTF it was, but I'd been tasked for Medical coverage on the DZ.

It was the middle of the night (of course) and darker than the inside of a boot (of course), and I was freezing my buns off after having arrived at (hopefully) the right spot several hours before. Moreover, those FLA jeeps ain't got a sign of a heater and no side curtains.

After several Ice Ages had seemed to elapse, I heard a C-130 approaching, and after a minute or so, could see the Team's parachutes drifting down. No lights, no nothing on the DZ.

Now, they were supposed to be jumping in a long, skinny field with a wooded hillside on the left side as they flew the approach. On the right side was a crooked black-topped country road and then a small creek.

I suppose the Team had been briefed about the creek (ditch??) prior to the jump. One of the jumpers appeared to be drifting towards where I was parked alongside the road. In addition, he kept coming closer and closer.

Directly, I heard a loud "CLANK ..... THUD" and a whole bunch of cussing. I decided that I'd best walk down the road about 50 yards to the guy to see if he was alive.

He told me he had looked down and saw that crooked, black thing on the ground, thought it was the creek, and executed a perfect water landing.... on the blacktop.

The only damage was to his dignity.

Fresh Tattoos
by Ray Flaherty

We had a guy in our class who went in to Columbus/Phenix City and got his self tattooed with all kinds of airborne stuff. He was one mean looking mutha.

On our first jump there was a guy laying on the DZ with his eyes closed, screaming that his chute wasn't gonna open. One of the instructors politely informed him it had; and to gather his stuff and get off the DZ. Guess who?

If you guessed it was the guy with the fresh tattoos, score yourself with a direct hit and pick up a candy bar on the way out.

It's odd that he wasn't around for the second jump. I wonder what he did with all those tattoos.

One Little Root
by Robert Pryor

It was a Hollywood jump all the way. It was a beautiful North Carolina spring day with a slight breeze, but not a cloud in the sky. We were jumping one of the DZs that are like a giant beach. Perhaps it was Holland, but CRS. Anyway, the DZ was hundreds of acres of sand with nary a shrub on it.

The jump was uneventful and I did my PLF into the breeze, still no problems. Then I started to get dragged, but what the hell, it was soft sand, right? Well, I soon decided enough of that shit and popped one of my cape wells. The chute immediately deflated. Jump, PLF, and ride over. Right? Wrong!

I jumped up and started to run around the chute in order to secure it. Well the DZ may have looked like a giant beach, but it did, in fact, have one little root sticking up out of the sand - perhaps a half inch. One of my suspension lines snagged on that root and my chute instantly inflated. Instead of running around my chute, I now found myself doing cartwheels down the DZ.

Trying to undo your one remaining cape well while heading down the DZ, ass over tea kettle at about 15 or 20 mph is not a pretty picture, let me tell you.

Jeepcrusher
by Reggie Manning

My very first jump at Fort Benning, I landed on the hood of the DZSO's (or somebody's) jeep. Mashed the hood right down on top of the air cleaner.

AWOL RB15s
by Robert Stepanian

In 1967, on a water jump at Camp Hardy an SFC drowned in front of an audience when he failed to release his risers. He became entangled. By the time we got to him in an RB 15 it was too late.

We disregarded the RB 15 when we got him to the beach so the docs on hand could work on him. The RB, only one of two at Hardy, was drifting out. So Greg L., Don N., Myself and one other guy hoppd into the other RB 15 to bring the drifting one back. By the time we caught up to it we were way off shore and fighting an outgoing tide.

We wound up out till the next morning. When they came to get us in a Navy Chopper, Greg was the first one up on a Cable. The cable failed, and in he went from about fifty feet. The rescue was done with the pilot timing his dips to get us in the bird between swells.

Moreover, shit, they left both RB15s out there.

Exotic DZs
by Richard Hayes

Try landing in a GD pineapple field on Oahu or lava bed on the big island sometime. Both suck! Didn't we manage to find some exotic places for DZs? Always wondered what the advance parties were thinking when they chose some of them.

St. Mere
by Terry Dahling

We were taking off from Neubiburg German AFB outside of Munich. Immediately upon lift-off it became apparent that something wasn't right. The Air Force crewmen put on their chutes, said something to the Jump Master, and we were immediately stood up, hooked up and stood in the door. I was the first in the door, and when the crew chief opened the door I looked out and saw beautiful downtown Munich only about 200 feet below. Right in the center were the spires of the Frauen Kirsch. The C-123 had lost an engine upon take off and couldn't gain altitude. The pilot decided to lighten the load - us!

All I could think of was a scene from "The Longest Day" where that trooper got hung-up on the spire of a church in St. Mere Eglise. I guess they decided that unloading us in downtown Munich wasn't a good idea. They got us seated and into the KYAG (kiss your ass goodbye) attitude. The plane made a very steep descent and I just knew we were gone to the big DZ in the sky. At the last minute it flared out and made one of the smoothest landings I have experienced. The crew acted like there was never anything to worry about. Right!! That's why they had their parachutes on. This reminded me of a cartoon I had seen where the airline Capt. and Co-Pilot were casually walking down the isle whistling while putting on chutes.

Otis AFB Lookin' Good!
by Tom Long

I was on Delbert Hayes team in the early 70's on a flight that took off from Otis AFB in a C-123K for some sort of FTX. We had just lifted off and were out over the water when the port side engine took a dump. Hayes had made me JM so I could get my master wings; and when the load master came back, I walked back to the area aft of the doors to see what he had to say. He ignored Hayes and I both, and opened the doors which we both recognized as a bad sign. It was early spring and I figured the water temperature was in the mid 30's, so getting out there wasn't going to work. The pilot got us overland just south of Boston and they told us to get ready to unass the plane.

I looked out the door and recognized the big highway that goes down to the Cape. It was full of traffic, but I figured most of us would come down in the median or off to the sides of the road and the rest were going to cause a huge traffic jam. About that time, he got the little jets to light and we flew back to Otis. At that point, I would have gladly walked to Vermont or wherever we were going.

North Andover Incident
by Tom Long

There was the North Andover incident in the early 70's at Devens. It was one of those "Fly Away" things and the pilots were reserve pilots. They thought a garbage dump fire outside North Andover was the DZ & dumped everybody out in town at about 2200 hrs. It scared the piss out of the town folk as guys were bouncing off house tops etc. Some guy went thru a large window into a living room where a family was watching TV.

Turn in Truck
by Tom Schultz

Summer '67: a Saturday "Grab Ass" jump by SWS. Two Hueys and Willie Williams J/M on one, me on the other. Willie and I decided we would be nice guys and get the pilots to fly a track so the guys would land as close as possible to the turn in truck.

Somehow it developed into a contest between the two teams, absolutely no idea how that happened. Anyhoo, after three or four guys had to kick off the sides of the deuce and a half, we were met by LTC O'Shaughnessy after that landing. He waved us over to him, looked at us and said "Knock it off, assholes".

Willie and I saluted, said "yes sir", and continued the jumps.

All jumpers after that had to walk a bit to the turn in trucks, not too far, but some bit farther than the others.

1967 and 1969
by John Cleckner

I was in Saigon attending a JUSPO Orientation Course that should have only had Colonels participating in it. I was a 2nd Lt. and had so much time on my hands I spent much of it shopping and finding out about Saigon, and also hanging out at the Sporting Bar, and at the club in the "SF Villa" and generally taking advantage of being in the big city. Maggie came into the "BAR" with a SGM from some Army Unit and one from the British Embassy.

We all linked up and commenced drinking and playing games. It was crazy; it was like being in an adult kindergarten booze party. Maggie walked up to me, put her arm around me and said, "Come on kid, you're with me." Apparently the Army SGM was too drunk (mid day) to do his escort duties and I was pegged. The British SGM (I believe he was a SAS SGM) was a really great guy and hung in there with us as evening approached.

Maggie jumped up and said, "By god, were taking this party to the British Embassy". I reminded her that there was a curfew and I had no orders authorizing me to leave the SF Compound. No problem. The British SGM and Maggie put me in the back of their land rover and covered me with blankets and away we went.

We made it through town and into the compound. As I recall it was pretty fancy. That is when I got married up with a couple of the horniest British female soldiers I ever met. The rest is history. The Brits brought me back in the morning with a pretty good hangover and a very large smile on my face. I never even got to say good-bye to Maggie.

She was last seen in the wee hours making her way to her room with a bottle of Vodka and alone.

In 1969 I was in Da Nang on Team business (A 102) when she came in and asked the C1 Cmdr for an escort over to CCN. It was a day, night, and next morning kind of deal. I was there when the call came in, and told her I was the man when she wanted me.

I met her at the Mike Force Bar and over to CCN we went.

Colonel Warren met us and gave us the red carpet treatment. Maggie and I got a through briefing and tour of the area. Then everyone assembled at the Bar and they went wild when she came in. She talked for a while, told a bunch of jokes and started to sing. Of course, a lot of conversation took place in the mean time. The drinks rolled big time.

We went from the bar to the billets/whatever and she talked with some of the guys individually - sometimes by themselves, sometime with me along. It was all very touching. She was a very caring person and the real deal.

Beside Col Warren at CCN at this time, there was Bill Angel, Cpt Brown, the major with the BIG muscles and a big head of black hair (CRS). Doug Welsh (sp) had the RTs. I armed wrestled the big major that night and Maggie kept putting her bets on my back. I was drunk enough to beat him.

I saw a lot of guys who had been in my Company in SFTG. They obviously took my advice and went to SOG. I often have problems with my decision to push the men with that assignment, two of them being Ben Lyons and Jimmy Pruitt.

It was very late and Colonel Warren told Maggie that a team was going out shortly. She asked to meet with them alone. She was granted her wish and we went into this dark room. I remember the guys looked too young to be doing this. I believe there were two Spec4s and an E5. She talked quietly with them and sang Gaelic songs to them. She hugged them and kissed them. We left and I took her to her room. I heard that the team was lost. This would have been early in January 1969 for those of you who were there then or monitor this sort of thing.

Maggie and I left the next day and I took her to the airport. She called my wife in Fayetteville and told her about "our night out". Sally got a big kick out of that.

Maggiebird
by Bill Coombs

I was at the Project Delta bar in Nha Trang one night when the guys presented Martha Raye with a medal that they had designed. It had some type of ribbon and on it hung a Full Colonel's eagle. They called it the first and only presentation of the 'Maggiebird'. She said, "This is the proudest day of my life."

Several weeks later, I was watching the Academy Awards program. We got it about a month late on AFVN. Bob Hope presented her a special Academy Award. She sniffled a bit and then said, "This is proudest day of my life." Then there was a pause and she added, "Stateside."

Drunk, Not Dead
by Bill Coombs

Walt Connell was a fellow member of Chapter 8 of the SFA. He told me that he got shot up pretty badly in Vietnam, and had been transferred to either Bien Hoa or Saigon (I don't recall which) for further med-evac out of the country. His plane was going to leave in the morning and he had to spend the night in Vietnam. Members of his team came to visit him and brought booze and got him plastered.

The next morning, a young doctor who had just arrived in Vietnam looked at Walt who turned out to be his first patient in Vietnam and declared him dead. They covered him up with a sheet. A little while later, Martha Raye came into the hospital and was told that one of her Green Berets just died. Maggie went over and pulled the sheet back to see who it was. Walt was still plastered and could not even grunt. All he could do was just barely wink at her. She saw that and said, "This guy isn't dead, he's drunk." Everyone jumped through their asses then and starting hooking him up to all sorts of stuff and they got him med evac'd to the Philippines.

When Martha Raye came over to Hawaii in 1982 with Rosemary Clooney, Helen O'Connell and Kay Starr for their NEW FOUR GIRLS SHOW, Walt and Maggie got together and had a ball talking about it.

Maggie's Escort
by Bill Coombs

General Abrams and a whole bunch of dignitaries met Maggie when she arrived in Saigon. They invited her to attend the New Year's Eve Party either at MACV or the embassy. I don't recall which.

A full colonel told her escort officer that the uniform he would wear that night was dress whites. The officer told the colonel he did not have dress whites with him in Vietnam, and was told he had plenty of time to get them there since New Year's Eve was a couple of months off.

As the story goes, he told Maggie and she told him that she would be wearing fatigues that night and he should wear what she was wearing.

New Years Eve arrived. Maggie and the escort officer arrived at the party in fatigues. During the course of the evening, the O-6 asked the escort officer if he had forgotten their conversation about the uniform. The escort officer explained that Colonel Raye told him to wear fatigues. The colonel got pissed and told the escort officer to forget the Colonel Raye crap; she was a movie star and nothing else, and indicated the escort officer's shit was in the street.

The escort officer told Maggie. Maggie told Abrams who called the colonel off.

Martha Raye Award
by Gary Lamberty

I'm not an expert on Maggie, and only met her once, but here are a few things, which I think, put her a cut above other celebrities who've spent time entertaining troops. First, I believe she took it upon herself to begin entertaining troops before the USO was even created during WWII. Second, she was one of the old-fashioned type super stars with a lot of broad talents, e.g. singing, dancing, acting, and esp. gifted as a comedienne. IMHO, I think there have been many, maybe even the majority of, stars who only did USO stints in the rear areas for the sake of more PR and "ticket punching" to further their own careers. Maggie, on the other hand, seemed more concerned with getting out in the boonies with the troops.

There must be hundreds, probably thousands, of guys who met her at A Teams, but I've never heard much about her being part of the really big rear-echelon productions put on like Bob Hope would do. I'm sure she's done those too; but it sounds more like she preferred to get out where the fighting troops were, and I don't think she traveled with a huge entourage and a bunch of production stuff. I've also heard she was wounded a few times, received two or three purple hearts, and would use her nursing skills to treat the wounded. Judging by all the reports and photos I've seen from others in SF, it seems like she was over in Nam during the whole thing. Either that or she sure kept bouncing back and forth between there and wherever.

When I met her at Bien Hoa, she turned to me and made a remark about shaved pussy. Later she sorta singled me out and came over to my table for most of the rest of the evening. CRS if that was the same night or the next night, because on the night of the strip show, I was sitting up front in the tables reserved for the A Teams and Mike Force. When she came and sat at my table it was toward the back of the club where I sat. She got on stage and sang a couple songs, including, "I Left My Heart In San Francisco". During her impromptu show, she said something about not letting the protesters back home get us down, and they weren't good enough shine our boots. At one point, a bunch of sirens started going off which I guess meant there was supposed to be incoming somewhere in the area. She said something to the effect of "Don't worry about that, they can't hit what they want anyhow." and just went on unphased. She drank vodka and lime all the sitting at my table; and never turned anyone away who came to talk to her, and never refused a dance with anyone either. As a matter of fact, she got on stage and danced with all the guys who formed a line to get a turn. I think everyone got a hug and kiss after each dance, too.

Times with Maggie
by Bill Adams

I last saw Walt C'nell at one of those chapter meetings we had up on the ridge at Ft. Shafter; or, it might have been over at Wainae where he needed a room and I gave him mine and went back home. "I'll pay you next time I see you", says Walt.

I have long kissed the money good-bye. When Maggie came over to Honolulu for that Four Girls Show, she called me and said I was still her number one sweet mutha. I live on the Big Island and couldn't get away. I asked her how in hell she got my number and she said, Oh that's easy. All I had to do was call some other sweet muthas. I think it was Tom Campbell (RIP) that gave her the Chapter roster.

In '73 Maggie came out to our camp at Ravenna, Ohio Arsenal after I sent a single rose and a bottle of vodka up to her room. She was doing a dinner show in Akron and I couldn't miss the chance. We were at Ravenna doing a domestic action project for Kent State University just across the highway.

Maggie spent the better part of three nights playing poker and drinking with us at the campsite. We picked her up and took her back to her hotel in a NG 2.5 ton truck. We talked of many things, but I don't remember us talking much of VN. I could be wrong as my memory didn't work right when I was drinking.

Almost Died
by Ben Roberts

As the SOG folks like to say, "You have never lived until you have almost died". As an A Team puke, I can honestly add you have never lived until you have almost died, when you fire three consecutive WWII 4.2 Mortar rounds with those yellow plastic explosive increments that cause the round to sit in the tube screaming and then turning a 90 degree angle when leaving the tube,
slamming into the sandbag walls of your mortar pit in a rainstorm...My Heart is still thumping! God bless the person who decided to put safety arming devices on mortar rounds. They still need to issue 75 mg of Valium before a crew starts firing old ammo, as well as ear plugs.

1962, Villa Teamhouse/Safe house in DaNang
by William Foxworth

The new team had arrived, and was being briefed and orientated to the area. One of the weapons men was showing his counter part how a Swedish K was operated. I was walking by at the time and glanced over as the weapons man had the bolt open and a fully loaded magazine in the weapon. Suddenly he fired it into the tile leaving bits of stone on the floor. Two or three fragments of the bullets hit me in the leg. Everyone was lucky that time. I heard several weeks later that the counterpart from the new team was killed on an operation with the Swedish K. He had accidentally shot himself. He had it loaded, the stock was extended, the bolt back and in the lock notch. He went to squat down with the weapon in front of him with the muzzle up. He put the stock on the ground hard; it unseated the bolt from the lock notch and put a couple of rounds up thru the chin and head.

One Stupid Mistake
by Bill Adams

I remember SSG R'rock from C 2/5 in 74 or was it 75. R'rock was a riffed Cpt and was a pretty good SF troop. He went on leave and at Ft Leonard Wood, Misery he called MPs, identified himself as General Somebody, and asked for an MP escort from Landing Strip Suchandsuch.
Two MPs showed up. R'rock drew down on them, took one MP's MP regalia, bound and gagged them and tied them up against a tree. He took the MP sedan, and waited outside post finance for a payroll officer to depart, followed the officer, pulled the officer over and instructed the officer that there had been a mistake and he would return the officer to post finance. The officer's driver was dismissed. R'rock held a gun on him while he took the officer to a remote location where he again bound and gagged him, then egressed the post. No problem until he bragged about it to an old Army buddy who thought little of R'rock's detailed direct action mission. His buddy promptly turned him in. LTC Larry Stearns declared at the Group's PT formation what had transpired with R'rock's adventure. We all realized the planning and execution phases were flawless, but security stunk to high heaven. Stearns told all that we should all go see R'rock who was in the post stockade. I did go see him and he whispered that he had contingencies and alternate plans for the entire operation, and that he made one stupid mistake.

Grass for Everyone!
by Bill Coombs

Before I admit my error, I have to ask if any of you SF guys received a shipment of grass seed at your camps.

One of the teams ordered the type of grass seed that is used on the green of a golf course. It grows very tightly and they wanted it to keep their berms from falling apart.

So I looked up the stock number and ordered 200 pounds of it. Well, it turns out that the unit of issue for the seed was not POUND - but BAG. Some clerk at CISO on Okinawa changed the unit of issue to BAG. Now, did he also change the quantity down from 200 to 1 or 2 bags? Noooo!

We ended up getting 200 bags of grass seed. Each bag weighed about 100 pounds. We could not return it and there were not many golf courses being built in Vietnam at the time.

So rather than being stuck with it, I thought about the reason we ordered it in the first place. Knowing the other teams had berms also, we force issued it to the four C-Team Logistic Supply Points (Da Nang, Pleiku, Bien Hoa and Can Tho); and they were to offer it to their subordinate teams. I think we even sent some of it to the Command Liaison Detachment at Camp Goodman in Saigon.

I swear, I never did another stupid thing. If you believe that to be true, I'll tell you another lie.

Camp Poli Prong
by William Foxworth

1963, Camp Poli Krong, due west of Kontum on the Dak Bla River: We ran an operation to the South of and West of the camp; did not run into any bad guys or yards. Saw plenty of tiger pugmarks. Returned to camp three days later without any contact. About a half hour to an hour after returning to camp, about 15-20 Yards, one old man and the rest women and children had followed us back to camp.

Our senior medic, James T, and one other American took another patrol out to the same area. We came to a old village site and killed a couple of water buffalo. A couple of days later, they came thru the site again and saw a tiger eating one of the dead buffalo. According to James, the whole point squad of yards and the two Americans opened fire on the Tiger. The tiger jumped up and ran into some tall grass. They closed in on the area the tiger had jumped into; James got up on one of the old pilings for a yard house so he could see over the high grass. He spotted the tiger lying down in the grass, and shot it in the head with his M2 Carbine. Then they skinned the tiger, rolled the skin up and put it in a waterproof bag.

The tiger had been hit by one bullet in the shoulder, in addition to the one in the head. When they arrived back at camp a couple of days later, the skin was really ripe. The team sergeant threw the bag and skin in the river.

Team Intel Sgt ran an operation, and we crossed a tributary chat fed into the Dak Bla River below Poli Krong. This tributary was a bout 20 feet across but very swift running in the rainy season. We strung a one-rope bridge across the stream, and had to tie most of the CIDG onto the rope so it would not be swept away. I went to the West side to get them off the rope and put them out on a perimeter. We had about 15 of them across and out on perimeter when we started receiving fire from up the hill.

Some of the CIDG returned fire, and like a fool I came out of the tree line at the stream to see what was going on. (Well there were no bullets kicking up dust around me, sooo I figgered I wasn't being shot at.) One of the CIDG came down the hill with his weapon on his shoulder asking for Bacsi. He was checked out; he had a crease across the top of one arm and had a round in his leg with no exit wound. W got him back across the stream. By this time our Intel. Sgt. had gotten across the stream and led an assault up the hill.

The few VC that had been there had departed. We found a blood trail, followed it but lost it. Two magazines were captured for a Chenault BAR.

Our wounded man was med-evac'd to the Pleiku CIDG hospital. At that time we were using HT-1 Radios that weren't worth two cents. They were the black square walkie-talkie type that took 6 or 8 "D" type batteries. A MEDEVAC was called for; at the other end they wanted to know if the WIA was an American or Indig. I told the ass hole it didn't make any difference. We had a WIA, and needed him to be evacued. That was when some one at a higher level had made the decision that if he was an indig, the RVN would do the evac. I do not know how long that policy was continued. At that time, the Huey's were just starting to become operational. The Army H-21 and the Marine Corps H-34 were the primary means of transportation.

CB Stat Team: We had a CB Team come to Poli Krong to assist us in the construction of an air strip. The CB Team Arrived with a big 5Ton truck with trailer, a jeep, a small bull dozer, and a sheeps foot roller. Do not remember how many men were on the team but they had an older chief and a young Lt. (Army Cpt, equivalent) who wanted his men to call him captain. Never happened.

Any who, when they arrived, with their equipment the first thing they did was try to send the 5Ton truck and trailer across the river still loaded with all their other equipment. Promptly sunk the ferry. First major job was to re-float the ferry.

This was an old French trail ferry that consisted of two barges with a deck built on them. In the event some may not know, what a Trail Ferry is or how it works. It is attached to a set of pulleys/rollers mounted on an overhead cable that is anchored on each side of the river. Another cable or line is attached to rollers and then attached to the ferry. Depending on which direction you wanted to go, you would have to move the cable/line from one end of the ferry to the other end. The current of the river is what powered the ferry. In the dry season when the river was low, it might take 10 to 15 minutes to go from one side to the other. On the other hand it would take only about 2 minutes to swing across the river.

After the CB's had completed the air strip. The Det Cdr asked them to clear the mine field on the south side of the camp and the airstrip. This mine field consisted of only the M-14 Toe Popper's and was put in by the Team that we had relived. Do not remember what group they were from. The field was probably 30-40 feet wide by the length of one side of the camp. There was no mine field plan made that I know of. It appeared there was no standard pattern and the mines were put in the ground as single, and double and triple stacked. We did not know this at the time when the CB's started to clear the field. They decided that the mines being M-14's, they would use the little D-4 bull dozer and the sheeps foot roller to run over the mines and detonate them. The driver of the dozer made a couple of passes and had to stop to refuel. While refueling he noticed that a few pads off the track missing, that was when we determined the mines had been stacked. Needless to say that stopped the mine clearing. My suggestion to the Detachment commander that we should use the dozer to either push them into the river or make a big pile of dirt in one place and put wire around the hill and mark it mined. That didn't happen either.

Who ever picked that site for an "A" Camp should have been court marshaled. It was on the west side of the river, on the river and no way across except the ferry, a couple of small hills that were higher than the camp on the north side. Subsequently the camp was overrun in 1964. The VC set up mortars on the west end of the airstrip and attacked from the west. The came had just received a new batch of CIDG from some place of which about 1/2 were reported to be VC after the camp was overrun.

Dumb
by Bob Smith

During a drunken party with the Ecuadorian SF (we had just made a 35,000 foot jump for their graduation), my team leader decides to shoot off his mouth and proceeds to tell one of the students, who happened to be their mountain team leader, that the gringos could do anything the mountain team could. The Ecuadorian Captain called his bet and proceeds to put together a climbing expedition for the next morning. I didn't find this crap out until we got back to our rooms that night. We were going to show the Ecuadorians just how "manly" we were by climbing Cotapoxi, an extinct volcano. We were to depart the hotel at 0500 for the 45-minute drive to the volcano. The mountain team leader provided us with a his best NCO and all the climbing gear to include down vest, boots, ice crampons (yes, there was fugging ice!) ice axes, etc.

As we approached the base of the volcano, I couldn't breathe! We were at 5,000 feet, still half-drunk, and in my opinion.... STUPID!

I took a few hits off an oxygen bottle and we began our slow climb. Climbing up a glacier is stupid! I wanted to embed my axe in the head of my stupid team leader! We finally started breaking through the clouds on the mountain and got up to about 17,000 feet when we saw someone coming down the mountain in front of us. As they neared, we stopped to take a break. Our visitors were a professional group of climbers who said it was too dangerous to go to the top. The sun was melting the ice and crevasses were opening up without warning. Nuff said! We moved over to a gentler sloping part of the ice and rode our axes down. We made it off the mountain fine. You might think this wasn't all that bad, but I found out a few days later just how bad it could have been. Seems as though there was another "extinct" volcano in country that had started acting up. British and French scientists battled to be the first to put monitoring equipment on top...the British won.... and lost. That damn thing blew up in their faces and all were lost except for one Brit. Now you see why I said doing this was dumb. My feelings were later reinforced when Mt. St. Helens blew up.

Vietnam the 1st Day…Say Wha?
By Bryan Furman

I arrived in Cam Ranh Bay, Vietnam, on January 16, 1969 with two other Special Forces medics Sgt.'s Neil Mayse and John Whisenant. Being only E-5 Buck Sergeants getting off the plane, we had to line up for Air Force luggage checks. They were looking for U.S. dollars and other things they didn't want in country.

I opened my bag and displayed, among other things, my 4" folding buck knife, and the young Air Force dude at the counter said, "That's mine".

"How so?" says I.

"It's mine, give it over," he says.

Angry at the dude's attitude and thinking, I wondered what the fook is this knife compared to all the weapons in country? Not wanting to give my knife over to him, I propped the now opened knife with the tip on the concrete floor and leaned the butt against the counter and stomped on it. I broke the blade into two pieces and from the handle. I picked up the three pieces and slid them across the counter saying: "There you go, now it's yours." Neil was watching, and just grinned at me.

Air Force went all frothy on me and said I had 'destroyed Government Property' and I was in 'big trouble.' Not saying a thing myself, just looking at him, he threatened to send me to his Commanding Officer (CO). I knew for sure now that the asshole would have pocketed the knife and maybe sold it on the black market if I hadn't broken it.

Dude kept his threat and called over a couple Army MP's and I was escorted to the CO's office. Turns up he is not in. Angry and wondering if they were all involved in this, I dutifully go with the MP's to see another officer, an Army 1st Lt. After answering some questions he stands up and starts yelling from behind his desk. While hollering, he gave me a clue and I said it was still my knife because he hadn't given me a receipt for it yet and said I wanted one. Far out, but it worked. I got my receipt for the broken knife.

The Lt was still pissed and sent me to KP. Relieved to be out of his office I left to report to the mess hall. I walked in the front door, reported in, and picked up some tableware. I slowly worked my way down table by table to the back door and out. I almost tripped over Neil. He was sitting on the back steps, sipping a beer and holding one up for me. I noticed he had brought my duffle. Looking down at his shit-eating grin I just sighed, sat down next to him and started whining, "Why me? Could you believe that? I mean….. "

"Bry" he said, interrupting me, "I could see it coming". We shared a couple of fuck you's with the beers, joined up with John and wandered off to find our quarters.

Roadcraters
by Bryan Furman

I heard a loud explosion while working in the dispensary; and two others and I took off south in the jeep. We found a huge crater in the road that had been blown through the canal bank, and a detonating wire stretched more than 100 yards east into a tree line. We found a MACV officer and his Vietnamese counterpart, still in one piece but with all their head openings bleeding. Their jeep was on its side, forward of the crater and almost jack-knifed up through the middle. We called a medevac; can't remember now which one was still breathing. It was maybe a mortar or 155.

Yes, road craters - I remember?

Swimming Vertical
Greg Hoisington

We were doing a lot of classroom, free-ascent tower, and pool work with the SEALS at Coronado. This included fun things like towel races and harassment swims, before we hit the ocean. There was one strap-hanger in the class who was more afraid of hungry things with teeth than I was..

As we were short one ossifer, and had only eleven men, the strap-hanger was assigned to my team. (Can't remember his name, but he knew the words to all the good German beer drinking songs. I mean, we'd be like sitting around having a quiet drink, when he'd start stomping his foot and pounding his glass on the table, and singing, "Auf die heimat stat ein kleines blumshenlein... clomp, clomp, clomp, clomp... und das heiss... clomp, clomp, clomp... Erika..." He'd get everyone going. Nevertheless, I digress and can't remember my German.)

Anyway, this guy starts quizzing the SEAL instructor about sharks, how to avoid them, etc. The instructor tells him to go to the bottom until the shark loses interest. Well, the questions go on until the instructor realizes that he has a live one, and plays him. The bottom line is that he tells this guy that sharks don't like to bite things that are vertical in the water. Well, how do you swim in a vertical position... get vertical when you see the shark... but... but...

Well, the next day was an ocean dive. We went down to the boat, started putting on our gear, and this strap-hanger pulls out his newly modified wet suit. Must have taken him most of the night. He had painted approx three inch wide bright yellow stripes around the arms, legs and torso of his wet suit. When he put it on, he looked like a giant yellow jacket. The Navy had a fit, and asked him WTF he was supposed to be. His response was that with the stripes, it would allow him to appear vertical, even when he was swimming horizontally... The SEALs were laughing so hard they forgot to give him the opportunity to do a little beach running.

To us, he looked like a big lure, so nobody wanted to swim anywhere near him. He ended up forming a threesome with other strap-hangers (expendable), while we let our extra man join one of our buddy teams.

Cleaning Side Arms
by Jack Moroney

On my way out of country for R&R I was making the rounds at B-24 trying to find a cot to crash on when I heard a gun shot. Two Yards came running from a barracks and pleaded with me to come with them. They led me to their fallen comrade who had been gut shot by a rather drunk troop who was still bending over the body with a .45 in his hand. Knowing that this must have been a stupid mistake by some guy fooling around, rather than aggressively trying to disarm this guy, I asked him to give me the gun and we could straighten this all out. He turned on me, raised the pistol and moving with all the lightning swiftness of a frigging slug, I some how managed to subdue him before he could get another shot off. Being a little ticked that this person with whom I had no quarrel had just tried to curtail my R&R, I snatched him up, told one of the Yards to pick up the weapon and follow me while I hauled this clown off to the SDNCO. Once inside the SDNCO office I asked for the weapon which the Yard sheepishly handed to me. It wasn't until after I tried to clear the weapon that I realized that the only reason why the shitbird hadn't shot me was because the cartridge case had failed to clear the slide port and was jammed into the barrel housing as it came forward to chamber another round. Kind of glad that the folks at B-24 spent more time hassling us folks at the A-sites and chasing their women than cleaning their side arms.

McIntire Story
by James McIntire

I was with Melvin at CCS and later at Mackal in '77. One day he and Satterlee came driving into camp. The compact pickup they were in was caved in and they had to hang out the windows. They had been over at Jack's drinking, the bridge was out and they were too drunk to find the dirt road. They drove along the railroad track and eventually got stuck in the sand. Well these two big ole boys rolled the truck out of the sand and crushed the top in. They were pretty proud of themselves because they had the presence of mind to lower the radio antennae so as not to break it.

Firefighting Mode
by Jim Lewis

In '66, we had a Viet village out at Sherman and managed to get a fire started one afternoon. When it got out of control someone called the fire department and they showed up with two trucks. They went into their best firefighting mode, rolling out hoses, giving attaboys, and turning on the water. There wasn't enough water in the trucks to put out a cigarette.

Grenade Training
John Cleckner

Here's one that almost got us all killed.

We had a great group of strikers at Dong Tre A-222. The only problem I had was that none of them could throw a grenade 10 feet and they always threw it up hill.

After getting clipped a couple of times and having a bunch of our strikers injured by our own people, I told our Wpns Sgt and Engineer Sgt to build a grenade course and re-train them, "as if they had ever been trained before". The problem continued, so I called a formation and took every grenade I could find away from them and told them they would get them back after they learned how to use them.

The next night the team notified me that ALL of the Strikers had "Gone Home". I said, "What the hell are you talking about?" Then the LLDB came over and said, "Way to go. Now what?" Sure enough all the strikers mutinied on me. Talk about thoughts swirling in your head. What the hell do I do now? They sure called my bluff.

To make a long story short the strikers had their grenades back the next morning. They all thanked me at a camp formation.

I retreated to my office with much egg on face.

Strikers Strike
by John Hauck

It's a Hell'uva feeling when you are the man in charge. I was put in that situation one morning at Xom Cat (A-312), 1966.

CPT Delano Reeves, Tm Ldr, had gone to Saigon leaving me in charge as the XO. One of the NCOs dragged my ass out of bed one morning and told me all the Strikers had quit. All four companies and recon platoon had lined up all there gear and weapons in nice neat formation, then walked off the job. Luckily, at Xom Cat there was no place to walk, except War Zone D. Xom Cat was located on the south western boundary of the D Zone. Only way in and out was by air or by boat. We had neither.

The reason for the strike was the B Team or C Team pulled a PFC, Cambode type, out of camp and sent somewhere. I don't remember. Problem was, this guy was the head hog Cambode, (how do you spell Kamer Seri?) He was in charge of all the III Corps Cambodes. No one was going to push this little guy around, so........they stacked arms and went back to their hooches.

Major David, who did not particularly care for me, nor me for him, kept stuttering on the radio telling me what to do. I told him to get the Cambode back to Xom Cat or he could send somebody to get the US types out of there. As a 1LT I had a hard time convincing the good Major to send the little guy back and everything would be hunky dorry. Finally, he conceded. The little people arrived at Xom Cat in a Huey, and life went back to normal at the intersection of the Song Be and the Song Dong Nai, not too far north of Bien Hoa. I miss those days.................

RUN
by Joseph Waskas

While serving with a four-man Mobile Advisory Team (RF/PF) in IV Corps, the weapons man and I were taking a squad of Popular Force troops down along a canal, SW of a town called Tram Chim. We were looking for a good ambush site and were trying to find signs of recent traffic. We came upon a small sampan with one of the motors that had the symbol "crossed hands" on it. These were supposed to be provided to friendlies by the "Hands Across the Sea" organization or some such name like that. Well, since someone had intended to hide this little bugger, my partner decided to drop a grenade in it. About the time he released the grenade from his hand, I noticed that the sampan was sitting much too low in the water to be empty. I yelled RUN and took off as fast as I could. The explosions lasted about 15 seconds and a small piece of wood lodged in my ear. I decided that I would be super-extra careful about processing what I was seeing before I acted in the future. This proves the old adage "ain't no use being stupid unless you show it."

Dropped the Hammer
by Kevin R.C. "Hognose" O'Brien

In about 1992 or so, we were doing the usual 12-mile rucksack march (now given the politically-correct name, "endurance event", but you guys would all recognize the march, if not perhaps some of the rucksacks).

At the finish point the various teams had organized adult beverages (now replaced with politically-correct Gatorade, at least in sight of higher-ups) and rides of one type or another back to the team house. Now, in the days of the Army Reserve SF, you didn't have no stinking deuce-n-a-half for something piddly like a ruck march. You used POVs, so we always straggled back in looking like the Taxicab March to the Marne or the Bonus Army or something.

My team had Charlie Mello's open stake truck, so we looked especially like Third Worldian migrant labourers. However, the scuba team had a van, and that's how the dog got killed.

See, [Name Redacted -- he's still in another SF unit] was playing with his new toy, an M1911A1, and he was doing it carelessly enough that his teammates got a little windy. They began telling him to chill out. He chilled not. They began telling him louder and slower (proof positive that SF language training is effective!). He continued to finger-f--k the Government Model.

"Look you guys," [Name] said. "I'm SF, AND I'm a cop. I know what I'm doing!"

This did not quiet the team. Their consensus: "Knock it off with the gun."

Finally, the team sergeant spoke, with the Voice of Stentor: "Dammit, [Name], you're being a shithead. Knock it off with the gun."

"Awwww, Top, dammit, it's not loaded. See?"; and he dropped the hammer on his beloved Golden Retriever.

They say the shot was very loud inside that tin van.

Weapons Safety Class
by Leamon Ratterree

We were on an MTT to 5th Brigade, San Vicente, El Slober-door, - a guy from MA, named John N., SSG, SF Medic type and I. We had just finished giving a weapons safety class to a bunch of new recruits. John had 3rd company, and I had second company. We turned the troops back over to their respective commanders, and were walking out the gate when we heard the loud bang. John and I looked at each other and made a bet that it was the other guy's company.

I won the bet. It was one of N.'s kids. Those folks liked to rest the muzzle on their boots. The lad did and pulled the trigger. We rounded the corner, and saw the soldiers cartin' their comrade to the hospital. Nolan was furious - he had lost the bet. Screamed at the lad, he did! "You know what you are? A training aid!"

He gathered the rest of the battalion to show the youngsters what happens to folks who rest the muzzle on their boot. This guy did better than most. The round went between his toes. Nasty burns, but the boot was still serviceable.

Dumpsters, Choppers, and DZs
by Kevin "Hognose" O'Brien

Lee (Bert) R. went into the dumpster on Turner DZ. Rather inexcusable as he was driving a -1. His story was that he lost his glasses on opening; or maybe that was his fallback story when we didn't buy the one about the dumpster chasing him. The medics stitched him up, but he got a lot of razzing.

I hit a helicopter - was futzing with a ruck that would not leg go my leg, and the wind would drift me towards the chopper; so I'd turn the chute, and resume futzing with the leg tie, looking up to see the GD copter was boresighted. I finally wound up hitting the machine while my ruck was still attached to one ankle, thanks to trying to solve both problems instead of just dealing with them one at a time. The aircrew was really pissed -- paratroopers are cheap but helicopters cost lots of money. It was a CH-54 (Skycrane) broken down on the DZ; and we flew around for an hour before jumping, while they tried to fix whatever was wrong with it.

In 1981, I had a run of about five tree jumps. Then a year or two after that I flunked out of jumpmaster school and broke my ankle and tailbone all at once. Sometime after that I pulled my head out of my aching ass and usually hit something resembling the Zone, although my Swamp Thing jump was a notable exception.

Blowing Up Duds
by Mike Berry

My favorite dud-round story from Bong Son was when the First Cav was in camp for an assault up the An Lao Valley. I had learned from experience to divide my duds into three piles instead of one big one. Quite unintentionally, I piled them about thirty meters apart in a line heading toward camp. In addition and quite unintentionally, I blew them in order from furthest to nearest about thirty seconds apart. I then retired to the teamhouse for a beer only to find about twenty First Cav troops hunkering down in the internal trenches. They yelled, "Get in here quick, they're coming!" The CO was not too happy with me. But we never fessed up to the Cav.

Demo Guy Blasts a Hole
by Terry Dahling

A Demo guy decided to help in the digging of a new well. Against saner advice he put a 40 lb. shaped charge in the hole. It was about three feet wide and ten to fifteen feet deep. When he detonated it, it picked up the A-frame used to haul buckets of dirt out of the well and went through the roof of the dispensary. Lucky no one got hurt. I distinctly remember the medic coming into the team room with tears in his eyes and saying, "Would anyone care to look at my dispensary?"

A6 Machine Gun Demo
by Terry Dahling

I was giving a class on the A6 machine gun to the Bru of Special Projects in Kontum. It was raining, so we were in a big tent. Keep in mind I was commo - not weapons. I had the gun set up on a table, pointing down the aisle between the seats.

As my grand finale, I was going to demonstrate that you have to cock the gun twice to get a round in the chamber. Unfortunately this is only true if you feed the belt from the side rather than raise the top cover like I had. I cocked the weapon once and was about to pull the trigger when something told me to also demonstrate that even though you know the weapon is empty, you always point it in a safe direction.

I pulled the trigger and the damned thing went off. I about soiled my drawers. The Captain came running in and asked what had happened. As calmly and coolly as possible, I looked him right in the eye and explained I was giving a lesson in gun safety, showing that you always point a gun in a safe direction even though you "know" it isn't loaded. The captain said: "Good job!" and left.

OOPS!
by Terry Dahling

The team sergeant told his demo man to load up the 3/4-ton with expired 60 mm rounds, and take it down to the range and blow it. A little later we heard the blast. A little later the demo man came in and opened a beer. Later the tm sgt asked where the truck was.

The demo man said: "Oops!"

The same demo man, shortly before being escorted out of the AO decided to help in the digging of a new well. Against saner advice he put a 40# shaped charge in the hole. It was about three feet wide and 10 - 15 feet deep. When he detonated it, it picked up the A-frame used to haul buckets of dirt out of the well and the A-frame went through the roof of the dispensary. Lucky no one got hurt. I distinctly remember the medic coming into the team room with tears in his eyes and saying: "Would anyone care to look at my dispensary?"

TWO THOUSAND ONE, NINE ELEVEN
submitted by Ben Roberts

THIS IS A MUST READ - THIS PERSON SHOULD STEP FORWARD AND CLAIM THIS POEM. THE WORDS ARE VERY POWERFUL!

Two thousand one, nine eleven
Five-thousand plus arrive in heaven.
As they pass through the gate,
Thousands more appear in wait
A bearded man with stovepipe hat
Steps forward saying, "Lets sit, lets chat."
They settle down in seats of clouds.
A man named Martin shouts out proud,
"I have a dream!" and once he did.
The Newcomer said, "Your dream still lives."

Groups of soldiers in blue and gray
Others in khaki, and green.
They say,"We're from Bull Run, Yorktown, the Maine."
The Newcomer said, "You died not in vain."

From a man on sticks, one could hear,
"The only thing we have is fear."
The Newcomer said, "We know the rest,
Trust us sir, we've passed that test."

"Courage doesn't hide in caves
You can't bury freedom in a grave."
The Newcomers had heard this voice before.
A distinct Yankees twang from Hyannisport shores.

A silence fell within the mist
Somehow the Newcomer knew that this

Meant time had come for her to say
What was in the hearts of the five-thousand plus that day.

"Back on Earth, we wrote reports,
Watched our children play in sports.
Worked our gardens, sang our songs.
Went to church and clipped coupons.
We smiled, we laughed, we cried, we fought.
Unlike you, great we're not."
The tall man in the stovepipe hat
Stood and said, "Don't talk like that!
Look at your country, look and see.
You died for freedom, just like me."

Then, before them all appeared a scene
Of rubbled streets and twisted beams.
Death, destruction, smoke and dust
And people working just 'cause they must.
Hauling ash, lifting stones,
Knee deep in hell, but not alone.

"Look! Blackman, Whiteman, Brownman, Yellowman.
Side by side helping their fellow man!"
So said Martin, as he watched the scene.
"Even from nightmares, can be born a dream."

Down below three firemen raised
The colors high into ashen haze.
The soldiers above had seen it before
On Iwo Jima back in '44.

The man on sticks studied everything closely
Then shared his perceptions on what he saw mostly.
"I see pain, I see tears,
I see sorrow - but I don't see fear.
You left behind husbands and wives,

Daughters and sons, and so many lives
Are suffering now because of this wrong.
But look very closely. You're not really gone.
All of those people, even those who've never met you,
All of their lives, they'll never forget you.

Don't you see what has happened?
Don't you see what you've done?
You've brought them together, together as one."

With that, the man in the stovepipe hat said,
"Take my hand," and from there he led
Five-thousand plus heroes, Newcomers to heaven
On this day, two thousand one, nine eleven.

(A toast) To War...
by Greg Hoisington

I drink to War,
   and all its glory,
      and pain,
         and decimation;

To War of terror
   and endless death,
      a child of man's creation.

For only in War
   the whole-man finds
      his heart,
         his love,
            and worth;

And truly in War
   life seeps from him,
      his blood to nurture the earth.

I raise my glass
   to War and death --
      may neither ever cease;

And to the monuments
   to War's lost heroes...
      erected in the name of PEACE.

Illegal Poem
by Hugh Johnson

I come for visit, get treated regal,
So I stay, who care I illegal?
I cross border, poor and broke,
Take bus, see employment folk.
Nice man treat me good in there,
Say I need to see welfare.
Welfare say, "You come no more,
We send cash right to your door."
Welfare checks, they make you wealthy,
Medicaid it keep you healthy!
By and by, I got plenty money,
Thanks to you, American dummy.
Write to friends in motherland,
Tell them come as fast as you can.
They come in rags and Chebby trucks,
I buy big house with welfare bucks.
They come here, we live together,
More welfare checks, it gets better!
Fourteen families they moving in,
But neighbor's patience wearing thin.
Finally, white guy moves away,
Now I buy his house, and then I say,
"Find more aliens for house to rent."
And in the yard I put a tent.
Send for family (they just trash),
But they, too, draw the welfare cash!
Everything is mucho good,
And soon we own the neighborhood.
We have hobby--it's called breeding,
Welfare pay for baby feeding.
Kids need dentist? Wife need pills?
We get free! We got no bills!
American crazy! He pay all year,
To keep welfare running here.
We think America darn good place!

Too darn good for the white man race.
If they no like us, they can go,
Got lots of room in Mexico.

Samuel Adams' Boston Lager Prayer
by Bill Adams

Our lager, Which art in barrels, Hallowed be thy drink, Thy will be drunk, (I will be drunk), At home as I am in the VFW. Give us this day our foamy head, And forgive us our spillages, As we forgive those who spill against us, and lead us not to incarceration, But deliver us from hangovers, For thine is the beer, The bitter and the lager, Forever and ever, Barmen.

The Final Inspection
submitted by James Carey

The soldier stood and faced God
  Which must always come to pass.
He hoped his shoes were shining
  Just as brightly as his brass.

Step forward now, you soldier,
  how shall I deal with you?
Have you always turned the other cheek?
  To My Church have you been true?

The soldier squared his shoulders And said,
  No Lord, I guess I ain't
Because those of us who carry guns
  Can't always be a saint

I've had to work most Sundays,
  And at times my talk was tough;
And sometimes I've been violent,
  Because the world is awfully rough.

But, I never took a penny
  That wasn't mine to keep...
Though I worked a lot of overtime
  When the bills just got too steep.

And I never passed a cry for help;
  Though at times I shook with fear.
And sometimes, God forgive me,
  I've wept unmanly tears.

I know I don't deserve a place,
  Among the people here.
They never wanted me around
  Except to calm their fear.

If you've a place for me here, Lord,
  It needn't be so grand.
I never expected or had too much;
  But if not, I'll understand.

There was a silence all around the throne
  Where the saints had often trod.
As the soldier waited quietly
  For the judgment of the Lord.

Step forward now, you soldier,
  You've borne your burdens well.
Walk peacefully on Heaven's streets;
for ..... You've done your time in Hell.

Puke and Beer
by Ben Fenske

When on my way to Germany the first time, two of my kids came down with the chicken pox, and they quarantined the whole family except me at the St George Hotel in Brooklyn. I had already taken my car to Caven Pt, NJ and had to rely on the subways to get to the ferry to Governors Island after sneaking the kids out the back door through the kitchen, and taking them to the hospital at Governors Island. I had never been to New York before. In the next week, I traveled as far as those subways would take me, just to get out of that hotel room and see the kids every day.

I was stuck there for seven days before the kids were released, and we sailed on the troop transport ROSE. Then the wife got seasick. That caused the kids to lose their cookies also. What a f—ked up trip that was. Their food was delivered to the room and they couldn't eat for three of the five days. If they did, I would be sliding through puke all over the stateroom. Of course, I got to eat with the top shelf, ship's Captain and all. I was one of the few eating; all the dependents were seasick and all that good chow was going to waste.

When I finally got to Munich, one of the other platoon sergeants in my unit was my sponsor. We had only been there one week. The first thing he handed me was an American can opener and a pop-top bottle of Lowenbrau. Being a lifetime kraut by birth and having used those bottles at my house for canning, I threw the bottle opener back to him and popped off the top with a whack from a forefinger. He almost shit in his pants. He asked how I did that. "Comes with the territory," I replied.

Their unit had already flunked the first practice alert, and the day before my arrival passed the 2nd one. I was stationed in Will Kaserne on that trip until the 11th Abn Div went ROTAD and I ended up in the 503d at Warner Kaserne the rest of that tour.

Enough already.

Sitting Dead
by Ben Fenske

I was on a trip with a bunch of local friends a few years back and went by bus, near the twin cities (MPLS & ST PAUL, MN), to a small town located on the Apple River where they rented inner tubes and everyone brought coolers and lashed them to a spare rental inner tube. At almost every turn in this narrow creek or "river" there was a painted target where you could fill your empty beer can and throw it at the target. The locals and renters of inner tubes made a small fortune from the aluminum which varies from 32 cents a lb to 51 cents depending on how many pounds you had. No bottled beer is permitted and in case somebody does sneak bottles onto these trips downriver, everyone must wear old shoes or tennis shoes as the average depth is only about three to four feet. After the floating was over, we departed and halfway home stopped at a restaurant in a very small town when a storm began to brew. After we entered and ordered drinks we sat down to eat, and the lights went out. The power outage was not from lightning, but caused by a local boy who was speeding outside of town, lost control, hit a telephone pole and was killed.

Most of the people on the bus were half to 3/4 wasted from excessive consumption of alcohol, ordered our meals and the proprietor lit candles for all tables. We had a good time. Luckily the kitchen stoves were gas operated and we were unable to open the cash registers; but used a cigar box, pad and pencil, and money from a slush fund the owner kept in his office.

After enjoying a great meal we departed and it was then that we came upon the kid in the red convertible still smashed inside his car. No jaws of life existed at that time. The police were waiting for the ambulance to come from over 30 miles away. The little towns were not more than 100 population and just small hick towns (no ambulance service). The sight of the car and the kid sitting dead in it sobered up most of our people; and it got quiet the rest of the way home.

"Cold" Night
By Ben Roberts

We made our way through the night vision course in the winter of 1965 at Ft Benning, Georgia. I was listening to President Johnson's speech about the ongoing war in Vietnam. I was 22 years old hoping to graduate from jump school, and the Special Forces Medical School while listening to his speech on the little earpiece speaker attached to my ear from a 2x2" radio.

The temperature was only 40 degrees as we blindly tried to follow the wet paths through the forest in the dark, stumbling and falling with loud grunts as we made our way. This was probably my most surrealistic part of the war because it would be over a year before I would even participate in it; yet, what was happening in Vietnam was being received in my ear. I was feeling rather patriotic and privy to the speech because no one else had little AM-FM radios on them.

We were freezing our asses off. Every man was behind the other, blowing into their numb hands, trying to warm those leaving clouds of heated air from their breaths behind them. As a future medic, I had support from one of the young basic medics who ran sick call. I had acquired a private stockpile of almost a quart of small Turban Hydrate used for coughs and colds.

The elixir of Turpin Hydrate and Codeine was probably the equivalent of a narcotic version of Nyquil. I assumed the role of dispenser of drugs to help my teammates around me while distributing the small, four-ounce bottles among the squad.

Before long, we felt little pain, and enjoyed the warm feeling as the drug for colds and coughs was absorbed in our stomachs. We made our way through the rest of the night in great spirits with occasional giggles heard from a few of the other airborne candidates. All of us enjoyed the medicinal properties for colds, and were able to complete our course in great spirits. Things have changed since those days. The army is not what it used to be. Restrictions on medicine are much greater. It was one of those times when a person wanting to be a medic actually helped out his squad before medical training.

Memories of C's
by Bill Adams

I could remember only a few times when we were permitted to build a small fire. Usually, the tactical situation was such that we'd have to eat cold C's everyday for one to two weeks before we'd get hot chow or allowed to heat the Cs. I do remember after a few years in the Army, we were issued those trioxane tablets. Nevertheless, if we somehow managed to heat something, we'd move out and have to choke it down, throw the trash away, grab our stuff, and beat it.

I remember a night we road marched for 3-4 hours and stopped. The terrible weather decided to get worse. I was sweaty from the forced march, so I put on my poncho to try to keep the wind and hawk out. Didn't work, so I sat cross legged and lit one trioxane tablet between my legs and the warmth under that poncho was heavenly. If only I could breathe air instead of choking on the fumes. Aha, says I. I put my trusty M17 protective mask on, and for the first time in days felt comfortable. At daylight we continued our road march at a healthy pace, and I felt myself having difficulty breathing. All that day this was the case, so I ruled the trioxane, poncho, protective mask shelter out of my bag of tricks.

When in Germany, I could place a can of Cs over the hot air exhaust of my M114 scout car and it would be heated in a few minutes. In addition, that 5K BTU gas heater was a splendid plus, not to mention I never needed to buy lighter fluid, because I had all the MoGas I needed for my Zippo.

I never knew what Texas Pete was until after my 4th or 5th year in the Army when the Mess Sgt put a bottle on each table in the Mess Hall. Course, they quickly started disappearing. Texas Pete did have a way of making one look forward to his Cs. I take that back. I don't think anyone favorably anticipated eating Cs, but Texas Pete did help.

Last SF Post Detail
by Ben Roberts

I had just finished SF Med school and was in C/7th SFG, but somewhere around 1965-66 our company got one a post detail assignment. We were assigned to those huge, I am talking REAL BIG here, warehouses where everything was stored for supplying all operations on at Ft Bragg. There were miles of aisles stacked fifty feet high with every part of anything that that moved on Ft Bragg including survival Kits full of amphetamines, parachutes, truck parts, etc. They told us to fill requested items by serial number, and put them in bags to be picked up by anyone on post ordering stuff.

We were all bummed out about this warehouse assignment, and started grabbing anything, and sticking it into the paper sacks, sending things off. If a cook ordered a spoon he got a truck axle sort of thing. It got so bad; they were losing a lot of sport parachutes, etc. They pulled us off the detail after a week, and called in the FBI who to my knowledge wasn't too interested in the miles of aisles issue either. After that, we all went happily off on FTX's and other schools. I think that was the last time SF was ever chosen for post details other then policing their own areas and helping out at Gabriel Demonstrations.

Mad Dog 20-20
by Bill Adams

Your eyes are getting tired.....it is difficult to keep them open....you are going back in time......you are now asleep. You will remember everything about that night at Mackall. Think back, think back, think back......was there another person sitting there while this group of great men, (May some of them now rest in peace), who put together this plan and war-gamed it from all chance of failure? Think back, and remember who else sat there. "Fighting Phil" Mc. was with R'edge's team somewhere out there fixin' to do a DA prisoner snatch on us. Now, who would be sitting there with you folks, because he would rather be with you than stumbling around in the dark with R'edge and McC? Remember? Now, when I snap my fingers you will awaken feeling refreshed and alert.

How else would I remember all those details? It was all bullshit, and gun smoke as we sat around that fire with all our "what ifs." Jim C'tle was there, too.

Actually, I had forgotten all about this until just after they took R'rock away, Bob Al'n stopped in my office and asked, "Do you remember that night at Mackall when we passed that bottle of Mad Dog 20-20 around the fire?" OH MY GOD! It dawned on me. Does that make me a part of this thing (accessory), I thought. Suddenly, overwhelmed by a mild pucker factor, I asked C'tle what he thought, and he responded with a "Sgt Schultz" on me. After all, it was just bullshit and gun smoke. How was I to know Larry R'rock or anyone else was gonna do it? I will say this for R'rock. He has very good recall, but I must also say his security was found wanting.

8th SFG IG Inspection
by Bill Coombs

I was the Supply Sergeant of Co E (Signal) of the 8th in 1965-1966. During that time, we were very short of troops because almost everyone was being sent to Vietnam. We got to the point where we had less than 30 guys in the company. If you were familiar with the Signal Company of a SF group at that time, then you know that we had a lot of vehicles. For maintenance, one soldier would be responsible for three trucks.

The group had an IG inspection coming up and the Group Commander wanted all of the buildings painted on the outsides. My company commander did not agree. He told the commander that he did not have the troops to do that.

He told me that we were not going to paint the building but everything inside would be straight. I went through the building and put in job orders for everything that needed work. The Post Engineers came and fixed cracks in the walls, the shower heads and all of that other stuff. I heard that the Captain and the Group Commander were having words over painting the building. Guys, if you have never been to Fort Guluck, these were not little one story jobs. They were three or four story high stucco buildings.

Well, the IG comes through and looks us over.

Fast forward to the IG's exit report where he said and I paraphrase, "Notably, Company E's building was the best in the group because they repaired problems; they did not paint over them." That did not go over too well with the Group Commander.

I wondered why the Captain did not seem to worry about things. Captain B've was a big guy and I understand he played football for West Point.

A short time after the IG inspection, I was working on some report that HQ on the other side of the isthmus wanted. I did it two or three times and they kept sending it back for changes. The Company Commander got tired of signing them and made arrangements for him and me to meet with a major in the G-4 of USARSO.

The major was very polite and explained that DA was dropping changes on them and they just had to pass them down to us; but they finally got it figured out and he explained to us. When he finished, the captain asked me if I completely understood, and I said I did. Then he said to the major, "This is the last f--king time we were going to do it. If you want anything else done, you will have to do it yourself." I couldn't believe my ears. I had never heard a captain address a major like that. The major asked me to step outside.

A few minutes later, my commander comes out and we get into his convertible and head back to Fort Guluck. He knew I had a question and he answered for me before I asked. He said he was visiting an officer's club one time. It was in the afternoon and he was sitting at the bar. He went to the john and when he returned, some guy in civvies was in his seat. He told him that he wanted his seat back. The guy told him it was HIS seat. The captain said, "No it is not. That is my drink right there."

He leaned towards the guy to get his drink and the guy pushed him away. So the captain decked him. I guess I should stop referring to the guy as "the guy" and start calling him the "General".

B've told me as soon as had decked the General, the bartender came over and apologized for not telling him the chair in question was always the General's after 4:00 PM, and he thought B've had left.

The captain's career was ruined and he knew he had only one more year to go in the Army and they would not let him stay in after that. He did come over to the 5th SFG, and I think he commanded Signal Company there also. He was a terrific guy who looked after his people but should have kept his fists to himself.

Where Do We Get The Berets?
By Bill Coombs

They say everyone will get 15 minutes of fame. I got about one minute for this. I was a SP4 working at the S-4 of the 10th Special Forces Group in Bad Toelz. This was before the berets were authorized even though we were wearing them unofficially in Germany.

I used to buy berets from a company in Canada where I would get thirteen of them if I ordered a dozen. I sold them for $5 each. My boss, CW2 Paul F. Lusk, was our Property Book Officer and knew that I sold berets.

One day, Mr. Lusk asked me, "Where do we get the berets?"
After informing him that I purchased them from the Dorothea Knitting Mills in Toronto, Ontario, Canada, I did not think anymore about it.

Unbeknownst to me, we had been authorized to wear the beret by President Kennedy and Mr. Lusk was preparing a response to a TWX from the Department of the Army. The folks at DA knew that we wore the beret in Germany and sent a TWX requesting the source of supply. Mr. Lusk sent a TWX back telling DA where we got them.

A couple of days later, the official message arrived from DA authorizing two berets per SF soldier and further authorizing us to request them.

The message went on to say, "The only known source is the Dorothea Knitting Mills in Toronto." I asked Mr. Lusk where they got that idea. Certainly, an American firm could make berets.

He said, "That's what you told me, Coombs." I had no idea when I answered his question that he would pass the information onto DA and they probably placed an order for 6,000 of them. So, if any of you still have berets with the Dorothea Knitting Mill label inside of them, you probably have one of the originals.

Broke Before Payday
by Bill Coombs

I recall, one night I hitchhiked from Fort Campbell down to the Rendezvous Bar in Clarksville. I had only one dollar and a beer cost thirty-five cents, so I had enough for two beers. I bought a beer and had only sixty-five cents left. A man sat next to me at the bar and we started talking. He bought me a beer. As I did not have enough money to buy a round (seventy cents), I sucked on my beer; and when he was getting finished with his, I was going to buy him a beer and then head back to Campbell.

The guy said to me, "You're broke, aren't you?"

I said, "Yeah."

He slid a five dollar bill over to me and told me that it was mine. I said to myself, "Oh, Oh. I wonder what this guy wants for his five bucks." I almost expected to feel a hand on my knee. He finished his beer, stood up and said, "Someday, you are going to run into another GI who is broke. Give him those five dollars." Then he left.

There I was...a couple of days before payday and I was RICH. That happened in 1959.

About ten years later, I was on TDY to Okinawa from Nha Trang. Almost the same thing happened. A Marine asked me if I could convert 500 yen into American money. He was broke. After talking with him for awhile, I found out he was on TDY from Hon Shu. I gave him a ten dollar bill and the look I saw on his face must have been the same one I had on mine when the guy gave me the fin. I used almost the same words when I told him to give the ten to some broke GI that he might run into one day.

Prop Blast
by Bill Coombs

Don't know how many of you were prop blasted. It used to be a tradition in the Airborne, but they don't allow it anymore as people really got drunk. They mixed up something that consisted of all sorts of booze plus onion juice and whatever other nasty tasting thing you can think of. Every time you turned around, you were handed a glass of this stuff and had to drink it. Sometimes, they tricked you into drinking it.

I was Prop Blasted in 1966 at the NCO Club at Fort Guluck in Panama when with the 8th SFG. I recall they sent me to one station and there was a sign on the ceiling that said "WAAT SINE?" They asked me to tell them what the sign said and I answered (so they say) "What Sign?" They told me I needed glasses if I could not see the sign, and sent me on sick call to the 'dispensary' where they gave me glasses -- (two glasses of that piss we were drinking). I think it was wine and onion juice to begin with and then they added the other potions.

The evil person who was in charge of all this was list member, Jim Lewis.

As drunk as I was when it was finished, and I was blasted, I went to town and ended up in the part of Colon where white soldiers did not normally frequent. What got me to go down there, I do not know.

Anyway, I was in a bar drinking with a bunch of the Panamanians when a black sergeant from my company came in. When he saw me, he could not believe his eyes. I saw him before he saw me and I of course invited him to join us. He asked me what in the hell I was doing there and I told him I was drinking with my new friends.

He immediately took me out of there and drove me back to the Fort, and the next thing I remember was waking up in the BEQ the next afternoon. When I saw the sergeant at work on Monday, he told me I would probably have gotten beaten up or worse if he had not come in. Apparently, I was making a speech about some subject, and the long knives almost came out.

One did get blasted at prop blasts. I understand that a lieutenant drunk himself to death at one of them and they are now taboo.

Special Forces Wives
by Bill Coombs

I was a young SP4 in Bad Toelz, and saw a woman at the club who looked familiar. I saw her husband, and then recognized SFC and Mrs. Bob R. Bob had been my Platoon Sergeant in Recon, 502nd and was just reporting in to the 10th SFG. She used to pick him up at Fort Campbell, and that's how I recognized her.

A few months later, I was visiting them and during the discussion, I referred to her as a dependent. She told me that she was not a dependent but an SF wife. I asked her what the difference was, and she gave me three examples:

You will not find an SF wife at the American Express on payday spending time buying money orders while the guys are waiting to cash their checks and get out of there. The dependents will be in there holding things up. The SF wives will wait a day or two.

You will not find an SF wife at the Post Exchange on pay day when the troops are in there buying their cigarettes and other things for the month. Of course, the dependents, which could certainly wait a day or two, will be in there.

For those of you who have never been stationed at Toelz, about 9:30 in the morning, everyone hits the snack bar for a cup of coffee. We did not have a whole lot of time to do that. She told me I would see dependents in there at that time holding things up. She said that Bob told her that if he ever saw her in the snack bar between 9:30 and 10:00, he would divorce her.

About SF wives not shopping at the PX on pay day, she informed me that she did not want to see any bachelors at the commissary that day. What's fair is fair, I guess.

Missing Files
by Bill Coombs

Back in 1959, when I was with 101st Airborne, a personnel clerk told me of a dirty trick in which he was involved. Seems there was a First Sergeant that no one liked. The guys in the Finance section sent his finance records to Korea with a package of others for guys who had been transferred there.

Of course, when the First Sergeant did not show up in Korea with the others, they assumed he was delayed for some reason, put his finance records in an in-coming box and forgot about them. Several months later, someone contacted Fort Campbell about the First Sergeant and was told he was still at Campbell. The records were returned, but for several months, the First Sergeant existed on partial payments. I wonder if the First Sergeant figured out what happened. He must have known if he came down hard on the Finance types, it could happen again.

There was another time that the troops 'got even' with someone. When I sailed to Germany on the USNS Rose, I befriended one of the US Navy guys assigned to the ship. There were just a few of them. He told me that on their last trip back from Germany, there was a little celebration going on at the back of the ship. He noticed that every couple of minutes, a sheet of paper was thrown to the fishes to roars of applause.

It seems the happy passengers had someone's 201 File and finance records; and page by page, they felt they were getting even with someone they did not like.

Some Things Never Change
Awards and Decorations
(Roman Style)
Author unknown
(provided by Bill Coombs)

Who has not thrilled to the story of Horatius at the bridge? How he and two other Romans stood off the Army of Lars Porsena until the bridge to Rome could be destroyed? How his companions ran to safety as the bridge began to fall? How Horatius, only after the bridge was down, quit his post and swam the Tiber to safety? Here is a translation of a papyrus found recently which requested an award for Horatius:

....

Rome, II Calends, April CCCLX
SUBJECT: Recommendation for Senate Medal of Honor

TO: Department of War, Republic of Rome

I. Recommend Caius Horatius, Captain of Foot, CMCMXIV, for the Senate Medal of Honor.

II. Captain Horatius has served XVI years, all honorable.

III. On the II day of March, during the attack on the city by Lars Porsena of Clausium and his Tuscan Army of CMX men, Captain Horatius, with Sergeant Sporius Laritus and Corporal Julius Herminius, held the entire
Tuscan army at the far end of the bridge until the structure could be
destroyed thereby saving the city.

IV. Captain Horatius did valiantly fight and kill one Major Picus of Clausium
in individual combat.

V. The exemplary courage and the outstanding leadership of Captain
Horatius are in the highest tradition of the Roman Army.

JULIUS ANTINOUS,
Commander, II Foot Legion

****
    Ist, Ind, AG IV Calends, April CCCLX

TO: G-III

For comment.

G.C.

****
    IInd Ind, G-III IX Calends, May CCC

TO: G-II

I. For comment and forwarding.

II. Change end of paragraph III from "saving the city" to "lessened the effectiveness of the enemy attack." The Roman Army was well dis- persed tactically; the reserve has not been committed. The phrase as written might be construed to cast aspersions on our fine army.

III. Change paragraph V from "outstanding leadership" to read "commendable initiative." Captain Horatius's command was II men, only I/IV of a squad.

J.D.

****
　　IIId Ind, G-II II Ides, June CCCLX

TO: G-I

I. Omit strength of Tuscan forces in paragraph III. This information is classified.

II. A report evaluated as B-II states that the officer was a Captain Picus of Tifernum. Recommend change to "an officer of the enemy forces."

J.H.

****
　　IVth Ind, G-I IX Ides, January CCCLXI

TO: JAG

I. Full name is Caius Claudius Horatius.

II. Change service from XVI to XV years. One year in Romulus
Chapter BPOE, has been given credit for military service in error.

E.J.

****
　　Vth Ind, JAG II, February CCCLXI

TO: AG

I. The Porsena raid was not during wartime; the temple of Janus
was closed.

II. The action against the Porsena raid, ipso facto, was a police action.

III. The Senate Medal of Honor cannot be awarded in peacetime
(AB/CVIII-XXV, paragraph XII, C).

IV. Suggest consideration for Soldier's Medal.

P.B.

****

    VIth Ind, AF IV Calends, April CCCLXI

TO: G-I

Concur in paragraph IV, Vth Ind.

L.J.

****

    VIIth Ind, G-I I May CCCLXI

TO: AG

Soldier's medal is given for saving lives; suggest star of bronze as appropriate.

E.J.

****

    VIIIth Ind, JAG II Calends, June CCCLXI

TO: JAG

For opinion.

G.C.

****

IXth Ind, JAG II Calends, September CCCLXI

I. XVIII months have elapsed since event described in basic letter.
Star of bronze cannot be awarded after XV months have elapsed.

II. Officer is eligible for Papyrus Scroll with Metal Pendant.

P.B.

****

X Ind, AG I Calends, October CCCLXI

TO: G-I

For draft of citation for Papyrus Scroll with Metal Pendant.

P.B.

****

XI Ind, G-I III Calends, October CCCLXI

TO: G-II

I. Do not concur.

II. Our currently fine relations with Tuscany would suffer and current delicate negotiations might be jeopardized if publicity were given to Captain Horatius' actions at this time.

T.J.

****
    XII Ind, G-II VI November CCCLXI

TO: G-I

A report rated D-IV, partially verified, states that Lars Porsena is very sensitive about the Horatius affair.

E.T.

****
    XIIIth Ind, G-I X November CCCLXI

TO: AG

I. In view of information contained in preceding XI and XIII the endorsements, you will prepare immediate orders of Captain C. C. Horatius to one of our overseas stations (remote).

II. His attention will be directed to paragraph XII, POM, which prohibits interviews or conversations with newsmen prior to arrival at final destination.

L.T.

****
    Rome   II Calends, I April CCCLXII

SUBJECT: Survey, Report of, Department of War

TO: Captain Caius Horatius, III Legion, V Phalanx, APO XIX, C/O Postmaster, Rome.

I. Your statements concerning the loss of your shield and sword in the Tiber River of III March CCCLX have been carefully considered.

II. It is admitted that you were briefly in action against certain unfriendly elements on that day. However, Sergeant Lartius and Corporal Herminius were in the same action and did not lose any government property.

III. The Finance Officer has been directed to reduce your next pay by II-I/IV talents (I-III/IV talents cost on each sword, officers; III/IV talent cost of one each shield, M-II).

IV. You are enjoined and admonished to pay strict attention to conservation of government funds and property. The budget must be balanced next year.

H. MARCUS AURELIUS
Lieutenant of Horse
Survey Officer

Never Forget
by Bob Smith

On 09/11/01, I was on station at the JFKSWCS Base Station doin' my regular contractor stuff when we heard on the radio about a plane crash into one of the towers of the World Trade Center. Tragedy, I thought.....then later we heard about the second plane.....no coincidence thinks I.

Later the NCOIC of the signal site called and asked me what kind of radios I could gather up in a hurry for deployment in support of the rescue effort in NY. I told 'em and he told me to do it. Now, as a contractor I don't usually do nuttin' 'ceptin what's on the contract; but I have good relations with these guys and proceeded to call up the support battalion at the SWC and get a whole bunch of stuff consisting of VHF, HF, SATCOM and whatever else we could haul in a van. I even managed to get some INMARSAT units from a private company that said they would foot the bill.

We ended up shootin' up to NYC, Ft. Hamilton, that night and set up an Emergency Operations Center. Along with us were cadre from the Medics Course with plans to bring up their EMT qualified students. They had been doing their training with the NYC fire department and had already established relations. Things were confusing as hell. The only way things worked as well as they did during those times is because there was so much manpower and equipment volunteered that nothing was left wanting....except survivors.

Well, FEMA got control and they decided that SF medics and commo weren't needed even though the NYCFD wanted us, and we were back at Bragg in a week.

These pictures will never leave my mind. The smell of the smoke and the look in the eyes of the workers will remain. I guess some people could forget unless they'd seen the tears of those who worked so hard those first few hours with little success.

Better Living Through Chemistry
by David Stafford

I ran a 5K road race at Palmerola in 1985. Two brazen boneheads opted to take on the oppressive heat with full, sandbagged rucks. One was William Joseph G.; a California boy and one of the most intelligent men I've ever been blessed to meet. (Active Reserve medic at present) The other Bozo was me.

Prior to the competition, Geppy and I journeyed into the medical facility and attempted to obtain some lidocaine to inject into my busted pinkie toe. Our slick ways were observed by a female captain named Shakelford. Nice woman. Pretty too.

She didn't see the need for any desensitization, proceeded to demand that I put my ass up on her examination table, and began manipulating my tarsal (foot bone) in a way that caused some serious discomfort.

Wild Bill (Geppy) Gephart whispered to me after she completed her examination and was standing nearby in all her fine smelling, feminine, very attractive, yet somewhat sadistic splendor, "Dave. Why'd you let her do that to you? Christ, you're as white as a ghost now."

"Wildest," said I with clammy sweat beads on my brow. "Let me tell you something, brother. For a moment there I didn't know whether I was going to pass out or ejaculate." The captain-doctor overheard my deliberate volume, and turned away trying to hide her smirking, comely grin. She failed.

She then learned that we were going to do the 5K in about twenty minutes or so, she started changing her mindset and said, "Sergeant Stafford, if you really deem it necessary, I think it'll be alright if you inject half a milliliter at the base (of the toe).

"No thanks," said I tremulously. "You just gave me a reminder of what legitimate pain feels like. I don't believe I need it now."

She grinned; Gepper and I went on to strap on our sand bag carriers. We finished ahead of some people that marveled at either our conditioning or our tenacity, and I'm writing you this to tell you I wish I had taken her offer very shortly after the race began. That busted little piggy needed to go to sleep.

Never Quit Attitude
by Dave Stafford

Can't say that I've had the pleasure of getting triple teamed by bouncers at the Town Pump in San Antonio; but I did happen to catch a throttling from the Mississippi Golden Gloves champ though by a boy by the name of Wayne W.

Wilcox broke his leg on a jump at Bragg and got recycled. His fame didn't come from his brand of PLF though. Wayne was our class's chronic sock filler. He liked to drop little presents on the blanket of the poor bastard in the bunk below him named Rosado.

This trained boxing champ lit me up pretty good because he felt I was laughing at his choice of female mammoths that night. The bastard clipped me seven times in the face and head before I got to him. He was a damned good boxer I believe. I finally reached him, knocked him into the River Walk River, and refused to let him out before I deliberately bitch-slapped him numerous times in front of the gathering crowd of our fellow late night boozers.

I was sore for about a week. He ended up with seven stitches over his right eye, some good color around his socket; and then spent more time kissing my ass than he spent pulling on himself. Being raised poor in Massachusetts gives you that never-quit-even-when-you're-supposedly-whipped kind of nature, they tell me.

I never enjoyed the Pump boozery, but my time was spent at Rick's and Hay Street, dodging the straight razors carried by those with more melanin than myself, and watching the backs of those I valued. SF was like that in the mid eighties. Still is, I hear.

Chased by MPs
by "Yukon Don" Shipman

July 1971. While most of you were running around in the jungles of SEA, a friend and I were being chased on foot by an MP through a dark housing area in Bad Nauhiem for throwing firecrackers. As we sped around the corner of one of the apartment buildings, laughing gleefully at how slow the MP was, we slammed into his partner, who promptly locked us in his sedan. It was our first experience with being "flushed like gamebirds into the guns."

Imagine my distress (and that of the MPs) when they delivered my 12-year old ass to my front doorstep, and my dad (the BDE CSM) opened the door in his Dress Blues (he was enroute to a Dining-In). To put it mildly, my kaka lacked vigor.

Paratrooper Future
by "Yukon Don" Shipman

My first trip to the Mess Hall was in '63 or '64. My dad was an ISG at Benning at the time. He and I went to the Mess Hall for breakfast. I still remember how "cool" I thought it was to slide those big steel trays along that shiny steel tubing and stop at each place for eggs, biscuits, and SOS. After chow, dad took me to the Arms Room and taught me how to take apart an M-60. Getting in the harness and doing the 34 ft. tower topped the day off. I do believe that gave me my first boner. I was in 2nd grade at the time. <G> The Black Hat that caught me (might have been one of you FOGs) asked me if I was going to be a Paratrooper when I grew up. I responded with, "Yes, Sergeant!" and took off back to dad. Man! Good memories.

I Hate Subs!
by Don "Val" Valentine

In April of 1963, my entire B Team was sent on submarine training. As I recall, the name of the sub was the "Perch." It was a World War II diesel sub that had been converted into a troop ship for Special Forces, intelligence, and ranger-type operations.

The forward and aft torpedo compartments had been emptied, and about fifty canvass bunks, just like those on troopships had been installed. They were stacked four or five high and were very, very close to one another. The ropes that interlaced the canvass to the metal form were slack and the canvas sagged a great deal which made them even closer.

We boarded the sub early one rainy morning at the port in Naha. My group was assigned to the forward troop compartment, and I took a bottom bunk on the left hand side against the wall. Sailors call the left hand side of the ship, the "port side" and the right hand side, the "starboard side." They also refer to a wall as a "bulkhead," the floor as a "deck," the front of the ship as the "bow" or "forward," the rear of the ship as "aft" or the "fantail," the door as a "hatch," and for some strange reason, they refer to a latrine as a "head."

The canvass on my bunk was so slack I was actually lying on the floor. The bunk above me sagged so much its canvass was only about two inches above my chest. If I wanted to roll over, the guy above me had to either get out of his bunk, pull himself up out of my way or I had to push him up. There were two men above me, and the top two bunks were full of our gear.

The rain had soaked our clothes while we were boarding ship. Some of the guys draped their wet fatigues over the hatch that connected our compartment to the rest of that tub to dry. While we were heading out of the harbor a sailor came through and started raising hell about those fatigues, and jerked them off the hatch. When he walked by where I lay, I grabbed the cuff of his trousers because that's all I could see and asked those navy oxfords, "Hey buddy, why are you so upset? The guys didn't mean any harm."

The oxfords replied, "If we ram something and spring a leak up here we have to be able to close that hatch and seal it off from the rest of the sub." Well sir, with my left hand I pushed up all the bunks above me, which were occupied at the time, and rolled out into the aisle. Maybe all of those damn pushups had done me some good after all. Then this East Tennessee boy found himself another bunk closer to that damn hatch. It was also a bottom bunk, but a lot closer to that hatch. In fact, I was right next to it. I vowed to myself, "They might seal somebody in this compartment, but it won't be me. The only part of me that they will ever lock in this compartment will be the heel of my boot as I go through that damn hatch."

Shortly after we cleared the harbor and made it out into the open sea, we submerged. In all fairness, there was one good point about traveling submerged; that damn boat didn't rock!

Within five minutes after we submerged, the captain came on the loudspeaker system and announced, "The Thresher is officially lost at sea." Those navy oxfords passed by again and I tugged on the cuff of their trousers and asked them, "What is a Thresher? Did we lose a part off this damn sardine can?" The oxfords replied, "The Thresher was a brand new nuclear submarine that just sank on its test dive." It was about then that I began to suspect that I was not going to enjoy training in this rickety-ass old World War II sardine can.

That's when I noticed the loud squeaking; actually it was so loud it sounded more like a twisting or binding of metal. It had been in the background ever since shortly after we had submerged, but I was not paying much attention to such things then. When those oxfords passed by on their way back out of our compartment, I tugged on the cuff of their trousers again and asked them, "What is all of that squeaking?" and they replied, "What squeaking? Oh, that. That's just the pressure of the ocean. It's trying to squash us." Well that confirmed it: I definitely was not going to enjoy a trip in a sub. That damn noise caused by all of the stress on the hull of our sub never ceased as long as we were submerged.

All of this caused my bladder to notify me that it required my full attention and I wriggled out of my bunk and went in search of the latrine. After I didn't find anything that remotely resembled a latrine, I asked the first sailor I met where it was. He showed me. (By the way, his voice matched that of the oxfords to which I had been speaking.)

He opened a door on the port side of our compartment and about half way forward, there "it" was. It resembled a metal commode in a wall locker with three knobs on the wall behind it. There was no water in the bowl, in fact the bowl did not have exactly the same appearance as a landlubbers commode; similar but not the same.

I asked, "Why so many knobs?"

He quickly explained, "Turn that knob and do your business, turn this knob after you do your business and then turn that knob. If performed in proper sequence, the pipes and the commode will be sealed and sea water will come in and wash the mess out into the ocean." Then he left.

I squeezed into that tiny wall locker, stood there and stared at that machine like a hog starring at a watch while I ran the instructions through my mind again and again. There were no instructions posted in that damn wall locker, nor were the knobs marked in any way. I wasn't sure I had the instructions right. So, I opened the door and looked around for that sailor again. No luck, he was already gone. That was okay. My bladder had already changed its mind; it was in no rush now. I figure my bladder had decided it would rather expand to the size of a basketball than risk drowning in a wall locker full of body waste and sea water.

Later we went topside to train on entering the RB-15s (rubber boats) from the sub. I took advantage of this opportunity and pissed off the aft end of the deck. One learns to spit, puke, and piss "with the wind," when one is aboard ship and topside.

The rubber boats and oars were stored (lashed down) inside a part of the conning tower. Sailors held the rubber boats alongside the sub so that we could leap into them. We discovered that this seemingly simple act required a keen sense of timing. The more you weighed, the more accurate your timing had better be. You could find yourself going right through the bottom of that rubber boat or being bounced like a ping pong ball right out into the ocean. You jumped when the rubber boat is at the "bottom" of the swell and the farthest from you. As you fell, the rubber boat would rise on the next swell to meet you. If you jumped when the rubber boat was on top of the swell, you and the boat fell together all the way to the bottom of the swell where both came to a teeth-jarring stop.

The sailors enjoyed watching us learn this simple task, and they especially enjoyed fishing some of the careless ones out of the ocean. After we got the boat loaded, we then shoved off, paddled around in a large circle, and returned to unload. Unloading was one hell of a lot better than loading.

The next day we tried a second method. In this technique, you sit in your little rubber boat and let the sub sink from under you. First we ran a dry run. The sailors lashed the boats to the aft deck and we got in and practiced releasing the tie downs. We were great at this, after all it was daylight and sitting on the deck, not in the water. Then they did it for real and the sub blew its ballast tanks and sank from under us. That wasn't so bad. In fact, it was a lot easier than jumping into the boats.

For our next trick, we were to meet the sub and let it tow us while it was still running at periscope depth before we came back aboard. Using this trick, the sub could meet us closer to shore and then tow us farther out to sea before it surfaced, and that way remain undetected. We lashed our little rubber boats together one behind the other. From my position as the last man on the right in the very last boat, I could just barely see the periscope moving through the water out to the front of our forward-most rubber boat. It amazed me how damn fast that sub could travel while submerged. The periscope was leaving a wake that was as high as I was. Someone in the front boat tried to lasso the periscope as it flew past, but missed. The periscope started to make a large circle to make another pass. Another guy on the front boat who was a cowboy from somewhere out west took charge of that chore.

All five of the rubber boats had been tied bow-to-aft, bow-to-aft in a line, but while just sitting there they were not aligned. The boats were just floating on the swells, some facing this way and some that way. Our cowboy stood up and rested one foot on the inflated side of the rubber boat's bow, re-tied the knot and made himself a real noose; and when that sub passed that time, he nailed that periscope in one try. As soon as that noose fell over that periscope, those little rubber boats literally "snapped" into a straight line and the bow of the front boat popped up out of the water. In fact, about half of the front boat came out of the water and our cowboy, who had been standing in the bow of that front boat, did a back flip (maybe a double back flip) and landed in the ocean. We were flat hauling ass in our little rubber boats. As we flew past him, I held my oar out to John Wayne, he grabbed it and two of us pulled him over the ass-end of our rubber boat. He was grinning from ear-to-ear as he shouted, "This is great fun, almost as much fun as bull-riding." Yeah, Right! Our illustrious leaders had more of this great fun planned for us. As a matter of fact, we were going to be lucky enough to try this same trick that night. Whoopee! After we were back aboard the sub, the sailors deflated the boats and re-stored them and the oars; we submerged and had supper.

It takes a while for a sub to feed its crew plus fifty or so troops. The galley and mess hall are unbelievably small. Everything inside that sub is unbelievably small. They have storage areas built into every place possible. The freezer and cooler are beneath the galley with access through a trap door. The benches in the mess hall are hollow and that is where they store potatoes and maybe apples.

Some of the offices are so small, the users must back into them, sit down, and then turn under their desks. All of the hatches are built for midgets. Anyone assigned to sub duty should not be allowed to be over 5' tall, and I'm serious.

By the time we left that damn sardine can, I had half a dozen scars on my bald head from trying to squeeze through those damn itty-bitty hatches. The chow was great and you could have all you wanted. That was the second (and last) good thing about sub duty. It was said that sub mess officers got first pick of chow when issued. Submariners had great chow, but it wasn't good enough to justify me being in a sub.

The sailors loved to kid us, "You guys have to jump out of airplanes, sleep in mud, and eat c-rations. Look at what we got. We always have clean sheets and good food."

I told them, "I wouldn't voluntarily live in a damn wall locker under the water for all the clean sheets and hot chow in the world."

During the afternoon a storm came our way. The sub captain advised our idiot B Team Commander not to put us off the sub in that weather because it was very stormy and rough. Our fearless leader was a Missile Command officer who had zero special forces training. He had just been "assigned" directly to SF duty and hated every minute of it. Our precious Major decided to put us out anyway. The sub captain told him, "I have never put troops off in rubber boats in this kind of weather, and you as their commander must assume full responsibility for that decision." Of course us enlisted folks were unaware of all this at the time. It came to light in our After Action Report.

The Missile Major made a command decision. He designated my boat as the Safety

Boat, and I would carry a radio set, I believe it was a Prick 25 [AN/PRC-25]. That was the only difference between our boat and the rest. Big deal, we were all powered the same way - hand-operated oars. Our mission was, "Disembark via Method #2. Then rendezvous with one another and travel together towards shore to a point just outside the breakers. And finally, return and rendezvous with the sub using flashlights."

When we popped up onto that deck, it was pitch black and raining so hard you couldn't see a flashlight fifty feet away, had we been allowed to use one. It was one of those nights where you can touch your nose with your hand without seeing your hand. We felt our way to the boats and felt our way from one boat to another until we came to our boat (well, at least we all hoped it was the correct boat).

The boats were aft and sitting side-by-side on the deck. Ours was the very last boat. We climbed in and unlashed it. Shortly afterwards, we heard the sub blow its ballast tanks; and at night, that is a scary sound. The sub started to sink from under us. The ocean began to lash out at us a little at a time, closer and closer as the sub left us. We heard a commotion in the boat beside us, and I could hear guys higher than us on the forward end of that boat and other guys who were at the same level as us, or maybe even a little lower on the aft end.

Then someone in that boat made a command decision and yelled over the storm, "Damn it! Somebody cut that fucking rope!" Somebody had overlooked one of the ropes that had been used to lash the boat to the deck. The sinking sub was pulling the itty-bitty rubber boat down with it. The free end of the rubber boat had been stuck almost straight up in the air with our guys clinging to it like rats fighting to stay on a log. Somebody cut the rope just in time. The fun had already begun and we hadn't even cleared the sub yet.

The other boats assembled on our safety boat by shouting in order for the boats to locate us; and then we all headed for shore with the safety boat in the rear. The stormy night was so dark we could not see each other; in fact, we couldn't even see our hand if we touched our nose, much less any shore lights. We just followed a compass heading.

Using the only rope in our rubber boat, I lashed down my radio set. Ma Baker was a friend of mine from Laos, but I didn't want to explain how I lost a damn radio. There would never be an end to that lecture. We rowed towards shore for what seemed like an hour or maybe two. Then, we got close enough to the breakers to hear them and decided to turn around. Unfortunately, we were a lot closer to the breakers than we thought; but because of the noise from the storm we didn't know that.

Three of our rubber boats made it, but one was having a problem overcoming the current. They had come too close to the breakers. The safety boat leader, Master Sergeant Billy W., told me to give him my rope so he could throw it to them and help tow them back out to sea. Billy also ordered us to row towards them. He was a damn good SF soldier. I seem to recall that he was one of the characters in Robin Moore's novel "The Green Berets". Billy was known for having brass balls the size of a basketball. I can't recall hearing anyone brag on his intelligence.

If one boat-load couldn't overcome the current and waves with its oars, putting another oar-powered boat into the same situation would not possibly solve the problem, even if they were tied together. As soon as Billy managed to get one end of the rope to the other boat, he directed me to radio one end of the rope to the other boat, he directed me to radio the sub and tell them what we were doing. The water was getting rougher, so I operated the hand mike with my right hand and grabbed the nearest carrying-handle with the left. Once I keyed the sub's call sign, a white horizontal streak appeared about six feet above me and to my right. Instinctively I tightened my grip on the handle and the radio handset. The call sign was all I transmitted because a black wet briny wall smacked into us, and ass-over-the-tea kettle we went.

The next thing I knew, I was suspended beneath the water, hanging to the carrying handle of our rubber boat with one hand and clinging to the handset of my radio set suspended beneath me with the other. Desperately, I tried to pull the radio set high enough to get it between my legs. A Ma Baker lecture on supply economy motivated me to try again and again, but I could not pull the radio high enough to grab it between my legs. The handset cord was stretched out to its maximum length, and my arms and legs weren't long enough to reach the radio transceiver. Try as I might, I could not pull my nose above the surface to get some air. The carrying handles were now on the very bottom of our upside down itty-bitty rubber boat and a good six to eight inches below the surface of the water. I couldn't lift that much weight high enough out of the water. Finally, I relented and released the radio set. I figured I needed air more than we needed that damn radio; and Ma Baker could just rant and rave all he wanted.

We had one guy with us, Doc B., who somehow managed to cheat on the SF swim test. In order to qualify for SF, you had to be able to swim 8 laps non-stop in an Olympic-sized pool. Doc B. could not swim, and out of everyone in those two capsized boats, his B-4 life vest was the only one that did not work.

Our luck was running true to form. We formed a human chain linked hand-to-hand with a guy at one end clinging with one hand to the boat while the guy on the other end struggled towards Doc B.'s cries for help. As I recall, Doc's cries for help weren't panicky. He was cursing. He cursed his life vest because that damn thing didn't work, he cussed because he couldn't swim, and in between he yelled for somebody to come get his fat ass before he drowned. Someone managed to reach Doc B. before he drowned.

Meanwhile, we heard another guy hollering for help between gurgles. We had no idea who the hell he was, but somebody reached him also. This was a young black soldier on his first hitch in the army and I can not now recall his name. In fact, Billy W. and Doc B. are the only two names I still remember. Anyway, he discovered that he had activated his inflatable life preserver alright, but because he was flailing his arms about in the water, it popped up behind him instead of beneath each of his armpits. The inflated vest then tilted him forward face-down in the water and that's when he hit the panic button.

We then righted our boats and got back into them, but we could only salvage three oars between the two boats. Then, Billy Waugh made another command decision, "We're going to use these three oars to row back through those breakers to the sub, and we're going to tow the other rubber boat behind us." We all chimed in, "Right, Billy!" I suspect we were all thinking, "Like shit we will." How Billy could think that three men could row two of those damn rubber boats full of troops back across those damn breakers is beyond my comprehension. Just a few short minutes before, eight men rowing couldn't overcome those breakers.

We rowed for several hours and never even got close to the breakers. We rowed until I was of the mind to jump Billy and strangle the life out of that little shit because I was using one of those damn oars the whole time. Finally, at about 0300 hours Billy made the best decision of his military career and ordered us to stop paddling and let the damn rubber boats just go on to shore, which we gladly did. Within five minutes after we stopped rowing, we were on the beach.

Billy and a couple of guys left to find a phone and the rest of us stayed with the boats. After we finally reached the beach, I must have pissed for 30 minutes, and my bladder just flat rebelled at the thought of going back out to that sub. It's a good thing that the fat ass Missile Major wasn't there when we hit shore. On a pitch black stormy night like that on a beach covered with slippery rocks, that clumsy asshole could have had a serious accident. We finally got out of there about daylight when the trucks came for us. The trucks took us to the barracks instead of back to the port to meet that damn sub and my bladder was elated. We returned to our company and the rest of our teams came back in on the sub and brought along our gear which was still aboard. That fiasco cancelled the rest of our sub training.

Because I had lost that damn radio, I heard about supply economy for a damned month from Ma Baker; but true to form, he finally helped me fill out the proper forms so he could officially write it off as a training accident. However, for a while Ma had me wondering how much that radio set cost and how long it would take me to pay for it.

About a week after we "beached" our little rubber boats during sub training, the company scheduled our B Team for another 3 days of sub training with the Perch. Maybe the idea was to compensate us because our training had been cut short on our first sub training exercise. I don't know and really didn't care because my bladder went spastic at the mention of the word sub.

I quickly informed our brilliant Missile-Major, "Major, our IG Inspection is due next week and if I stay here, I could have all of the communications gear in our B Team and also that of our A Teams ready for inspection." He quickly agreed and my bladder was once again its cheerful self. Officers just love neat IG Inspections. So I sadly missed the second session of sub training and my bladder and colon both agreed that I had done a wise thing. All I had to do was wipe the dust off the damn radio equipment, but I thought of my brave teammates and the Missile Major every time I hoisted a cold one.

Mechanized Dandruff
by Don Valentine
Still Walking Bowlegged

William 'Ma' B., who was of medium height and a tad on the chunky side, was from Kentucky where he used to work for the railroad. He was nicknamed Ma because he acted like your mom. He lectured you on Supply Economy every time you requested anything, but if you patiently endured his lecture, repented, and promised to mend your wasteful ways, he eventually relented and gave you whatever you needed.

One day Ma served pizza for supper. Two pieces per person. The topping was from a box that he bought at the commissary in Vientiane. About an hour after supper, I started itching all over. Large welts appeared all over my body, I could barely breathe and nearly died. Doc Thomas thought it was nerves, but it wasn't, because I've never been what you would call a nervous person.

The next night we had pizza again. Same reaction - Same diagnosis. Doc was afraid that I wouldn't survive and I was afraid that I would. When I recovered that time, I decided that I didn't need anymore of that damn pizza. That was the only connection that I could make between the two attacks. When I asked Ma for a box of that damn pizza mix, he didn't have anymore, and the garbage had already been burned. Nevertheless, I decided that there must have been some kind of preservative in that pizza topping that I was allergic to. Therefore, because I never knew for sure what was in that pizza mix that I was allergic to, I stopped eating pizza of any kind for the next twenty years.

This was never put into my medical records because our records were not with us; and I never requested that it be included after I returned to Oki because SF had to be able to eat any kind of food and I was afraid that they would kick me out of SF. At that point, I preferred to risk death rather than risking leaving SF. I had found a home in SF - they were family.

One night a bunch of us went to Mimi's Restaurant in downtown Luang Prabang,
Laos [LP]. For a Lao, Mimi was as cute as they come and she owned and ran a very tiny restaurant on the far side of LP. You have to understand, by this time the south end of a northbound water buffalo looked cute. We sat next to a table of Lao Officers. She served them a large steaming platter of something and shortly afterwards the place was filled with an awful sulphur-like smell. We couldn't figure out where that awful smell was coming from until I glanced over my shoulder and saw a huge plate of boiled eggs sitting in the middle of the table behind me. I saw one of the officers crack an egg and eat it; it was "rotten" with the boiled chick or duck still inside. Come to find out they consider that crap a delicacy. They lay the eggs out in the sun for several days until they are rotten and then they boil them. Ugh! That called for more booze.

Mimi ran out of the local beer so we drank Mekong, the local whiskey. That proved to be even worse than the local beer. The next morning, I awoke in a GI canvas cot in the back room of Mimi's with Mimi lying atop me. We were both buck naked, so I guess something had happened. What ever it was, I figured it was better than eating those damned eggs.

A couple of days later while I was taking a shower, I noticed a lot of small particles of dirt in my pubic hair and dutifully began scrubbing away at the dirt. Much to my surprise, those damn dirt particles began to race around my crotch like crazy. "Oh shit, mechanized dandruff (crabs), ala Mimi." I ran to Doc Thomas for some Crab Powder. He did not have any crab powder and could not get any until the next milk run - maybe a week. "Shit, the whole team will be infested with crabs in a week. I can't have that."

Next, I went to Ma B. for help. Nothing, all he had was a couple of army-issued DDT Bombs. Being desperate, I took one. Hell, anything was worth trying, so I stripped and sprayed it all over my crotch and ass - balls and all. You could see those damned crabs doing swan dives off of my body. About two seconds later, the pain hit me and I wished that I could do a swan dive off of me. I started hopping around like the Easter Bunny. As I passed by a table, I grabbed a magazine and hopped all over the place fanning my crotch and cursing at the top of my lungs.

My teammates found my antics very entertaining. I should have waited a week for the crab powder and let that mechanized dandruff invade their bodies too. The treatment worked and according to Doc Thomas, it worked a lot faster than GI Crab Powder, but I can't say that I really recommend it.

Ma B. retired from the army and returned to Ravena, Kentucky where he went back to work for the railroad and later retired from it also.

Riot Control Course 101
Don "Val" Valentine

About one month or so after we returned from MACV-SOG duty in Vietnam in August 1968, several of us were goofing off at the Stag Bar in the American Legion. They announced over the public address system that all Special Forces personnel were to report back to their unit immediately. When we arrived at our company, we were told that the Okinawans were rioting, and we began to draw weapons and prepare for riot control duty. The 1st Special Forces Group had never received any riot control training.

We loaded onto trucks and off we went. My truck went to a road intersection where the US camp bordered the civilian highway and out we hopped. Our company had issued us live ammunition, but they left it in the wooden case on the truck.

We did have our rifles and bayonets. A group of Okinawan men was standing on our side of the highway waving flags and shouting something in Japanese. Our officer jumped out of the cab of the truck, observed the situation, and told us, "Our orders are to eject any rioters from US property, and those people are on US property." Then he said, "Move them off US property!"

Without a word spoken between us, we looked at each other, shrugged our shoulders, fixed bayonets, and then, screaming like a bunch of blood thirsty maniacs, we charged. Those protesters disappeared like a wisp of smoke.

Someone else radioed for help. According to the radio message, there was a huge mob trying to push their way onto the Sukiran Marine Base from Highway 1. So we loaded back up on our trucks and away we raced. We were the first troops to arrive at the besieged gate. We already had our orders, so as soon as the truck screeched to a stop, we leaped off, charged past the Marine MPs, and went after the mob with fixed bayonets. It was a race to see who would get the honor of drawing first blood.

If you want to be a leader in SF, you must be fleet of foot. We were in pretty good physical condition and some of our guys were fast, but none of us could get close enough to a protester to stick him. We chased them across Highway 1, through the alleys and side streets, and into and in a couple of case "through" the houses. Those protesters scattered like a flock of geese. We still couldn't get within bayonet range and no one got stuck, which really frustrated some of our guys. They really wanted to "mix it up."

Our fearless leader received another radio call and we were ordered to go to the gate at the American Legion. Now that's carrying things too damn far. The American Legion was Group's favorite watering hole on the island. This time it took us a while to round up our troops because they had chased protestors to the four winds and some were reluctant to give up the chase. When we finally arrived at the American Legion, there were several trucks of SF troops already there.

Thousands of protesters were along the civilian highway, but outside our fence. Our company commander stationed one twelve-man A Team outside our fence along our side of the highway right of way and told the rest of us, "Stack arms and take a break." What better place to take a break than our favorite watering hole. We left one man to guard our weapons and the rest retrieved a cold beer or soda pop.

I really don't recall which. Of course we provided our guard with refreshments also.

The size of the mob continued to increase. They began to Dragon Dance and the line of dancers started weaving closer and closer to our guys that were standing at parade rest on our side of the highway. To the best of my memory, the Island Commander at the time was a general that we had nick-named "Small Paul." Anyway, the Island Commander, whoever the hell he was, decided to intervene and interject his inspirational leadership and wisdom into the situation. The general landed in the parking lot, hopped out of his itty-bitty "bubble" chopper and ran to meet our company commander. Our Colonel ran to meet the general as if he was overjoyed to meet with his much-adored superior officer and inquire as to his recent bowel movements. The general surmised the situation and noted the protesters slowly working their way closer to the men we had stationed outside the fence.

By this time the line of Dragon Dancers were weaving within three to six feet of our guys who were standing at parade rest - and practically defenseless in that position. The general made a command decision. He told our CO, "Move your troops out Colonel!" (He later explained that he really meant for our CO to bring that A Team "back inside" the fence. However, what our CO heard was "Charge!") Our Colonel shouted, "Move 'em out!" Our twelve brave men on the outside of the fence immediately "snapped to" and charged that mob with fixed bayonets. This time those bastards couldn't escape and at least one of that A Team drew blood. The protesters in the front of the mob literally climbed over the top of the protesters behind them in an effort to avoid being stabbed in the ass.

We snatched up our rifles and raced towards the gate to help our guys on guard there. Before we could reach the gate those twelve guys had already broken that mob up and sent them fleeing in all directions trampling each other in the process. The general nearly had a damn heart attack right there on the spot. He quickly clarified his order and had our troops withdraw back inside the wire. He then jumped back on his itty-bitty chopper and flew away.

When the civilian paper hit the stands the next day, almost the entire edition was devoted to the protest and the brutality of the American forces. The very next day the entire 1st Special Forces Group began mandatory riot and mob control training that was conducted by the local military police battalion. With bayonets affixed to our rifles, we marched around in formation at a half-step for several hours while wearing helmets and gas masks.

Even after we had riot control training, from that moment on, SF troops were not allowed to directly confront protesters unless the protestors broke through the military police lines and actually entered a US base. When our company was called out for riot control duty afterwards, they would always place us in the center of the air base that was threatened and tell us to stay there. They told us, "If the protesters jump the fence or overrun the MPs, we'll radio you and tell you where they are. Then they belong to you. Until then, stay put."

Using the approved and politically correct riot control techniques, the US eventually lost control of Okinawa and returned it to the Japanese Government. Hell, the Japanese did not want Okinawa. Financially speaking, without the US subsidy, that island was a losing proposition. The US greatly reduced their "payments subsidizing the local economy" and prices have soared. How the typical

Okinawan benefited from the Japanese takeover, is a mystery to me.

So much for politically correct and DA-approved riot control techniques. Personally, I preferred SF's riot destruction technique. At least it worked. The protesters threw rocks of all sizes, shouted obscenities in English, and threw paper bags full of shit at the riot control troops and they just stood there and took it. If they had put an SF unit in a situation like that, I think somebody would have been killed.

Summer Camp
Don "Val" Valentine

Early in the summer of 1969, I was selected to be the Assistant Camp Counselor for Summer Camp at Camp Hardy for some army brats [dependent children]. In this case they were boys between seven and fifteen years old. At least, that's the age bracket in which they were supposed to have been. One little squirt that I nicknamed "Pee Wee" had trouble walking with a full canteen of water on his pistol belt. Later, I found out that an exception had been granted for "Pee Wee" - he was only five years old.

A married master sergeant was originally assigned as the Camp Counselor, but two days after we arrived at Camp Hardy, he had family problems. He returned to base and I was promoted to Camp Counselor. Lucky me; a bachelor with no experience with kids, was left in charge of 80 boys at Summer Camp for the next three weeks. That was an experience I will never forget.

Camp Hardy was the pre-mission training camp for the 1st Group. We all slept in squad tents that were erected on concrete slabs. We began each day at the crack of dawn with reveille followed by breakfast; and then we took a little time to clean up our tents before we took physical training.

From that point on the curriculum varied from day-to-day. We put those kids through a "gentle" version of pre-mission training, but, I really worked their little butts off. I tried my best to wear those kids out so they would go to sleep at nights and not get into trouble. You see, we had no television and very few of the boys even had a radio. There were also very few books available. However, regardless of how hard I worked them, you could hear them horse-playing until taps, and sometimes afterwards. Usually, I had to make only one visit to one tent to calm them down after taps because I was loud enough for all the tents to benefit from it. Hell, I was pooped and that saved me some time so I could get some sleep too. Riding herd all day on eighty young boys can wear a person out.

We trained them in marksmanship using BB Rifles; we trained them in the art of tracking humans; we trained them in using little rubber boats; we ran them through a modified version of the Camp Hardy infiltration course; we gave them swimming lessons in the ocean; and most of the third week we spent camping out. The rest of the third week, we spent at the Basic Airborne Course at Sukiran where they got to jump out of the 34 foot training tower. We also offered scuba-diving lessons to any boy that could pass the swimming test, but no one passed it. Every kid tried their best to pass that swimming test, even Pee Wee. We had to pull some of them to safety because they would have drowned before they would have quit. If they were members of the boy scouts, they received credit toward merit badges for successfully completing the swimming lessons, weapons classes, for erecting a sleeping shelter, and cooking when they camped out.

If they did well with the BB rifles, they got the same training with a .22 caliber rifle. They were taught "Quick Fire" techniques. That is where you lift your rifle and fire without using the sights. Those little snot-nosed brats did pretty damn good. They put everything they had into it because they all dearly wanted to shoot the 22s. On the infiltration course, blanks were fired over their heads instead of bullets and firecrackers were set off here and there instead of plastic explosives.

Survival training was included in the camping trip. After we arrived at our bivouac site, I assigned each squad a section of the woods and told them to build their shelters. On the very first day, we assigned the oldest kids to be squad leaders and the next oldest to be their assistants; and made them responsible for taking care of the younger members of their squads, just like in the army. They had hatchets, knives and army field gear. I told them, "I will grade each shelter tomorrow morning." In addition, I issued each squad their rations for that evening and the next day. They scurried off into the woods like a bunch of newly hatched chicks, and pretty soon all you could hear was chopping and squeals of laughter all through the woods.

Those little guys were having a ball. Most of the boys had built sleeping platforms off the ground in the trees. All during the night, you could hear a tree begin to crack, and then a snap and crash as the platform came down amid cries of fear. No calls for help came, so I knew nobody was hurt. Shortly after each platform crashed, you would see flashlights through the trees, and the chopping and laughter would begin anew as the hapless camper and his team mates set about re-building his platform. Those kids were having the adventure of their life.

None of their food was cooked for them. It was all issued raw. Sometimes they got hot dogs, sometimes it was hamburger meat and sometimes it was chicken. They had to prepare their meals themselves.

While they were camped out, I was required to taste and approve one meal by each boy who wanted credit for a Boy Scout badge. That took guts. Pee Wee was too young to be in the scouts, but he wanted to do everything that the "big boys" did, so I just had to eat a meal with him also. Pee Wee served hamburgers in that meal; and as he picked my burger off of his makeshift grill, he dropped it into the ashes. That little guy never blinked an eye. I thought sure he would break down and cry, but he didn't. He plucked my burger from the ashes, wiped it off the best that he could, and proudly presented that little piece of charcoal to me.

Boy, was he proud of that burger. Oh well, I like my meat well done anyway, and besides, charcoal is a great remedy for the shits. Of course I didn't have the shits yet, but you never know when they might strike; and I figured it wouldn't hurt to have a little extra protection already inside me, just in case. In addition, I had to inspect and approve each shelter before the Boy Scouts would award them credit for that. Thankfully, I was not required to sleep in them.

We returned the boys home each Saturday afternoon and picked them up early each Monday. The second time I picked them up, several of the mothers approached me and asked me what I was doing with their boy. I asked, "Why? What's wrong?" The most common reply was, "Nothing's wrong, he's just changed. He's not the same boy that I sent to you. He's independent now and wants to do everything for himself."

Well, it seemed that the mothers didn't have as many kids to "mother" anymore and that bothered them. Well, I took it as a compliment, but I'm not sure that's how it was intended. However, I couldn't help but wonder if I was going to get another one of those damn "letters of apology" that I "must" sign and send back through channels like happened after my Taiwan trip.

There were a lot of hard things being said about American kids at that time because of the drugs, hippies, flower children and protesters. There wasn't a damn thing wrong with any of those boys. They were all crackerjacks. All they needed was just a little leadership, a lot of challenge, and enough freedom to make mistakes. I hope they also had enough wisdom to learn from their mistakes.

Believe me; I learned more from those kids than they learned from me - a lot more. For the first time in my life, I regretted not living a normal life and having a family of my own with my own kids; but that feeling wore off in about two days.

Several times since then, I have wondered how those young men turned out and how their experiences at summer camp affected their lives.

Defeating a Threat
by Catherine Fitzpatrick
of the Journal Sentinel staff

Gary Lamberty embodies both types of hero. He flinches at the term, but his reaction in a desperate situation gained him recognition by the Carnegie Fund.

Much of Lamberty's adult life has been spent in service to others. He is a former member of the U.S. Army Special Forces, and a former teacher at a school for troubled teens. He was finishing his first year as a gym teacher at Racine's McKinley Middle School when, on an early June day in 1991, he heard a loud crash outside his apartment.

A deranged man had driven a pickup truck into four cars. The man emerged from the truck with a machete and began swinging wildly at an 80-year-old man and a woman. Firefighters and an off-duty rookie police officer, Russell Cera, tried to stop him. Just as the man began hacking at a woman curled on the ground in a fetal position, Lamberty stepped in. He lured the assailant away, bobbing and weaving to avoid being hit. When the assailant turned his back, Lamberty used his martial arts training to tackle him.

Today, Lamberty credits his response to that training, and service with the Green Berets in Vietnam and experience as a teacher of troubled teens.

"It didn't take a lot of guts for me to do it," Lamberty says. "I had a background for it. It was old hat for me. The rookie cop, Russ Cera - he was heroic. The firefighters. Those guys all had a lot of guts."

Bottles and Butts
by Greg Hoisington

The only time you'll see a squirrel shit is when you're raising it. Squirrels shit like rats; they drop little turds and never miss a beat, step or lick.

Seems like I'm always bottle feeding some little critter where I live, and they all require their little butts stimulated. I use a wash rag, with a bowl of warm water on the side. There is a connection between shitting and eating. For example, while a fawn is nursing from its mother, she will be licking its butt. Therefore, to get an orphaned fawn to accept a bottle, the old wash rag on the butt trick will help. White tails will usually readily take to a bottle, but some others will fight you for days.

I've got two baby wallabies (miniature kangaroos) on the bottle now. Every three hours is about as far as I can stretch out the feedings. And, yup, they need their butts stimulated also.

I am reminded of a woman who brought us baby possums. There was this dead possum in the road, and a woman decided to stop her car and toss it into the brush. When she did, she noticed the possum's pouch moving. There were nine (count 'em) tiny pink possums in the pouch. Where do you take possums? To the Deer Farm, of course! Unfortunately, she said she would check on them from time to time, so I was stuck. Anyway, I managed to raise seven out of the nine. I hate to admit it, but they were really fun critters until they got to be about half grown. When they were large enough to take care of themselves, I took them up toward a buddy's (Val's) AO and turned them loose… to enrich the gene pool of that area. Motherhood ain't easy.

SCUBA after Jaws
by Greg Hoisington

I don't know what SCUBA training was like at Key West, but with the BUDS/Marine folks at Coronado, it was cold, miserable, and sometimes terrifying. My team, and a few strap-hangers, went through SCUBA, Amphibious Recon, Methods of Water Infil and Exfil, Hydrographic Surveys and Beach Recon, and other courses/training that had to do with being wet and cold.

About half way through all this, the movie "JAWS" was released. Seeing that movie, particularly if you happen to have an active imagination, it was a big mistake. It visualized everything I had ever thought about sharks and other unknown monsters that prowled the waters, looking for things in black rubber suits to eat. It sure ruined my daytime dives. My head was always turning like a radar antenna, watching for the "big one" to suddenly appear in the low visibility of the CA water.

Night ops were worse. Once, we did a bottom and beach recon of a section of Pt. Loma, swam out about 2 klicks to the recovery point, inflated our bc's, turned on our lights, got lined up, and waited for the boat. In addition, we waited for the boat. No boat. After a half hour or so in 58-60 degree water, wearing a leaky wet suit and wishing you had drunk more coffee so you could pee in your suit again for that glorious thirty seconds of warmth, there were only a few things to think about: Where's the fucking boat? Would chattering teeth indicate weakness to a hungry shark? Do we look like a row of floating snacks with little lights on them to big hungry things?

Look at those cars going over the bay bridge. They don't know we're down here, about to be eaten. Bet they have their heaters on. The boat finally showed up about an hour late, by which time we were all too cold to hang onto the loop, and had to be fished out of the water by the Navy. That was the coldest I have ever been.

WETSU!
by Greg Hoisington

During the first night underwater navigation course, my buddy and I were swimming along in the blackness of Coronado Bay, too busy at first to think about hungry things with teeth. He had the tac board and had his mask buried in the compass, while I was the kick-counter, maintaining contact by holding onto his tank. We got into an area that was full of tiny critters that would phosphoresce with water motion. I noticed that I could see the leading edge of the tac board, then I looked over at my buddy and could see the outline of his mask, head and regulator. Wow, I had never seen anything like it. We stopped for a minute, flicked stardust from our fingers, waved our hands, and had our own little light show, like a couple of stoned hippies. Then, back to swimming the course. While counting kicks and thinking about the phosphorescence, I made the mistake of looking back at our fins agitating the water. Holy shit, we were literally blazing a trail through the water. We looked like two electric lures surrounded by blackness, a tasty snack for something...

At the completion of that thought, we crashed into the bottom of the bay. Two regulators immediately sucked in about 600 lbs of air, followed by many seconds of silence and noooo bubbles. We thought we had swum into some sleeping giant who was about to turn and eat us. When nothing happened, and we realized what we had done, we started breathing again, got back on the azimuth and continued the mission... humming the music from "JAWS" into our regulators. Oh yeah, WETSU!

(Coronado Bay is only about thirty feet deep where we were. If you get into a shallow descent and are focused on your compass, you can swim into the bottom before your ears tell you that you are going deeper.)

Correlation
Bruce "Hardcore" Koch

Melvin was my intel NCO when Rudy and I were running the MLS Quan Loi for CCS. That was in lat '69, early '70. In 1980 I was running Phase 2 at MacKall, and Melvin was part of my crew along with "Bata boot" Bennet, the senior NCO.

Melvin and I were sitting there one day, and I told him, "Melvin, 10 years ago we were in a little shack like this, and you were an E6 and I was a Major. 10 years later, the rank hasn't changed. When are you going to make E7?" He said, "About the same time you make O5, sir."

He did make E7. I understand that his long time in grade went back to when he was stationed in Thailand. They were having a picnic, and Melvin was barbequing. Some civilian pissed him off and he impaled him with the barbeque fork. Doesn't seem to me that that would warrant any kind of punishment???? Myself with 6 years EM time, one GCM, one Article 15. Wondering if there is any correlation???

CSM Edge
by Jack Tobin

Some of our list members may remember when I was at Benning in '97-99 training folks for Bosnia. A new Director showed up for the JPOM group. I was OIC of training; others were in personnel and logistics. This guy was the original horse's ass. He left me alone with my instruction, but continually screwed with the people. I would argue with him, win some - lose some; but was tiring of the BS, when they asked me to extend for another nine months. I happened to be talking with the CSM, and told him I was going to tell them to stick it. I didn't need the aggravation and wanted to go home to Charlotte to be with my family.

The CSM said "You're absolutely right. Tell them to go to hell; you don't have to tolerate their crap. Of course, that means the folks coming through there won't be trained when they deploy, but you will be at home and that's what counts."

Yep, felt like horse's ass. I didn't say much for a second, then quietly said, "Guess I better sign the extension in the morning."

He chuckled quietly, and said "Thought you were too old to start running from a fight. Guess you just had to be reminded."

He was a soldier, and will be missed.

V-ball
by Jim "Cerealman" Kellogg

I'm mostly a sand player, which is more or less recreational ball. (Six people on my court is at least 2 more than normal.)

We walked into the shit on Sunday playing Open trips (3's) on the grass. We knew that going in. We had some experience with this before and made it through approximately five matches in double elimination play. We never won, but didn't care as long as we played to our potential and didn't fold when things got shitty; we did care that we were out there in the middle of it, and never gave up shit, attitude-wise, except for the setter.

When the setting was good we were crushing balls. Blocking doesn't mean much when a ball was set well and the hitter looked at the court. When it was lacking, we were doing the best that we could.

We knew that we were facing the best of the best locally; but did this for a few years and our game was good. We did not have a great setter; nevertheless we were passing to him well, considering that our two hitters receiving serve, were dealing with hard incoming jump serves across court and straight down the line.

For those that don't know, some folks are hard pressed just to touch the f--king ball, much less get it up to setter in such a manner where he wasn't running his brains out trying to provide a decent set at this level.

Hitting was good, passing was OK, digging and blocking work was excellent, setting was ..ehhhh, challenged. <Grin>

Cowboy
by John Cleckner

Patton was truly a one man Army and accomplished much that is little known of this eccentric. Patton had found out that the Russians had possession of the Lipizzan Horses and knew they would eat them ending the "Line". Therefore, he came up with a plan to rustle them and thereby save them.

A few years ago a great local Veteran died. His name was Cowboy Southard. Cowboy had gotten out of the Army (101st Airborne) came back to Shasta Country CA and resumed his life as a "Cowboy".

He had befriended me about 15 years before he died because I was an ex-paratrooper. Cowboy had jumped in during the Normandy Invasion and I believe he had a total of three Combat Jumps and was also a survivor of Bastogne. He had the Silver Star and several purple hearts as I remember, and was quite a character. He told a story to me about General Patton asking him to round up a small group of guys that could ride horses and report back to him directly.

Cowboy did and General Patton told them about the Lipizzan Horse, and the fact that they needed to be rescued before the Soviets ate them. Well, Cowboy and his group of guys ran a recon, found the horses and brought everyone one of them out without a shot being fired and before the Soviets knew what hit them.

Patton decorated Cowboy for his actions.

Radio Watch
by John Cleckner

For some reason I never pulled radio watch. Anyway, I returned to A-102 early in July '69 after being wounded in May. I was still on crutches and of little use other than to voice my opinion on whatever was being discussed from time to time, and waiting for my leg to heal.

I was asked if I would mind pulling radio watch and I said, "Heck no." Being an old Commo Man, it couldn't be that difficult. I was briefed and got set up for a double shift, which I had volunteered for. I was particularly interested in the "Team's" Zenith World Oceanic Radio, and always wondered if one of those things worked.

It was July 20th 1969. As usual, most if not all of us on the A Teams didn't have a clue as to what was going on around the world, let alone across the next mountain top. Listening to the first station I was able to raise, I was taken by the drama that I was hearing. It took me a while, but finally I "Got It", and realized I was listening to the actual live broadcast of the "First Landing On the Moon".

It was momentous. I cheered and hollered, but no one in the Camp had a clue what was happening or was about to get up to see what all the commotion was about.

It is a moment in my life that I will never forget. It was a one in a million chance that some guy, on a Special Forces A-Team in the middle of the jungle of Vietnam, would turn on a Trans Oceanic Radio and catch the actual live broadcast of Man's first landing on the Moon.

The Siege of Tien Phuoc
by John Cleckner

I am reminded of an experience I had a number of years ago when my old A-102 Team Sergeant Lloyd "Doc" Lampkins called and invited my LYB and I to a SFA Mini Convention in Banning CA with Chapter 12. Doc Lampkins insisted we stay with him and his wife and he also invited an old Soggy, Lloyd Bylund, to stay with him as well. Both Lloyds served in the 8th SFGA for many years as I was told that evening as they related MTT story after story.

We finally got settled in, and the first night was all about us three guys talking about Vietnam and Panama.

The next morning, with the three of us experiencing 8.2 magnitude hangovers, we met again in the kitchen and Bylund asked, "Where are the snow shovels and 55 gallon drums?"

I looked at him trying to figure out what he was talking about. Then Doc started laughing and I said, "What the hell is going on?"

Bylund answered, "Well, John, we are standing in three feet of shell casings and grenade pins after all those war stories that were told last night". I finally got it and laughed my butt off. He was right on.

However, that isn't the story I am trying to tell here. What I found out the night before made me completely reassess how I was going to write a book about the siege of Tien Phuoc. Doc and I were just talking about things that happened during the two and a half months Doc was there. I added some other stuff before and after his time on site.

Then during the conversation it HIT me right between the eyes. My Team Sgt and I did not see the same things the same way during the same time regarding the same event in 1969. Both of us were well trained in O&I and I couldn't understand what was going on. I sat there and made sure he could talk out his points without interruptions. I listened intently. I didn't see one thing he said he saw. Our take on any number of battles were different.

I made sure I didn't correct him or say that he was wrong about anything he said. His descriptions were crisp and direct, and obviously not rehearsed in any way. They were in great detail and I could only think that every man that was "There" has his own perception of the Battle.

I knew that Doc had been a survivor of the Korean Invasion, the Choson Resivor; and he also assisted General Dean while he was MIA, before Dean was captured. In other words, he had a hell of a lot more experience in experiencing War than I did.

I didn't roll over though, and he never knew what I was thinking. The point is, what I was continuously experiencing was totally new to me. I realized that night the truth is two individuals looking at the same action will "Always" come up with a different opinion of what happened.

At that point in time I made a promise to myself to include as many individuals from as many Military Units and sources that participated in that Battle as I could. I wanted a book to reflect the Siege in every aspect: Air Support, Artillery, VN, SF, LLDB, Strikers, reinforcing Divisions etc.

Thacker
by John Cleckner

This is a skydiving story and I was reminded of it again because of the passing of Bill Edge.

Bill was my platoon Sergeant (1st Plt) in Jump School (1957). He and I laughed our asses off b/c regarding Blood Burns, who was 2d Plt Sgt, and the crazy antics he pulled. Bill had the 1st. Platoon and led the way. He was TDY from the 325 and I was assigned to HHC 325 at the time. I did graduate ("HONOR" Graduate) as a Private E2 from 1500 men of all ranks, Bill supported me but I earned it the hard way.

The deal is most of my Buddies are and were SOG, Scuba Sharks, and HALO Sky Gods.

Don't ask me why; that's just the way it worked out for me. I felt like the Forrest Gump of Special Forces sometimes.

I was the HHC Cmdr of the 2d Battalion, 508th Airborne Infantry Battalion, 1st Brigade, 82nd Airborne Division. (This was my HELL on earth)

After returning from Vietnam in late 1969 I cut a deal with DA to stay at Bragg because of my wife's mental condition. She had been visited by the Dept of the Army twice and informed I had been killed in action. She had a nervous breakdown and I wasn't about to move her to Ft. Carson in Colorado if I could help it.

As a consequence, after multiple commands (two in Combat) and demanding staff positions, and in their infinite wisdom, DA assigned me to the 82nd Abn Div. First as the

S3, 1/504, then as the S3 2/508. After a Battalion trip to Turkey, two Brass Strike demonstrations, (Which I was directed to command on Sicily by the XVIII Abn Cmdr, General Dean personally), I was finally rewarded with the Command of 285 + men of HHC, 2/508. I had HHC, 2/508 and the Command Group for the 1st Brigade, 82nd Abn.

It was easy. I told the First Sergeant and the XO that they would go to Leavenworth if they fucked up.

Then I called in the Platoon Sergeants of the Platoons in HHC, 2/508 (RECON, Medical, Assault Gun, Maintenance, Commo, etc and the beat goes on. I told them to beat to death any asshole that f--ked up in their platoons and I would not prosecute. I did not have one problem...

I would not tolerate one pay hurt in my Company as far as jump pay was concerned. I would not tolerate one AWOL. If any man had a legitimate personal issue, the Plt Sgt or Plt Ldr had better let me know; and if any son of a bitch didn't like those rules he could come in and command my Company after he wiped my ass.

I constantly bummed cigs from my troops, drank with them, and beat their asses at arm wresting and pool. I gave them a 3-day pass every time I could. However, what made it all happen was my First Sergeant, an E7 who had his shit together. Period. End of quote.

All of the E8s in the Battalion wanted his job, but I told Smoke S'mons that if he ever tried to replace him I would make sure he never got promoted to 06.

As an aside, I also told the CO of the 1st Bde that I would close down his Brigade if any of his panty waist, suck ass, f-

-king staff rats did anything that f--ked up my Company. He said he would support me.

Now let gets on with the story, my First Sergeant and Skydiving. "Top" and I were attached at the HIP. He and I played this Company like a Stradivarius.

I loved troops who excelled; who did more than was asked of them. Remember, we are talking 1970. Shit city for the Military. If it wasn't race related, then it was DRUG related.

I had an E4 who really had his shit together, and I did everything I could do to keep him in the military. He was also a recreational Skydiver. I promoted him to E5 and constantly counseled him to re-enlist. NO DICE. I did not fail very often, but this kid stopped me in my tracks.

Then, the First Shirt came into my office with a very strange look on his face. He said, "There is a guy in civvies in my office that scuffled in and said, "I want to speak to John Cleckner, tell him it is Jean Paul." I looked at the First Sergeant and told him to show him in. Top knew this guy was special.

Jean came in and I invited him to sit down. Thacker was, for most, the God of Skydiving. He also controlled MECCA, "Raeford Drop Zone".

Jean and I had gone back a long way. He said, "John, I need Chuck Collingwood." I said so do I and so does the US Army.

Jean said that Chuck would not re-enlist, but he had a plan. God I love a Plan. This one. however, meant the end of my career and possibly Leavenworth.

Jean wanted me to place him on Project Transition and give him to Jean for three months. In other words he would be AWOL for 3 months and I would be validating this action. During this time he would personally train him and ensure he would re-enlist and be a WORLD Champion Military Skydiver.

I agreed, did it, survived; and Chuck Collingwood re-enlisted, became a GOLDEN KNIGHT and became the WORLD CHAMPION Skydiver. There is a GOD.

Prop Blast
by Jim Stewart

I was Prop blasted in the 10th on 26 May 1959. I still have my qualification card and the Warning Order - signed by A. C. CWO for LUDWIG F., Captain, Infantry Adjutant.

The Official Prop Blast Mixture - not to be divulged to anyone who is not a qualified and blasted parachutist (guess I am safe, since the Prop Blast is outlawed now).

75% champagne and 25% vodka, fresh lemon juice and sugar added for flavoring. It will be served very cold.

I think that the Committee strayed from the recipe. For sure it got really drunk out that night.

Where Did We Go Wrong?
by John Cleckner

This is a subject that I have great knowledge of. There were two funds in most Teams that had their shit together. One was the "Team Fund" - ours; one was what was given to us by the CIA to Fund the operation of the Camp for a month. The amount varied depending on the size of the CIDG force, Intel money, food requirements, civilian payroll, Camp construction, etc.

I ran an "A" Team fund for Dong Tre, A-222 in 1966-67. This was during the "Kelly" era which put your ass under the gun so severe you had to be an imbecile to steal from it or be the cleverest-luckiest con man in VN. (An there were many of us) The FUND was Colonel K's number one priority.

Colonel Splash K. required every XO to go through a brief school to instruct them how to handle funds. Then you had a FUNDS Officer in SFOB, each "C" Team and "B" Team and of course the XO at the Team Level.

We received our "Piasters" from Air America birds that flew in and dropped off the money with "Fund" paperwork included, usually in a Gray Canvas Postal Bag the beginning of each Month..

It was up to the A Team XO to account for every penny. An XO had paid the CIDG and allocated the rest of the Funds, putting them in the safe for disbursement; then the XO took his Fund Paperwork through the Hoops and Whistles Col. Kelly had set up and refined to stop stealing. The XO would travel through the B & C teams on his way ultimately to SFOB where you went into the "Interrogation

Room" and either got a passing grade or sent to Jail. I shit you not!

This is where the LLDB got the bulk of their money from. GHOSTS!!! Soldiers on the rolls that didn't exist. It used to drive me crazy. A-222 was one of Father Hoa's camps. He also got his cut by selling me rice to feed soldiers that didn't exist.

I refused to pay the good Father the $85,000 he demanded for rice he said he had given our men. He got on Air Nucmom (sp), flew to Saigon, and complained to General Westmoreland. I kept my job, but Major Duke, B22 CO brought a black briefcase into the Camp and showed me the money he was going to pay the good Father as soon as he arrived by "Army" helicopter furnished by Westy.

Now to the "Team Fund" (Which varied from Team to Team depending on how aggressive those who ran it were in hustling money for the "A" Team members).

My theory was that we were sending most of our dough home; so I gave each Team member $250.00 on each In-Country R&R and $500.00 for Out of Country R&R. When a Team member left (DEROS or was moved to another Team or got wounded) he received an equal cut of the total amount in the fund at the time.

I had the CIDG build a Bar for us; then I would buy palates of beer for 2 1/2 cents a can and sell it for a dollar or more. I did the same thing with Soda Pop. Plus, I stole every thing that wasn't nailed down everywhere I went. When the 4th ID left our AO, they laterally transferred FIVE (5) brand new 2 1/2 ton trucks to our "A" Team. I opened up Hwy 6B from Dong Tre to Tuy Hoa and the rest is history. Our A team was like a paradise in the jungle, we even had a TV.

I also had my Montagnard Companies employed to make knives, crossbows and other Yard "Stuff" that I sold to Legs, and Pilots. Made a mint and our Team members always had a smile on their faces, and so did the Yards....This was a very unique camp in that it was half Yard and half VN.

The Most Memorable Wedding Anniversary of My Life
by Doris, John Cleckner's LYB

It was the day before my 14th wedding anniversary, and my husband John and I had made reservations for dinner the following evening. The next morning we woke up before 7:00 AM. My husband is very romantic and he is always planning something special for me on special days. We were lying in bed discussing what we would like to do that day to celebrate our wedding anniversary when the phone rang. It was ten minutes to seven and John, not being an early riser, let the recorder come on. A friend's voice said "John, turn the television on, America is being attacked"! We both knew that this man was not the type of person to play a joke. We jumped out of bed and turned the television on.

The reporter was saying a commercial jet had just crashed into one of the towers of the World Trade Center in New York. John and I were both asking one another how could a commercial jet have gotten that far off course. My god what a terrible accident!

Just then John screamed, "Oh my God here comes another one". The second plane had just hit the other World Trade Center Tower.

The two airlines that were involved with the crashes were American and United. I said, " John they are using the Airline names that symbolize our Country, United and American". I had chills from the thought of it. This attack was definitely intentional.

Then the reality hit me that we had friends and relative flying for both Airlines. By this time I was frantic. John and I immediately called everyone in the family. We were able to get the locations of our nieces and nephew and let my 87-year-old Mother know that everyone was ok.

Later reports said a man heard the explosions and had thought that a movie was being made. He recorded it from a high-rise tower apartment where he lived in New York City. He thought that Hollywood was filming another episode of Striking Distance, where they had actually blown up a building in downtown New York. He recorded the first part of the explosion without realizing what had really happened. My husband and I were in shock. We found out that everyone else who had just heard the news felt the same way. We continued to watch as the smoke bellowed out of the tall skyscrapers, covering Manhattan in a vale of white. A few minutes later the news media was reporting that firemen and police were running into the buildings to try and help save as many people as possible.

It was horrible to witness this event. People were falling out of the buildings, and jumping to their deaths. All kinds of debris fell from the air. A few minutes later a long line of firemen ran into the burning building to help save lives.

Moments later a huge explosion came down through the tower to the ground flour and the men disappeared.
The buildings started collapsing. People near the buildings started running for their lives. The firemen were trapped and buried alive trying to save other peoples lives.

Then the news came over the wires that a plane had crashed into the Pentagon. The United States was being attacked, there was no doubt about that. At the time no one knew who was responsible for this devastation. People were calling the news media letting them know that they had just talked to a loved one by cell phone from the planes.

I was glued to the television. I could not take my eyes off of what was happening. Terror was taking a hold of me.
It was mid-morning and I was consumed by emotions. It was my wedding anniversary, with all the wonderful memories, and plans for the day's celebrations spinning in my head. Then the reality, that this day in history would never be forgotten by America because of this attack, hit me.

Just then another plane, traveling from the Boston area, was reported to have flown to Pennsylvania. They didn't know anything about this plane only that there was another Airliner missing. I was sure this plane and maybe others had also been hijacked to hit other parts of America and in particular Washington DC. The latest missing plane was heading that way. More fear consumed me as I wondered if there were suicide planes flying all over America.
One of the passengers on that flight called his wife from his cell phone and told her that his plane had been hijacked.
The wife told him of the planes being flown into the World Trade Center and the Pentagon. Her husband told her that he loved her and that he and a few other men on the plane were going to get control of the airplane. She heard his last

words, "Lets Roll". A few minutes later the plane was on radar, and they could see that it was making a U-turn over Virginia. Then the plane crashed near a small town in Pennsylvania. The television reporters were telling us that the plane that crashed in Pennsylvania was headed for either the White House or the Capitol in Washington DC.

The TV reporters then informed the American people that the government had ordered all airlines to fly to the nearest airport and land their planes. Then we heard the commentators say that the airplanes had been hijacked by terrorist and flown into the World Trade Center, the Pentagon, and the Pennsylvania field.

 My husband John is a retired Green Beret Officer who had fought in combat around the world. His experiences and training with this elite unit automatically triggered him to start planning for our survival. He reassured me that no one would successfully destroy our country, but he said we had things we had to do just in case things got out of hand.
I was so upset and scared I couldn't think. John's strong arms and reassurance helped me get a grip on reality.
We have a large family and they were spread out over the country. We started calling our children and grand children to reassure them that everything was going to be Ok. Then we called our parents, brothers and sisters. John and I gave them advice on escape and evasion if necessary and how to survive. Each call was different because of where they lived.

As the day wore on I began taping every news report and keeping a diary. John and I also planned what we would do if anything were to happen in our geographical area.
We started filling water jugs and preparing food supplies if we had to evacuate. John had a location in the mountains for us to go to where we have our deer camp each year. It has

good water and plenty of shelter. It is also miles from anywhere and the safest place we could get to in a fairly short period of time.

John and I both said, "The Dam" at the same time. It seemed logical to us that if the terrorists wanted to take out California, Shasta Dam would be his number one target. I was terrified at the thought of what would happen if the terrorists attacked the "Dam". We figured we could live high enough to be safe from flooding, but we still planned for the worst.

In all honesty, by this time, I had completely forgotten about my Wedding Anniversary. My husband and I were doing all the things we felt we had to do, under the circumstances, to survive. The thought of survival consumed us and we moved like people possessed. Needless to say we did not go out to eat that night to celebrate our wedding anniversary. Like millions of other Americans we sat in front of our TV watching in disbelief and trying to understand what had happened and what was going to happen.

The report we initially heard was that over 10,000 deaths resulted from these attacks. Those numbers were incomprehensible to us.

September 11, 2001 was my 14th Wedding Anniversary, a day I will never forget and a day that will definitely live in infamy.

MP
by Big John Delavan

I wuz a broke assed leg MP back then, and about the only beverages I could afford wuz a few Cokes a month, one of which went down with mushroom soup. Since my head injury I can't remember the names of any of the clubs, bars and so forth except the Kaeglebahn (sp?) that was located on the right hand side of the road on the way into Toelz from Flint. I think I could find them all again if the town hasn't changed too much (hey, I don't think it had changed much in the previous 400 or so years...) but remember the names? HA!

Being there as a leg MP was what inspired me to find a way to get into SF. By the time I'd made that decision I had too many various MP schools under my belt and the official line was that I was "overqualified" as an MP, and wouldn't be allowed to change MOS.

So I got out at the end of my two-year mini-career and played civilian for about five more. Then, a recruiter told me that I could enlist for SF. Hooray!!! Only he screwed me and signed me up under my old MP MOS. If I could have found him I would have spent an entire career at Ft. Leavenworth. Again I was "overqualified" as an MP so I spent the next three years in MPI.

I came back to the outside world where I found 12th Group in So. CA. They took me in and let me train first as a medic and later in weapons. So there was a light at the end of chat tunnel. That was the one just before the train came rolling through – but that's another story.

Relieve Toenail Pain
by John Delavan

Step #1: First get a visual on the nail that is causing all that excruciating pain. This is an important step because burning a hole through another toe nail will not give the desired effect. It will give an effect, but not the one you really want right now.

Step #2: Once you have eye-balled the hurt nail and you are sure there is a lot of blood under it (you can tell this if the nail is dark purple instead of it's usual color), remember which toe it is. Tying a string around it usually helps in relocating that toe when you are ready to perform step number 5.

Step #3: Obtain a long, thin, cylindrically shaped piece of metal. A straightened paper clip will work fine.

Step #4: Heat the metal object over an open flame until it is red hot. It will probably help to hold the object with a pair of pliers while heating it. This prevents collateral damage to your finger tips.

Step #5: While holding the red hot metal object with the pliers in one hand, relocate the injured toe. It's the one that hurts really bad, has a purple nail and a piece of string tied around it.

Step #6: Gently push the red hot metal object directly through the TOP of the nail in the center of the purple area. It might take more than one heating of the red hot metal object to do this. You will know when you have passed through the nail because there will no longer be as much resistance when you push on it and when you remove the red hot metal object from your toe nail a quantity of dark red blood will follow it and begin dripping on mom's new beige carpet. The throbbing pain you had been feeling in your toe will immediately begin to lessen. You will not feel any pain from the red hot metal object unless you push it too far into the toe. Go back and read the "Gently push the red..." part again right now. Also, do NOT push the red hot metal object UNDER your toe nail from the front. You will know why you don't want to do this as soon as you do it. Trust me.

Step #7: Once you have finished pushing the red hot metal object through the top of your throbbing, purple, hurting like Hell toe nail and blood is dripping on mom's new beige carpet, place the red hot metal object in an ashtray or other safe place. Try to not accidentally grab it with your fingers or sit on it before it cools to room temperature. Please do not drop the red hot metal object on mom's new beige carpet that your toe is now dripping dark red blood on.

Step #8: Place a gauze pad over the nail that is now dripping blood on mom's new carpet and squeeze gently. Squeeze on either side of the hole you just made in the top of your toe nail. The excess blood that has built up under the damaged nail will come out into the gauze pad thus preventing an even bigger mess on mom's new carpet. But, WTF, you're already in trouble so don't worry too much about it.

Step #9: Remove the blood soaked gauze pad and drop it on mom's damn new beige carpet. Remember, you're already in trouble for bleeding on it and dropping the red hot metal object on it which burned a damn hole right in the middle when company can see it. Oh, Lordy are you in trouble now!

Step #9: Place a small amount of triple antibiotic ointment on the business side of a new Band-Aid, then place the business side of the new Band-Aid with the triple anti-biotic ointment on it on your previously damaged toe with the nice new hole in it.

Step #10: Put on your socks and jogging shoes then run like Hell before mom sees what you did to her nice new blood stained burned up used to be beige carpet.

A Journey West
John Hauck

I experienced the following phenomena in the desert of West Texas west of Marfa; then later in the area of Sanderson and Dryden, TX, at Terrell County International Airport which lies between these two sprawling metropolises.

A few days ago the dust devils chased me all over the desert west of Marfa; then a tremendous black thunderstorm with a heavy "black wall" rain tried to circle around and hit me from both sides and the rear at the same time. Twenty miles from Marfa I went WOT, held on to the seat with one hand and the other on the stick, and with a full bladder hauled ass for the little airport at Marfa. I made it just in time to find the FBO closed and no one for miles, or so I thought.

After scoping out the little airport, a friendly local showed up that had keys to the gas pump, and I was on my way east. By the time I got into Terrell County AP the thunder bumpers were booming and I spent the next two nights and day in the little FBO that had everything I needed but hot and cold running maids. During these thirty-six hours no other aircraft landed or took off from the airport. My little Kolb Mark III was the only airplane there. The only other human being I saw was CD Cairns the FBO Operator/local building contractor. I would see him in the morning and just before dark each night. During my stay there I experienced many downpours with thunderstorms, thunder and lightening. First time I had experienced floods in the dessert. This area normally experiences 6 to 11 inches of rain annually. I believe they got half that during my short stay.

During my flight I landed at Santa Ynez near Goleta, CA, home of Ben The Plunderer. Although I was able to make telephone contact with Ben, I was unable to get the logistics correct and failed to make eye ball to eye ball contact with him. I'm sorry we could not make it work. I truly enjoyed my visit with Ben two years prior when Nell and I came through the area pulling the old 5th Wheel.

I also struck out with Jim Hanke at Sierra Vista, AZ. I was making better time than I had expected and was on top of Sierra Vista before I realized it. Although I could not make telephone contact with Jim prior to landing at Sierra Vista, I went ahead and flew south in hopes I would, by chance, be able to meet up with him. No such luck.

However, I had no trouble meeting up with my buddy, Steve Antonelli, Auntie Nellie himself. By the time I landed at San Geronimo Air Park a few miles west of San Antonio, Steve had already recon'd the airstrip and local area. When I landed last Wednesday, Steve, his wife and kids were waiting for me at the airport. We had a good visit, Yvonne cooked a delicious supper, a welcome change to the MREs I had been consuming and supplied by Auntie Nellie, a good night's sleep, and I was on my way home the next day. Had a great 16 day flight: 5,250 miles (estimated),

75 mph average speed (estimated), 70.5 flight hours, 350 gal fuel (estimated), 12 States (I think. Got to take a look at the map to make sure).

Lowest elevation landed was 211 feet below sea level at Furnace Creek, Death Valley, California.

Highest altitude flown was 14,500 feet to cross the Sierra Nevadas and Yosemite National Park. Even at that altitude I only cleared the highest mountain in the area by aprx'ly 600 feet.

I finally got to see the Pacific Ocean from my airplane. In 1994 I flew the length of the coast from San Diego to Seattle without seeing the Pacific because of marine fog. Got the same thing last week, but when I got near San Luis Obispo and Oceana, California, I got a small break in the mountains where I could get a peak at the white breaking surf. I ducked under the marine fog and flew the beach and surf of the Pacific Ocean. First time to see the Pacific from my little Kolb Mark III experimental/homebuilt airplane.

Was a wonderful flight, thoroughly enjoyed by an old fart 64 years old. Who would have thought I would have been flying like this thirty years ago? I am grateful to be able to still do and enjoy it. I still fly cross countries the same as I did nineteen years ago when I started cross countrying ultralights - rough it - sleep under the wing - find hot chow when I can. Life is good. Would be even better if someone had done all my chores here at Hauck's Holler while I was away, rather than collecting them upon my return. Ugh!

Walk on the Moon
by John Hauck

I was on leave in transit to VN for my second one year tour. I got pretty excited getting to watch things unfold on the TV and watch Neil Armstrong step on to the moon.

A couple weeks later I was somewhere over the Pacific on my way to Saigon. After four or five months in-country it was fast approaching the Xmas season. Our Attack Helicopter Company had been selected to escort the CH-47's carrying the Bob Hope Show from Camp Eagle, Hue/Phu Bai, down south to Da Nang's Marble Mountain. We were quite proud to be able to do the duty. The morning of the show up at Eagle, twelve of us fired up six AH-1G's. We flew up to the VIP Pad at Eagle near the amphitheater where the show was to take place. Reserved seats were waiting on us. Man, this was the best I had been treated since arrival as a seasoned Captain from the States.

I had started off my Army career in the 101st at Campbell as a piss ant PVT2 in D Co/187. Went through jump school and on to fame as a 111.17 (I think that was the MOS in 1958). Needless to say, I felt much like a private the first month's in-country with the 101st. I tried to have me get ready for a foot and wall locker inspection. What????????????????

On with the story. I enjoyed the show with Bob Hope and the gang, but the highlight of the Xmas Show was when Neil Armstrong walked out on the stage. Wow! Here was the guy I had seen walk on the moon, and now I was looking up at him in person. I was truly in awe. That was 34 years ago this Xmas. Time sure flies.

Old Impala
by Jüri Estam

I bought an old Impala with Hawaiian plates for 75 dollars from a guy who had processed in from Hawaii. Never registered the damn thing, no post sticker, and no insurance. I was an anarchist bohemian SF-er, I suspect. It was strange; SF was a place where someone with problems submitting to authority could still fit in at that time, though I admire the current level of discipline. I am not sure we were a whole lot less professional; work was something we took seriously.

The empties would go over the shoulder into the back seat. That car was like a horse; it knew the way home from Boston by itself. I certainly didn't have any recollection of driving it. This is not shit that I am proud of, but it did happen. There was a back road that one could take on to post from somewhere along 2A out where the demo range was or thereabouts.

The heater didn't work on the Impala. It had a blanket for your lap and a candle in the windshield to warm up a small porthole of visibility. Copilot would yell out instructions, "Take a right turn in 75 meters. No, no, not yet. Now!"

Slipstream
by Jüri Estam

An old friend of mine used to speak of some women being as ugly as unpainted tanks before they plastered themselves with the makeup, and I think it was HL Mencken who wrote of Eleanor Roosevelt being so ugly that it made you want to burn every bed in the world. I hope Mencken and Ms. Eleanor were contemporaries; if not, it was someone else who said that.

One of my Estonian-American predecessors in SF was a butterbar named Viido Polikarpus who - as far as I know - was the officer equivalent of a candystriper. He had just been sent to Bad Tolz administratively, meaning on orders and not on the basis of the Q course.

Viido and I hung out together before my time in the Army, and there are numerous wild tales to tell. When we finished a period of several months of living a debauched life in San Francisco (It was women we debauched; on each other we were just bad influences.), we packed up and took a road trip across America and ended up doing some more debauchery in the lovely (?) out of the way burgh of Lakewood, New Jersey, just down the road from Ft. Dix, which I would come to know and love during Basic.

The four of us had been living in a San Francisco apartment. Upon unassing California, we made the mistake of putting Viido in the GTO, which was being towed. There were about eight cases of beer in the towed vehicle and we should have seen this coming. About 90 minutes outside of the city limits, half-drunk Viido begins honking the horn because his bladder is sending him full-up signals. We, being mean people, wouldn't stop. Finally, in desperation, he rolls his window down and voids into the slipstream, but aerodynamics and things being what they are, it all blew back into the car and drenched him.

Many misadventures later, we were in Tom's River, New Jersey. All people of Estonian extraction have a tacit agreement when a story that starts "this is no shit", you do not say at the outset "we was pissed". It goes without saying that you had been imbibing; to say so would be redundant, and it is a timesaving device to not emphasize the obvious.

The three or four of us, still hanging out together as a merry band, would do a little work and we would party a lot. One misspent Saturday or Sunday we were on the breakwater. I had decided to climb up 40 or 50 yards to the top of some sort of a tower that housed a navigational device or whatever. With no ill intent - honest - I began to drain the vestibules. (I do not know where that term comes from.) As soon as the hue and cry began from my colleagues below to the effect of "what in the hell are you doing" and "we are going to kick your ass" (I was about 19, they were "much older", as in 23 and 25), I obliged and stopped in mid-stream. You know how hard that is, to stop pissing if you are on a roll. How could I have known the wind would do chat; I was pissing to the other side of the tower. Even though out of the goodness of my heart I complied with their requests, there was little or nothing I could do about the 40 or 50 yards of said substance still making its way to the ground. I don't recall getting my ass kicked, which sort of surprises me.

Vietnam Whiners
by Larry McMillin

During the course of my work the last 30 years, after I retired from the Army, I have met some of the world's greatest whiners. I have always encouraged them to tell me their stories. Most of them seem to have come from rear area people. Now people in the Infantry bitch piss and moan, but there are very few whiners.

In late 1969 in Viet Nam there were over 500,000 American troops. I think most SF was having some enemy contact, but not all every day. I would say, of the line combat units, only about one-half were having enemy contact on a daily basis. Could be even less depending on where they were. What I am getting at is there were many idle folks and that weren't good for any army.

President Nixon announced he was going to end the war with dignity . The darn problem was trying to get 500,000 troops out of Vietnam in a hasty and orderly manner using air craft. Since 1965, troops had been returning to the states with little fan fair. Heck, people in SF were begging to go to Viet Nam so they didn't have to pick up pine cones.

I guess it was in 1966 that the word started getting around how bad everything was in RVN . In other words, the peaceniks' invasion started, and the Press started the bias broadcasting and planting seeds of discontent in the minds of the American people. If you tell a young soldier how bad and wrong something is long enough, he will start to believe it. Thus we started getting the whiners. There were whiners in WWII and Korea , however the way they whined was different from the way the Vietnam vets whined.

However, the real whiners of all time were the peace time vets who never heard or saw a shot fired in anger .You must remember, not all the troops in the large military of the Vietnam era went to Viet Nam and were really peace time veterans. Germany had so many screwed up troops that the stockades were running over. Rocky L. told me he tried to put at least two per week in jail and kicked the same amount of the army. Billy K. M. told me the same thing.

In 1972 I took a trip up from Bad Tolz and visited some of the Leg units in Germany. From what I saw on that trip, the Russians could have walked through Germany without a shot being fired. Darn Baseball caps were held on male heads with bobby pins. I swear I thought someone was issuing the troops pot. As the story goes, the troops got hooked in RVN and carried their habits to Germany. Now, pray tell how this happened when the guy had never been to Vietnam. I knew a guy in Spring Lake who went only to Germany, and he was a basket case for something the Army did to him over there. I'll bet Matterson knows the guy I am talking about. He hung around Parker plumbing but, his family were the whiners. He was so spaced out and had a low IQ to begin with he really didn't give a hoot. I think it's obvious the point I'm trying to make.

It was a time when whining was in style among many.

D.S.S.
by Leamon Ratterree

One of my "cases" in Lumberton NC was given a rented, furnished house, which was kept stocked with food. Dept of Social Services paid for all this.

Well, I went there for a visit one day with a young female Social Worker from DSS. The place was trashed, and stunk really bad. There had been complaints from the neighbors that a lot of street people had been hanging out there and being noisy all hours of the night.

Afterwards the DSS SW finished lecturing him on living responsibly. She made the mistake of asking him for "input." He went into a tirade against DSS, and "You people stop tellin' me how to live my life. I lived on the streets for 18 years and was just fine until you came along and messed it all up. I know how to dumpster shop, and cook MY kinda food." He knew when and where to pick up and cash his SSI check. He also knew if things got really bad, he could go to the homeless shelter.

The lad had all kinds of skills and was really living a good life. The SW was just putting her values above his. I didn't say anything but he occasionally looked over at me and got a reassuring nod.

As we were driving away, the SW asked me, "What do you think?"

I answered, "Number one law of social work - the self determination of the client comes first. He has told you what he wants. It is your duty to see to it that it happens. He wants to live on the streets. Let him."

She did.

PS. Next time I saw the lad out on the streets, he serenaded me with "A Country Boy Can Survive." He could have had a career in CW.

The Bodyguard
by Leamon Ratterree

In 1986, I was sent to El Salvador and after about 24 hours on the grid square, it was determined that I would need a bodyguard. So, was assigned a fine gentleman, the same age and approximate size as I, to serve as my personal security. The fine man, who appointed this private in the National Guard to me, said that he was the very best and the brightest. This proved to be true.

My Bodyguard was indeed a Private. He had been with the National Guard of El Salvador for ten years. He had gone to special training which qualified him for a position on the U.S. Embassy Protective Services Section (not sure of the title). He had gone to U.S. and Israeli qualifications courses. He was well versed in personal protection, countermeasures, and the fine art of building clearing. I asked him why he didn't go to Officer School. He said that if he went to officer school (which he would have likely been honor grad) he would probably been sent to some remote, under strength outpost to be killed along with the others manning the post. He also pointed out that he turned down the rank of Sergeant. I queried him on why he turned that down.

He gave the following reasons: He would be sent in place of a Lieutenant to a remote, under-strength outpost to be killed along with the others; he would get less pay; he would miss all the other benefits of being an Embassy Bodyguard.

What less pay? He was getting paid for being a Private with ten years in the National Guard, he was getting Special Duty Pay from the National Guard, for being a bodyguard, and he was drawing extra pay from the U.S. Embassy. Add it all up, and he was getting paid more than if he were a Sergeant or Lieutenant in the ranks of the regulars. What benefits? He got to go to all the fun events and eat the best chow with whomever he was assigned. We flew all over the country in helicopters. He was able to rub elbows with the hierarchy of the Embassy Officials and the USMILGROUP. Lots of the Americans in country knew him and liked him. He demonstrated a lot of wisdom and knowledge of tactics, techniques, and doctrine of the U.S. Army, as well as that of the guerrillas. So, I decided to tap into this resource.

I had to fly out to various brigades and military districts throughout the country to coordinate National Guard "training exercises" and operations with commanders and their staffs, as well as with the Americans working at these various sites. This required my bodyguard to accompany me on these trips. We both dressed in either civilian clothes or in "sterile" (no rank or unit insignia) jungle fatigues.

We arrived at the Cavalry Regiment for a coordination meeting with the Commander and his staff. The U.S. Advisor to the Regiment was an Armored Cavalry NCO from Ft. Bliss, Texas. He was very good at his job, and he knew about my bodyguard.

It was decided to hold the meeting in the Officer's Mess, and we all moved to the table at the front of the room. I managed to maneuver everyone into their seats, and the only seat left was at the head of the table. That was the seat reserved for the senior ranking officer. My bodyguard was forced to take the seat. All present assumed that he was my counterpart, which meant he was likely a Captain or Major. The bodyguard learned quickly what I was up to. The Cavalry NCO, my bodyguard, and I managed to keep a straight face throughout the planning meeting.
The local officers referred to him as "Sir" and were respectful of his assumed rank as he provided input and guidance to the upcoming operation – in this case, night zone reconnaissance.

The meeting was supposed to be finished before the lunch hour, but since we went longer than expected, other officers in the Regiment started showing up. In Central America, when a junior officer entered or departed the mess, he was required to report to the senior officer present, and ask permission to eat or permission to leave.

Well, my "Private-in-Charge" knew exactly what his reply to these requests was supposed to be, and he executed his responsibilities in a manner expected of a professional "officer" seated at the "senior officer's chair."

A few days later, we brought in the Special National Guard Company, issued their Operations Orders, and conducted our mission without incident. Much of the success of the mission was a result of the input and professionalism of a Private in the Guard.

Shark Story
by Marvin Crist

While at Key West, my dive buddy (Paul F.) and I saw this one small sand shark while out doing our practice compass swim. It was a surface swim with a snorkel and a wrist mounted compass. No problem with the shark, he was about 4-5 feet and swam away quickly.

Saturdays were the days make-up swims were done. If you failed a compass swim, either for time or by missing too much, you had to find someone to swim with you. There was an AF CCT (Dave) that asked me to swim with him on Saturday. Paul and I were swim team one and this guy was about half way in the pack. So come Saturday I was swimming with this guy daydreaming because I was not finning my ass off to keep up with Paul. All of sudden, Dave knocks the regulator out of my mouth and starts nudging me over. I put my regulator back in my mouth and look at him with a big question mark on my face. He gave the sign for big hungry. I looked at the bottom, there was the same shark Paul, and I had run into on Monday, just sitting on the bottom.

Dave and I finished the swim. When we get on shore, I asked Dave, "WTF are you doing? That shark was just sitting there.

He says" Not when I saw him." It appears Dave and the shark saw each other at the same time. Dave went vertical in the water and the shark went for the bottom. I'm not sure who was more scared of whom.

About a year after passing SCUBA school and going to HALO school, guess who else shows up? Dave.

Low Tide Fest
by Mel Thornton

I had just returned from a weekend party with my brother, and a group of my more rowdy friends, out at our cabin on Debob Bay. My 20 year old niece had been staying in my 5th wheel trailer along side the cabin for the last 6 months. So she invited all the young girls who work with her as maids at a local motel, to the party. All these girls proceeded to get very smashed, and over the course of the weekend we had them sucking down raw oysters, learning to appreciate designer beer, and starting to like music from the 50's and 60's. One exception was a cute little twenty-two year old bosomy blond, who only drank soda the whole weekend.

As this hung-over group left for work Sunday morning, my brother told my semi-alcoholic niece how nice it was to meet one of her friends who did not drink. My niece just laughed and said that Tracy was only invited after promising the other girls (who were afraid she would embarrass them in front of us old guys and wives) that she would not drink. This was because every time she got drunk, she took off all her clothes and was known for public displays of excessive affection!

Needless to say, those of us whose relationships would have survived a little live entertainment took this news very badly.

Records Out of Sequence
by Merlyn Eckles

A buddy of mine was a clerk typist before he went through 91B training, and was assigned to the 6th SF. Someone in HQ found out that he was doctoring the records, and he was pulled up to S-1 to "take up the slack".

One of his pet peeves was the 0-2s that were on orders to the 5TH would come into the section and say they wanted a new Form 55?(the green one) so that when their file went before the promotion board it would 'look good'. Naturally, they came in the day before they were to sign out. Therefore, he would fill it out, mark the little box down in the corner #1, and give it to them. He would not send the change in sequence numbers to DA. That meant that when the next change to records was sent forward, the numbers would be out of sequence, so the 201 File would be flagged, until the mess was straightened out. This could take several months.

Shucking and Jiving
by Paul Whitmore

If suddenly some of us were to become French, would that make us any less the soldiers that we were and dream of being again if necessary. It is not the tag that the individual wears – it is his individual commitment to the ideals that he is willing to fight for that will determine what kind of soldier he will be. Thinking back to Viet Nam, I each of us can remember someone whom we would never in a million years want to be in a war with. So just think of the adage "There but for the Grace of God, go I."

I can remember after a fire fight, there was SP4 Joel, medic in the 173rd (who was blacker than a piece of West Virginia coal) who earned his Medal of Honor.

That night the blacks were gathered together "shucking and jiving" and doing their 5, 10, and 15 minute "daps" all the while bad mouthing the entire white race, the military, and America in general. Him I want on my team; those others should have been shipped - all expenses paid to their "ancestral birth place".

Beanie Weenies
by Ray Flaherty

Recently, while grocery shopping with my wife I spotted a can of Beanie Weenies. Thinking it might remind me of other times I tossed a can into the shopping cart.

Today I heated them in the microwave and had them for lunch along with buttered fresh bread and milk. What a letdown! It was nothing like the C Rations I remembered.

Could it be because there was no rain running down the bridge of my nose? Was it because the temperature wasn't bitterly cold or extremely hot today? Or that I didn't hurry my meal in case the shooting started again? Was it because I warmed the contents of the can and washed it down with fresh milk?

I should have remembered they are best eaten cold out of an O.D. can with a not-so-clean spoon and washed down with flat tasting water from an aluminum canteen.

Seal Straphanger
by Richard Hayes

This was in 1981 during SPECWAREX in the Philippines. We (A-726), along with an Australian Clearance Dive Unit and the SEALs from NAVSPECWARUNIT-ONE out of Subic Bay, were using the Grayback (the UW diesel sub out of Subic Bay) and a SEAL team drowned in the large hanger trunk during a lock-in/-out evolution. They quit the lock-ins/-outs pending investigation but we continued with the operations. The Grayback was a lot easier to use than removing bolts and replacing them with eye-bolts to string all the lines on the "boomers" and making the Navy types nervous with what we were doing outside of their boats!

We had a young SEAL strap hanging with us on a night water jump and he lost our M-14A1 (an M14 with a separate pistol grip and folding front grip under the forearm, a hinged shoulder rest attached to the buttplate, a removable muzzle jump compensator, and a bipod; it was a good SAW type weapon we liked to carry before the Army came out with the M249). They had to transfer a replacement M-14A1 to the Army from the Navy's stocks and it pissed the Navy SEAL Cdr (an AH named Grabowski) off so badly that he had the young guy thrown out of the SEALs. The XO for the unit was pretty squared away, a black Lieutenant Commander named Greene (the guy who as an 0-6 made the news and got in trouble for some sexual harassment stuff a few years back). The SEALs I dealt with there were pretty good in the water and with doing PT or working out in the gym, less so in the jungle.

Brownie
by Robert Pryor

When I got to Jump school in early January 1968, I met up with and befriended Brownie. He had the gift of gab and was easy to make friends with. He was a few years older than I, so he always called me kid. I didn't mind, though, as I only looked about 14 or 15 years old anyway.

As jump school progressed, Brownie and I became one another's primary friend. Not that there was that much to do at jump school other than run, PT, and train. We would sit and bull shit from time to time, when we had a moment. On the second day of tower week, I busted up my jaw on the 34-foot tower. I rode it out but there was blood all over me, my harness, and the make-believe reserve. You probably think that I must have screwed up exiting the tower, but I did not.

After being released from the trolley risers, I reported to the training NCO and mumbled my number as best I could. He responded, "Satisfactory jump, recover and make another." I then pointed out my injury to him. He called me a sissy or something and told me to report to the medic. They too me to the hospital and my jaw was surgically repaired.

I don't know if it is true or not, but I had been told that if you miss 14 days of jump school you must go back and start the course all over again. I did not want to have to retake ground week, plus whatever portion of tower week I had completed, so I really leaned on the doctor to release me to duty. After a 13-day absence I found myself back in tower week. My friend Brownie was long gone. I thought that I would never see him again, but if that were the case, there wouldn't be much to this story.

Upon graduation from jump school, I was assigned to SF Training Group. I got on the bus to Ft. Bragg with a whole bunch of other cherries. Now being called a cherry wasn't so bad, as the alternative was being called a leg.

We got to Ft. Bragg late Saturday evening. They put is in some sort of transient billeting until we could get assigned to our company. I was assigned to B Company and reported in that Monday. One of the first persons I saw when I got there was Brownie.

Great! A friendly face! Man, was I ever wrong. So here I was a cherry and Brownie already had two weeks into Phase I. Brownie was going into commo and I was going to be a combat engineer. For the next four weeks I had to hear all about Phase I from the "experienced" Brownie. Wow, did that suck! His condescending "Wait 'til you get to this part" attitude. Here Brownie was an expert on Special Forces training, and I was the FNG. It only got worse.

When Brownie went to the Phase One Field Training Exercise, he made his cherry blast. Now I was in for it. Not only was Brownie heading into MOS training, he had his beret and was an "experienced" jumper while I was still just a cherry. Brownie received his beret at the completion of Phase I, so whenever he would see me in my baseball cap he would make remarks such as "Batter up, Cherry!" From the day Brownie got back from McKall, all the way up until the last time I ever saw him, he always called me cherry. It was his way of saying that he was always above me.

Brownie was in the Cornish commo program so he finished MOS training quickly. He then moved into Phase II training, still a few weeks ahead of me. It was the same crap every day. "Hey Cherry, wait 'til you get to this part and wait 'til you get to that part." I had been putting up with this crap for about four or five months now, and it was really becoming nauseating.

The next layer of insults was when Brownie completed Phase II a few weeks ahead of me and earned his "full flash". Brownie mercifully went to Seventh Group so I was spared his insults for a while. When I completed Phase II, they assigned me to Third Group while I cross trained in Operations and Intelligence.

I would see Brownie from time to time there on Smoke Bomb Hill. Again, it was same shit, different day. Brownie would brag how he was on a team and what his team was doing. How Seventh Group was so much better than Third Group was. Of course he would remind me that I was still just a trainee.

Then the day the came with mixed blessings. Brownie got his orders for Viet Nam. I had to listen to all of his crap about going off to war, while I was just a trainee. At least he would soon be on the other side of the world from me. As soon as I completed the O & I course, I was on orders for Viet Nam. It was a great day for me as that was all I ever wanted: To go get in the mix before all the fighting ended.

I got to Vietnam on December 19, 1968. I immediately headed for Nha Trang as I was scheduled for Recondo School prior to being sent to an A-team. I had already begun to forget about Brownie, but you just had to know who would be the first person I met at Recondo School - Good old Brownie. He was half way through the program, and again I had to listen to his crap over and over. "Hey

Cherry, wait 'til you get to this part... Wait 'til you get out to Hon Tre Island."

He mercifully completed the course and was sent away. I completed the course and received my orders for Bunard. I knew nothing about Bunard but some people teased me about it and said that there was little or no action in the AO. I head on down to Bien Hoa to report in to the C Team. This is really getting old, but I ran into Brownie. He had been assigned to Mike Force. Here I was just an A-Team puke at a camp with a reputation of little action at that time, and Brownie was a big bag Mike Force dude. Did I ever have to hear about it! Fortunately I was quickly sent out to my team.

I would return to Bien Hoa from time to time during my tour of duty, and as often as not I would run into Brownie. I had to listen to his tales of the adventures of Mike Force. I was getting to the point where I never wanted to hear the name Mike Force again.

On April 17, 1969 I was wounded for the first time. It was only a scratch. I continued to do my thing at Bunard. Then the following month someone got the bright idea to put me in for Soldier of the Month, representing our B-Team. I have never been a parade field trooper and I considered that type of thing to be for REMFs.

I had to go to Bien Hoa for the competition. I came in second, which says little or nothing for the competition, as I put forth no effort. Of course, one of the other guys in the competition was Brownie. He looked all spiffy in his spit shined boots while I looked like Hell since I had been extracted from a patrol to go back and play this game. I ran into Brownie the night before the competition and had to spend the evening listening to Mike Force tales. The next morning we all reported for the competition. My team Sergeant had taken a clean and pressed uniform to Bien Hoa for me to wear. He put forth the effort to have all the proper patches sewn on, which was something I did not bother to do previously.

So I reported, along with Brownie, and I believe three other suckers. Brownie was standing there telling me some more of his Mike Force Tales when suddenly he says, "I see you have the CIB."

Now after four months on a team, I figured that his statement was about the dumbest observation I had ever heard. I figured that with all of his Mike Force tales he must have about every award and decoration by now. In my amazement I responded, "Yes, and I have the Purple Heart too. What are you getting at?"

He responds, "I guess all I will ever have is the EIB." "What do you mean, Brownie? How come you can't get a CIB?"

"Well, I work in the commo bunker at Mike Force HQ and I never get to go on operations."

After a moment of stunned silence, I said, "Brownie, as long as you live, don't you ever speak to me again!"

Hey, I have no problems with the guys in support roles. We would have all died without them. It is just that Brownie turned out to be the first SF qualified wannabe I ever met. Brownie finished fifth out of five in the Soldier of the month Competition.

View of Somalia
by Stephen Antonelli

Garrison passed on Les Aspin's requirements for the intervention of Somali politics as the two factions declared civil war. This war caused a refugee problem and absence of food and medical supplies for the northern faction. This civil unrest was of common knowledge over the years that Russia, China and North Korea attempted to settle the political problems of the Somali culture. Somalia was left to find a solution without these communist countries.

Additionally, Somalia was, and still is, a strong Italian stronghold before WWII up to the present. Italy was the only nation that managed to keep Somalia from civil war by providing stability from almost full employment of all resources, both natural and labor intensive. HIV/AIDS issues have plagued the entire region, as many U.S. Missionaries took it upon themselves to assist Somalia, a Muslim country to come in the fold of Christianity. Naturally, the introduction of Christianity went over like a fart in church and the missionaries' over-zealous publication that Somalia was ground zero for HIV/AIDS and Christianity must prevail. Ground zero for Aids is true, but Somalia does not want or need outsiders to steal from the masters of that art, Somalis.

The missionaries of the United States managed to influence the African-American population to a point of activism to protect their black brothers. Somalia, like most countries on the continent has no respect for African Americans because they have no idea that Africa is a continent and not a nation, secondly the so called African Americans are considered inferior because their fore fathers did not fight to the death to prevent slavery and last, only the inferior tribes were enslaved because they did not know how to govern themselves or organized and defense by the Arab slave traders. The Somalis are and were great hunters and very involved in the slave trade centuries ago.

Upon the election of "Clinton" he promised the promenade black voters he would "take care of Somalia and Haiti". The United States busted into Somalia to save the day from a nation that did not want to be saved and considered their political issue private and wanted no interference. The newly elected president and his gang of political no nothings forced their way into Somalia to clean up a mess and force Somalia to live a clean life similar to all American because the American way was the only way.

All parties concerned advised the new administration to stay out of Somalia as the Somalis would look at our presence as an invasion also Italy warned the United States not to get involved. The Unites States begun with they humanitarian aid and the progressed to demanding that the United States would supervise to distribution of food an medicine that was in shortage because the two warring factions where hording all supplies. The civil war was an internal issue. My great uncle, Col in the Italian Army, surveyed the country before WWII around 1928. Because of the family name I was a welcomed guess at the Italian embassy and privileged to learn the Italian point of view and their insistence to stay out and let the entire issue die of a natural death. The new administration learned from several sources far more knowledgeable than my assessment to stay out.

The United States along with host nations invaded Somalia, in the eyes of the Somalis and at that point all factions set aside their differences and united to throw out the invaders. No one can say the United States was not warned.

During the planning of the invasion the existing OPPLAN was the guide to a projected successful short term occupation to insure the Somalis receive the free gifts and beads of the United Sates and soon to join the fold of that administration. General Garrison and the Marines briefed what was required and all was approved. However, at the last second while the equipment was being off loaded it was reloaded by the command of the POTUS. It was discovered by written documents that MFRs were exchanged from the 26 year old female Special Operations Advisor to the POTUS and Georgie Boy that armor was considered excessive and the rule of engagement were change to be politically correct. No other country would agree on the POTUS as a result they did not suffer the deaths experienced by the United States. Les Aspin agreed with both the female and Georgie boy and ordered Garrison to scrap his 10 year old standing OPPLAN for the region. I will not go into the details of an OPPLAN or its contents. The staffing involved moving a Marine and Army expeditionary force is complicated. This same plan was rehearse a year prior which I was the Plans Officer that did the 5th Group slice as a joint project. There is more to this that I have the time to write about and if anyone wants to challenge my message you may b/c me, however simply inquiring through Frank Hudson or MG Bowra will do. Additionally, I reserve the right not to answer your questions.

The entire event is a national embarrassment and I hold the "Clinton" administration responsible for the murder of great American Soldiers.

Western Front News
by Steve Shanahan

Gene, Merle, Lance, Ben, Vern, Larry, Bruce, Steve, Jon, Jim, Robert, (Did I miss anybody?), and I are holding down the shores of the Western Front, between Canada and Mexico. We are keeping an eye eastward to the rabble of DC, Westward to the lands of the hungry masses who covet our soil. We keep the other eye open in our own neighborhoods for the slimy underminers of our Nation's foundation....the sick, the mean, the ill-informed, and the One-World starry eyed dreamers, in their hemp shirts and trust fund Beamers and tree hugging mittens. We stand at the wall, ready for the call to action.

Page 1- The Antiwar Demonstration in San Francisco last Saturday, 18 Jan 03, drew a measly 150,000 demonstrators by police estimates. The spokesperson (read: new age commie) claims in excess of 200,000. Who cares? If I could count, I prolly wouldn't be a cop. A group of the anarchist, as predicted, broke off the scheduled route of March and tore up private property. Judges are busy today dismissing all charges for malicious mischief and resisting arrest.

For more of this story and the upcoming event on 15Feb03, when the Chinese New Years Parade is scheduled to coincide with another nationally organized antiwar demo, go to:

http://sfgate.com/cgi-bin/article.cgi?f=/c/a/2003/01/23/BA244094.DTL

My squad performed remarkably well as the professionals they are.

Page 2: Sports- The Raiders are playing the best they've played in 20 years. Their fans are a fricking embarrassment to humanity. Even though the game is going to be played in San Diego, Oakland will have public disturbances and property damage after the game simply because the town is a shithole. Watch for updates on TV coverage following Super Bowl. Sideshows and burning vehicles.
Is it time for another flood?

Page 3: Arclights remembered. I was a frightened skinny little numbnuts in 1969 at BuPrang #2 when I got to sit thru an Arclight directed at the 66 NVA Regt. The camp had been getting the shit shot out it with all manner of rocket and indirect fire and sappers. The arclight broke this Regt's will to fight and they didi maued back to Cambodia or WTF. This was the same Rgt that had attacked Ben Het and DucLap as it made its way south. These were some very tenacious and ballsy little soldiers if not dinkydau. The arclight rocked our hilltop camp in waves and made a continuous rumbling sound for about 30 seconds, shaking loose the red dust in the timber walls and ceiling of the TOC. It still stands as one of the most impressive events of my brief military career. I think we discussed this before; and as I recall, Rudy was out there with MF and called in one of the arclights. Arclights continued for weeks afterward, mostly south of BuPrang #2. In two months time, work on the BuPrang#3 began a few klicks to the East.

Page 4: Leeches in Quang Duc Provence. Blood thirsty, silent little commie parasites that were everywhere. About an inch long, dark brown or black, they could drop off a leaf as you passed by, crawl up from the ground below or swim to you in still water. They were blood magnets that could find your ears and your toes or ass crack, eat a fine lunch or O Pos and sit there relaxing before you noticed they latched on. Bug juice worked well to remove them. That stuff was DEET then or some primitive carcinogenic solvent in little bottles.

Page 5: Food News: Thinking about all this old stuff has made me hanker for a PIR. Maybe a dried shrimp with plenty of hot sauce and a sausage on the side. Jungle dining was an art form, and the CIDG sure knew how to supplement a bag of rice with roots and leaves and young bamboo and snake. Add some little red-hot peppers and you're in for some well earned NL dining.

Page 6: Classifieds: Responsible middle-aged gentleman seeking Thermite.
Specifically four file cabinet type top units, 12" x 20" with pull device. Wire Paladin in San Francisco. No, make that Steve @ Shanahan1818@aol.com.

Page 7: TV Listings: Nothing worth a crap on TV.

Chase on the High Seas
by Terry Dahling

In 1971, the OAS was evaluating the coastal security of their member countries. I was sent as a radio operator on a mission to attempt to penetrate Columbian waters. The boat was a converted PT boat. The original engines were replaced with diesels because of fuel consumption, the super structure was redone and the boat was made into a cruise/sport fisher. The crew consisted of four, and to this day I have no doubt that they were real live gun/drug runners.

We departed Coco Solo about 0100. It was very hot and I decided to sleep on the fantail. I woke up with a god-awful headache. I attributed it to the diesel exhaust but just recently (30 years later) realized it was carbon monoxide poisoning and I was fortunate to wake up. It took two or three days to reach Cartegena. Whenever we saw another vessel we would commence fishing, partying and acting "normal."

Some time around 1000 hrs. on the last day, a Columbian Destroyer hailed us and told us to heave to. They had been dogging us for quite some time. Our captain hove to like instructed and I figured we had had it. As soon as the destroyer was dead in the water the captain applied full power and off we went. It took some time for the destroyer to get up to speed. He pursued us at what appeared to be a couple of miles behind. It was hard to tell who was winning. The captain felt that if we could make it to dark we would have a chance.

About 1600 hrs. a Columbian Huey appeared on the scene. I waved and acted like we were having a good time. Then they cheated. All I saw was a bunch of guns point at us from the door of the chopper. I had heard stories of Columbians shooting up "friendly" boats in the past so my hands immediately went Arriba! We failed and the Columbians passed. When we saw the M-16's the captain decided to "give it up". They escorted us to Cartegena; we (the USSF) spent the night on the boat and returned to Coco Solo the next day. Luckily we had our own supply of cerveza. No party or congrats; we just returned home in defeat. Actually it wasn't a defeat for us but a victory for the Colombians. We were testing their coastal security. The chopper and destroyer escorted us to Cartegena. The worst part.

Disadvantages of Rank
by Terry Dahling

While on the SCUBA team in the Canal Zone we used to go on civic action missions up the coast. We would blow navigable channels in the coral reefs near villages to enable them to get larger fishing boats in and out of the villages. After introducing ourselves to the villagers we would survey the area and determine our course of action. As soon as the LCM was anchored and the ramp dropped, Sarge, my SCUBA dog, would go in the water and check the current and for nefarious creatures. As soon as he determined it was safe he would get back on the boat. The team sergeant and one other would set the first charges. Everything would go according to plan. Being the second ranking NCO on the team I "got" to check out the progress and set the next charges. By the time we got into the water every shark within hearing distance (from Alaska, Hawaii and Chile) was in the area investigating and looking for a meal. EVERYTIME! I remember seeing a Bull Shark who looked like he could swallow the Mike boat.

Decompression Sickness
by Terry Dahling

We had the only re-compression chamber in SEA. I think the nearest others were in Korea and Oki. I really don't know how we got it. Maybe it was because of the B-52 and U-2 flights out of U-Tapao. Ed Foushee, the team sergeant, was a school trained diving medic. I maintained the compressors, air banks and the chamber.

One day the AF brought five crewmen over. They were displaying symptoms which Foushee diagnosed as decompression sickness. Apparently the pressurization system in their aircraft had gone berserk and took them from sea-leval to around 35,000 feet several times in a short period of time. This shouldn't have affected them since they are supposed to purge their systems of nitrogen by breathing straight O2 until at altitude and pressurized, similar to purging one's system prior to using closed circuit systems. Apparently they didn't.

Foushee immediately put them in the chamber and we took them down until the symptoms were relieved. What amazed me was that the USAF doctor got on the phone and had direct voice communications with the USAF Hyperbarric Doctors back at Brooks Army Hospital. It turns out that Ed had properly diagnosed the problem and started the proper treatment. FYI, a diving medic takes precedence over a regular MD in diving diseases. The doctor at Brooks talked us through the entire procedure. Since the B-52 had no nitrogen in its system it didn't need treatment. This is the only time our chamber was ever used except for pre-school testing. Then it was for the USAF.

No lo comprendo
by Terry Dahling

There was a cat-house on the trans-ismithian hwy a little over half way to PC. There was a bar, a kitchen and a couple of pool-tables and several rooms out back. The mamasan paid off the Guardia and it was one of the few safe spots in the Republic. It was staffed mostly with Colombian girls.

I remember driving back one night (not the smartest thing) and coming to a little village a couple of KM from the check-point outside Colon. The posted speed limit was 10 KPH about 6mph. We could see a party going on and all of a sudden about five or six Guardia stopped us. I know I was going as slow as possible but they said we were speeding. I went into my "No lo comprendo" mode for self protection. I handed them my wallet, which I kept near empty for just such occasions, they emptied the wallet, said "Grassy Ass" and went back to their party. Loved Panama, and the Indians, but had no use for the Guardia, or city folk.

Privacy
by Terry Dahling

In 1970, prior to moving to Coco Solo, I lived in the "Beq" above Co A. It was basically a huge squad bay with slatted partitions between cubicles. About half of the residents were from the School of the Americas - mostly Puerto Ricans. Though I spoke Spanish I could never understand these suckers. They switched back and forth from English to Spanish several times in a sentence. My mind just couldn't switch that fast

Anywho, there was a distinct lack of noise privacy. The Porkchops would turn their TV's and stereos up to max and drive everyone nuts. One night SFC Smolz or Stolz (Can't remember, but he was an instructor in commo school in '63) asked one of them to please turn down the TV. No response. Again, he asked nicely. Again no response. Without a word he calmly walked into the guy's cubicle, picked up the TV and dropped it on the floor. He returned to his cubicle with nothing more than a chuckle and a smirk.

War Casualties
(A different perspective)

I had been out of the service for a few years when I saw or heard about a program for post-Vietnam Vets which made me realize that maybe I was a casualty.

The theory postulated that many troops in Vietnam were very young yet given tremendous responsibility for the lives of tens or hundreds of men. They became accustomed to making life and death decisions affecting the lives of themselves and their men on an almost daily basis.

Then, they return and all of a sudden they can't take a dump without permission. Many times they had to take orders from professional civilians and draft dodgers who were far less qualified and who even "feared" the competence of the Combat Vet. I probably fell into this group. As I said, I didn't adapt to the "peacetime army" very well. My philosophy was:" Tell me what to do and by god I'll get it done. Stand over my shoulder and scrutinize each and every step, and by god you can do it yourself." I may not be saying it was right; just describing my attitude in years past.

PH (Purple Heart)
by Terry Dahling

Please don't anyone take offense at what I am about to say. If I see someone wearing a PH he has my utmost respect until he proves otherwise. That goes for any award.

That being said, a famous philosopher named George Allen once told me he never wanted a PH because it meant he failed Basic Training.

There once was a recon man in Kontum named Glover. I don't recall, but I think he may even have been a leg -- yes there were leg's in SOG. He only went on three operations. Until his third and last he was quite a source of humor. On each of three missions he received a PH. Tragically the third was posthumous.

On his first mission an elephant stepped on him. Since it was a communist elephant, he received the PH.

When he returned from the hospital and his leg healed he went on his second mission. He thought to help clearing an LZ by knocking trees down with an M-79. Apparently he had never heard of "Iron Trees". He hit a tree and then suffered a frontal attack of frags. Off to the hospital again. Since it was a communist tree he received his second PH. End of humor.

On his third and final mission he was shot out of a chopper. Fred Zabitowski was on that mission and he got the MOH. Unfortunately, Glover got his third PH.

Payroll Heist
by Toby Todd

At SSG Larry R.'s courts-martial, MSG K. (TM Sgt, ODA-563) and I were detailed to be his escort. So we sat thru his trial, he was convicted, and got fifteen years.

Actually, he held up his old BCT Company payroll, where he had been a Drill, or maybe XO (CRS). Funny thing was, I remember sitting on a target in the Cp Mackall area one night with a buncha guys from C/2/5; and around the campfire, we talked about pulling off such a heist. Yes, Larry R. was amongst us, along with Jim G., Bob A., Phil Q. and yours truly, of course.

Damned if the next month or so, Larry didn't pull it off, pretty much like we talked about. So one Saturday morning, I'm driving into post for Bn Staff Duty, when I hear Johnny J. on the radio announcing that SSG Larry W. R. had been apprehended for the robbery of a BCT unit at Ft Leonard Wood.

Almost drove off 'a the f—kin' road.

1973
by Tom Marzillo

In October of 1971, I DEROS'ed from what had become TF1AE (formerly CCN) and returned to civilian life. I carried a bit of baggage from my time there as did many others. One of the items I carried was the fate of a Recon Company guy by the name of Danny Day Entrican whom I met at the 1-0 course Long Thanh, along with Robbie Robinson. He was simply a great guy to know and was thought captured in 1971, but listed as MIA as was standard for all who did not return but whose remains were not recovered. There is more than enough available on the Internet for any who need to look at the particular circumstances.

Shortly after arriving home I sought information on Danny's status and got the usual bureaucratic run around. This led to a series of letters to US Senators, DoD, etc., etc. As we were still bound by our security agreements there was very little I could directly address. By the end of 1972, SOG was history from an operational standpoint and there was much discussion of the return of US POWs and so I became slightly more hopeful of seeing him listed, but as we know now, nobody from SOG was listed as a potential returnee except for one guy who got captured while doing his E&E after 'Leghorn' fell and received the MoH for his troubles.

Early in 1973, DoD released information on the existence and mission of SOG, but fudged the casualty figures badly. Knowing that the only real shot there was for Danny (and the rest of the folks from SOG who might still be alive) was to have them listed as being suspected as captured-in-action. If they were not, Kissinger could not put their fates on the table when negotiating for the release of POWs.

So I went New York Times-public, on my own nickel, disputing the bogus casualty figures put out by DoD in the hopes I might finagle a way to get the names of 'our' guys on to the State Department's POW list. Well, this raised quite a bit of ruckus given the times, and I found myself in a very warm and muggy Washington DC, testifying before the Senate Armed Services Committee relative to CCN and SOG.

Just before being brought into the packed hearing chambers, I was taken aside by a senior staffer to Kissinger who asked me not reveal the MIA-CIA switch as 'the secretary' was dealing in a very delicate stage of negotiations and was trying to get them home. Being 23 years old and relatively ignorant but trusting that we would do the right thing, I took the proffered bait. The only thing regarding POW-MIAs I discussed was the case of Jerry Schriver who went missing just outside of the Katum AO. There had been a recovery team put into the area by CCS in 1970 and from the little they let slip to a few of us, they had found a set of headless remains, missing the right hand, as was rumored to have been done to Jerry's body. Oh yes, there was one other thing... I told the Senators that future generations of American fighting men would watch carefully what they did that day.

Well, as you know the questionable cases from SOG were never to see the official light of day in Washington. I will always deeply regret trusting the State department that day. In 1979, Jimmy Carter declared our unreturned POWs to be dead and the world moved on. But today, I am glad that State Department has been prevented from having its way again when deciding how we will treat our missing and captured service personnel; and I hope we never go back to the way it was.

Draining
by Tom Marzullo

In 1979, San Diego, I got cheap-shot-ed in a flag-feetsball game after the play was over and it ruptured the major ligament as well as doing other very bad things. I was in the ortho clinic on a Sunday afternoon with a couple of residents who decided to drain the knee that was alarmingly large at that point. One almost-a-quack sez to da udder... "Let's take the anterior approach to drain this one." This means instead of going laterally where the draining can be done easily and with minimum discomfort, they intend to stick an 4 inch 8 gauge needle through the big tendon, go under the knee cap and thence into the joint capsule - and all without the benefit of anesthesia, mind you. At the moment of insertion, I sit straight up and swing hard for the resident with the syringe, missing his face by a couple of thousands. Then pluck the syringe w / log out of my knee and chuck it at the other resident who smartly ducks it, having gotten a little distance betwixt he and I by that time.

I then proceed to get up, muttering something about "give your souls to god..." when I am restrained (with difficulty) by a couple of staffers.

Suffice it to say, they chose to drain the knee laterally.

Squidly Activities
by Tom Marzullo

I can recall a certain LCDR (O-4) who was very, very unpopular with his sub crew. He also displayed untoward pride in his near-race tricked out beemer; so things being what they were, they sugared his gas-tank with expected results. When the car came back from the shop (where the LCDR was diverting most of his earnings to), within the week the culprits very carefully opened his fuel tank door and poured a bit of sugar 'around' the gas cap, making sure to spill a little on the ground. The wary LCDR always checked his car before driving away, and this, of course, prompted yet another trip to the shop to remove and clean the gas tank and fuel lines.

After three more of these go a rounds, he finally transferred. I am, of course, innocent and pure as the driven snow on this one... Honest!

Upon graduation from sub school, they assigned me to my first boat where the executive officer was much hated; to the point of several thousand being raised to have him killed while the boat was doing a South America run, but the cash was found and the plot foiled.

The Yeoman, having looked through my records, passed the word as to my previous service and I was quietly approached on the mess decks. "If youse wanted ta killa guy, howudja do it?"

My response was: "Do you just want him dead or do you want to have some fun with him first?" Well, the eyes around me lit up like Christmas tree lights. Therefore, I tell them to buy Ipecac and super-glue. Then take the guy out to a spaghetti supper with red wine and all the trimmings being sure to get him a bit drunk. In his last glass of red wine, add the Ipecac and do a toast so that he drains it. Then each of them gets a firm hold of each corner of him and super-glue his lips shut. The watch as he tries to puke all the strands of spaghetti out of his nose, aspirates his stomach contents and over several days dies. I was a popular guy.

Ramblings of an Old Man
by Joe Galloway
sent by Zoltan Krompecher

Provided by Joe Galloway, author of 'We Were Soldiers' and posted as an item of possible interest. This one is definitely NOT tongue in cheek. The author, was a teen-aged Marine who marched and fought as a rifleman to and from the Chosin reservoir in Korea in 1950. He switched to the Army, and served as a Special Forces officer in Vietnam. After Vietnam he joined the CIA, and went back to Korea. He's been there, done that, and has some specific thoughts on countries that don't "like" us.

Is there anyone else out there who's sick and tired of all the polls being taken in foreign countries as to whether or not they "like" us? The last time I looked, the word "like" had nothing to do with foreign policy. I prefer 'respect' or 'fear'. That worked for Rome, which civilized and kept the peace in the known world a hell of a lot longer than our puny two centuries-plus.

I see a left-wing German got elected to office recently by campaigning against the foreign policy of the United States. Yeah, that's what I want, to be lectured about war and being a "good neighbor" by a German. Their head honcho said they wouldn't take part in a war against Iraq. It's kind of nice, to see them taking a pass on a war once in while. Perhaps we needed to have the word "World" in front of War. I think it's time to bring our boys home from Germany. Outside of the money we'd save, we'd make the Germans "like" us a lot more, after they started paying the bills for their own defense.

Last time I checked, France isn't too fond of us either. They sort of liked us back on June 6th, 1944, though, didn't they? If you don't think so, see how nicely they take care of the enormous American cemeteries up above the Normandy beaches. For those of you who've studied history, we also have a few cemeteries in places like Belleau Woods and Chateau Thierry also. For those of you who haven't studied it that was from World War One, the first time Europe screwed up and we bailed out the French.

That's where the US Marines got the title 'Devil Dogs' or, if you still care about what the Germans think, "Teufelhunde". I hope I spelled that right; sure wouldn't want to offend anyone, least of all a German.

Come to think of it, when Europe couldn't take care of their recent Bosnian problem, guess who had to help out there also. Last time I checked, our kids are still there. I sort of remember they said they would be out in a year. Gee, how time flies when you're having fun.

Now we hear that the South Koreans aren't too happy with us either. They "liked" us a lot better, of course, in June, 1950. It took more than 50,000 Americans killed in Korea to help give them the lifestyle they currently enjoy, but then who's counting? I think it's also time to bring the boys home from there. There are about 37,000 young Americans on the DMZ separating the South Koreans from their "brothers" up North. Maybe if we leave, they can begin to participate in the "good life" that North Korea currently enjoys.

Uh huh. Sure.

I also understand that a good portion of the Arab/Moslem world now doesn't "like" us either. Did anyone ever sit down and determine what we would have to do to get them to like us? Ask them what they would like us to do. Die? Commit ritual suicide? Bend over?

Maybe we should follow the advice of our dimwitted, dullest knife in the drawer, Senator Patty Murray, and build more roads, hospitals, day care centers, and orphanages like Osama bin Laden does. What with all the orphans Osama has created, the least he can do is build some places to put them.

Senator Stupid says if we would only "emulate" Osama, the Arab world would love us. Sorry, Patty; in addition to the fact that we already do all of those things around the world and have been doing them for over sixty years, I don't take public transportation, and I certainly wouldn't take it with a bomb strapped to the guy next to me.

Don't get me wrong: I'm not in favor of going to war. Been there, done that. Several times, in fact. However, I think we ought to have some polls in this country about other countries, and see if we "like" THEM. Problem is, if you listed the countries, not only wouldn't the average American know if he liked them or not, he wouldn't be able to find them. If we're supposed to worry about them, how about them worrying about us?

We were nice to the North Koreans in 1994, as we followed the policies of Neville Clinton. Moreover, it seemed to work; they didn't re-start nuclear weapons program for a whole year or so. In the meantime, we fed them when they were starving, and put oil in their stoves when they were freezing.

In a recent visit to Norway, I engaged in a really fun debate with my cousin's son, a student at a Norwegian University. This thankless squirt lectured me about the American

"Empire", and scolded about dropping the atomic bomb on the Japanese. I reminded him that empires usually keep the stuff they take; we don't, and back in 1945 most Norwegians thought dropping ANY kind of bomb on Germany or Japan was a good idea. I also reminded him that my uncle, his grandfather, and others in our family spent a significant time in Sachsenhausen concentration camp, courtesy of the Germans, and they didn't all survive. I further reminded him that if it wasn't for the "American Empire" he would probably be speaking German or Russian.

Sorry about the rambling, but I just took an unofficial poll here at our house, and we don't seem to like anyone.

Baptism in S.F. Land
by Zoltan Kompelher

The year was 1989. I was 22 years old and sure of myself that is until I reported to the USAJFKSWC, and reported in for the SFQC. The buildings were all nondescript-those old WWII barracks with peeling paint, open stalls in the latrine (of which one was always waiting for a work order t fix it), metal bunks and a screen door that, when used, slammed shut with a wheezing sound that still managed a cacophony that stirred one awake during those precious moments of sleep. The buildings had outlasted most of their purposes except for those who decided to give of themselves (more than I would ever imagine) in service of their country and comrades. Funny, I expected "The Schoolhouse" to be girded with steel and concertina wire with armed guards on patrol instead of buildings falling into ruin. I guess this was the impression of SF-never show your bravado.

I walked into the Company Headquarters, I think it was Charlie Company, and was quickly relegated to feeling "out of place". The office itself was cooled by a single air conditioner, and was adorned with old "Soldier" magazines, a coffee pot with that mornings 40-weight sludge, Chain of Command pictures on the wall, and a quiet 1SG who had more ribbons and badges on his class A's than a variegated montage of colors in a modern painting. In short, he reduced me. Not by barking orders, but by his very demeanor-cool. He, the 1SG, introduced me to my platoon sergeant. He, the PSG, was a skinny black man who also looked very non-descript. My initial thoughts were, "Surely this man is a clerk because he is too small and skinny, in my eyes, to carry a ruck. Three hours later, I was in the need for the course, i.e. moleskin, camo make-up, overpriced 550 cord, boot polish, bug repellant, wind-up clock (still works today) and handkerchiefs (every other school instructed me to buy handkerchiefs). I also bought the most recent issue of Soldier of Fortune and had to catch my breath when I looked at it because there, right on the cover, was a picture of my skinny platoon sergeant. This was my initial baptism into SF.

I tried to fit in with the other soldiers. Imagine that. Me? An E4 artilleryman trying to find my place amongst all the former Rangers, combat veterans, "The Nordic Prince" Sonner became my companions. Others followed. Most notably Scott "Elvis" Barkalow, Dave Shepherd, Tim Hogan, and Randy Perry- hard guys with a flair to go all out. Most are still serving in SF (Scott lost a leg in Afghanistan) and, with the exception of Martyn, I have kept in close touch with all of them- such is one of the most important lessons I learned in SF: the bond of brotherhood.

PT sucked because the 1SG was all "lungs and legs", and I was not. However, training was exhilarating because I feel that I was serving a purpose that extended far beyond any feelings that I was doing this for myself. I felt comfortable and wanted to serve with these guys anywhere.

I learned many lessons about SF, myself, and life in general. One in particular occurred in a seemingly innocuous environment, and could have been easily dismissed by the average soldier- we were not average soldiers. It happened while we were sitting on the ground bitching while we waited to head out to Camp McKall. Out of nowhere came this giant of a man. He was a giant of a man whose name escapes me at this time. Needless to say, he was intimidating. Anyway, this guy caught us in a near ambush, and told us in his loud Jamaican-tinged dialect that he did not care if we bitched, but he had never, ever, catch us bitching while we "sat on our asses." Score one for the CSM. It is a lesson I impart to all my soldiers.

For years now, I have been out of the SF community. However, like I said before, I maintain contact with many of my SF brethren. They keep me grounded. I realize that no matter where I serve; as an MI officer in Korea, even as an English instructor at West Point, the tab opens doors and inquiring looks. As such, I shed the early bravado I acquired as a newly minted SF sergeant, and instead try to act as a professional soldier by helping out others, volunteering to train, and using my SF experience as a tool to help "grow" others. I will carry the things I learned in SF all my days and, I believe, it shows in all I do both in and out of the uniform. In fact, though, I am now an MI officer, the tab had allowed me access to missions and people whose doors would have otherwise remained closed. Despite my nominal missions in SF (as compared to most), I am proud of my SF heritage. My baptism into SF-land had been one of the most life-altering experiences of my life. The tab defines me.

Damned Good Luck
by Ben Roberts

I never saw it but as we were coming upon a VC village using only hand signals, SSGT Ivan Bomark behind me says, "Jesus Christ!"

I am too close to look down, or turn around; my eyes are looking at the village in front of me. I am less than 100 feet from the village which turned out to be empty before we walked in. When it was safe, I turned back to Ivan and asked, "Why were you talking as we approached the village?"

Ivan remarked..."Ben, you just stepped over the biggest God damn Cobra I have ever seen."

Fortunately, I did not step on the damn thing. As I was sneaking up on the village with my rifle on full auto, I would have probably shot my feet off, let alone gotten bit and given our position away. I did always carry the multi venom serum shots, but I would have died of a heart attack or no feet either way. Luckily, some things are just meant not to happen.

Medics Cross Training in Explosives
by Ben Roberts

Bong Son 1966 ...Central Highlands A-227...Demo man. SP-4 Mike Berry asked me to help the Jr. Medic in the camp blow a large assortment of dud ammo, mainly 4.2 mortar rounds and miscellaneous explosives he had assembled in a large pile off the end of our runway in Bong Son. Being a Medic, I was eager to play with firecrackers and larger explosives, and cross train in explosives. We drove our large duce and a half over to the bad ammo dump and wrapped the chord and some sticks of C-4 around everything. After looking around and seeing no one, we lit a five-minute fuse, jumped into the truck and drove about 200 yards away. Then we went out and hid behind the heavy truck tires.

We watched the runway and pile of explosives, waiting for things to blow. A Montagnard farmer walked out of the bushes, and started walking across the red dirt runway carrying a huge stack of Bamboo on his back. We yelled at him, waving our arms, and jumping up and down. We fell on the ground to demonstrate our demands, yelling Dung Li, and trying everything to get his attention. He saw us but continued to walk to the stack of dud ammo that was about to blow.

In desperation, I pulled a small useless 25. cal. Beretta out of my pocket, smuggled into Vietnam in a can of pipe tobacco, and carefully tried to kick up dust in front of him. At 200 yards a 25 cal. round is about as accurate as a closing your eyes and throwing a rock. I emptied the magazine, kicking up little puffs of dust across the runway in front of him. Finally, he was in the center of the runway, and perhaps 100 yds. from the dud stack of ammo with the fuse burning close to setting off the C-4 and exploding everything, he finally got the idea that we trying to get him to lay down fast.

As soon as he hit the ground it seemed like the world blew up! Red dust and rocks were falling all over the place. The heavy smell of cordite and acrid smoke blew in our direction. It blew the windshield out of the truck. Shrapnel was everywhere, and we were sure the hapless farmer was killed.

Suddenly, the farmer got up with his tied bamboo, and continued his journey across the runway as if nothing happened. Mike looked at me and asked," Do you suppose we used too much explosive to blow up all of that stuff?"

I looked at him and said, "Nope! It looks like we blew things up real nice."

We drove back to camp, got out of the truck, parked it near the other trucks in the compound, and went to have a beer in the team house. We agreed to change our story and say, "We used a different truck. What happened to that other one?"

Eyelids Awake
by Greg Hoisington

My dad flew B-29's over the "Hump." He said that the missions were so long and they would get so tired that they would take pieces of cigarette tobacco and put them in their eyelids to keep them awake.

I always thought I was hardcore, but that trick was beyond my limits.

"Float & Bloat"
by Bruce "Hardcore" Koch

Getting my thoughts together and packing for the "Float & Bloat". Having serious second thoughts...

Let me see if I got this right. I am going on a three and one half day raft trip with 10 other troops down a secluded river. Most will be packing firearms and copious quantities of booze. The majority of these guys was "Special Needs" types and most was "baby killers" at some time in their early lifetimes.

Some are still suffering shell shock from too many incoming rounds. One took a round through the head. A couple of them manifest their previous problems by imbibing ungodly amounts of cheap assed wine. One is a former medic who wandered back to Vietnam last year for a friendly visit. One is an aspiring writer, retired Warrant Officer who just happens to be Hare Krishna qualified. He is also an expert at barrel rolls down escalators. I can just see him in class 4 rapids.

The perpetrator of this affair was kicked out of every college on the west coast. "Spider Man" cannot tolerate cold water, and takes umbrage when someone steals the punch lines from his jokes. He also is a licensed firearms dealer and carries class three weapons. The commo man for this affair is code named Shakey???? All of these guys pack knives and other sharp instruments, and we are using inflatable craft??? One was a helicopter crew chief named DasTurdly?????

The only reasons I am invited???? They want me to bring firewood, and lots of GBNP. I am qualified because I am a former Specialist and did cross border Ops. No mention as to who is going to be the Couth Control Officer for this little soiree. Guess who will get the blame when the tribal police on the Warm Springs reservation incarcerate the whole crew???

In addition to all of this, I could be spending that time playing hide the sausage and other fun games with my newly acquainted young ladies. So, what is the logical decision here??? Bet your ass, I am going! Packing my camera AND tape recorder.

PM of W
(Portuguese Man of War)
by Jerry Braudrick

At Key West, we had do several surface swims. These were done side stroke so no one splashed, not wanting to alert the enemy of our approach. On one typical perfect day in Key West, there was a pretty good breeze blowing up from the South. The instructors informed us as the landing boats took us out to the 1600 m buoys, that this was the type of wind that would bring the P M of W out from the Saragossa Sea. (spelling?) The only place in the world they breed.

Sure enough, as we approached the buoy we saw the instructors laughing and pointing out the frilly pinkish blue sails on top of the almost clear bloated little basket ball size P M of W. Like me, I think almost everyone was thinkin' "No problem. They're on the outside of the buoy. Just let me out of this damn thing before the wind brings them any closer." Wrong, of course. The first wave had gone by the buoy long before we got there. This may explain why the instructors were late in getting us out there. Naw, they wouldn't screw with ya like that, would they?

Most surface swims were done "Hollywood", no fins, mask, nothing but your shorts with T shirt optional. I spent my high school and college days in Southern California, on the beaches from San Diego to Huntington. No way was I going to get sun burned without a T shirt. Good for me but you could not tell a jar head (Force Recon type) that he should wear his shirt. They all were trying to be first on the beach and did not want any dumb old shirt to act as drag in the water.

About half way in, my swim buddy spotted a P M of W dead ahead about 20 feet. The wind was kicking up just enough wave action that we were all bobbing up and down like cheap bobbers on cane poles. With each up, I could see more and more of those damn frilly sails. By now the screams of pure pain were starting to sound off all around my swim buddy and me. Not that I'm brave or even stupid, but I turned to my swim buddy and said "F--k it man, we got to get to the beach. Follow me."

I may have made five strokes before it hit me. No shit, my body came out of the water like a bass on Saturday mooring fishing show. Splashing is not allowed, my ass. Partly fear of the unknown and the rest due to pure pain, that MFer hurt like hell, up and down both arms and around my neck. Thank God for the T shirt. Thirty seconds later my swim buddy got hit. After the initial shock, it was just pain, and the beach was still there. So, the only thing you could do was keep swimming.

We were lucky. We made it the rest of the in without getting hit a second time. From all the yelling I could tell others were not so lucky.

At about twenty five yards before the beach, you could stand up and wade on in. As I started to wade, I noticed a pair of the Marines in front of me starting to stand up too. They never stood up till it was too shallow to swim because it cut down on their speed. (Timed events) They were about twenty yards ahead of us. I could not believe it when they stood up. One guy was wearing a PM of W on his right shoulder!! Remember that Marines don't need no stinkin' T shirts? Even the instructors were in total awe of this guy. He made it about ten feet up the beach before he collapsed. He had made about half the swim wearing the damn thing cause he didn't want to loose any time on his swim.

You can say what you want about all the different SO types, Army, Navy, Air Force, but from the ones I went to school with in Key West and the ones I got to take on their first combat patrol in VN. (cherry popping' patrol), no one could match a Forces Recon Marine when it comes to havin' a set of balls! They may not be the brightest bulbs in the batch, due to their indoctrination by the Corp, but they are the most physically fit hardcore brain washed MFer's I have ever meet.

The Ft. Benning Bridge
by Jerry Braudrick

During WWII, the troops from Benning would go across the bridge to gamble, drink, and of course get laid. They were spending a lot of money in the little nothing town. This was not good enough for some of the locals as they started rolling the GI's on their way back across the bridge and actually throwing guys off the bridge. They just wanted to make sure they didn't get back to Benning with any money. The attitude in town was dogs and GI's stay off the grass. The cops were either in on it or at least looking the other way. The General of Ft Benning, (? name) put the town off limits and parked a tank at the entrance to the bridge. The locals complained all the way to D.C. to get the ban lifted. I believe it took about 4 weeks before D.C. was able to get the Gen. to open the bridge up. Of course the towns people were very happy to have the GI's back. And only rolled about every 10th drunk instead of each and every one of them.

That was the story that we heard while in jump school in 1962. Do not know if it is completely true or not as I was still shitting green in non-disposable diapers at the time this would have taken place.

We were told not to cross that bridge. Even if we ever got any time off while at jump school. Of course, we never got weekend passes in jump school, so we couldn't have gone if we had wanted to.

Tellin' it I remember it was told to me.

C119 Joys
by John Cleckner

I had just left OCS and was assigned to Special Forces Training Group. Shortly after I arrived, I was selected to go on this "mission" and it was a classic, especially for a "new guy".

The Mission was to fly to San Antonio, Texas and jump the Basic Medical Students attending school at Fort Sam Houston. We took off from Green Ramp, Pope AFB NC aboard an ancient C-119 Flying Boxcar. It was now being used by some reserve Air Force unit. I was thinking that this was the same "Bird" I made my first 10 jumps out of almost a decade earlier.

The C-119 was full of legendary jumpers and Green Beret heroes. (No shit). I didn't realize this until we got to the motel at San Antonio and everyone slipped into his "special uniform". Bata Boot B. was an old enlisted friend, and he filled me in.

Major Bill A. was the Commander on the trip. That is until we got there and the Martinis started to flow. (I had seen him once in a bar, and then again on the Bird coming back with an 8.2 magnitude hangover sleeping on all the expended chutes.) I was the XO and the "new guy". I have no idea who the NCOIC was, but I'll bet someone out there knew who he was. As I said, we flew a Reserve C-119 with 3 Air Force 06s at the controls. (They called one another by their first names and treated us real nice).

I had no idea what was going on other than we had a mission. I was a new 2nd Lt. and had a flame 3 feet long shooting out my ass, by God. We had to jump the Basic Special Forces Medical Students on Hondo DZ so they wouldn't lose jump pay. Talk about focused.

We landed after a very long and uneventful trip. When we got off the Bird, we had a fleet of rental cars waiting for us to take us to the nicest motel you ever saw in San Antonio. I remember riding in a Mustang Convertible behind Bata Boot and his female friend, who were leading us to the motel. She was giving him head all the way. He was in the Median more than he was on the road.

We accomplished our mission, and were returning home to Ft. Bragg and glorious Green Ramp when we hit "weather". I was trying to sleep beside Dick B. who kept telling me to put on my chute. I eventually did, and then the A/C Cmdr decided to get above the soup. He went into a max climb, as much as a C119 can climb. B. went nuts; he thought we were going in. He screamed to everyone, "We are going in, lets get out of here!" He convinced me; after all, he was an ex-marine and had 10,000 more sky dives than I had as a Stupid 2nd Lt. I followed him to the door and tried to get it open. (We couldn't get it open, thank god, or we would have ended up someplace in north Georgia). Then I became aware of the fact that everyone else on the "Bird" was looking at us and laughing their butts off.

Later Father T. was in the clamshell listening in on the headset to the Pilots' conversations. T. motioned to Bill "Bata Boot" to listen in, and when I saw their eyes get as big a silver dollars I thought I had better find out what was going on.

The conversations went something like this:

from the Pilot. "Hey Bill (the 06 Navigator) where are we?"

"I think we are over South Carolina".

"Bill, what do you mean you think?" At that point the Pilot broke through the clouds and all we saw was water. He immediately radioed to Shaw AFB for an emergency landing, because they were extremely low on fuel.

When we got to Air Ops at Shaw we were about a thousand hours overdue at Pope AFB. Everyone asked to use the phone to call home and assure our loved ones we were still alive.

Bill B. and I were walking back to the bird behind the Pilot and Co-Pilot when we heard the Pilot say, "God, I hope they didn't fill those out board tanks, with all the weight we are carrying we'll never get off the ground if they did".

I don't know whether they saw us back there and were screwing with us, but Bill believed it and so did I.

I only remember 3 things from that point on: we hit the trees at the end of one of the longest TAC Air runways I ever saw, we made it home and Bill A. was still passed out on the expended chutes when we got there. Oh and by the way, that was the last time I ever flew in a C119.

Donning Berets
by John Cleckner

This is a true story, about a group of Special Forces Retirees (SFA Members) flying from the mainland of the United States to Hawaii for the SFA Annual Convention in 1978. Hosts that year were Chapter 8 (VIII), Honolulu Hawaii.

Bill C. met us as we deplaned and can verify what I am writing, so this story can be rated higher than an F6.

I was still living in Fayetteville, N.C. in 1978, and Pappy G. (SFA Administrator then, before Jimmy D.) asked if I was going to go to the SFA Convention in Hawaii. I had thought about it, but hadn't made a firm decision yet. He said if you go I want you to be the Chapter I representative and make the check presentation at the Banquet. That did it. I could never tell him "No" to anything, so I went down to Major Travel on Reilly Rd and bought my tickets. That was the year Clyde was the outgoing and Charlie was the incoming President.

Charlie was having some health problems, so my wife and I took him under our wing and helped him get from plane to plane until we finally took off from LA.

Well, quite a few guys and gals joined us there (at least a couple of "A" Teams) for our flight from LA to Hawaii. The 747 flight was long and uneventful,l and we all were anxious to land and get on with the festivities.

When the plane finally came to a stop all of the SFA members got up, "As On Cue", reached into their "Carry On Luggage", pulled out their **Green Berets** and proceeded to put them on. It looked to me like it was orchestrated, but of course it was not.

Several of us were on the Starboard side of the 747 and the rest of us were on the Port side. Ten to twenty people in the center rows stood up and started screaming, "Don't hurt us, we will cooperate", "It's a High Jacking", "Oh my god they are taking over the plane", and of course some of the women just screamed. This went on as we (SFA Members) looked on, never said a word, finished donning our Green Berets and exited the plane.

I looked at my wife before we left the plane and stated something to the effect that I never imagined people would react that way just because a bunch of guys put on a Beret.

As we cleared the plane, there was Bill C.'s smiling face with tons of lovely ladies waiting to lay us.

Coke Smugglers
by John Cleckner

The following is to illustrate how wide spread coke smuggling was in the late 70s. A friend of mine and I were approached by an active duty SF E8 to move a load of coke from the Dry Tortugas to a location on the west side of Fla.

I was offered $100,000 to provide security, and my friend was offered a $150,000 to drive the boat because of his expertise in that area and knowledge of the geography. I sat there in disbelief that this guy had the balls to approach my friend, let alone me on this venture.

We looked at one another and just got up and walked out.

Confessions of a Lawnmower Gone Bad
by Mel Thornton

Talk of lawnmowers has caused me to remember back in 1966, when one disappeared at the Dog Lab, prior to an I.G. inspection of the old hospital barracks. The cadre Sergeants had somewhere borrowed a new power mower to cut the grass around all the barracks. Someone, when finished mowing had left it right in front of the Dog Lab.

A few of us had just finished getting the dog pens ready for the I.G., and were ready to leave for the week end. One of the cadre seeing the lawnmower, yelled to me
"Get rid of that f--king lawnmower".

I looked around in both directions, and there was nothing but boarded-up barracks connected by boarded-up hallways, as far as I could see; and no place to stash a lawnmower! So, I had no choice, but to temporarily put it inside one of the empty dumpsters…just until the inspection was over.

Then I proceeded to go downtown and spent the weekend drinking at the Holiday Inn. I of course, had forgotten about the lawnmower. It was not mentioned for a couple of weeks, until all were mustered by a very angry Sergeant, who was trying to remember, which one of us he had told to remove the lawnmower; and threatening to make us all pay for it. As my class (to a man) denied any knowledge of the lawnmower; and, furthermore, declined his offer for each of us to donate $5.00 towards replacing it. I of course, had no choice but to go along with my classmates.

As you might imagine, this left some pissed off Sergeants to pay for the lawnmower. They in turn dedicated themselves to making our last couple of weeks of Dog Lab, hell. After a few days on our hands and knees cutting grass with bandage scissors, and diving into full hospital dumpsters, looking for anything the Sergeants thought might be missing from the operating rooms, everyone in my class was ready to kill whoever had stolen, then possibly even pawned the lawnmower.

In this very charged atmosphere, I thought it best not to volunteer the fact that the lawnmower might only be misplaced. And only once, did I even think about telling this story; when after returning from RVN, I was sitting on the balcony of the Student Union Building, on the U.C. Berkeley campus, with fellow ex-medic Ken U., watching the daily Anti-war riots, between the Alameda County Sheriffs and the so-called students.

We started talking about Dog Lab, and the subject of cutting grass with scissors came up.
Kenny volunteered that he would still like to know who the ass-hole was who had taken the lawnmower. Now Kenny was not a person you wanted pissed off at you, so I just left the story untold, until now.

Why Rhythm is Important
by Bill Pelletier

It was to be my first taste of real combat.

November 1970: in Tay Ninh Province it was a beautiful day, sun was shinning, hot, but not like it had been. I was a DASL (Dumb Ass Second Lt.) and had been monitoring the net traffic all morning. Things were quiet all over, so I thought I would take a jeep and drive from our base just west from the old SF A Camp at Tri Bi to our base up on the Cambodian border to drop off some mail and goodies for the American advisor. (Tri Bi had been abandoned for several years. All that was left were a few small remnants of the outer bunker line).

I was at that time an advisor to the Vietnamese Airborne Division. We only had one American with each Company, and I was with 94 Company. The Co. CDR was Cpt Lam, a Veteran with seven yrs with the Airborne. Advisor at this time was not a true description of our job. We were there to provide Air, Artillery medevac and logistical support. When a fight got underway, my job was to get with the Co. Cdr and see where he wanted the fire to hit. I was with SSG Don Wertz; he had been in country for a while and with the ABN. for six months. I was with Wertz because I had not seen any action as yet. We did not turn any advisor loose until he had worked a couple of fights with an experienced Advisor, and had been cleared for combat. Rank was not a consideration - only ability.

Anyway, on the way back from the Bode border I had just passed Tien Ngon (Star shaped A-Camp) when the radio came to life. It was my Boss, Cpt. Jim McMonigle yelling, "Get your young ass back here NOW!" After a couple of

"Yes sirs" and "on the way sir", I got a quick brief of what I was supposed to do.

It seemed that the NVA/VC had set up a classic road ambush from the tree line south of Tri Bi. I was to hook up with Wertz and 94 Company on the road and get ready to go in. A Bn. of the bad guys were set up in the trees 240 - 300 yards from the road. They had a couple of Chinese 57mm Recoilless rifles supported by three 51 cal MG and a whole bunch of infantry. Between the tree line and the road, they had dug in a shallow hole for the assault team to hide until it was their turn. A convoy of civilian and military vehicles was headed for us and the Camp at Tien Ngon.

"Charlie" did it right. He hit the first truck in the convoy and another one about 10 back with the 57s. It stopped both. Their assault team jumped up from their camouflaged hole and ran up to the stalled convoy, tossing grenades and satchel charges into everything that was not already burning. Then they moved on through the kill zone and kept on going off to the north. It would have been almost a perfect text book operation except the men manning the 57's and .51's, along with support, stayed where they were instead of beating feet back to Cambodia, only about 2 Clicks to the south . This f**kup cost them dearly. At the end of the second day we finally got through their lines and encountered 92 'step-ons'. I got to the assembly point at about noon.

The road was a raised one with a roadbed about four to five feet above the surrounding semi-cleared field. Rhome plows had done their stuff during the Cambodian invasion in the spring of 70. There were several shot up deuce and half trucks and jeeps on the road. We already had one company at the tree line fighting their asses off with some very good NVA/VC.

We had eight or so KIA and 20+ WIA on the road bed behind the jeeps and trucks. The Bn. Co and my boss were standing behind a burnt out APC discussing the situation. I was with Wertz about 75 -100 yards away, and decided to go see what and where we were going to step into the mess. I stood up and started walking down the road to the APC. My RTO, Wertz and about 20 Paratroopers were on the reverse side of the road hunched over running in spurts to the HQ. Don't forget I was a DASL. I was walking in the middle of what had been a kill zone only a few minutes ago.

I started hearing strange noises. A series of short loud "cracks" were announcing their presence. I got up to the ABC and wondered why all the ""Gomers"" were looking at me with a strange look on their faces. It was a combination of awe, amazement and that all encompassing look of "what a dumbass".

The cracks had been following me during my "stroll". I asked Wertz, "What the f**k is that noise, are we using silencers or what?" With all couth and respect for superior Officers, he yelled at me to get my dumb ass down. I was being shot at!

Hell, that was news to me. The shooting was way far away (yea, right!) It was all of 250 yards away. The grenades were a dull thump; the MGs were not too loud either (remember DASL). My "Gomers" were looking at me wondering if I was crazy or just had Balls the size of basketballs. I never did let on that I was just plain ignorant. To them I was another crazy, brave COVAN (Vn for advisor).

McMonigle gave Wertz and me our assignments, and I went with Don and 94th Company across the flatland to the fight. This time I was acting just like all the Vn Troopers. Moving in jerks and spurts hiding behind fallen trees to catch our breath, we finally got to the woodline. By this time the diffused noises from 250 yards became a very loud roar. A constant stream of fire came and went from both sides, with short periods of total quiet.

The quiet was eerie; one shot was followed by hundreds more. The Thumpers (M-79) were banging away. The M-60's kept up a continuous roar, and single shots of the M-16s were all around. As this was my first fight I had not learned the difference in sounds made by M-16s and AKs, between RPDs and M-60s. I kept hearing these loud bangs from RPGs. (After this fight, I quickly learned so well that I could eventually tell within a matter of a few feet how close the fire was to me.) By this time the Cavalry had arrived. We had several Cobra's and Huey gunships on station asking where to put their stuff. Wertz was on the radio directing air assets.

Don was putting in gunships up and down the tree line with considerable success. I was lying close by, listening to his conversation with the gunships. Every once in a while, Don would tell me to throw another smoke. Sometimes to the left, sometimes to the right. I saw one 57 RR on our left flank take a direct hit with something. It took off into the air, flipped once before coming back to earth. Another rocket hit 50 yards into the tree line. I was not sure what it had hit but it caused a huge smoky secondary. The blast sent a shock wave back to us, knocking some of our "Gomers" over on their backs. I was lying down behind a low rise in the ground, so all I felt was the concussion. It left me a little breathless, but unhurt. The blast was so large and loud that both sides stopped shooting for what seemed minutes. (Probably only 30-40 seconds.)

Then it started again, one shot, another shot, then two or three more, and then bedlam again. An M60 mg on my right and a little to my rear opened up with an extended burst. No fire discipline here. My Vn Paratroopers loved hand grenades and they proceeded to use all they could. Explosions were all over the place. Screams and yelling were erupting from both sides. It seemed as if mass confusion had taken over. The M-60 stopped firing. The gunner was hit in the upper chest, and was gasping and grunting. He needed help, so I scooped him up in a fireman's carry and took him over to a spot where our medics were set up. While carrying him, I heard SSG Wertz yell at me, "KEEP YOU ASS DOWN." Still a DASL, I grinned over at him and continued to carry the Gunner. On the way back to Wertz, I saw another guy who was gut shot. He was curled up in a fetal position groaning and rocking back and forth. Well, I had done it once, so I did it again. Again Wertz yelled at me ,"KEEP YOUR ASS DOWN".

Well Wertz was busy bringing in Guns, so I went back up the line and helped a couple of others back to the medics. We had been in contact for about 45 min to an hour by then and the fire started to slack up. It looked like we had the situation under control (ha), so Wertz threw me the hand set and told me it was my turn. I took the hand set and started to get a new set of gunships lined up for a gun run. I got them lined up and they started with their 20mm and rockets. It was not anything like the training I had received in OCS or SFOC. This was the real thing and it was confusing at first.

I got my shit together and got the hang of it. We had gunships all over the place waiting their turn to fire up the enemy. (I forgot to mention that I think this was the only firefight going on in VN that day while Wertz was bringing in Gunships, the FAC would tell us that he had some 'Fast Movers' from Danang with only a few minutes of station time left. Wertz told the FAC to put in the heavy stuff to the rear of the NVA position to prevent them from running back to Cambodia. We were getting Diverts from all over VN, some from Danang, some Navy A-4s from a carrier, and Black Pony Navy Gunships from IV Corps.)

I continued to bring in air support. Every once in a while, I would pop off a couple of un-aimed shots with my CAR 15. No aimed fire, it just felt comforting to shoot. The smoke and debris and dust was real thick at this point, so I told Wertz that I was going to move from my position behind the small rise to another spot where I could see better. Again Wertz, "WATCH YOUR ASS". I was hunched over (no more of that hero shit I had done while on the road). Half running, half crawling, I started to move again.

That's when it happened. I felt a blast of heat and at the same time I thought that someone had thrown a fast-ball at my head. I went over on my right shoulder in a daze. The left side of my cheek and neck was sore. It was like I had received a sucker punch with a baseball bat. Not real painful, just real sore. I must have been knocked out for a few seconds because the next thing I felt was my RTO pulling on my right ring finger. I am still sure he was going for my college grad ring.

I reached up with my left hand feeling for my cheek. I came away with a palm full of blood. I don't know why, but then I used my right hand to check my right cheek. Again, fresh blood. A sick realization came to me that I had been shot through the mouth. I rolled my tongue around the inside of my mouth feeling for broken teeth, extra holes, etc. Nothing, thank God. Wertz came over and I asked him how bad was it, did I need a medevac, what the f**k happened? Don told me I was hit by a grenade. He saw it coming toward me from behind the little rise I was hiding behind. He said I didn't need a medevac, but I had a bunch of little holes in my cheek and upper neck. I was alive, bleeding like a stuck pig, but I was alive. Don put a field dressing around my cheek and we got back to work. It throbbed, but no real sharp pain.

The fight went on for a long time, maybe 4 hours. We were still getting a bunch of fire from inside the tree line. We had only gotten about 30 - 40 ft inside the trees and still could not advance. Another Company had tried to flank around the right but was also stopped. We decided to pull back across the road and set up for the night. Take care of our injured, re-arm and get some more help. By that time the artillery (105's) were on target. We had Fast movers stacked up so we decided to let them do their job.

We set up in the old Tri Bi perimeter. We got a call from "Spooky", a C-47 gunship; and between the 105's and the mini-guns we kept up fire on the NVA positions all night. We wanted to keep them out of position so we could go at them again in the morning.

It was a strange morning, no urgency. Everyone was calm (not me). We got some hot sweet rice, a Cafe sua and rucked up. I went in with the scout platoon, expecting the whole world to explode around me at any minute. Nothing. SILENCE. Except for the crackling of some fires burning, it was quiet. Strange.... eerie ....smelly..... Then we started to see them, not moving, in weird positions all dead, no wounded. There were 8 lined up in a fighting trench, some were still 1/2 standing 1/2 leaning up against the front of the trench. If they still had rifles, you would think they were waiting to ambush us. They had been hit by "nails" from a Cobra 2.75 in a Flechette round. It looked they had small pox or measles. Some were in pieces.

I walked over to the low rise I had been hiding behind and looked at the reverse side. It was a fighting position with 2 dead NVA in it. They were hugging each other in a final show of mutual support in a time of terror. I was lucky they did not just roll the grenade over the top. I would not have stood a chance. I was walking around staring at the carnage in a stupor. It was not anything like I had expected. The smell was the smell of death. This was the first time I had smelt it, but not the last by any means.

We killed 92 brave soldiers that day and lost 23 of our own. Both sides were brave dedicated men. I still wonder what would have happened to us if we did not have all the Air and Artillery support that day in November 1971.

Oh yeah, what does this have to do with RHYTHM? Well soon after this I got my own Company (94 Company, 9th Airborne battalion, Vietnamese Airborne Division, The finest Airborne infantry in Vietnam, bar none). I did not get to work with SSG Don Wertz for another 7 months. This time we were on the ridge line outside Dak To, trying to break the siege the NVA had on Firebase # 5. I hooked up with Wertz's Company. We got in some shit again and had a 4 day fight with the 66th NVA Regiment. This time Wertz yelled at me to "KEEP YOUR HEAD DOWN THIS TIME EL TEE". To keep this short, I kept my head down but got hit in the ass this time.

I Figure if I had gotten the RHYTHM correct I would not have gotten hit the 1st two times.

SO HELP ME GOD.